A MILITARY HIST

This book represents a new, expanded and substantially updated edition of one of the most acclaimed overviews of Australian military history available. As well as providing a detailed chronological narrative of the wars in which Australia has been involved, it discusses the evolution of defence policy in peace and war, and the impact of war and military service on civilian society. It maps the development of the Australian armed forces as institutions and the relationship of military policy to government. It covers the major theatres of war in which Australia has engaged – from Gallipoli to the Gulf War. The author also examines armed conflict that has taken place on Australian soil between indigenous Australians and European settlers. In addition, the book considers how national security and defence policy is being shaped at the end of the twentieth century in a rapidly changing world.

JEFFREY GREY is Associate Professor of History at University College, Australian Defence Force Academy. He is the co-author of *The Oxford Companion to Australian Military History* (1995) and author of *Vietnam Days: Australia and the Impact of Vietnam* (1991); *Australian Brass: The Career of Lieutenant General Sir Horace Robertson* (Cambridge University Press, 1992); *Emergency and Confrontation: Australian Military Operations in Malaya and Borneo 1955–1966* (1996); and *Up Top: The Royal Australian Navy in Southeast Asian Conflicts 1955–72* (1998).

War is not a polite recreation, but the vilest thing in life, and we ought to understand that and not play at war. We ought to accept it sternly and solemnly as a fearful necessity.

Leo Tolstoy, *War and Peace*

The military system of a nation is not an independent section of the social system but an aspect of it in its entirety.

Michael Howard, *The Franco-Prussian War*

This is a people that has been tempered by war, and for whom the memories of war have permeated the years of peace.

T. B. Millar, *Australia's Defence*

For T. B. Millar (1925–1994)
who paved the way, and
Ian McNeill (1933–1998)

A MILITARY HISTORY
OF AUSTRALIA

JEFFREY GREY

University College
Australian Defence Force Academy

PUBLISHED BY THE PRESS SYNDICATE OF THE UNIVERSITY OF CAMBRIDGE
The Pitt Building, Trumpington Street, Cambridge, United Kingdom

CAMBRIDGE UNIVERSITY PRESS
The Edinburgh Building, Cambridge CB2 2RU, UK   http://www.cup.cam.ac.uk
40 West 20th Street, New York, NY 10011–4211, USA   http://www.cup.org
10 Stamford Road, Oakleigh, Melbourne 3166, Australia

First published 1990
Revised edition 1999

Printed in Australia by Brown Prior Anderson

Typeset in New Baskerville 10/12 pt

A catalogue record for this book is available from the British Library

National Library of Australia Cataloguing in Publication data

Grey, Jeffrey, 1959–   .
A military history of Australia.
Revised ed.
Bibliography.
Includes index.
ISBN 0 521 64283 3.
ISBN 0 521 64483 6 (pbk.).
1. Australia – History, Military. I. Title.
355.00994

Library of Congress Cataloguing in Publication data

Grey Jeffrey.
A military history of Australia/Jeffrey Grey – revised ed.
p.   cm.
Includes bibliographical references and index.
ISBN 0-521-64283-3 (hardbound: alk. paper).
ISBN 0-521-64483-6 (pbk.: alk. paper).
1. Australia – History, Military. 2. Australia – Armed Forces –
History. 3. Australia – Military policy. 4. Australia – History,
Military – Sources. 5. Australia – Armed Forces – History – Sources.
6. Australia – Military policy – Sources. I. Title.
DU112.3.G74 1999
355'.00994–dc21   98–54959

ISBN 0 521 64283 3 hardback
ISBN 0 521 64483 6 paperback

Contents

List of Maps, Tables and Figures

Maps

Tables

Figures

Note on money and measurement

Money Australia used pounds, shillings and pence for much of the period covered by this book. There were 12 pennies (d.) in one shilling (s.), and 20 shillings in one pound (£). A guinea was £1 1s. When Australia changed to decimal currency in 1966, $2 was equal to £1.

Measurement Metric equivalents to imperial measures are as follows:

1 inch = 25.4 cm	1 acre = 0.405 ha
1 yard = 0.914 m	1 ton = 1.02 t
1 mile = 1.61 km	1 bushel = 35.2 L

Acknowledgements

The debts I incurred in preparing the first edition of this book a decade ago remain, others have accrued since.

In reviews and correspondence after the first edition was published, various readers kindly drew my attention to errors in fact or interpretation, or suggested alternative readings of the issues. I have incorporated as many of these as I could into the revised edition, and record my thanks in particular to Eric Andrews, Joan Beaumont, Carl Bridge, John Bullen, John Coates, John Connor, Alastair Cooper, Kent Fedorowich, James Goldrick, David Horner, Neil James, Peter Londey, Robert O'Neill, the late Geoffrey Serle, Peter Stanley and Craig Wilcox. I have learned a lot from the work of many of the students who have passed through my hands, from fourth year honours to PhD level, over the last ten years, and offer further thanks to Richard Bushby, Ian Campbell, Stephen Clarke, Alastair Cooper, Mark Edmonds, Bruce Faraday, Gavin Keating, Dayton McCarthy, Jasmin Northey, Jason Sears, John Sholl, Craig Stockings, Alison Vincent, Glen Wahlert and Mark Welburn. I accept the blame for such errors of fact or quirks of interpretation as remain.

My editor at Cambridge University Press, Phillipa McGuinness, has kept me honest and she and the people at CUP have reminded me again of just how good Australian publishers can be.

The debt which I can never repay is that to my wife, Gina, and to Victoria and Duncan.

Introduction

Australians do not generally think of themselves as a military people. Our heroes play at full-forward or scrum-half or open the batting, and when we do acknowledge the heroic qualities of someone in a military uniform it is more likely to be for self-sacrificial mateship than deeds of martial virtue. We have statues in the national capital to Simpson and the donkey and to 'Weary' Dunlop, both of them symbols of suffering and its alleviation, but none to Albert Jacka, the first Australian to win the Victoria Cross at Gallipoli for single-handedly holding a trench against a Turkish raiding party. Yet in his day Jacka was as great a public figure as Dunlop became in more recent times, and his funeral in Melbourne was attended by thousands, as Dunlop's was. But there, it seems, the similarities end.

Sporting teams and primary produce have not been our only notable exports. In the twentieth century we have been known equally for the quality of our soldiers and our willingness to send them overseas to fight alongside our allies in a variety of causes. At home, we have frequently differed over the necessity to do so, and if the voices raised in dissent have often been in the minority (sometimes distinctly so), in most periods such dissension has been tolerated (though sometimes barely so). If we have been prepared to make considerable sacrifices in time of war, we have been equally ready to ignore defence issues in time of peace, with most of the usual lamentable consequences.

War and military service have been among the great defining influences in our history. It is increasingly a commonplace to observe that our genuine national day is 25 April, Anzac Day, rather than 26 January, which marks merely the first settlement of New South Wales. A majority of Australians still define an important part of the national ethos and national identity in terms of the Australian experience of war, and even those who criticise the martial dimensions of the national heritage, such as some feminist critics, often accept the argument on its own terms. Nor is Anzac Day and the Digger cult confined to the pre-baby boomer generation, or to members of the Anglo–Celtic tribes. Attendances at Anzac Day commemorations around Australia attest to the continuing vitality of the Anzac tradition, and of its capacity for reinvention with each new generation, a point further underscored during the 'Australia Remembers' commemorations of significant anniversaries from the Second World War held between 1992–95. Likewise, the interment of the Unknown Australian Soldier at the Australian War Memorial in November 1993 prompted enormous crowds of purposeful watchers for whom the event resonated in ways which surprised even those who had argued long and hard for the repatriation of this last symbolic Digger. The rear of the Sydney Anzac Day march is becoming longer each year, as the veteran population within the various post-1945 communities of migration asserts its right to a share in the imagery of Anzac, a clear signal that participation and legitimation are linked.

All of this is readily recognisable, and has been the source of comment and analysis for some decades concerning the manner and outcome of the development of white Australia. But at the heart of white settlement in Australia, as elsewhere, lies the violent dispossession of the previous tenants, an aspect of our history with which many Australians have still to come to terms. The conflict between whites and blacks on the frontier of settlement was neither unique, nor uniquely horrible, but the failure to acknowledge its existence and the baleful consequences for Aboriginal people which flow from it is not only a profound discredit to us as a community, but suggests something of the insecurity which has run through sections of the white population since the mid-nineteenth century: as we took this country, might not it yet be taken from us?

The United States was created in one war – a war for independence – and was confirmed and renewed in a still greater one, the Civil War. Australians acquired their independence peacefully and in stages, by dint of legislation, and our disagreements have never been so great that we have felt the need to kill each other over an opinion. But war has defined us just as clearly, and if we want to understand ourselves as a community then we must understand the place of war and the military in our past and our present.

War has shaped some of our most bitter domestic political debates, especially over conscription during the Great War and for Vietnam. It has helped to transform us as a society, from something narrowly British and provincial by opening Australia up to American influence and to the great waves of non-British migration after 1945, both of which are consequences of the Second World War. For most of the present century, military service has been the single greatest shared experience of white Australian males, whether as volunteers abroad for the duration, as trainees either voluntarily or compulsorily enlisted in the citizen forces at home, or as a regular or a national serviceman in the postwar conflicts in our region. That common denominator of experience is now changing, but the influence of a major war is generally held to continue to shape a society for a century after its end and the cultural, if not the physical, impact of past military endeavours is likely to continue in Australia well beyond 2001.

There is a certain irony in this. In most post-industrial societies in the West, war is seen more often as an aberration, an unfortunate and undesirable resort of final choice in regulating relations between states. This holds true to some extent in Australia, too. Public support for the decision to join the United Nations coalition forces in the Gulf War of 1990–91 was widespread, but it was noticeably less solid when the Australian government chose to send a small and largely token contribution to the Gulf again at the beginning of 1998, when the need for an armed response to Iraqi actions was ostensibly less clear. There would be near-unanimous support for the proposition that peacekeeping, especially under United Nations auspices, is an appropriate use of the Australian Defence Force, but little understanding that too great an emphasis on peacekeeping corrupts armed forces and unfits them both for their primary purpose and as peacekeepers, as the Canadians have found to their shock in recent years.

This is a book about the place of war and the military in our history. It pays due regard to what is known as the 'war and society' school of historical issues, and readers will find in its pages consistent, if scattered, reference to the role of women, the impact of veterans, the outcomes for indigenous peoples, the parts played by industry and the consequences of war for economic activity. There is considerable discussion of the policy context without which the role and functions of the military will make little sense. But at its heart lies the idea of war as a human activity, and the military as human institutions studied in their Australian manifestations.

In the first edition of this book I noted that there were numerous silences in the literature of Australians and war, and voiced the hope that before long other scholars would help to fill the gaps. In preparing this edition, and especially while revising the bibliographic chapter,

I have been struck by the ways in which scholarship in the field has moved forward dramatically in some areas, but hardly at all in others. In part this reflects the movement in the '30 year rule' which governs access to official records, in part the continuing interest in Australian history as grist for the PhD mill in the universities. But there is still so much we do not know, and so much still to be said, that perhaps the things which this book does not deal with, or deals with inadequately, will prompt renewed and continuing activity across the board. In which case, a further edition may well be called for.

CHAPTER 1

The Colonial Period, 1788–1870

Early colonial society bore the stamp of the British military to a marked degree. Indeed, the first colony of New South Wales owed its foundation in large part to strategic considerations. With the opening of the colonies to free settlement from around the 1820s, the military stamp of early Australian life diminished, but the British naval and military presence continued to be an important one until the final removal of the garrison in 1870. Although the military duties of the British regiments were always low-scale, the military played an important role in virtually all areas of colonial life.

The argument that Australia was founded as a dumping ground for the scum of the Georgian prison system has long been recognised as too simple an explanation. With increasing sophistication, historians have come to recognise the importance of international trade rivalries in eighteenth-century British policy, and the emerging importance of global seapower. The decision to colonise New South Wales cannot be isolated from the strategic imperatives of the world's first truly global struggle, the Seven Years' War (1757–63). This is not to suggest that the 'convict dumping' explanation has been overturned entirely, but to it have been added what might be characterised as 'trade' and 'navalist' interpretations of Australia's origins. Certainly, the British government welcomed the chance to establish an entrepôt for the furtherance of the East Indies and China trade, and the Admiralty sought to exploit the abundant stocks of timber and flax in New Zealand and on Norfolk Island to furnish naval stores to vessels of the Royal Navy in the East. An even more immediate imperative, however, following the failure of plans for various African alternatives, was the need for a naval base in wartime from which the British might interdict the maritime communications of the French, Dutch and Spanish.

There was a pleasing harmony between these considerations and the need to find a new destination for convicts previously shipped off to the American colonies. Convicts were an acceptable form of expendable labour with which to establish a naval base, and to the negative value of reducing social tension in early industrial Britain was added the prospect of strengthening Britain's hand in the trading and imperial rivalries which existed between Britain and the continental powers, especially France. As Lord Sydney told the chairmen of the East India Company, such a settlement would prevent 'the emigration of Our European Neighbours to that Quarter'. Given what we know of Anglo-French imperial rivalry in India, North America and elsewhere in the course of the eighteenth century, it seems reasonable to assume that the Australian colonies owed their foundation in large measure to the strategic perspectives in Whitehall. In this sense, then, the history of white settlement in Australia has an important military dimension from its very beginning.

That military dimension was reinforced by the nature of settlement itself. The garrison troops that arrived with Captain Arthur Phillip in January 1788 comprised three companies of the Marines, 212 all ranks, commanded by Major Robert Ross. The leading officials of the infant colony were all officers of the garrison, and the governor himself exercised supreme military and civil authority. As the senior command-ing officer, Ross was appointed lieutenant governor, a combination of posts which continued for the first half-century of the colony. The early governors in New South Wales were all military men, naval officers like Captains Arthur Phillip, John Hunter, Philip Gidley King and William Bligh, or soldiers like Colonel Lachlan Macquarie, Major General Sir Thomas Brisbane, Lieutenant General Sir Ralph Darling and Lieutenant General Sir Richard Bourke – and all except Brisbane and Bourke were men of relatively humble origins who had risen through dint of their own efforts and often considerable abilities. Other colonies were ruled by military officers also: Captain David Collins, Colonel George Arthur and Captain Sir John Franklin in Tasmania, Captain James Stirling in Western Australia, Captain John Hindmarsh and Captain Sir George Grey in South Australia. Of thirty-four gov-ernors, lieutenant governors and administrators of New South Wales, Tasmania and Victoria between 1788 and 1855, only three were civilians, and more than one-third of all such posts in the first century of white settlement were filled by serving military officers.

Just as the fact of the military presence influenced the settlement, so too the nature of that military force influenced the shape which the early colonies took. The early colony has been depicted as a sump of squalor and venality, and the soldiers, sailors and marines who made up a sizeable proportion of the population are often equated with Wellington's famous description of his army in Spain: 'scum of the earth, enlisted for drink'. The New South Wales Corps is singled out for special attention in this regard, but the judgement is held to apply to the military in general, from private soldier to officer, and to extend perhaps even to the senior officers who were charged with responsibility for the conduct of affairs in the colony.

The term of foreign service for the First Fleet marines was fixed at three years, but it was four years before the first contingent was relieved in 1791, and that after enduring considerable privation through inadequate rations, poor quarters, and the hard physical labour attending the establishment of the settlement. They were replaced by the New South Wales Corps. Specially raised in 1789 for service as a colonial garrison force, this unit has had a particularly bad press in Australian history, but in fact the overall quality of the regiment was not demonstrably worse than that pertaining elsewhere in the British army of the day. The officers, experienced men drawn from other regiments, raised their own companies, receiving three guineas for each approved recruit, and a proportion of the rank and file were drawn from the Savoy military prison or were convicts of good character recruited locally in the colony. Governor Bligh, not the most objective witness in the circumstances, remarked on the large number of 'soldiers from the Savoy and other characters who have been considered as disgraceful to every other regiment', but in 1807 there were only twenty-five ex-Savoy recruits in the ranks, and such men never reached 10 per cent of the Corps' strength (see Table 1.1). By way of comparison, in 1787 regiments detailed for Indian service were reinforced with prisoners from Gloucester gaol, and the 60th Regiment in the West Indies was often brought up to strength with Irish deserters from other regiments. Throughout the British Army, the abuse of patronage by officers was commonplace prior to the gradual reforms initiated by Generals Sir Ralph Abercrombie and Sir John Moore and the appointment of Frederick, Duke of York as Commander-in-Chief in 1795. The involvement of officers in business, which so scandalises later critics of the 'Rum Corps', remained accepted practice among officers in India into the nineteenth century. On the other hand, many of these same officers were skilled artists, farmers, botanists, surveyors and engineers, and keepers of detailed journals and diaries. Such men laid much of the civilian infrastructure of the early colony, as well as discharging their military functions and profiting from their land and business interests.

The commissioning and promotion of army officers was by purchase, and this remained the case until the Cardwell reforms of 1870–72. In no sense was the officer corps a professional one. Many took their cue from

Table 1.1 Composition of the New South Wales Corps, 1790–1810

Year	Total corps strength	No. of convicts	No. of ex-Savoy	Commissioned officers in NSW
1790	–	–	–	10
1791	192	5	–	14
1792	358	5	4	21
1793	436	30	9	21
1794	496	41	21	22
1795	516	58	25	21
1796	522	54	24	21
1797	535	59	25	20
1798	564	72	38	20
1799	564	76	40(a)	23
1800	577	76	38	23
1801	635	93	35	25
1802	685	96(b)	34	24
1803	682	86	32	25
1804	563	71	26	25
1805	579	70	26	26
1806	587	69	26	24
1807	596	65	25	22
1808	601	63	21	26
1809	802	62	21	33
1810	794	57	21	34(c)

Source: Pamela Statham, *Ins and Outs: The Composition and Disposal of the NSW Corps 1790–1810*, Canberra, 1988.
(a)   Maximum representation, 7.09 per cent.
(b)   Maximum representation, 14.01 per cent.
(c)   A total of 82 active in the Corps during the period.

the Duke of Wellington, who thought that all military education was nonsense, notwithstanding the establishment of the Royal Military College in 1802. Many officers were frequently absent from their regiments, often insubordinate, and just as frequently drunk. Their attitude to their military duties was casual, and day-to-day administration and training was very largely the province of NCOs. Officers had little to do with the rank and file who were in any case separated from their superiors by a yawning social gulf. 'Whoever "listed for a soldier"', wrote one such in 1805, 'was at once set down among the catalogue of persons who had turned out ill'. Another ex-soldier, writing in the 1840s, noted that the British Army 'as is well known, is the *dernier resort* of the idle, the depraved, and the destitute'.

The conditions endured by the other ranks were frequently appalling. Enlistment was for twenty-one years, twenty-four in the cavalry. With low life expectancies and the prospect of years of service in a fever-ridden station in the West Indies, desertion was widespread. The standard wage of a shilling a day was increased to thirteen pence in 1800, and this remained the basic wage until 1867. Sixpence a day was stopped for rations, and a soldier was subject to other stoppages of pay for lost kit or the milder scale of punishment. As part of the reform of the British Army, soldiers began to be housed in barracks in the 1790s, but the earlier system of billeting troops on local inhabitants persisted into the nineteenth century. Punishments were ferocious and usually physical, and included the wooden horse, the black hole, porcupine drill, the branding of deserters, and transportation. At the pinnacle of the disciplinary code was hanging which was awarded for a range of offences, but the most common punishment for several centuries was flogging. Twenty-five lashes was the minimum, with a theoretical maximum of 1500 lashes although there are records of 2000 lashes being awarded late in the eighteenth century. Flogging was well known to civil as well as military law. During the Napoleonic Wars protests were made in the House of Commons against flogging in the army, and in 1812 the Duke of York forbade regimental courts martial from awarding more than 300 lashes, although district and general courts martial retained the discretionary award of more severe punishment. In 1855 the maximum number of lashes awarded by any court martial was reduced to fifty, and in 1868 this was restricted further to crimes committed on active service. Total abolition did not come until 1881.

The British Army of the late eighteenth and part of the nineteenth centuries largely comprised an officer corps of often aristocratic amateurs in command of the social sweepings of the industrial cities and the dispossessed rural poor, and many men enlisted as a means of escaping debt, poverty, or gaol. 'I do not know what the enemy will make of them', Wellington once said, 'but by God they frighten me'. Poorly trained, inadequately led and abominably treated, the British Army was not a formidable military force. Successive defeats in the Low Countries in the 1790s and at the hands of the infant regular army of the United States in 1814–15 were a better general indication of the state of the army than were Wellington's victories in Spain.

Life in the Royal Navy was equally harsh. Discipline was upheld by hanging, keelhauling and the lash. Life between decks was wretched in the extreme, characterised by cramped and insanitary quarters, monotonous and unhealthy diet and dangerous work. Ships were often at sea for months, even years, at a time. The food was frequently inedible, and many seamen served against their will, having been 'pressed' into service to meet the manpower shortage which afflicted the navy during every major war. Many deserted at the first opportunity, and it was Britain's insistence on searching neutral ships in order to apprehend absconders which contributed to the outbreak of war with the United States in 1812.

The Royal Navy was wracked by mutinies at Spithead and the Nore in 1797. Discontent had been growing over rates of pay (which had not changed since 1685) and the overdue disbursement of prize money, but mutineers at Spithead also demanded an improvement in medical services, extra shore leave, the removal of unpopular officers and protection from embezzlement by pursers, who often cheated them of their rations. The government accepted the demands for pay and prize money, but twenty-nine of the ringleaders at the Nore were hanged at the yardarm. At the Peace of Amiens in 1802, several smaller mutinies over the paying off of ships were dealt with in exemplary fashion also, the leaders once again being hanged.

The navy was regarded more highly than the army, at least by those who were not in it. Samuel Johnson, acerbic as ever, thought that 'no man will be a sailor who has contrivance enough to get himself into jail', but 'Jolly Jack Tar' enjoyed popular hero status during the Napoleonic Wars and after, although he remained largely a figment of the public imagination. Following the Napoleonic Wars the Royal Navy was severely run-down, as was the army, but unlike the latter the navy found a new and clear-cut role for itself as guardian of sea-borne trade and police-man of the expanding empire. After 1815 all those who served in the fleet did so as volunteers – the press gang vanished, never to reappear, and the practice of sending minor criminals to sea rather than to gaol also ceased. The worst physical punishments had been opposed firmly by Nelson and others, and in the first half of the nineteenth century their use declined as their application was regulated strictly, although flogging was not 'suspended' until 1870. Food and conditions improved gradually, as did the incidence of shore leave, and even uniforms were introduced, finally, in 1857. In some senses, the long peace after 1815 was harder on the officers than on the ordinary seamen. They were not paid off at the end of the war, and in 1818 there were 5797 commis-sioned officers in the navy, four out of five of whom lived ashore on half pay with nothing to do. (The navy had been reduced overall to 121 ships and 20 000 seamen, from a total in 1813 of 658 ships and 140 000 seamen. The number of officers had in fact increased.)

The thoroughly military character of the foundation years of the Australian colony was justified by the parlous state of the settlement and the nature of the garrison's duties, which entailed mostly the guarding and supervision of the convicts. From time to time the soldiers of New South Wales were called on to also discharge their military function against Aborigines, escapees and rebellious convicts. The nature of the conflict with the Aborigines merits separate treatment (see Chapter 2). The early use of force in the colony, at Vinegar Hill in March 1804, was militarily insignificant on one level, but doubtless contributed to the unwholesome image which the military enjoyed in early colonial society. Some 200 convicts, mostly Irish, rebelled at the government farm at Castle Hill, seizing some arms and rousing convicts on nearby properties. Three-hundred strong, they moved off towards the Hawkesbury settlement to the northwest of Parramatta where they were intercepted by Major George Johnston and a company of the New South Wales Corps. Johnston called upon the rebel leaders to meet him in parley and, when they did so, promptly arrested them. A platoon of soldiers gave the rebels a volley, and then charged their line. The convicts fled, pursued by soldiers and some bands of armed settlers. Most gave themselves up in the succeeding twenty-four hours. Fifty-one were punished, nine of them hanged. The 'battle' became known as 'Vinegar Hill' after the site of an earlier and bloodier engagement in County Wexford during the Irish rebellion of 1798. Governor King and his officers believed that the rebellion was a manifestation of Irish Catholic political and religious revolt, although it is clear that a number of non-Irish convicts were among the leaders and that sectarian issues played hardly any part. Amongst other measures taken in the aftermath of the rebellion, Catholic worship was prohibited in the colony. Johnston received a land grant of 2000 acres for services rendered.

It was ironic therefore that in January 1808 he should have led the New South Wales Corps in rebellion against the governor, by this time Captain William Bligh. Bligh sought to bring an end to the involvement of officers in trade, especially the monopoly over spirits, and to transfer the Corps away from the convict colony and to restrain the activities of John Macarthur, formerly a junior officer who used his connections within the military to further his pastoral and commercial activities. Johnston intervened when Bligh attempted to charge six officers with treasonous practices after they protested Bligh's conduct of a court martial against Macarthur. No shots were fired, no-one was injured, but much effort was expended in justification and condemnation by both sides. Eventually Johnston was court-martialled in England, but suffered no greater penalty than to be forced to leave the army. Both he and Macarthur were allowed to return to their lands in New South Wales in 1813 and 1817 respectively. Bligh was retired. The incident lacks nearly all the modern connotations of coup d'état and should be seen in the context of officer insubordination which was a hallmark of the eighteenth-century British Army. The governor of Madras had been deposed and imprisoned by his Council in 1776, and insubordination had compromised the Duke of York's command in the Low Countries in 1794–95. Even the Duke of Wellington was forced to suffer unruly subordinates in the Peninsula in 1807–08 while in 1809 there occurred a 'white mutiny' among European officers of the Madras Army, a phenomenon repeated in mid-century within the East India Company's Army. A tiny ruling oligarchy, isolated and inward-looking, enjoying a relatively high standard of living and resentful of the impositions of an outsider, reacted to the stresses placed on it in a manner which all – save Bligh – understood as vouchsafed by custom if not by law.

The New South Wales Corps was an important presence in the infant colony across a twenty year period. Over 1600 men served in its ranks in that time, and the unit had an average strength of 550, making up almost 15 per cent of the male population of New South Wales. Some 442 men took their discharges in the colony, a welcome injection of skilled manpower in a period before the widespread migration of free settlers. A large proportion of the officers (thirty-seven of the eighty-two who served) likewise settled in New South Wales, and their trading and farming activities both during and after their service in the Corps were 'the principal means by which the colony arrived at that state of improvement in which I have found it', in Governor Hunter's words. As the New South Wales Corps' most careful and eloquent student, Pamela Statham, has concluded, far from being 'the blot on early New South Wales history that has been portrayed in the past, the New South Wales Corps should be seen as having been a positive stimulus to early growth and a major determinant of the Colony's survival'. It is time we set this record against the relentless portrayal of greed, self-interest and abuse of office which has been presented as the New South Wales Corps' only legacy.

The regularisation of the military presence in the colonies dates from Macquarie's arrival as governor in 1809. The New South Wales Corps was returned to England, becoming the 102nd Regiment and fighting in the Napoleonic Wars before being disbanded in 1818. Macquarie brought with him his own regiment – the 73rd – and from then until 1870 the colonies were garrisoned by regular units of the British army which were rotated through the colonies in keeping with the policies and needs of the Horse Guards (Whitehall headquarters of the British army), and whose primary duties were police work and the super-vision and construction of fortifications and barracks. Twenty-six regiments served in this capacity together with detachments of the Royal Engineers and the Royal Artillery; the number serving here varied, especially during periods of crisis such as the New Zealand Wars of the 1860s when troops from the Australian colonies went abroad on active service. In the early 1820s the garrison grew from a single regiment at any one time, to three by 1824, to between four and six from the mid-1820s to the mid-1840s. By the 1850s it had reverted to two, and after 1857 to a single regiment again at any one time.

The posting policy of the line regiments of the army in the nineteenth century is a complicated process. Australia and New Zealand were remote stations, Australia at least being arduous but not especially dangerous. The conditions of the rank and file between Waterloo and the Crimean War were characterised by hardship, brutality, disease and early deaths, and service in the fever-ridden garrisons of the West Indies, for example, produced appalling mortality rates among officers and men alike. Other imperial outposts were little better: service in Ceylon produced a mortality rate five times higher than that pertaining in Britain, while West Africa was a regimental graveyard, half the men perishing within three months of arrival and few men surviving fifteen months' service. The death rate in the Gold Coast (in West Africa) between 1823 and 1826 was 668 per thousand per annum, the highest anywhere in the empire. By comparison, service in Canada ('healthy but dull'), the Cape Colony and Australia was far preferable. But although the Australian colonies might be a relative backwater in military terms, the regiments sent there went with a purpose. For as much as thirty years after 1815, veterans of the wars against Napoleon continued to serve in the ranks of British units across the empire and a regiment such as the 48th, which arrived in Sydney in 1817, had over 200 veterans of the Peninsular War in its ranks while every officer above the rank of ensign had seen active service against the French.

Only infantry regiments served in Australia; the cavalry served in the Crimean War and in India and rarely elsewhere, while in the nineteenth century the Guards regiments served overseas only in the Crimea, and briefly in Canada in 1837. Because of the distances involved and the slowness of communications, a regiment would serve overseas for a lengthy period of time and in several posts or garrisons before returning to Britain for a period of home service and refitting. Postings were often long, although there were anomalies within the system. Units might be dispatched from Britain to Australia, serve a period of six years there and in New Zealand, and then embark for India and another period of seven years or so before returning to Britain. India accounted for the largest number of British regiments, followed by Britain itself, North America, the West Indies and the Mediterranean. Being based in these areas, of course, could entail service in all sorts of places against all sorts of foes. Regiments in India found themselves fighting in Burma, East Africa and China in the first half of the nineteenth century, and emergencies like the Indian Mutiny and the Crimean War could throw out the regular pattern of regimental movements quite considerably.

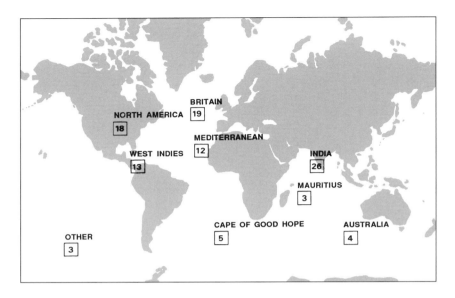

Map 1   Distribution of infantry battalions around the empire, c. 1840

Until the cessation of transportation of convicts to New South Wales in the early 1840s, the movement of troops to Australia was dictated by the transportation system, and this continued to be the case in Tasmania until transportation ceased there in 1852. The guard aboard the transports was provided by a regiment being dispatched for service in Australia, although it would often include men being sent as reinforcements for existing regiments already serving there. This meant, of course, that it took time to concentrate a regiment in its new station: in the early 1840s the 96th and 99th Regiments took nearly two years to bring their sub-units together in Sydney. Troop strengths in Australia fluctuated, influenced by the need for men in various colonial campaigns around the world. Consider, for example, the figures for the decade of the 1840s, a period marked by several large wars fought in India, Afghanistan and New Zealand and in which strenuous attempts were made in London to reduce the overall size of the army for financial and other reasons. In 1839 the total of other ranks' strength in the Australian colonies stood at 2971; in 1841 it had dropped to 2623 due to the hiatus in regimental reliefs. It peaked in 1847 at 5369, declining again by 1851 to 3035 as a result of the advent of a Liberal administration in Britain bent on reducing the strength and expenditure of the army. To this effect at the end of 1849 the Australian Command had received instructions to reduce the strength of most regiments in the colonies, to enrol military pensioners for use as convict guards, and to hand over barracks, buildings and stores to the colonial authorities, who were expected henceforth to maintain them.

Works and facilities had been the responsibility of the Board of Ordnance, which had initiated and overseen much construction in the colonies in the thirty years before the Crimean War. Although responsible for such important items of civil and military infrastructure as the construction and running of the Rideau Canal in Upper Canada and the surveying of land for settlement in Tasmania and South Australia (the latter under the Wakefield system), the existence of the Board interposed another layer of military authority over commanding officers in the colonies, who answered both to the Ordnance and the Horse Guards and, in the case of military officers who were colonial governors, to the Colonial Office as well. In addition, the Board increasingly failed to discharge its duties efficiently in the course of the 1840s and incurred enormous financial losses in North America, leading to the setting up of the select committee on Army and Ordnance expenditure in 1849–50 which recommended major economies. Sir George Grey, one of the principal critics of the Ordnance, began the process of divesting its responsibilities in the colonies, first in New South Wales and South Australia, backed by the Treasury and without consulting the colonial governments. 'N. S. Wales kicked a good deal at first but the people there are beginning to understand that they cannot have the advantages without the burdens of self-government', he wrote; 'I am refusing to undertake any works unless the colonies will pay for them'.

Regiments arrived in Sydney, but did not necessarily spend their time only, or even mainly, in New South Wales. Many sent detachments to the other settlements. The 40th Regiment, for example, spent almost the whole of its first period of service – between 1824 and 1829 – in Tasmania, embarking for service in India in the latter year; in its second period, between 1852 and 1860, it was based in Melbourne and acted as an escort for the gold dispatched from the goldfields to Melbourne, and maintained law and order on the diggings. In this capacity it was involved in the armed melée at Eureka near Ballarat in December 1854, acting in aid to the civil power and in support of the police in putting down the miners. The 3rd Regiment had its headquarters in Sydney between 1822 and 1827, but companies were dispatched continuously to various outstations, serving in Tasmania and with other detachments at Newcastle, Liverpool, Parramatta, Port Macquarie and Bathurst. This regiment was also shipped to India at the end of its service in the Australian colonies. The 21st Regiment had its headquarters in Hobart between 1833 and 1839, but dispatched two companies to the infant settlement at Swan River in Western Australia, before proceeding to

India. The 28th Regiment arrived in Sydney in 1835, several detachments serving as guards to the penal settlement at Brisbane, before being sent to India in 1842 following the disaster to British arms in the First Afghan War. The 58th Regiment reached Sydney in 1844, but was sent to New Zealand to fight Hone Heke in April 1845. It returned to Sydney in late 1846, but was sent back to New Zealand in 1847 to campaign around Wanganui, and it did not return to New South Wales. The 12th Regiment served in New South Wales from 1854 to 1860 before being ordered to New Zealand in 1860 where it remained until departing for India in 1866. The 77th Regiment served in New South Wales very briefly, during 1857–58. Wanted for service in Hong Kong, it was diverted to India when news of the Mutiny reached Sydney. This pattern was typical of regimental experience in the Australian colonies.

Far less typical was the experience of the men of the 12th and 40th Regiments, who aided the police troopers in the suppression of the miners' rising at Ballarat in December 1854. Thirty or forty miners were killed in the assault on the stockade at Eureka, along with one officer and four soldiers. Twelve soldiers, one policeman and an unknown number of miners were wounded. The action lasted perhaps a quarter of an hour – like Vinegar Hill it was militarily insignificant. The miners claimed to be fighting for liberty, but equally it may be argued that they rose in defence of economic interest as small capitalists. The image of red-coated soldiers bayoneting sturdy but essentially defenceless miners is a common one, both then and now. But the miners came from all over Europe and the Americas, and numbered in their ranks men who had more than their share of military experience in assorted revolutions and lost causes, while such bayoneting as was done was carried out equally by the blue-coated mounted police, who like as not were Australian-born. Like Vinegar Hill, Eureka is a reminder of the rarity with which white men in the colonies settled their differences through organised violence.

But officers and men did not contribute only military skills to the colonies, or serve only military ends. The army and navy played an important part in economic and social life and, in the early period at least, sometimes resorted to coercion in both areas. The early economic life of New South Wales was founded on the military commissariat. It became the chief market for colonial produce and paid with receipts drawn on the government store. These became a kind of generally circulating government note issue. In a short time the store became the chief source of capital loans, advancing stock, equipment and, of course, rations. While many transactions were made through barter, they were carried on in monetary terms. Thus there grew a distinction between 'sterling', or money equal to bills drawn on the Treasury in

London, and 'currency', or money acceptable purely in the local environment such as store receipts. During the governorships of King, Bligh and Macquarie, private economic activity flourished, led by officers like Johnston and his predecessor Major Francis Grose and former officers like Macarthur. Of equal – perhaps even greater – importance was Macquarie's decision to encourage development and a free economy in the interests of furthering the growth of New South Wales as something other than a penal settlement, and to use authoritarian methods as necessary to bring this about.

Military intervention in the social life of the colonies was usually more benign. The 28th Regiment had a particularly fine band, much sought after for concerts in the Sydney Domain and used to accompany oratorios and other similar performances in St Mary's Cathedral. The 57th Regiment helped to introduce cricket to the colony in the 1820s, and in the 1830s the officers of the regiment fielded a side in regular competition against the gentlemen of Sydney. Captain Ward of the Royal Engineers was a noted cricketer who convinced Governor Denison to alienate part of the Domain by enclosing it for cricket matches. He was also in charge of the sapper detachment which ran the Sydney Mint, and was nominated to the Legislative Council in 1861. The 11th Regiment first used the site of the Sydney Cricket Ground for sporting purposes, enclosing the area as a regimental recreation area and maintaining the grounds through a subscription system. The 11th were also called upon regularly as fire-fighters.

The officers of the Royal Engineers were responsible not only for the building of fine permanent military works, such as Victoria Barracks in Sydney and Fort Denison in the harbour, but contributed much to the creation of essential civilian and economic infrastructure. The process of land surveying in South Australia has been mentioned already; to this might be added the building of the breakwater at Newcastle and the clearing of mudflats in the Parramatta river as aids to commerce and navigation in the late 1830s, and the supervision of roads and bridges which was added to the responsibilities of the Colonial Engineer, Captain George Barney, at the insistence of the governor in 1837.

All this was in addition to Barney's responsibilities to the Board of Ordnance and as the Commanding Royal Engineer in the colony. After retiring from the army, Barney became Chief Commissioner of Crown Lands for New South Wales and, in 1855, Surveyor-General for the colony. He was an exceptional man, but scarcely unique among sapper officers in the colonies. Major General Sir Andrew Clarke became Surveyor-General of Victoria in 1843 and was Agent-General for Victoria in London from 1899 until his death in 1902. Captain John Hawkins surveyed the first railway line from Sydney in 1856, becoming a railway commissioner in 1857. Numerous others combined duties as commissioners of public works, commissioners of railways, roads and telegraphs, and even involvement in the governance of the Melbourne Mint with their regular tasks as military engineers responsible for the construction and maintenance of barracks, stores and fortifications.

The cessation of transportation to New South Wales after 1840 and the subsequent advent of free settlement in the other colonies changed the military situation quite markedly, and altered attitudes towards the soldiers on the part of the civilian population. There was a general colonial antipathy to the 'brutal and licentious soldiery', born from a mix of the traditional Anglo-Saxon mistrust of standing armies – arguably with us still – and the views of emancipists within the civilian population who resented the coercive and disciplinary role which the army played in relation to the convicts. After 1840 this changed. Not only did the strength of the garrison decline gradually, but as we have noted, the duties became much less arduous. The growth of organised police forces from the 1830s meant that many of the tasks performed originally by the soldiers, combating Aborigines or maintaining law and order, were now performed by others.

The army became less evident and hence less threatening. Increasingly the Australian colonists perceived threats as externally derived in any case, and the need for an efficient army and navy in meeting such threats was not disputed. This was underlined by the decision of the Colonial Secretary in 1848 that garrison strength would be dictated by the likelihood of external threat. War scares were frequent and plentiful in the nineteenth-century colonies. Many were over-reactions fuelled by the slow and primitive nature of communications, while others were an extension of wars or periods of international tension between Britain and other colonial powers such as Russia and France. That the colonies were vulnerable was not pure fantasy on the colonists' part. The famous incident in November 1839 when two American warships, under Commander Charles Wilkes, USN, entered Sydney Harbour in darkness and anchored without being detected until next morning illustrated the potential for raiders to wreak havoc among colonial seaborne trade, and to hold the settlements 'hostage' under threat of bombardment.

The usual response to such scares was a frenzied period of activity in which fortifications were begun or upgraded and interest flickered in the formation of citizens' corps, followed by a rapid waning of activity and interest as the immediate commotion passed. The warship incident in 1839 led the governor, Sir George Gipps, to renew pleas for upgraded defences for the port, which meant increased expenditure upon coastal guns and the trained manpower to utilise them, pleas which were ignored by London as earlier requests had been. The question of coastal defences remained an issue for most of the 1840s, with construction of harbour defences on Bradley's Head and Pinchgut Island in Sydney being undertaken without sanction from London.

Similar concerns were expressed in the other colonies and settlements. Suggestions were made for the erection of Martello Towers to protect the Swan River settlement in 1837. There was agitation for the construction of ordnance storehouses and magazines for guns to protect the approaches to Port Adelaide in 1846, and for the renewal of new powder magazines at Hobart in 1844. Argument with London over the provision of such facilities took place in the context of Whitehall's attempts to divest much of the cost of colonial fixed defences onto the colonies themselves, and all of these projects foundered for lack of funds. Colonial capacity to assume this task was given a considerable fillip by the discovery of gold, and the advent of the Crimean War lent the process at least a temporary strategic imperative. The advent of responsible self-government concomitant upon the passage of the *Australian Colonies Government Act 1850* evidently strengthened the hand of Whitehall in its argument with the colonists about the funding of colonial defence.

One measure of colonial self-reliance and self-assertion in matters of defence was the existence of bands of volunteer soldiers raised from the citizenry itself. The first such local forces had been raised as early as September 1800 as the Sydney and Parramatta Loyal Associations, in response to fears of an Irish rising in Sydney. They were disbanded in 1801, a decision modified by Governor King to permit partial embodiment under which they were exercised one month a year; in 1803 they re-formed on receipt of news of the war with France, and during the convict rising the following year were used to guard strategic points in Sydney while the New South Wales Corps marched off to deal with the rebels. In July 1819 Governor Macquarie made some proposals about the formation of a colonial militia, largely in response to cuts in the strength of the army at the end of the Napoleonic Wars. He recommended in particular the raising of militia cavalry, but the Treasury in London decided against the plan in view of the recently sanctioned increase in the size of the army in August 1820. Such suggestions were revived by Captain Edward Macarthur of the 19th Regiment in 1825, but again met with little success. Governor Darling's view was that an efficient mounted police force was more valuable for the maintenance of law and order, and again the idea of a militia was not proceeded with, not least because the formation of the mounted police obviated the need. There was talk of raising local forces again in the 1840s, but this too came to nothing.

Volunteer militia existed already in New Zealand, where the need was greater, and in November 1846 Grey had instructed the governor, Sir

Charles Fitzroy, to bring the question of a local militia before the NSW Legislative Council, a move which the governor declined to make, referring the matter instead to the Select Committee on Police. W. C. Wentworth used the issue to further the cause of self-government, arguing that the formation of a militia was the right of the citizens, and that formation was made all the more necessary by the denuding of the garrison in the Australian colonies as a result of the demands of the New Zealand wars. The stirrings of national sentiments thus went hand in hand with the British quest for fiscal stringencies, and the drive for self-government abetted Grey's attempts to reduce the cost of garrisoning those colonies which, in the view of many in London, were in no danger of attack. The discovery of gold altered evaluations of colonial vulnerability, however. While the colonies became more desirable targets, many members of the police forces deserted their posts and headed for the diggings, and colonial insecurity was fostered by war scares following the advent of Louis Napoleon in France. Ironically the discovery of gold, which greatly increased the colonial capacity to invest in self-defence, actually prompted Whitehall to dispatch an additional infantry regiment to Victoria.

The Crimean War was a catalyst for defence preparedness and the raising of local forces. A Select Committee of Inquiry in New South Wales in 1853 recommended the establishment of fortifications at Georges, Middle and South Heads and an additional line of defences inside the harbour at Dawes Point, Bradley's Head and Pinchgut. The governor of Victoria, Captain Sir Charles Hotham, RN, ordered the purchase of a steam ship, HMCS *Victoria*, for the defence of the colony. The advent of war saw the passing in 1854 of a Volunteer Act in Victoria, leading to the formation of several volunteer rifle units in Melbourne and Geelong and a volunteer Yeomanry Cavalry Corps. An Act was passed in New South Wales also for the raising of a battery of artillery, a troop of yeomanry and a battalion of rifles, to be drawn from 'highly respectable classes of persons'. As with the volunteer movement in Britain and Canada at this time, the members paid for their own uniforms and all the other expenses of part-time soldiering, while the government supplied arms and instruction. The artillery, however, was never issued with guns. With the passing of the threat the units so raised declined quickly.

New forces of volunteers greeted later war scares. There was a flurry of activity in 1859, although not all sections of colonial society shared the sense of urgency which led to the raising of volunteer corps. The upsurge in activity across the Tasman in the 1860s kept the volunteer movement alive in the eastern colonies, but the limitations of relying on volunteer corps was well illustrated in Tasmania, whose defence appropriation for 1860 totalled just £6. Nonetheless, at the end of 1861 there were some 9000 men in the Volunteers, or about one in every fifty men of working age in the colonies; at about the same time, an attempt to raise a volunteer force in Western Australia, following the announcement in 1860 that imperial troops would be withdrawn from that colony, foundered upon a lack of arms and a lack of volunteers to bear them.

The Treasury view of colonial defence problems reached its logical conclusion in the 1860s with the deliberations of the Mills Committee, whose findings were presented to the British parliament in March 1862. Dividing the empire into 'colonies proper' and 'dependencies', the committee came to the view that 'the responsibility and cost of military defence ... ought plainly to devolve upon [the colonists] themselves'. Local expenditure on defence in the Australian colonies in 1861 had varied from approximately £10 000 in New South Wales and £23 408 5s. in Victoria to just £800 in Queensland and nothing at all in Western Australia. In implementing the Mills Committee report, the Colonial Secretary advised the colonies in 1863 that London proposed to allot the Australian colonies fifteen companies of infantry to be spread between them in designated fashion, for which service the colonies would pay a specified annual sum of £40 per head. If the colonies wanted more men than the total allotted, they would be required to pay £70 per head, 'a sum which more nearly approaches the real cost to the Imperial government of each soldier'. No troops were to be sent to Western Australia.

Not only did the greatly increased cost of imperial protection fail to commend itself to the colonial administrations, but the fact that the same troops for whom the colonies paid could be removed to areas of greater need in the event of hostilities also provoked adverse comment. Opinion had it that the provision of artillery would more closely match the defence needs of the colonies in any case, and reorganisations of the volunteer troops followed in order to meet the perceived deficiencies in coastal artillery. By 1863 the two largest colonies mustered over 5000 volunteers between them, the preponderance being in Victoria which by now was the largest and wealthiest of the colonies. Increased complacency characterised the second half of the 1860s, and in New South Wales volunteers became so hard to attract that the government was forced to pass a new Volunteer Act in 1867. A standard of efficiency was set for individual officers and men, and every volunteer who completed five years of 'efficient' service became entitled to a grant of fifty acres of land. The 'Land Grant' scheme did not survive the end of the following decade, but the principle was established by which men would receive some remuneration in return for the efficient discharge of their duties. Victoria had already adopted such a scheme, and other colonies followed suit. This largely solved the personnel problems of the colonial forces. The resolution of the matter was timely, for in 1869 the Governor of Victoria advised London that imperial troops could no longer be maintained at public expense in the colonies unless artillery units were substituted for infantry and guarantees were forthcoming regarding the deployment of units in the event of hostilities. That same year the British government announced that all troops bar a single regiment would be withdrawn and that the capitation fee would be raised. In May 1870 the Secretary of State for the Colonies, Lord Granville, advised that the troop needs of the various colonies did not amount to a single regiment and, accordingly, at the end of September, the last British soldiers of the 18th (Royal Irish) Regiment departed for Britain, although some hundreds took their discharges and remained to settle in the colony. The *Sydney Morning Herald* commented upon the severing of the eighty-year link between the colonies and the British army that 'it is the first step towards nationality, not the result of direful conflicts and years of suffering, but the well considered conclusion of men who rule the destiny of a great nation'. In fact, it had more to do with a desire in Britain to spread the burden of colonial defence and a matching reluctance within colonial administrations to pay any increased premium for Australia's defence.

In the course of the 1860s the eastern colonies at least had begun to flex their military muscles, after a fashion. The Waikato War saw the recruitment of some 2500 Australians for service in the Waikato militia against the Maoris; after arduous service against an accomplished enemy, many of the volunteers took advantage of the offer of land and settled in New Zealand, although by the end of the decade a good number of these had drifted back across the Tasman. The government of Victoria had made HMCS *Victoria* available to the authorities in New Zealand (for a fee), and the warship was used to ferry troops and supplies from Australia and took part also in a number of operations against Maori *pa* (fortified camps). The existence of a colonial naval warship caused the British some problems; the status and protection enjoyed by ships of the Royal Navy could not be extended to it when it operated outside of colonial territorial waters, since all Royal Navy ships had to be commanded by officers holding commissions from the Crown. The Admiralty was also fearful that a colonial naval vessel, through inexperience or bravado, might embroil the Royal Navy in an international incident.

Yet for much of the period under discussion the Royal Navy played a constant but undramatic role in the defence of the Australian colonies. From 1821 a ship was detached routinely from the East India Station for service at Sydney, and at times the number of ships so detached increased as the navy was called on to perform various functions in regard to the infant colonies. Circumstances in the western Pacific and the deteriorating situation in New Zealand in the late 1830s and early 1840s led to the permanent detachment of a larger part of the East Indies Station to duty in Australasian waters. Naval forces played a distinguished part in the New Zealand wars of the 1840s, both afloat and ashore, and in 1847 as part of a general review of naval functions it was decided to base a distinct force on the Australian part of the station under the command of a captain. In 1859 the division became a station in its own right – the Australia Station – under the command of a commodore, in response to the defence demands of the newly self-governing colonies, the growing need to police the trade in indentured native labour, and the greater ability it gave to extend protection to the islands of the western Pacific. The ships based there, however, were, in general, neither large, modern nor numerous.

Until the second half of the nineteenth century, imperial defence needs tended to be seen in London as a collection of more or less discrete colonial problems. It was not until later in the century that attempts were made to erect a unitary system of empire defence. In the naval sphere as in the military one, steps were taken to devolve some of the costs of defence to the colonies, through passage of the *Colonial Naval Defence Act 1865*. This empowered those colonies which sought to

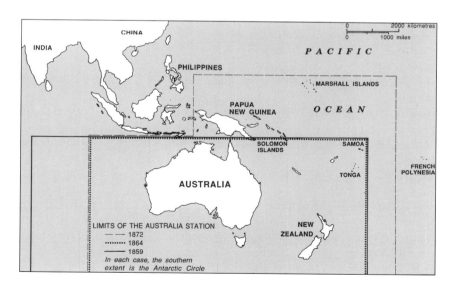

Map 2 Boundaries of the Australia Station, 1859–72. Note that the boundaries were changed again, slightly, in 1893 and 1908

do so to raise their own naval forces for coastal defence purposes. Only Victoria took advantage of this offer, partly because the question of the defence of Port Phillip remained unresolved, certainly because Victoria could afford such measures as the richest of the colonies. The colony ordered the construction in Britain of the armoured monitor, or warship, *Cerberus*, at a cost of £25 000. There was a general lack of colonial enthusiasm otherwise; indeed New Zealand protested that the passage of the Act eroded its own claims to naval protection by fostering a fragmentary approach to naval defence of the colonies.

The importance of the 1865 Act was that it set the terms of the debate over naval defence between London and the colonies for the rest of the century, as the British sought increasingly to redeploy the Royal Navy for strategic as well as fiscal reasons. Colonial naval forces in the nineteenth century could never assume the overall defensive role which the ships of the Royal Navy discharged; their usefulness lay in the degree to which they freed the Royal Navy to make use of its power elsewhere. This cut directly across one of the most entrenched of all colonial concerns, namely the desire for effective defence at the lowest possible price to the colonies themselves.

By the time the regiments departed, the Australian colonies had long since shed the overtly military stamp which had characterised them at their foundation, and which proved transitory. But the economic and social impact of the military in the colonies had gone far beyond the overt duties which they had discharged in the maintenance of law and order and the defence of the colonies from external threat. They had played an important part in the creation of various export industries – most obviously the remount trade with India which kept the British army there supplied with horses – and supplied much of the original administrative infrastructure which made possible colonial economic development. Colonisation by Britain, as opposed to some other European power, meant involvement from the very beginning of white settlement in the world's first industrialising economy. It also determined that Australian military institutions would be modelled upon British patterns. The pool of skills upon which the colony was able to draw, the sheer depth of organisational and administrative talent which the military brought to bear, was a benign outcome of the application of military power in a colonial context. The role of force as a negative factor in our early history is a commonly told tale, while the more prosaic record of prodigious nation-building has been eclipsed. Neither reality, however, is complete without the other.

CHAPTER 2

The Military and the Frontier, 1788–1901

The nations produced by the settler capitalism of an expanding Europe were founded on the dispossession of the original inhabitants. The white immigrant societies in Australia, New Zealand, southern Africa, Canada, the United States, and South America fought indigenous peoples for control of the land, and successfully wrested it from them. This was a gradual process in which the indigenous peoples fell victim as much to disease, cultural deprivation and starvation as to organised violence.

In Australia's case the frontier conflict between European settlement and the Aborigines was, for much of our history, greatly downplayed. Nineteenth-century Australians fostered the belief in the uniquely peaceful settlement of Australia and the victory of science and industry in taming and cultivating the land. The premise, sometimes unspoken, was either that the original inhabitants had simply made way for the white man, or that the Aborigines had no title to the land; the resulting 'history' characterised their opposition to dispossession as occasional, sporadic and ineffectual. Unlike the Maori, the Zulu or the North American Indian, they were not conceded the dignity due to worthy opponents.

We now know that Aboriginal resistance was widespread, consistent and determined, and the debate has moved on to consider whether resistance should properly be called 'warfare'. It centres on the nature, not the fact, of the armed conflict which occurred. To deny the existence of a state of war is to deny the status of combatant to Aborigines, with all the important attendant psychological ramifications. Yet to debate the existence of a state of war or otherwise is to miss the point. The great Prussian theorist of war, Carl von Clausewitz, defined war as 'an act of force to compel our enemy to do our will', and elsewhere

25

wrote that 'war is an act of violence pushed to its utmost limits'. In fact, 'war' is an almost infinitely expandable term and the conflict between native inhabitants and white settlers over the possession and utilisation of land can readily be described as 'war'. That indeed is where the real analysis begins. What matters is the reality of profound conflict. We must ask how it was fought and why the outcome was so decisive. Nor are the answers always obvious or unanimously agreed upon. The argument over black–white conflict has led to absurd claims on both sides, and in seeking to establish the fact of Aboriginal resistance some writers have advanced positions as distorted as those which they seek to refute.

Fundamental to the problem is an understanding of the military application of technology and organisation. It is often assumed, wrongly, that European settlers defeated indigenous peoples through superior firepower. This assumption ignores two things: the history of the military application of technology in the nineteenth century, and the adaptation or otherwise of European technology *and military methods* by native peoples. In general, there were three possible armed responses to European expansion. The first, and that which characterised the later stages of Aboriginal response in Australia, was the use of traditional methods of warfare. These were capable of some refinement and development, but only within their own context. Second was an imitative and sometimes comprehensive copying of the European system. The British fought such armies in India in the 1840s during the Anglo-Sikh Wars. Finally, there was what Belich identifies as adaptive innovation, 'a system which ideally transcended the stratification of both others, and which was specifically designed to cope with European methods – not as a copy of them'. This category covers the Maori military system with the development of the modern *pa*, to which might be added the ready adoption of firearms and the horse by North American Indians in both the eighteenth and nineteenth centuries.

Western development in firearms technology in the nineteenth century was dramatic, if one places the smooth-bore muzzle-loading muskets carried at Waterloo alongside the .303 short magazine Lee Enfield rifle introduced as the standard British infantry weapon in 1902. But this is not the whole picture. Progress in firearms development consisted of a series of incremental advances with a quantum leap occurring only once, in the 1860s, with the wholesale shifting from muzzle-loaders to breech-loaders. Before this, the technological equation could favour the indigenous peoples as often as their European opponents. And none of this explains why some indigenous peoples adopted Western weaponry while others did not. There was no inherent reason why firearms technology should be confined to its creators; indeed, it was not, as the Maoris among many others demonstrated.

Aboriginal peoples were faced with organisational and cultural problems in resisting the British, and at least initially these were more important than technological disadvantages. Traditional warfare was highly ritualised, and localised, and Aboriginal society in Australia had no military class as such. This is linked almost certainly to the fact that Aboriginal societies were not based on surplus-producing economies – the basis of all standing armies. The Aboriginal 'nation' was also very fragmented. If one assumes that linguistic groupings approximated to tribal differences in other cultures, there were perhaps 700 distinct 'nations' in Australia at the time of white contact. While highly complex in their internal structure, they appear to have had no basis for persistent alliances of the kind necessary for successful, long-term military resistance. Thus although the Aborigines outnumbered the whites for at least the first half century of settlement, they were usually incapable of turning this fact to their advantage.

A central element of the Aboriginal failure to resist white incursions successfully was a shared cultural system within which the concept of dispossession was not just unfamiliar but totally incomprehensible. An initial failure to resist implacably was partly a failure fully to grasp the enormity of the European pretension. This expressed itself at a number of levels. Combined with the organisational and technological disadvantages under which Aborigines laboured, this cultural reality explains in large degree why Aborigines failed to pose the significant level of military threat which their numbers and mastery of the country should have presented. Ironically, this failure to defend their land effectively reflected the very profundity of their attachment to it. The truth remained, for too long, literally unthinkable.

Aborigines 'belong' to their land. Land and culture are virtually indivisible. Each territorial group recognised both a central estate and a range over which they hunted and foraged. It was in keeping with tradition for some outsiders to use the resources of the land, provided permission was obtained and certain local laws and taboos were observed. Questions of kinship also involved certain rights in another's domain, and certain restrictions, and family groups would come to blows if these were not observed. The areas 'owned' by individual families were precisely delineated in the minds of all concerned, and penalties for transgression could include ritual spearing and even death. Disputes arose not only over property rights, but also over women, and could be and were settled violently. Aboriginal society was not disadvantaged in its conflict with whites by an exaggerated pacifism.

Despite a complex system of domain rights, the Aborigines lacked a notion of 'invasion' in the sense of a permanent occupation and expropriation of the land. They were familiar with unauthorised incursions ranging from discourtesy to serious breaches of hunting, foraging or travelling rights, and treated them as crimes of varying seriousness. Hence white actions were readily discounted, initially, from acts of war to acts of felony. In some regions in the early post-contact period it is possible that Aborigines were disinclined even to offer violence to whites because they were outside Aboriginal society. Traditional methods may have been deemed inappropriate in a non-traditional setting. Others attempted to deal with white incursions by use of such traditional means as sorcery and pre-arranged battle. Neither was effective, for obvious reasons. In an attempt to explain to themselves the presence and actions of white settlers, some Aborigines assumed them to be returned ancestors and even assigned them the names of former members of the group – how else did one justify their obvious assumption of territorial prerogatives? That whites proved impervious to sorcery must have been another factor in their gaining ascendancy over the Aborigines.

The domination of one group by another, in war as elsewhere, is as much a function of morale as of the preponderance of force. There is clear evidence of the strength of Aboriginal resistance being sapped by disease more than by the force of European arms. Aborigines had no immunity against European diseases. The greatest of these was smallpox, although Aborigines also succumbed to diseases like measles, influenza, tuberculosis and the common cold which were rarely fatal to Europeans. Captain John Hunter, commander of the *Sirius*, noted in his journal that initially the tribes of the Port Jackson region met the settlers of the First Fleet with almost unrelieved hostility. Foraging parties were attacked, often after being lured ashore by friendly gestures or the offer of women. The British strayed from their settlement only in armed parties. After one such attempt to trick them into coming into range, Hunter wrote:

> [w]hat reason they could have had for this treacherous kind of conduct, I am wholly at a loss to guess, for nothing hostile or mischievous had appeared on our part; on the contrary, the most friendly disposition had been manifested in every thing we said or did; even when their women took the alarm upon our approach, I spoke to them, and made such signs of friendship as we judged they would understand, and went round at a distance to prevent their apprehension of any insult. It was perhaps fortunate that my gun did not go off [it missed fire after the party was attacked]; as I was so displeased at their treachery, that it is highly probable I might have shot one of them.

Once smallpox entered the equation, this changed. Perhaps half the population of the Port Jackson region died in a few months. Hunter had been absent on a resupply mission to the Cape when the outbreak occurred. When he returned, he noted 'much surprise, at not having seen a single native on the shore, or a canoe as we came up in the ship; the reason of which I could not comprehend'. On arrival, he learned of a major outbreak of smallpox. It was 'truly shocking to go round the coves of this harbour, which were formerly so frequented by the natives; where, in the caves of the rocks which used to shelter whole families in bad weather, were now to be seen men, women, and children, lying dead'.

Henceforth, the disease preceded the wave of white settlement. On an expedition in-country to the Hawkesbury in April 1791, Governor Phillip found that most of the occupants of the country around Richmond 'were dead of the smallpox'. The disease spread rapidly, and did not require white settlers to facilitate it. In about 1789, and certainly in 1829, a wave of smallpox ravaged the Wiradjuri people along the Murrumbidgee River, killing perhaps 60 per cent of the total Wiradjuri population. When the explorer Charles Sturt came down the river in 1829 he was moving already among survivors of the epidemic. The Wiradjuri fought white settlement for some six years, but their numbers and social organisation had been shattered by the disease and this, as much as the muskets and mounted tactics of the settlers and police, broke their resistance. A series of influenza epidemics in 1847–48 completed the process of demoralisation and social disintegration.

Aboriginal warfare was a form of tribal warfare, an extension of the hunt. It emphasised ambush, skirmishing, hit-and-run attacks, and there is no evidence of any coherent tactical system. Several accounts report parties of Aborigines advancing in a crescent-shaped formation, for example, but there is no indication that this was utilised for any tactical advantage which it might give. It is suggested sometimes that Aboriginal warfare took the form of a guerrilla war, but this is best understood as a description of tactics rather than as any strategic system and certainly bears no resemblance to guerrilla warfare in its post-1945 manifestations. In any case, wars are not won by guerrilla methods alone. Aborigines often selected economic targets, such as livestock, crops and buildings, in their attempt to drive back white settlement, but if this was a strategy it was deeply flawed, since it provoked the Europeans without really altering the balance of military force.

One observer in 1839, during the Wiradjuri wars along the Murrumbidgee, thought it 'not an open fight, but a regular guerrilla warfare'. Stock losses were certainly high. In the same area the Commissioner of Crown Lands, Henry Cosby, noted in his report of May 1839 that Aborigines had killed or run off 980 head of cattle in less than six months. In July alone they accounted for over 1000 more. 'The Blacks have gone so far', he wrote, 'and struck Such Terror into the minds of

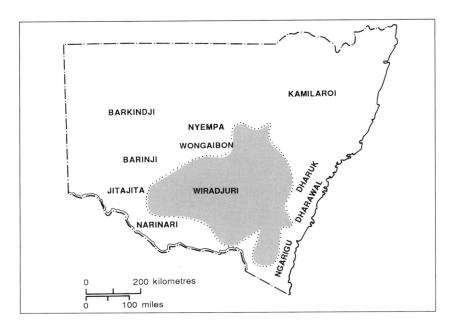

Map 3   Wiradjuri domain and major tribes in pre-contact New South Wales

the Settlers that the White Inhabitants will be compelled to abandon at least 50 miles of the River'. Indeed, it appears that the Wiradjuri not only halted the spread of settlement in their district, but may even have forced a temporary retreat on the part of the settlers – large stations along the Murrumbidgee were abandoned by their occupants. But the settlers were back in force within the year, killing large numbers of Aborigines and reimposing the westward march of the pastoral frontier.

While there is evidence that Aborigines had access to firearms, and in some places even adopted them for hunting, in general guns were not used in war. This emphasised the power of the 'spear tradition': 'killing was traditionally a highly ritualised procedure and it was natural that it was still largely done in a traditional way'. In addition, Aborigines may have preferred traditional weaponry over the unreliable pre-1850 firearms. This latter concern did not influence the Maoris, who acquired large numbers of guns in the 1830s and 1840s and used them to good effect.

Not only did the traditional indigenous methods impose great limitations upon Aboriginal warriors; the Aboriginal way of thinking about war itself was a serious limitation. It was quite possible to adapt firearms to an indigenous method of war, as the Zulus did, or to adapt the method of war to incorporate the new weaponry, as the Maoris did. But the Aborigines generally did neither, certainly in the period when effective opposition might have been possible. Late in the nineteenth century some of the most serious threats to whites were posed by Aborigines who had acquired guns and 'white' skills as native police or trackers, and who then turned these against white settlers in northern and western Australia. But these men were detribalised individuals among whom the power of the 'spear tradition' presumably held no sway.

The other feature which distinguished the wars against the Aborigines from those waged in other areas of British settlement was that in Australia the major part of the conflict was fought by settlers and police, not by the soldiers of the British garrison. This is not to suggest that soldiers took no part. In Tasmania, Governor Arthur declared limited martial law in November 1838 and detailed 100 soldiers to mount a punitive expedition against local Aborigines in the centre of the island, while in October 1830 more than 500 troops drawn from a number of regiments were mobilised under a declaration of full martial law to take part in the infamous 'black drive'. Soldiers were used against the local inhabitants on several occasions in the Swan River colony in the 1830s, Governor Stirling and a detachment of the 21st Regiment assisting the Mounted Police under Captain Ellis at the 'Battle' of Pinjarra in 1834. A detachment of eighty soldiers of the 96th Regiment was sent from Port Arthur to South Australia in October 1841 in response to increased hostility from the Aborigines, and some of them manned isolated garrisons on the Murray and at Port Lincoln. But from the 1840s the Mounted Police and the Native Police Corps were used increasingly to put down the Aborigines and pacify areas of recent settlement and the army, in general, withdrew from this role.

It in no way belittles the fact of Aboriginal resistance to say that this was possible because the Aborigines were not a serious military threat, however gravely the settlers in various areas might fear for their safety. Some 18 000 troops had to be mobilised for the largest of the New Zealand Wars which were fought between 1845 and 1872. Had the Aborigines possessed anything like the same level of military effectiveness, the puny garrison which comprised the Australia Command would have been hopelessly inadequate to the task. But the severe limitations imposed by traditional forms of war meant that bands of settlers suitably armed and equipped, to which were added later the skills of the Native Police, were sufficient to deal with the resistance offered by the indigenous peoples. In 1843 a party of armed settlers set out to 'deal with' a Maori chief at Wairau; they were routed, with twenty-two of their number killed. To believe that New Zealand settlers did not treat the

Maoris as their Australian counterparts did the Aborigines because, when they tried, they got killed is to understate the effectiveness of Aboriginal resistance on occasions. But the point is well made and applies equally to the lessons taught to the Afrikaners by the Zulu and to early French and British settlers in North America by the Iroquois.

Initially, of course, Mounted Police units were raised from the ranks of the army, so that distinctions drawn between the two do not necessarily mean very much. The Mounted Police was formed first in New South Wales in 1825, when Colonel William Stuart transferred a dozen men from his 3rd Regiment to help meet the rise in bushranging. By 1830 their number had risen to about 100, and they were used in conjunction with parties of infantry in operations against Aborigines, as in the Hunter region in 1826. They were modelled loosely on the Royal Irish Constabulary, which flourished between 1814 and 1836 and which was used in Ireland for many of the same purposes, and regiments embarking for service in Australia would recruit an extra fifty men above their establishment for mounted police duties. In 1838 Governor Gipps formed the Border Police to supplement the Mounted Police in the frontier areas of New South Wales. Drawn from military deserters transported to New South Wales from the garrisons at the Cape and in India, they were corrupt and inefficient, and noted for their brutality towards the native population. In 1846 they were disbanded. While the expedient of mounting some members of the garrison gave the security forces a useful element of mobility, a group of stockmen was at least as adept tactically as the soldiers and it remained the case that the military was called upon to deal with the Aborigines only in cases of serious resistance to white encroachments.

The pattern of conflict in Australia ran parallel to the pattern of settlement. From the early days around Sydney Cove the hostility of the Aborigines to the depredations of the whites was clear to all. As settlement spread along the Hawkesbury and Georges Rivers and to Parramatta, the pattern of harassment, crop-burning and ambush increased, and was reciprocated. In some places the Aborigines resisted for years, usually because the area which they inhabited afforded some particular advantage in terrain which enabled them to maintain food resources while at the same time making it difficult for Europeans to operate against them. In many places, however, the local population was defeated quickly, reduced in numbers by exotic diseases and declining food resources and unable to withstand the relentless pressures of a constantly increasing European population.

By the time the Aborigines had begun to think of white settlement in terms of invasion and expropriation of their land, they lacked some of the advantages which had accrued naturally to them in the early years of

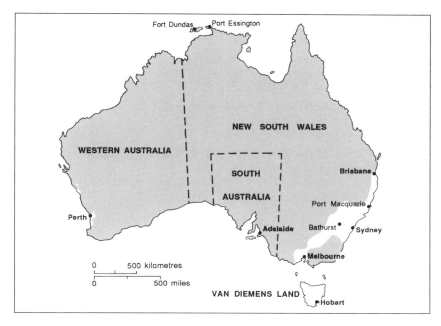

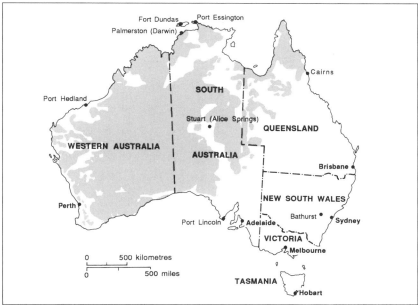

Map 4 Spread of white settlement in Australia in 1838 (top) and 1888 (bottom).
Source: Australians: A Historical Atlas, Sydney, 1987, 42

settlement. The Hawkesbury sandstone country of the Sydney region was close, often wooded and marked by heavy scrub. It gave the British little opportunity to use the mobility which horses provided, and equalled the odds of combat by providing the Aborigines with many sites from which to ambush their opponents. Once settlement had broken out of the mountains to the west of Sydney, the open plains enabled the settlers to maximise their strength and pit it against Aboriginal weaknesses in technology and organisation.

As settlement extended beyond the environs of Sydney the dimensions of the conflict grew nonetheless. In the Liverpool Plains region, sixteen whites were killed between 1832 and 1838, and many hundreds of blacks were killed in the two-year span 1836–38, including those at the notorious Myall Creek massacre in June 1838 and the even worse killings of large numbers at Slaughterhouse Creek and other places along the Gwydir River. This second wave of settlement in New South Wales was also characterised by the occasional declaration of martial law and the utilisation of soldiers to hunt down marauding bands of Aboriginals, but far more often the killing was done by civilians, as at Myall Creek, or by the police. Seven Europeans were hanged for their part in the Myall Creek killings, but no such fate was awarded Major Nunn and the detachment of Mounted Police who had shot down anywhere between twelve and eighty (the official estimates) or as many as 200–300 Aborigines at Waterloo Creek in January the same year. The 'war of extirpation' waged against the Aborigines in various parts of the colonies was never any part of central government policy, a view supported by the Myall Creek trial and verdict. But the effects of unofficial action were real enough to contemporary observers: Edmund Denny Day, a local magistrate, reported a 'war of extirpation' on the Gwydir in mid-1838, and wrote that Aborigines in the district were repeatedly 'pursued by parties of mounted and armed stockmen, assembled for the purpose, and that great numbers of them had been killed at various spots'. Although he himself had not witnessed the events concerned, clearly they were open knowledge in the area. Such actions received sanction in the press. In November 1838 the *Sydney Thunderer* exhorted its readers to protect themselves from 'the filthy brutal cannibals of New Holland', and that since the government made 'inadequate exertion' to protect life and property, to shoot the 'ferocious savages' as they would 'any white robbers or murderers'. That many Aboriginal tribes were wiped out in the course of the conflict tells us much about the nature of that conflict, and of some of those who waged it, but rather less about the intentions of British and colonial government policy.

Certainly by the middle of the century attitudes were hardening. A crude social Darwinism was increasingly influential, propagating the belief that the Aborigines were an inferior race whose fate was to be assimilation and redemption (literally, from the point of view of the Christian missionaries), or a gradual dying away in the face of progress. Equally, the edge of the frontier spread north of the Tropic of Capricorn after 1850, encountering much larger concentrations of indigenous peoples far from the centres of colonial civilisation. After mid-century, violence was perhaps more easily rationalised in British minds than it had been, not least as a result of the fears generated by the Indian Mutiny. The massacre at Cawnpore and the siege of Lucknow sent a frisson of horror down the collective Victorian spine, and the massacres in Queensland of the Frasers at Hornetbank in October 1857 and of the Wills party on the Nogoa River in October 1861, both of which involved white women and children, tapped some of the deepest racial fears of nineteenth-century Englishmen.

At the same time, the widespread introduction of breech-loading weapons was giving the settlers an overwhelming technological advantage over the Aborigines, and the quasi-military organisation of a Native Police Force was copied from the southern colonies. Native Police had been formed in Victoria and New South Wales in the early 1840s, and had been used to great effect in pacifying the tribes of the Western District of Victoria and the northern rivers of New South Wales. In Victoria, at least, they had been seen as a means of civilising the Aborigine as well as employing the skills of bushcraft and tracking against recalcitrant groups. Under the efficient and fairly ruthless command of Commandant Henry Edmund Pulteney Dana, a corps of indigenous police was raised in the Port Phillip district in January 1842. Active in the Western District and along the Murray, Dana's men provided a cheap and effective means of checking Aboriginal depredations against settlers' flocks, properties and lives. They were responsible also for wholesale killings of recalcitrant blacks. Upon Dana's death in November 1852 the corps was disbanded, by which time it had fulfilled its intended function admirably, but other divisions of Native Police were active still in New South Wales where settlement had extended northwards into the Darling Downs region. Resistance was widespread once again: 174 Europeans were killed in the Moreton Bay–Darling Downs area by 1852, 250 by 1860. A detachment of native police was raised in the Moreton Bay settlement in 1848. This force, at least, was not even a government institution. It was sanctioned from Sydney, but it was raised and run by the squatters themselves and was commanded by Frederick Walker, who became Commandant of Police and who was well known for his ruthlessness towards threatening, or even potentially threatening, Aborigines. It was disbanded in 1855, but the region was by no means pacified and various units of Native Mounted Police were set up and run by the squatters at their own expense and with minimal direction from Sydney. After separation of the colony in 1859 the new government of Queensland instituted an inquiry into the native forces, and the Native Police was placed on a more regular footing under the Police Act of 1863. The force had its headquarters near Rockhampton, and deployed 137 all ranks in fourteen detachments across the colony.

The greatest and most sustained incidents of violence between whites and Aborigines occurred in northern Queensland, where resistance offered to settlement was universal and determined, constituting 'a major obstacle to the economic exploitation of newly-opened regions'. There were 470 deaths at Aboriginal hands in North Queensland alone after 1860, two-thirds of them white, and at least 4000 Aborigines were killed. In Queensland overall, between 1840 and 1897 perhaps 850 Europeans and their allies were killed. The main instrument of reaction to Aboriginal resistance was the Native Police. Its numbers rose to around 200 by 1875, and it was responsible for many punitive actions against Queensland Aborigines, to which were added countless private reprisals mounted by settlers and miners. The other great attraction of the force was its relative cheapness; its annual budget in the 1860s was about £14 000, which constituted 5 per cent of the colonial budget but which was far less than the cost of maintaining an equivalent force of Europeans. Between 1860 and 1880 the total outlay involved was about £300 000, a large sum justified by the fact that the Native Police made possible the rapid settlement of the pastoral frontier. Indeed, from 1864 the Police Commissioner in Queensland was entrusted with the implementation of frontier policy in the colony.

The frontier conflict continued into the present century in the Northern Territory and the far northwest of the country, with several notorious reprisal massacres of Aborigines being perpetrated into the 1920s. It is all but impossible to arrive at casualty figures for the whole period. We do not know with certainty what the pre-contact population was. Some of the violence is well documented; some, by its very nature, is not documented at all. It is likely that between 2000 and 2500 Europeans died at the hands of Aborigines; with 20 000 a conservative estimate of black deaths in violent circumstances associated with aggression or reprisal on behalf of the settler society. Many times that number died of introduced diseases, starvation, and hopelessness.

The fact of concerted Aboriginal resistance to white encroachment gives the lie to the belief in the peaceful and unopposed settlement of Australia after 1788. But the literature which has revised our view of the subject is in danger of imposing distortions of its own. Claims of an official policy of genocide in the nineteenth century are refuted by the evidence. To describe every encounter as a 'massacre' under-estimates the resolve of both sides to fight to the finish and casts the Aborigines in the role of passive victims. Finally, some of the claims made for an Aboriginal 'system' of warfare complete with 'battles' and 'battlefields' misrepresents the nature of Aboriginal–non-Aboriginal conflict in Australia. The attempt to turn a figure like Pemulwuy into an Aboriginal Hector is pointless, and cannot be sustained. It does not require this sort of embellishment for white Australians to concede the geographical spread and effectiveness of Aboriginal resistance. To understand why Aborigines never presented the type of military threat to the British which the Maoris or Zulus mounted elsewhere is to grasp some of the essential realities of a unique and ancient culture. Ironically, the beliefs, values and expectations which had made Aboriginal societies at home in Australia for tens of thousands of years, together with the biological and military vulnerability produced by long isolation, left Aborigines profoundly ill-equipped to meet the challenge of white society.

Although it forms no direct part of the establishment of the frontier and the armed contest for control of the land discussed above, the revelations over the 'stolen generations' of Aboriginal children in the twentieth century – and more especially the reaction of denial and belittling of those revelations by some white Australians – illustrates the extent to which the issue of white dispossession of black Australia remains a contested one in Australian history, and in contemporary politics. To label the recognition of profound conflict on the frontier a 'black armband' view of the past is to risk replacing it with a 'white blindfold' interpretation, as a number of observers have stated. The latter position is simply unsustainable.

CHAPTER 3

The Colonial Period, 1870–1901

The withdrawal of the main body of British troops from the Australian Colonies in August 1870 caused no great perturbation. Some newspaper editorials praised the opportunity the change had created for serious thinking about the defence of the colonies, but the second Intercolonial Conference meeting in Melbourne in July – after reminding the British government of its duty to provide for their maritime defence needs – returned to its usual round of squabbling over free trade, tariffs and a customs union. If the motivation in London behind the troop with-drawal had been to instil a more mature appreciation of colonial defence responsibilities in the Australian colonies at least, the period until Federation in 1901 was to prove a disappointment.

The last thirty years of the nineteenth century saw a period of enormous prosperity up to 1888, followed by a devastating bust in the Australian colonies. The 1870s and, even more, the 1880s were a time of great expansion in the economy marked by the inflow of British capital and its utilisation in land booms and speculation. Sophisticated com-munications networks and considerable building activity refashioned the major cities, especially Melbourne, which became the financial capital of the country and a great Victorian city. Population growth had tapered off after the end of the gold rush and was not to experience a further spurt until the wave of assisted passages in the decade before the Great War. The early 1890s saw an economic depression which only the crash of 1929 would surpass in severity. The bubble burst, banks failed especially in Victoria and politicians fell with them as harsh economic realities exposed their own financial dealings. The decade was marked by intense dispute and bitterness between capital and labour, wide-spread strikes and lockouts bordering on armed confrontation between the two sides. Prices for primary produce fell disastrously, taking wages and conditions with them.

The orthodox response to the economic crisis was applied by all colonial governments, and the impact of the resultant reductions in public expenditure was felt by the infant colonial defence forces. Against this background the colonies moved hesitantly towards Federation and, in both the 1880s and at the end of the century, took their first steps towards the development of that expeditionary force mentality which was to characterise so much of Australian defence policy for the succeeding sixty years.

Developments in the colonies in this period must be seen also in the context of the policy of imperial defence which sought to spread the military burdens of empire. This, after all, had been the overt justification for the withdrawal of troops from the self-governing colonies in the first place. Such a policy did not leap fully formed from the brow of Whitehall; the idea attracted much talk but painfully little action. Benjamin Disraeli's Crystal Palace speech in 1872, in which he spoke of the creation of a military code for the colonies, was not followed by any action in this direction when the Conservatives came to power after the 1874 election. Of course, from London's perspective there were many pressures and issues more important than the views and requirements of the antipodean colonies. The principal imperial military needs of the age were home defence and the defence of India; and the acquisition of new interests and possessions such as the Suez Canal placed further demands upon those resources. There was pressure too from the Admiralty to end the dispersal of the Royal Navy, brought about by the role of world policeman which the navy characteristically played but which would give way increasingly to other roles closer to home as the century drew to a close. And the picture was further complicated still by the fact that the self-governing colonies did not speak with one voice, nor present one set of strategic problems.

The departure of the British army created a particular requirement for the establishment of standing defence forces in the colonies, to stand in relation to the volunteer forces in the same way as the British regulars had done before 1870. The results were not impressive, at least initially, and although the opportunity might have been taken to move towards a federal system, at least for defence or in imitation of Canadian Confederation, inter-colonial rivalry ensured that defence measures continued on a colony-by-colony basis until the end of the nineteenth century.

If the strategic environment in which the Australian colonies operated had changed little, the basis on which to construct colonial defence forces was less than promising. The Volunteers continued, of course, although the Land Grant schemes were discontinued in most of the colonies by the mid-1870s. The first colony to set about raising a permanent paid defence force was New South Wales in 1871, a move which resulted in the formation of a battery of artillery and two companies of infantry. This was in addition to the twenty-eight companies of the Volunteer Rifles and the nine batteries of artillery volunteers which existed on a colony-wide basis. Victoria created a small permanent unit which may have fulfilled some role as garrison artillery but whose primary function appears to have been as a recruiting force for the colonial police and prisons service. Here too the Volunteers continued in existence, manning batteries at various sites around Port Phillip Bay and fielding detachments at various centres. Of significance too was the purchase of the ironclad monitor *Cerberus*, ordered from, and partly paid for by, the Admiralty, and sailed from Chatham by a colonial crew. It arrived in Port Phillip Bay on 9 April 1871 and saw out its service as a port defence vessel and as flagship of the Victorian Colonial Navy. With a top speed of six knots, no sea-going capacity worth speaking of, and a consumption of thirty tons of coal per day on its commissioning voyage to Melbourne, it was hardly the basis for the projection of colonial naval power.

The periodic war scares and alarms by which colonial defence preparations may be charted in the first half of the century continued after 1870. A further war scare in 1878 saw Disraeli reinforce the garrison on Malta with drafts of troops from India. It affected colonial defences in two ways. First, it prompted a statement by the Colonial Secretary in the House of Commons that the colonial forces maintained by the self-governing colonies were liable for service not only in the colonies which raised and maintained them, but also for dispatch and service outside the colony according to regulations drawn up by the governor. Secondly, the debate over Disraeli's move led to the setting up of a Royal Commission by the Colonial Secretary to enquire into the state of the defences of British possessions abroad, and this necessitated the expression of some colonial opinion. The second volume of the commission's report dealt with the defence problems of the Australasian colonies.

The recommendations of the Carnarvon Commission set the tone for the discussion of defence matters between London and the Australian colonies for the rest of the century and into the first decade of the next. This was especially true of naval policies. The Commission quoted with approval the findings of an imperial officer, Major General Sir William Jervois, that the defence of commerce and communication should remain an imperial responsibility and that the colonies should contribute to the defence of ports and coaling stations from their own resources. Localised colonial naval forces were opposed, strongly, but the principle of colonial financial contributions to the costs of naval protection was introduced, despite the objections of the premier of New South Wales, Sir Henry Parkes. Parkes appeared before the Commission and stated that, while the colonies would doubtless make their resources available for the common defence in time of war, the principle of shared costs through subsidy would carry with it a claim for shared responsibility in decision-making. Not all the colonial dignitaries echoed this view, but it was a foretaste of things to come and was to be reflected by Canadian as well as Australian colonial statesmen in subsequent years.

Parkes was not the only colonial political figure to take an interest in local defence. In 1876 the premier of New South Wales, John Robertson, had forwarded to London a request, on behalf of his government and those of Queensland, Victoria and South Australia, for the services of an imperial officer who might give the colonial administrations 'good professional advice' on the state of their defences. The request went so far as to specify the officer desired, Sir William Drummond Jervois of the Royal Engineers. At that time Chief Administrator of the Straits Settlements, he had already acted as adviser to the Canadian government and had a background in planning for the defence of Britain itself. He was an uncommonly well-qualified and senior officer for the job required. Unfortunately he was also unavailable in the short term, but when the colonies declined the proffered services of another imperial inspector, Lord Carnarvon, the Colonial Secretary, released him early from his term as Chief Administrator in the interests of facilitating colonial interest in colonial defence matters.

Jervois was assisted by another Royal Engineer, Lieutenant Colonel Peter Scratchley, who had experience of the Australian colonies (his wife came from Victoria) and of the usual fate of reports into their defences. This highly able pair demonstrated once again the enormously influential role played by a handful of Royal Engineer officers in the nineteenth-century colonies, whether in helping to establish their economic infrastructure or in more specifically military matters. At the time of their investigations, several of the colonies had recently completed Royal Commissions of inquiry into the state of their defence forces, but the Jervois–Scratchley mission was the first time that a systematic survey of all the colonies (except Western Australia) was completed on the ground by the same team of investigators.

As noted, the basis of their reports was the understanding that the defence of the Australian colonies was linked to the wider concerns of empire defence, and that the Royal Navy was the guarantor of security. Both officers were navalists, and believed that the distance of the colonies from potential aggressors and the shield provided by the Royal

Navy meant that the threat to the colonies would take the form commonly of raids and short-term lodgements. As engineers, they tended to adopt the 'bricks and mortar' solution to the defence of ports and other strategic sites which, given their assumptions and the technology of the day, was good sense. Fortifications served by batteries of guns would be supported by mobile field forces to guard against enemy landings which might outflank the defenders. The recommendations were acted upon, in general, and the colonial administrations embarked upon a building program in Sydney, Newcastle, Port Phillip Bay, Hobart, Moreton Bay, and Adelaide, the fruits of which can still be seen on South and Middle Heads in Sydney, at Fort Scratchley in Newcastle, at Queenscliff in Victoria and elsewhere. Although the size and detail of the colonial defence forces themselves would fluctuate, this scheme remained the basis of territorial defence in the colonies until Federation.

Direct payment schemes were introduced in the course of the late 1870s and 1880s, in order to open the part-time units to men of the working classes for whom the costs of providing uniform and equipment, coupled with the wages lost through attendance at parades, precluded involvement. These partially paid volunteers, the militia, often existed alongside 'pure' volunteer units. By the mid-1880s all the colonies except Western Australia enjoyed this mix of militia and volunteer soldiers, although the volunteers went into temporary decline until the middle of the following decade. Victoria in fact disbanded all volunteer units as part of the defence reorganisation of 1884, incorporating some into the newly raised militia units. In Queensland the payment of volunteers while in annual camp was abolished in 1880, and in 1884 under the provisions of the Queensland Defence Act the colony set up a dual system of paid militia in the metropolitan area, unpaid volunteers in rural areas, and a reserve of former militia members. Officers were almost always men of standing in their communities, members of the professions, retired imperial officers and politicians. In rural areas the officers were often the sons of the local squattocracy, with the other ranks provided from the rural labour force which worked the pastoral stations. Other units were formed by groups and organisations within colonial society; early rifle companies in Tasmania were provided by the Masonic lodges, and the Australian Natives' Association raised a company in Adelaide. Private patronage played a part also, and the Victorian Horse Artillery (the Rupertswood battery) was formed and paid for by Sir William Clarke, partly as a plaything for his son.

There was little uniformity in arms and equipment between the various colonies. All bought their arms from Britain, often being sold obsolescent models which were in the process of being phased out of British service. Thus the various forts around Australia continued to use rifled muzzle-loading (RML) guns long after breech-loading ordnance had been introduced elsewhere; many of the infantry companies were issued with the old Martini–Henry single-shot rifle, while the British army was being equipped with the magazine fed Lee Metford and Lee Enfield. The units themselves borrowed heavily from British patterns, and several colonies boasted Scottish and Irish regiments ('national corps' as they were known), complete with kilts and bonnets, and cavalry regiments dressed like dragoons or equipped with lances. By the 1890s this was giving way to khaki drab and the slouch hat, although the national corps continued to exist until the advent of compulsory military training early in the next century.

The depression of the 1890s had a marked effect upon the fortunes of the colonial forces, some units folding for lack of funds and men. In South Australia the navy, comprising HMCS *Protector*, was paid off, and the military forces suffered a reduction in the budget of £12 000. In 1893 the annual camp was made voluntary, to save costs, and men who left were not replaced. In Tasmania half the permanent force was discharged and all funds for training were withdrawn. In Victoria the permanent force was reduced and those remaining suffered a cut in pay – the militia rate dropped from £12 per annum in 1891 to £6 5s. in 1894. In New South Wales the annual camps were cancelled in 1892 and 1893, and pay for the militia likewise was reduced. All these measures led to resignations from both the permanent and militia forces, which reduced costs, and effectiveness, still further. The early 1890s was marked by widespread industrial unrest in the wider community, and units of the colonial defence forces were used in strike-breaking roles in Queensland 'in aid of the civil power' and in support of the pastoralists who had imported non-union labour to work in the shearing sheds. In Victoria the forces were called out during the Great Maritime Strike in 1890, best remembered perhaps for the ill-chosen words of Colonel Tom Price, who allegedly instructed his men to 'fire low and lay the bastards out' should the order to fire be given (it wasn't, and he later claimed to have been misquoted). There was a revival of the Volunteers after the middle of the decade, and many of those who had been forced by economic circumstance to reduce their involvement in the part-time forces were able to resume their interest. But the depression of the 1890s was severe and many like John Monash, a Melbourne engineer and captain in the Victorian garrison artillery, did not fully recover financially until the decade's end.

For all the efforts of the colonists themselves, the cornerstone of Australian defence remained the ships of the Royal Navy, beginning with those based on the Australia Station. The navy itself had undergone change as a result of reforms overseen by the First Lord of the

Admiralty, Hugh Childers, in 1869. These had begun to reverse the decline in size and quality which had set in and which had seen most of the major developments in naval architecture and technology in mid-century pioneered by the French. They led also to the redistribution of naval vessels. This was motivated as much by desires for economy as any predominant naval strategy, but in the course of the 1870s and 1880s, under the influence of Admiral Sir John Colomb and other apostles of sea power, the notion of the interdependence of the empire and the need to protect the empire's lines of communications became accepted as the basis of imperial defence. In addition, by the 1880s the security of the metropolitan centre was seen as paramount, a notion which did not necessarily contradict the concerns of imperial defence but which was to introduce strains within the relationship between Britain and the dominions, since colonial politicians were disinclined to accept that the navy's brief included the defence of the empire as a whole and not only or merely that of the Australian colonies. At the Intercolonial Conference in 1881, for example, the Australian colonies had sought an enhanced naval presence in Australian waters, but had rejected the principle of colonial contribution. These various trends were to culminate in the Naval Defence Agreement of 1887 and the Naval Defence Act of 1889, which by British legislative fiat established the 'two-power standard' and which laid down that the strength of the Royal Navy was to be maintained at a level sufficient to beat the navies of any other two powers combined.

One of Jervois' recommendations had concerned the acquisition of local naval defence capabilities by the colonies themselves, a recommendation adopted by a number of the colonial administrations. Jervois' idea was that this would then free the ships of the Royal Navy for wider duties. The Admiralty resisted strenuously attempts to break up the squadron in Sydney and disperse it among the various colonial ports, but were happy to agree to the provision of colonial naval forces as a means of humouring the colonists and ensuring that they did not become so disenchanted with British arrangements for their security as to consider severing relations. But the Sea Lords took a sufficiently jaundiced view of colonial navies to refuse the sanction of the White Ensign for colonial naval vessels, not wishing to be embroiled in an incident or, worse, a war, as the result of the actions of an inexperienced colonial officer.

The 1887 Agreement was a step towards a cooperative scheme for imperial defence. At heart it sought to resolve two problems – should colonial navies be an alternative to or a part of the Royal Navy squadron, and should naval defence be provided at imperial or colonial expense? The Russian scare of 1885 had added urgency to sporadically surfacing colonial defence concerns, and the agreement itself was the fruit of long negotiations between the Flag Officer commanding the Australia Station, Rear Admiral Sir George Tryon, and the colonial governments. The agreement, which had been the major defence issue placed before the first Colonial Conference held in London in April 1887, required the Admiralty to station an additional squadron of five fast cruisers and two torpedo gunboats for the defence of Australasian maritime trade. The colonies were to pay £126 000 annually towards its costs, with New Zealand's share being £20 000. The auxiliary squadron was not to leave Australian waters without the agreement of the colonial governments, and the agreement was to run for ten years. The New Zealanders wanted two of the ships based in New Zealand waters, but had to settle for regular visits.

The Admiralty regarded the colonial veto on deployment of the auxiliary squadron as a fundamental hindrance to sensible naval strategy, and soon sought to have it revoked. Their fears were aided by the pro-prietorial attitude of the colonies to 'their' ships, and by the complaints received whenever one or other colony felt that it received insufficiently frequent visits. In fact, the colonies got the better end of the deal and it was to take the Admiralty sixteen years to remove the worst of the restrictions. But the agreement had the effect also of killing off any desires to form colonial blue-water navies. The colonists wanted defence on the cheap, and they got it; the Admiralty preserved most of the elements of undivided command and control which were important to it, and received some assistance in bearing the burden of naval expenditure. One thing the agreement did not do was to spark en-thusiasm in other self-governing colonies for similar schemes, a blow to those who hoped for a naval contribution from the whole empire, and who dreamed even of imperial federation.

Such dreams, and the hopes entertained in London about colonial willingness to serve in the cause of empire, were given a considerable fillip by the events of 1885. Too much weight should not be placed upon the dispatch of a New South Wales contingent to the Sudan that year. It was a relatively minor incident, but it provides evidence both of the growing willingness of colonial society to take part in the wars of empire in certain circumstances, and tells us something about the attitudes of colonial society to war and empire at this time.

The circumstances in which the force was raised may be dealt with briefly. The news of the death of General Sir Charles Gordon at Khartoum at the hands of the Mahdi's forces reached Australia on 6 February, sparking a wave of public grief and outrage of which perhaps only the Victorian age was capable. The very next morning a retired British officer, Major General Sir Edward Strickland, suggested via the pages of the morning newspaper that the colony should offer to field an expeditionary force to help revenge Gordon. The idea was seized upon by the acting Premier, William Bede Dalley, and, without recourse to parliament, the raising of a force of infantry and artillery was at once undertaken. Thirty officers, 740 men and 218 horses were embarked within two weeks of Dalley's offer to London. This was the first occasion on which forces in the pay of a self-governing colony had served in an imperial war; offers had been made before, and had been rejected, and the offers received from Victoria, South Australia, New Zealand and Canada on this occasion, likewise, were rejected. The offer from New South Wales was accepted through a mix of judicious timing, the particular circumstances of Gordon's death and the resultant criticism of William Ewart Gladstone's administration in London, and the urgings of the governor of New South Wales, Lord Augustus Loftus, who cabled London that refusal of the offer of assistance would 'be deeply felt in the colony'. With an eye to morale both in London and Sydney, the British government accepted the offer, more or less graciously.

The contingent was dispatched amid enormous crowds and considerable celebration on 3 March. It reached the Sudan at the end of March, but in approximately two months of 'operations' the men saw practically no fighting, spending much of their time providing guard details for the railway which was being constructed by native labour to meet the logistic requirements of Sir Garnet Wolseley's Anglo-Egyptian army. It was not that there was no fighting to be done, rather that the New South Wales contingent missed out on nearly all of it. A couple of men were wounded slightly in the concluding stages of the Battle of Tamai (little more than a punitive skirmish), but the fatalities among the force were entirely the result of disease and accident. The force returned to Sydney on 23 June, to a very muted reception indeed. The great hopes which the good citizens of New South Wales had placed in their contingent had not been realised – through no fault of the men, it should be added – and the derision and parsimony with which they were received on their return was in marked contrast to the scenes which had heralded their dispatch.

The significance of the event lies in two aspects, the existence of opposition to the sending of the contingent and the disinclination of the colony and the troops to serve elsewhere at the discretion of imperial authorities. The crisis in relations with Russia which led to the diversion of troops from the Sudan to India and the postponement (by thirteen years) of a settling of scores with the Mahdi prompted Dalley to offer the services of the contingent for use in India, 'to assert the arms of England wherever our help is needed'. The mood in the colony had shifted, however, and opinion held that in the event of war with Russia the place of the contingent was in New South Wales, assisting in the defence of home and hearth. The men themselves were asked whether they would volunteer to serve elsewhere, but the result was disappointing, with few men coming forward. In part it was prompted by concerns for the defence of their own colony, but there is evidence to suggest that many of the men who declined to volunteer for possible service in India were casting a vote of no confidence in the contingent's officers. The change of attitude in the colony itself suggests strongly that at this stage at least the colonial Australians were not prepared blindly to send forces to any and every imperial emergency.

The question of opposition to the dispatch of the contingent is more difficult. The claims for a nascent 'peace' or 'anti-war' movement at this time seem exaggerated, and owe not a little to the efforts of later generations to create a tradition of anti-war activism back to the dispatch of the first expeditionary force. The serious opposition to Dalley's efforts came from within the mainstream political process, headed by Parkes who used the occasion as a means of getting back into public life, from which he had 'retired' in 1884. Opposition from this source in fact centred not on the contingent itself but on the manner in which it had been sent; the government had failed to consult the legislature or the full Cabinet and had acted without the approval of the Colonial Treasurer. When the matter was placed before the parliament, the Australian Military Contingent Bill was passed by a wide margin. Within the parliamentary sphere, support for the contingent tended to come from native-born Australians – men like Dalley, frequently with convict ancestry and, in his case, a Catholic to boot – while opposition came often from those with close English connections who echoed liberal sentiments opposed to the subjugation of the Sudan. In that sense the dispatch of troops became a nationalist issue, one in which amends were to be made for the 'convict stain'. On the other hand, opposition from journals like the *Bulletin* stemmed from the radical, anti-imperial nationalism which was to find its chief expression in literary and artistic forms in the 1890s. The dropping away of popular support for the contingent had less to do with any anti-war or pacifist sentiment than with the frustration of popular expectations, which had been pitched impossibly high in the emotional and jingoistic atmosphere of the early months of 1885.

The last fifteen years of the century were marked by attempts both by the British and the colonies themselves to impose some measure of cohesion upon defence matters. The creation of the Colonial Defence Committee in April 1885 was the first attempt in London to establish a permanent agency charged with guiding the colonies on defence matters. The system of itinerant and irregular reporting, of the kind which Scratchley and Jervois had undertaken, was replaced now with a small standing committee of the Colonial Office to which all the colonies could refer their defence arrangements for discussion, guidance and approval. Its first task was to discuss the defence of the West Indies, but in August 1885 the Colonial Defence Committee circulated a request to all colonial authorities asking for details of their defence forces and infrastructure, largely in the interests of collecting for the first time a systematic body of information concerning colonial defence. Colonial governments were requested also to forward copies of their defence plans.

The committee laboured busily on its task, reviewing the local defence needs of the empire. Within two years it had prepared twenty-six memoranda on such issues, and had made recommendations in a further fifty-three cases. Between 1885 and 1891 it met on fifty-eight occasions, considered 470 items of business, scrutinised the defences of thirty-seven colonies, and assisted a further nineteen to draw up defence plans of their own. In 1890 it even composed a memorandum on the advantages of Federation in the defence of Australia. The Colonial Defence Committee aroused some antagonism from both the Admiralty and the War Office, which it resisted successfully, but equally found the self-governing colonies disinclined to cooperate on occasions; the Canadians repeatedly delayed drawing up plans for their defence, the New Zealanders reported regularly but nonetheless did not submit their first defence scheme until 1899, while the government of Tasmania never submitted one at all! When the new Commonwealth government in Australia made it clear that it would establish a national fleet of its own early in the new century, the countervailing views of the Committee could not sway them. But the establishment of the Committee was an important step in the systematisation of imperial defence, and it remained a useful tool until it was subsumed by the Committee of Imperial Defence in the aftermath of the Haldane reforms in 1904 by which the British army, and the governmental machinery for strategic direction, were brought into the twentieth century.

Colonial reactions were prompted by the pressures for political Federation and the renewed spectre of European colonial expansion close to Australian territory. To fears of the French, Russians and Americans were added the Germans, whose claims to the Solomons and the northern part of New Guinea in August 1884 led to the declaration of a British protectorate over south-east New Guinea. This region was of greater concern to the colonial authorities than it was to the imperial ones and earlier demands in 1883, especially from Queensland, that imperial authority be asserted in the area had been rejected. Although the outcome had proven satisfactory in some senses, the experience generated considerable criticism of British 'tardiness' in protecting what was seen in the colonies as a legitimate area of interest, and led directly to the formation of the Federal Council. Formed to speak to Whitehall 'with a united voice' on matters of 'foreign relations' which affected the colonies, the Council had no powers over the defence forces of the colonies and was not representative, since New South Wales and New Zealand declined to join. It became widely discredited in the 1890s, and was of greater significance in the gathering movement leading to Federation than in the growth of systematic organisation for defence.

One further consequence of these events was the formation in Victoria of a Department of Defence. Created as part of the defence reorganisation pushed through by the premier, James Service, in 1883–84 and formalised in the Defence Act of 1883, it was the only colonial department of state created to deal solely with defence matters. F. T. Sargood, a member of the Legislative Council and a major in the Volunteers, had been made minister without portfolio in 1883 with responsibility for defence matters; in the following year he was made the first Minister for Defence. Initially the day-to-day running of the Victorian forces was placed in the hands of a Council of Defence, but in April 1885 the position was regularised with the appointment of the first secretary of the department, Major General M. F. Downes, the former Commandant of South Australia. The appointment was used also to assert the primacy of representative civil power over the military, a position contested actively by the Commandant, Colonel T. R. Disney, RA. The military and naval Commandants reported to the minister through the permanent head, although they remained responsible to the minister and thence the government. Other colonies continued to entrust administration and control of their defence forces to ministers whose primary responsibilities were in other spheres.

The drive for Federation nonetheless had an effect upon defence issues, although the commonly held belief that a concern for strong, centrally directed defences was a prime motivation for Federation is not borne out by the evidence. The 1887 Colonial Conference produced not only the Naval Agreement, but concern on the part of the Australian colonies for regular, periodic inspection of their forces. The premier of Queensland and the defence minister of Victoria, Samuel Griffith and Sir James Lorimer respectively, both urged this course upon their fellow delegates, finding general agreement from all except Parkes, who asserted that the colonies should act for themselves and on the basis of their own estimates. Ironically, it was Parkes who was to make the greatest use of the report of Major General J. Bevan Edwards which resulted.

Edwards' *Proposed Organisation of the Military Forces of the Australian Colonies* conflicted with the views of earlier reports, not least in that he did not discount the possibility of a strong attack being launched against the Australian colonies by powerful enemy fleets. The overall thrust of his report was that the colonies should federate in the interests of efficient defence. The colonial militias, he argued, which could not operate outside the borders of their own colony, would need to be concentrated to meet an invasion; arms, equipment, training, legislation and rail gauges should all be standardised; the whole should be commanded by an imperial officer in the interests of a unified command, replacing the system whereby each colony's forces had its own Commandant who acted as commander-in-chief. Cooperation was to be the order of the day.

This report did not find great favour with the Colonial Defence Committee which, in common with advice from all sections of Whitehall, had been arguing that the Australian colonies did not face a significant threat because of the global efforts of the Royal Navy and the clear lack of any bases from which potentially hostile forces might stage an invasion. The federation of colonial defence efforts clearly was desirable, however, and the Colonial Defence Committee encouraged this development by commenting favourably upon a general plan for Australian defence drafted by a committee of all the military Commandants which met in October 1894. These plans were duly revised by the Inter-Colonial Military Committee which met in 1896 and which recommended their implementation to the colonial premiers. By that stage, however, the impetus for political federation had grown such that military federation was seen increasingly as a consequence rather than as a progenitor of a federal Australia.

Parkes' famed Tenterfield Oration in October 1889 used defence as a convenient hook on which to hang the wider issue, and he mentioned this before Edwards had issued his report on the desirability of a federally based defence scheme, indeed before Edwards had even left Hong Kong on his way to Australia. It seems likely that there was some degree of collusion between the two, with Edwards hoping to fill the appointment of Inspector General of the forces which he had recommended should be created, and Parkes requiring an issue which would highlight the 'common need' which would help to crystallise the general but as yet unfocused consensus on the Federation issue. That the security of the colonies was not a pressing issue in the 1890s is underscored further by the significant reductions effected in colonial defence budgets as a result of the depression, and by the fact that the great debates in the Federal Conventions which met to argue the case for Federation were more concerned with the role and strength of the

Senate, finance, immigration, and the use and misuse of the federal power. Defence featured in the two referendum campaigns, but not prominently.

Support for federal defences and the negotiation of the 1887 Naval Agreement were two parts of a British program to spread the burden of imperial defence and draw upon the potential contribution which the colonies could make to British military capabilities. The third aspect was the attachment of imperial officers to colonial forces. The Commandants of the military forces in the Australian colonies were all British officers, but it was only in 1893 that New South Wales selected its first Commandant from the active list, Lieutenant Colonel E. T. H. Hutton. Other colonies had appointed officers from the active list before this – South Australia's forces were commanded by Lieutenant Colonel M. F. Downes, an officer of the Royal Artillery, between 1877–85 and 1888–93 – but it was more common for the Commandants to be drawn from retired or half-pay officers, and in fact Downes never returned to the British army, retiring in 1884. The British government exerted pressure against the employment of retired officers, initially by ruling that officers employed by colonial governments were not eligible to draw service pensions during their period of colonial employment. The move was effected by passage of the Superannuation Act of 1887, which had the effect of depriving retired officers of their pensions if they took up colonial appointments, and it is clear that by 1889 the War Office was following an explicit policy favouring the employment in the colonies of officers on the active list.

There has been some argument, based largely on conjecture, about the role of these officers in the evolution of imperial defence. Hutton proposed a scheme for federal defence upon his arrival, including a proposal for a Defence Council in wartime which would comprise the naval and military commandants and other representatives from each colony, and which would have the power to formulate and implement defence policy. This idea was not adopted, but it does seem clear that Hutton supported the federal idea because of the possibilities which this would provide for utilising Australian manpower in imperial missions and under British command in the event of a war elsewhere in the empire. The Commandant of Victoria, Major General Sir Alexander Tulloch, admitted as much. As in Canada, and again in Australia after Federation, Hutton's period in New South Wales was marked by public brawling with his nominal political superior, the premier, over cuts to the defence budget and 'interference' in personnel matters.

Other measures for integrating the colonial contribution to empire defence were discussed and adopted also. At the Colonial Conference in 1897, timed to coincide with the queen's diamond jubilee – the celebrations for which involved over 70 000 colonial troops from all parts of the empire – defence issues featured prominently. The Naval Agreement was renewed, but the restrictions on the deployment of the Auxiliary Squadron which the Admiralty found so irksome were not removed, and there was little support from the Australian delegates for an increase in the subsidy. Hopes for a scheme of exchanges of military units foundered also. The desire of the War Office to raise the standard of efficiency of colonial units could not overcome the differing require- ments of colonial military legislation, and the program of exchanges which was suggested finally in August 1898 was restricted to forces on the regular establishment. Among the Australian colonies only Queens- land and New South Wales agreed to participate, and even then the idea was reduced finally to an exchange of a few officers and NCOs from the Queensland permanent artillery, which did not proceed in any case owing to the war scare in South Africa. It is too simple, however, to see the Commandants merely as agents of London. They were Imperial officers to a man, and this obviously shaped their views, but so did their own service in other parts of the empire in colonial campaigns and the conditions which they encountered in the Australian colonies. It is probably more realistic to see them as occupying a position somewhere between the aspirations of the metropolitan government and the politics of the colonial ones.

At the end of the nineteenth century, therefore, the probability of an effective scheme of imperial defence seemed low, while the attention of the Australian colonies was directed to political Federation and the consequences of the depression rather than to any great level of concern with defence and the security of the colonies. The involvement of New South Wales in the Sudan expedition had not presaged any inclination on the part of the Colonies to become involved auto- matically in the war effort of the empire, and the condition and preparedness of the local forces had fluctuated wildly depending on the level of threat, real or imagined, pertaining at any given time. The war in South Africa did not change this.

The crisis in South Africa grew over a number of years, and the declaration of war in 1899 was not unexpected. Afrikaners indeed regarded the Jameson Raid in late 1895 as the real declaration of war, one merely followed by a four-year armed truce. The structural flaws in the British army, which would lead to early disasters to British arms and a long and drawn-out conflict which followed, were not readily apparent to the casual observer in October 1899, and had nothing to do with the offers of assistance which the colonies made. Indeed the very nature of these offers must be scrutinised, for it is clear that the old explan- ations of popular imperialism and empire loyalism are not sufficient to explain the manner in which colonial soldiers found themselves in South Africa.

The spontaneous gestures of support for Britain really came after the string of disasters at Magersfontein, Stormberg and Colenso in December 1899, dubbed 'Black Week'. Before the outbreak of war, however, the gestures of support were more calculated and manufactured. In early July the Secretary of State for the Colonies, Joseph Chamberlain, instructed the governors of Canada, Victoria and New South Wales to request of their ministries 'spontaneous' offers of troops in the event of hostilities. All three administrations refused. But on 11 July the Queensland government offered 250 mounted infantry with machine guns. This offer may have been unsolicited; it also seems likely that the volunteers did not at that stage exist and that the recommendation for the action had come from the Queensland Commandant, Major General Howel Gunter. The offer was made on the understanding that the British would foot the bill, and at least one historian has argued that the unwillingness of Victoria and New South Wales may have stemmed from considerations of military expenditure as well. On 4 September the premier of South Australia offered volunteers 'for service beyond the colony', although again it is unclear whether the offer was prompted by unofficial communication with the governor. Although the colonial premiers were divided in their views over the desirability of offering troops, the various colonial Commandants appear to have suffered no such doubts (although they disagreed initially about the form which a contribution might take), and in conference in Melbourne from 30 September to 4 October they devised a scheme whereby the colonies would send a combined Australian contingent of 2000 men. Chamberlain vetoed the idea, however, because the War Office wanted only small contingents which could be parcelled out among imperial units, and because in any case Chamberlain's concern at this stage was with appearances.

By various means, including an undertaking that the imperial authorities would bear all costs associated with the dispatch of contingents, the government of New South Wales was induced to offer the services of a detachment of the New South Wales Lancers, at that time preparing to return to Australia after some months' training in Britain at their own expense. By 6 October all governments had offered contingents of troops, subject to parliamentary consent; clearly no-one wished to repeat Dalley's experience in 1885. In all colonies such approval was forthcoming, although in Queensland and South Australia the voting was close. The rather hesitant manner in which the pledge of troops was made reflected both financial stringency so soon after the depression and a sense that the war in South Africa, if and when it came, did not represent any crisis. Once colonial administrations began to make offers, inter-colonial rivalry and self-image meant that all would follow suit. The role of the Commandants should not be under-estimated, but neither should the enthusiasm of colonial officers faced with the prospect of active service. Of popular support or agitation for involvement there was, at this stage, little sign.

The Colonial Office laid down that Australian contingents were to number 125 men, two contingents each from New South Wales and Victoria, one each from the other colonies. For reasons which mystify still, the stipulation was for infantry units, not mounted ones, although after the war it was stated that the term 'infantry' had been held to include 'mounted infantry'. The confusion may simply have been the result of a badly worded cable. Equally, the War Office distrusted 'irregular cavalry' and General Sir Redvers Buller, who commanded initially in South Africa, had not been impressed by the standard of the NSW Lancers when he had observed them at Aldershot that year. In any case, within months of arrival the colonial foot were turned into mounted rifles. Enlistment for the contingents was slower than expected among the militia and permanent forces which had been expected to furnish recruits for the forces. Applications for commissions on the other hand were heavily oversubscribed, and political influence played as much part in selection as prior military experience. In all, eight contingents left Australia for South Africa, a total of 16 175 men. (This figure reflects gross, not nett, enlistments since it counts men who re-joined subsequent contingents as separate enlistments. The number of individual Australians who served in South Africa is not known, but is in the vicinity of 10 000.) The second contingent was raised after the news of Black Week, and subsequent ones – the Citizens' Bushmen and the Imperial Bushmen – were recruited in response to public support in 1900 and to the pressing need for mounted troops in a campaign in which mobility was the key factor. The final units to sail did so after Federation, as battalions of the Australian Commonwealth Horse, although the last of these arrived too late to see any action. The total numbers involved do not suggest a strenuous military effort on the part of the Australian colonies, and if the will had existed there seems little reason to doubt that a very much larger force could have been sent. (New Zealand, with a much smaller population base, sent ten con-tingents totalling 6500 men.)

The question of popular attitudes to involvement in the Boer War has occupied historians rather more than has the actual involvement itself. In part this stems from a concern with opposition to later conflicts, but it is clear that there was concerted opposition to involvement in South Africa associated both with the rise of the Australian Labor Party and the labour movement generally, and which drew some of its impetus from

Table 3.1 Strength of contingents sent to the Boer War, 1899–1902

State	State troops at state expense	State troops at imperial expense	Commonwealth troops	Total
NSW	3377	1384	1349	6110
Vic	798	1646	1121	3565
Qld	733	1419	736	2888
SA	346	690	490	1526
WA	349	574	306	1229
Tas	179	375	303	857
Total				16 175 (a)

Source: L. M. Field, *The Forgotten War*, Melbourne, 1979, and *Australian Year Book*, No. 12, 1919.

(a) Comprising 848 officers and 15 327 other ranks. This figure includes re-enlistments. The contingents were accompanied by 16 314 horses.

the very much greater division over the war in Britain itself. By the end of 1899 there was a concerted campaign against 'pro-Boers' and 'disloyal elements'; G. Arnold Wood nearly lost his Chair in History at Sydney University because of his opposition to involvement, and politicians who agreed with him were vilified as traitors at rowdy public meetings, although there is little evidence that this translated into votes. As in most of Australia's wars, the extreme poles of opinion were occupied by a small but highly vocal minority and their influence with the wider public was exaggerated by them for their own purposes. In so far as generalisations can be made, it is clear that the ALP was strongly opposed, but it is not necessarily the case that working-class opinion mirrored this opposition. The radical nationalist school centred on the *Bulletin* was opposed vociferously, but like intellectuals in most periods of Australian history their influence was confined largely to those already convinced, and in any case even they modified their opposition during the crisis which followed the initial Boer victories. Irish-Catholic opinion, traditionally regarded as the single greatest source of dissenting viewpoints, does not lend itself to simplistic classification either. Class was an important factor, but so too was the issue of native-born versus Irish-born; the clergy were largely Irish born, and this was an important determinant in their opposition to British actions in South Africa, as it would be again after the Easter Rising in Ireland in 1916. Whether such 'official' opinion can be regarded as representative of the views of those whom it seeks to represent is a problem in assessing both pro- and anti-war cases, and not only in relation to South Africa.

Popular support was probably widespread, especially at the war's outset and after the early disasters in December 1899. By early 1901 the public was becoming disenchanted with a long war, one moreover which did not conform to the pattern of rousing charges and climactic battles which popular belief identified with war. Australian casualties cannot be used to explain this falling off in popular enthusiasm, since these were very low and affected few of those who remained behind. The Morant–Handcock affair and the fiasco at Wilmansrust (see below) came too late in the war to have much effect, and in any case were not really digested until after the conclusion of hostilities.

The sense in which the experience of war in South Africa failed to match popular expectations affected those Australians who fought there also. The South African war may be divided into three phases: the first months of the war to early 1900, in which the Boers scored a number of impressive early victories; the period after the appointment of Lord Roberts as commander-in-chief, during which the British relieved Boer pressure on isolated positions like Ladysmith and Mafeking, conquered the territory of the Boer Republics themselves, and won the conventional war; and the period under Kitchener from late 1900, in which the remaining Boer commandos fought a savage guerrilla struggle and the veldt was fenced, depopulated and scorched in an effort to bring the 'bitter enders' to the peace table. Australians took little part in the first phase, the first contingent arriving at the Cape just before 'Black Week' and the majority being assigned initially to lines of communication duties. The first significant action involved 200 men of the Queensland Mounted Infantry, together with Canadians and some British regulars, in an attack on a laager at Sunnyside in the Cape Colony on 1 January 1900. A tiny firefight, it nonetheless buoyed the reputation of the Australians, who had acquitted themselves well in their first action. Lord Roberts arrived in January 1900, and promptly began to alter the strategy and dispositions of his forces. In an attempt to increase the mobility of his striking force, he raised irregular companies of mounted rifles from among the Cape colonists and requested that the five companies of Australian infantry then in camp at Enslin be converted to mounted infantry. The newly mounted unit proved its worth in the operations around Colesberg and in actions at Slingersfontein and Pink Hill.

Such successful actions were used as occasions to hail the arrival of the Australian soldier. The war correspondent A. B. Paterson reported that the British authorities were eager to obtain more troops from Canada and Australia because of the fighting qualities demonstrated by those of the first contingent. After Pink Hill Australian correspondents waxed lyrical. The Melbourne *Argus* suggested a great monument to the Victorian dead in the action to remind future generations of 'the heroic measure ... which they could never surpass but from which they must

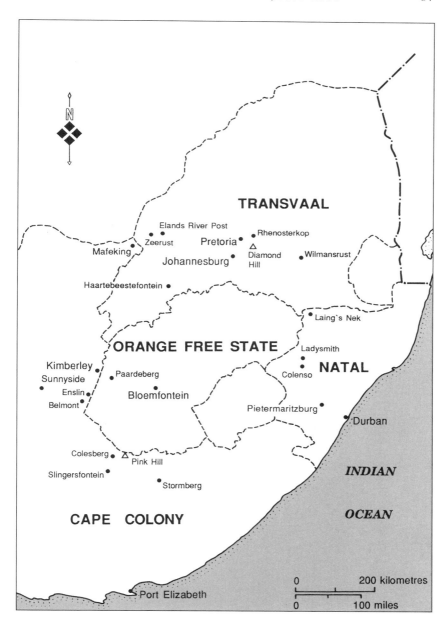

Map 5   Theatre of operations, South Africa, 1899–1902

never decline'. The Adelaide *Advertiser* expressed pride that Australia's military representatives had displayed the highest military qualities in the field: 'plainly wool and wheat are not our greatest products'. More important still, British observers heralded it as 'an exhibition of resolute courage'. Major G. A. Eddy, the Victorian commander killed in the fight, was given a hero's burial and flags flew at half mast in many Victorian towns. But there was a fundamental mismatch between the relatively insignificant nature of the actions and the overwhelming reactions of many Australians to them.

The second contingent arrived in February 1900, and the Australians took part in Roberts' great drive to Bloemfontein and Kimberley, in the war of manoeuvre against the Boers which would culminate in the capture of Pretoria. The last major set-piece battle of the war was fought at Paardeberg on 18 February, in which a force of 6000 Boers under General Piet Cronje was defeated but in which the Australian units played little part. Although the remainder of this phase of the war would see a number of skirmishes and actions involving the Australians, such as at Diamond Hill, the main fighting was over, to be replaced by long periods in the saddle during the advance to the Boer capitals. The mounted infantry units were placed under the command of Brigadier General E. T. H. Hutton where they dominated the force, comprising one-third of his 6000 men. Four of Hutton's eight staff officers were Australians, and the men wore a large letter 'A' sewn on the side of their helmets. Hutton was a great believer in the virtues of mounted infantry and in the capacities of colonial troops; 'fine looking work-manlike men', who nonetheless were 'ignorant of their own value'. Casualties from battle were light, those from disease far heavier and heavier still among the horses. Hutton's brigade lost one man killed and thirty-five wounded in the drive on Pretoria, but lost 18 per cent of their horses.

The lack of any real fighting and the transformation of the war into a guerrilla war in which the civilian population was the main target of operations led to disillusionment among the Australians. Burning farms and herding women and children into concentration camps was not what the colonial volunteers had joined for, and by late 1900 there was widespread disaffection among them. In October Lord Roberts ordered that the first colonial contingents could return home should they desire to do so. This led to further disaffection among men of the second contingent, who had to wait for the anniversary of their arrival in South Africa before being eligible to return to Australia. The first contingent reached Australia in December 1900, to a nation in the flush of Federation and cheered by Roberts' praise of their soldiers' efforts. The approbation of imperial officers which these Austral Britons sought so eagerly was given freely, and the returning men received a rousing homecoming which was in fact to be the last major outpouring of public enthusiasm for the war.

The subsequent Bushmen's and draft contingents were raised from a much larger section of the population than the first two had been, and the vacancies in them were oversubscribed. It was in these contingents that the romantic bush figures who featured in the literature of the 1890s were fused with the citizen soldier who was to take their place as the embodiment of the Australian ethos. Having discovered the virtues of colonial mounted units, the imperial authorities could not get enough of them. Calls went out to Australia, Canada and New Zealand for more mounted soldiers, and the Imperial Bushmen of the fourth contingent were raised on the basis of just such a direct appeal from Chamberlain. Once again the colonials won praise for their dash and gallantry at actions such as Elands River (4–16 August 1900), Rhenosterkop (29 November) and Haartebeestefontein (21 March 1901), but these were small-scale actions in which the Boers were occasionally brought to battle in the long sweeps across the veldt. It was hard work, and occasionally dangerous, but almost never glamorous.

That the Boer was not defeated and was still capable of hitting back was demonstrated to a unit of the fifth contingent, the 5th Victorian Mounted Rifles, at Wilmansrust on 12 June 1901. Surprised after dark by a party of 140 enemy, eighteen Australians were killed and forty-two wounded within minutes, the rest fleeing in panic or being captured. Since the Boers had no use for prisoners the latter were released quickly, but more than one hundred horses were killed and the same number taken to replenish enemy stocks. It was a rout and a humiliation but one which made little difference to the final outcome, although it certainly lifted Boer morale. Its sequel, however, was even less happy. Abused by a senior British officer for 'a lot of white-livered curs', three Victorians were charged with incitement to mutiny after suggesting to their comrades that they should not take the field again under such a commander. They were court-martialled and sentenced to death, the sentences being commuted. The men were later released before the completion of their sentences, and the matter caused questions to be asked in federal parliament. Little sympathy was evinced for the men, who were under the jurisdiction of the British *Army Act* in any case, but the incident prompted Barton to request from the British authorities details of courts martial involving Australians. The Wilmansrust affair was notable also for the alacrity with which the shortcomings of the raw Australian troops were blamed upon alleged deficiencies in the imperial officers placed over them. No such special pleading applied in the cases of Lieutenants Morant and Handcock, tried and executed in February

1902 for shooting prisoners and for the murder of a German missionary suspected of acting as a courier for the Boers. The fact that they were officers may explain why their sentences were carried out, rather than commuted. There was little sympathy for them in Australia, and the executions only became a *cause célèbre* for later and rather different generations.

The final contingents sent to South Africa went as the Australian Commonwealth Horse. Unfortunately these first truly Australian units contributed little to Australian military history, the war having ended before half of the eight battalions involved even reached the Cape. Many Australians served against the Boers in other than Australian units. Many of the gold prospectors on the Rand fields before the war had been Australians, and they joined the Cape colonial units and other irregular forces. Precise figures are impossible to ascertain, but such enlistments must have numbered several thousand.

The Australian contribution to the South African war is difficult to assess. At no time did they make a contribution in their own right, serving always as part of other forces which included Canadians, New Zealanders, Cape colonials, British Yeomanry and regular units. Nearly 450 000 British and empire troops took the field in South Africa, of whom 31 000 were colonial volunteers from outside South Africa, with some 52 000 coming from South Africa itself. It is difficult to generalise about the Australian contingents also. The first two, drawn largely from the part-time militias of the colonies, had some military background and acquitted themselves well, and it was they who set the standard by which Australian troops were judged in' this war. But comparisons with later contingents are made more difficult by the very different nature of the fighting. Later contingents were marked by some indiscipline: men of the third contingent burned the offices of a Cape Town newspaper which favoured the Boer cause and there were disturbances on some of the troopships, but there had been incidents involving grievances over pay among the first contingent also. The rout at Wilmansrust and the Morant–Handcock affair were incidents specific to time and place, and not indications of general weakness or shortcomings in colonial troops.

Weaknesses there were nonetheless. The Australians were noted as good horsemen but bad horse masters, and their standards of marksmanship were deficient. Several witnesses before the Elgin Commission which inquired into the conduct of the war thought the Australians to be soldiers of great potential. Their officers were singled out for criticism, however, as poorly trained and generally inadequate. This was a complaint voiced by the New South Wales contingent in the Sudan, and would feature again during Hamilton's tour of inspection just before the outbreak of war in 1914. The dash, initiative and courage of the colonials – and not just the Australians – was commented upon widely, a judgement supported in the case of the Australians by the award of five Victoria Crosses, all gained for rescuing wounded men under fire. Other decorations were handed out rather freely (twenty-three awards of the CB and no fewer than sixty-two awards of the DSO), which debased the currency and led to at least one celebrated libel suit.

Australian casualties were light. Officially, twenty-nine officers and 222 other ranks were killed in action or died of wounds, and nine officers and 258 others died of disease. (As with all casualty statistics, these figures are open to challenge, and a revised total of 606 dead has been suggested, almost exactly divided between battle and non-battle casualties. This figure, however, includes Australians serving in non-Australian units.) Seventy-seven officers and 658 men were wounded, five officers and ninety-nine others taken prisoner, and forty-three men were listed as missing, for a total casualty list of 120 officers and 1280 men. By comparison, South African volunteers suffered over 8000 casualties, and there were more than 100 000 casualties of all kinds among the British and empire forces, 22 000 of them fatal. More than 400 000 horses (237 456) and mules (196 674) died on the British side alone.

From the viewpoint of the Australian colonies, the Boer War is seen best as the logical outcome of a process which had been building for several decades. The same urges and pressures in the popular mind which manifested themselves in Australia were seen in New Zealand and Canada, with certain Francophone variations in the latter case. Enthusiasm for empire and the wars of empire was not a specifically Australian phenomenon, and neither was the desire to dispatch contingents to assist the mother country. The granting of self-governing status and the removal of British garrisons carried with it the need to provide for local defence from local resources. Inevitably, given that the Australian colonies remained part of a great and expanding empire, those forces would ultimately be involved in the wars of that empire as maturing colonial societies sought to share the costs as well as the fruits of empire. Further evidence for this was provided by involvement in the Boxer rebellion in China. Not only did the colonial governments agree to an Admiralty request for the deployment of ships from the Australian and Auxiliary Squadrons to Chinese waters, but Victoria, South Australia and New South Wales sent naval brigades and a colonial warship to join the international Field Force for the relief of the Peking legations. As in the Sudan earlier, the colonials arrived too late to see much real action, but the 'bluejackets' stayed on in various non-combatant roles until April 1901.

What is often overlooked by those who lament the readiness to volunteer which Australians allegedly displayed is the lack of willingness of Australians (and Canadians for that matter) to become part of an imperial federation or to surrender totally the control of such forces as they possessed to the metropolitan power. The restrictions placed upon the Auxiliary Squadron demonstrated this, as did the provisions of the first federal Defence Act which restricted the forces to service in Australian territory and which itself was a direct descendant of similar provisions in colonial legislation. The later refusal of the Commonwealth to place Australian soldiers under the capital courts martial system of the British Army Act likewise was a direct consequence of earlier colonial legislation (and owed little if anything to the execution of Morant and Handcock). And the moves at the 1902 Colonial Conference to form an imperial military reserve, supported by the New Zealand prime minister, Richard Seddon, in the hope of translating the military support fielded in South Africa into a permanent scheme, foundered upon the nationalist content of the imperial sentiment in Australia and Canada which Seddon and others sought to harness.

CHAPTER 4

A New Nation and its Military Forces, 1901–1914

The outbreak of war in 1914 found the dominions in agreement with Britain in matters of defence and foreign policy, at least in so far as the fighting and winning of the war was concerned. In one sense this was not remarkable, since the British government had long enjoyed the right to make empire foreign policy and the dominions, in general, had not disputed this. But the pattern of defence relations in the decade and a half before the Great War qualifies this view; the self-governing dominions enjoyed the right of control of their own armed forces and in the years following Federation the government of the Commonwealth of Australia gradually established and enlarged those forces, in a manner which at times ran contrary to British views and which did not always follow British patterns.

Defence was not a prominent issue in the early days of the first parliament, and in so far as the country's early legislators took an interest in the subject they were motivated by a desire to reduce spending on defence, not increase it. For some, the federation of the colonies provided an opportunity to rationalise the existing colonial defence forces and reduce their size and expense. Amalgamation was to bring about heightened efficiency, and efficiency was equated with reducing expenditure.

The states did not hand over their defence forces to the Commonwealth immediately on 1 January 1901; it was necessary first for the federal government to make various administrative arrangements before assuming its defence responsibilities. The Defence Minister, Sir John Forrest, had moved to that portfolio from the more demanding office of Postmaster-General following the death of the previous minister, J. R. Dickson of Queensland, just nine days after taking office. Forrest oversaw the drafting of a Defence Act and the necessary military regulations under which the states' forces would be incorporated. In the interests of economy Forrest was one of those who favoured a small permanent military force and a part-time militia, and was opposed to the creation of a large and expensive military headquarters. On 1 March 1901 the naval and military forces of the states were transferred to the control of the Commonwealth. The government was negotiating with the British for the services of a British regular officer to command the infant military forces, but until the appointment was made the Commandants of the various state forces, meeting as the Federal Military Committee, remained responsible for those forces to the new federal minister. Like the parliament and the rest of the government, the Defence Minister and the service headquarters were based in Melbourne at Victoria Barracks where they were to remain until after the Second World War. Victoria had been the only colony before Federation to create a separate Department of Defence and upon the creation of a federal department the existing colonial organisation was absorbed into the new; it involved the transfer of just twelve people including the permanent head of the Victorian department, Captain R. H. M. Collins, RN, who became the first secretary of the department.

The forces which the Commonwealth took over were small and disorganised. There were colonial contingents totalling 5000 men still fighting in South Africa, and the last waves of volunteers for that war would serve as members of the Commonwealth Horse, although most arrived in the theatre too late to see action. The military forces at the Commonwealth's disposal numbered 28 886 in 1901, of whom just 1500 were permanent soldiers. The naval forces mustered around 2000 men, only 250 of whom were on full-time duty manning an assorted collection of vessels in various stages of obsolescence.

The Defence Bill had been drafted by the Federal Military Committee in Sydney, and was presented to the parliament by Forrest in the first session. It was not a success, an outcome assisted by the minister who introduced it with the admission that he felt 'somewhat nervous on having entrusted to me a subject on which my experience has not been very great in the past'. It was a mess; inadequately worded and giving the impression of merely having stitched together the various pieces of colonial legislation which had preceded it. It was referred back for amendment, which the Federal Military Committee duly considered in Melbourne in June, but so poor were its chances of passing the various stages of reading that the government allowed the Bill to lapse, despite enjoying a majority in the House. It was withdrawn on 26 March 1902, an inauspicious beginning for the Australian forces.

The objections to the Bill in many ways set the tone for much of the defence debate in ensuing decades. Forrest told the parliament that he found himself in 'the unfortunate position of controlling a department which takes everything in the way of money and gives nothing back and therefore, not a department to receive that support and assistance from the general public on ordinary occasions which are received by what are called paying departments'. This attitude had been mirrored in the Governor-General's speech at the opening of parliament when he had declared that 'extravagant expenditure will be avoided'. Fifty-two amendments were proposed during the Bill's first reading; the clauses permitting the dispatch overseas of the permanent forces, the calling up of citizens in 'times of emergency', the discretionary powers given to the Commandants were all attacked. In general, the Bill aroused the hostility of the left of the House, suspicious always of 'militarism'.

The officer chosen to head the Commonwealth's forces was Major General Sir Edward 'Curly' Hutton, former Commandant of the New South Wales Forces and the Canadian Militia, a member of Wolseley's 'Ashanti ring' who had commanded Australian soldiers in South Africa, and one with a highly controversial record of ignoring his colonial political masters and referring matters of dominion or colonial defence policy direct to his superiors in London. He was in fact the third choice for the position, the preferred candidates having declined on the grounds that the salary was insufficient and career prospects limited. There had been calls within parliament for preferment of an Australian with experience in South Africa. Hutton's appointment was made with effect from 26 December 1901, and he was charged with organising the six colonial forces into a homogeneous federal force. He believed that a national army of citizen soldiers was 'the true form for an army for an Anglo-Saxon state to possess', a large standing army being 'an unnecessary and unwarranted expense'. This preference for a paid militia did not prevent him from promoting the interests of Lieutenant Colonel W. T. Bridges and Captain C. B. B. White, both regular officers, nor from passing over militia officers for commands when he considered them 'weak, ignorant and inexperienced'. Never a man to tolerate those he perceived as fools, he described the Australian parliament in March 1904 as 'ill-informed', possessing 'neither the training nor … the Military instincts to qualify them as critics in so difficult a profession'. On one celebrated occasion while Commandant of New South Wales he had attended a meeting with the premier with a loaded pistol in his pocket, though what he thought to do with it is not recorded.

As Australia possessed neither a General Staff nor a Military Board at this stage, Hutton was answerable directly to the minister, Forrest. His appointment as General Officer Commanding, Commonwealth Military Forces, also had the effect of downgrading the standing of the

Commandants, who henceforth were responsible for their commands directly to Hutton and not the minister. This was despite the fact that the Defence Acts of the various colonies were not repealed until the *Defence Act 1903* had passed through federal parliament, and that as a result all regulations and statutes governing the military and naval forces of the Commonwealth continued to be made under the provisions of the colonial legislation. Hutton also tried to insist that the Officer Commanding the Commonwealth Naval Forces should be subordinate to him, but Captain W. R. Creswell, the first naval officer to occupy the position, successfully resisted this bid for army supremacy within the defence organisation.

The Defence Act was proclaimed on 1 March 1904, together with the Military Regulations and Orders and the first Military Forces List, which set out the seniority of all serving officers. The forces now had a statutory basis on which to operate. The Act allowed also for a Board of Advice to be nominated by the Governor-General and intended to discuss defence matters referred to it by the minister. The Board was never formed, and during Forrest's tenure (1901–03) of the Defence Ministry all defence matters were discussed by the minister with the two Officers Commanding, usually separately. A later minister, J. W. McCay (1904–05), moved to regularise the matter in August 1904 with the creation of the Council of Defence, based on a colonial precedent in Victoria. The 1904 amendments to the Defence Act did not specify the duties of the Council, and at the same time set up the service Boards of Administration – the Military Board and the Naval Board – to govern the services themselves. This action also had the effect of cancelling the positions occupied by Hutton and Creswell. The membership of the Council of Defence comprised the minister, who acted as president, the Treasurer, the Inspector General of the Military Forces and the Director of the Naval Forces (positions created to replace that of GOC and OC Naval Forces), and the Chief of Intelligence. Provision was made for consultative members, and the permanent head of the Defence Department was to act as secretary to the Council. Although it was a brave attempt to institute machinery for the discussion and formulation of defence policy, the Council of Defence met only twelve times between 1905 and 1915; Cabinet was not obliged to take up its recommendations, and rarely did. Its meetings often became bogged down in administrative minutiae better left to the service boards of administration.

As noted, a distinguishing feature of Hutton's imperial service had been an inability, or disinclination, to see as his first duty an obligation to the defence minister of the colonial government whose forces he commanded. The habits of a lifetime are not easily broken, and in

Australia Hutton continued to see his duty in imperial and not national terms. The system by which imperial officers like Hutton, Alexander Godley, Henry Finn, G. A. French, J. M. Kirkpatrick and many others were posted around the empire to oversee the development of the colonial and dominion military forces is too little understood. It is not clear whether the attempts to impose a policy whereby dominion forces were raised and trained to act as a wartime reserve to imperial forces was in response to the promptings of local politicians, the urgings of London, or the individual advocacy of the imperial officers themselves, but the last was probably the decisive influence. As we shall see, Creswell was to act very much as a nationalist in naval matters, and to earn the displeasure of the Admiralty as a result. But the Royal Navy provided the first line in the defence of the empire, and the situation of the land forces is not strictly analogous.

Whatever Hutton's faults, he was energetic and possessed of drive and organisational talent. However, his term as GOC was characterised by fiscal restraint, and military policy was dictated by Treasury. In his famous *Minute upon the Defence of Australia* of 7 April 1902, Hutton accepted the general premise of imperial strategy, namely that the risks posed to Australia were minimal as a result of the defensive shield provided by the Royal Navy. No invasion force could hope to reach these shores unless the Royal Navy had first been defeated, and the threat to Australian territory therefore consisted of raids upon defended ports. As a result, the naval base at Sydney and the principal ports and cities should be garrisoned and provided with fixed defences to deny them to an enemy. All militia and other partly paid units were to be formed into a mobile field force for concentration at threatened points for 'the defence of Australian soil'.

Hutton's argument that the field force was to be used for the defence of Australian interests almost certainly was duplicitous. He went on to state in his report that the defence of Australian territory was not sufficient to safeguard those interests: 'the surest and best defence is by a vigorous offence'. In light of the objections to the draft Defence Bill this was bound to provoke a hostile response, which was duly forth-coming. Collins informed Hutton that Forrest would not agree to any proposal, actual or implicit, to surrender control of the forces to imperial authorities. Hutton amended the proposal by calling for a smaller force of 13 831 men, but the government made it clear that the role envisaged for the forces was a restricted one of local defence, and despite Hutton's best and worst endeavours – for he was not an excessively tactful man – the Commonwealth would not be drawn into furthering British government defence policies through the creation in peacetime of an imperial reserve in a self-governing dominion. In any

case, the whole scheme foundered upon the unwillingness of both parliament and government to sanction the levels of expenditure called for.
Hutton had based his estimates on the number of troops serving in the
colonies at Federation and on the combined total of their military
expenditure, some £937 000. The Opposition had proposed a reduction
to £500 000, Batchelor of the ALP suggested a reduction of nearly 50 per
cent, and Forrest succeeded in getting the (reduced) estimates for
1902–03 through the Committee on Supply only by undertaking to
deliver cuts of £131 000 the following year. 'It was unmistakenly shown
during the debate', he told Collins, 'that a still larger reduction was
desired'. Recruitment was stopped, the strength of the permanent
Artillery and the Staff falling by 39 per cent the following year; on
30 June 1903 the strength of the military forces stood at 22 346, down
from the 25 844 called for in Hutton's scheme while the estimates for
1902–03 were in fact £175 198 below the level existing in 1901 and actual
expenditure in that year saved a further £84 525.

In a real sense then Hutton lost the fight with the Executive and the
Legislature, for his grand scheme for a field force of six brigades of
light horse and three brigades of infantry remained largely on paper.
Parliament never endorsed his 1902 report, while he dismissed them as
'ill-informed'. His case was fatally weakened by the views of the Colonial
Defence Committee in London, which admitted to the Commonwealth
government that the proposed force structure served no useful purpose
within Australia itself. Although the government approved his reorganisation of the forces in July 1903, only the administrative and financial
provisions of Hutton's scheme were ever followed through, although the
permanent artillery was organised for the garrisoning of defended
ports. This much in itself was a considerable achievement, however,
since six disparate colonial forces had been welded into one which was
now available for the defence of the country regardless of internal
boundaries and which functioned on a single administrative, financial
and organisational pattern and with a common system of training. But
the demands of economy had won out also, and the level of Commonwealth defence expenditure did not exceed the colonial total until
1906–07. Most significant of all in terms of Hutton's desire to enmesh
Australia's forces into a system of imperial defence, the 1903 Defence
Act precluded any but volunteers from serving outside Australia.

Hutton's attempts to overhaul the Commonwealth's ground forces
nonetheless bore some fruit, although they also engendered a certain
amount of confusion and resentment on the part of those reorganised.
In New South Wales, for example, six regiments of light horse were
created from existing mounted units, supplemented by men transferred
from the 2nd, 3rd and 4th Infantry Regiments. The artillery and

engineers were reformed into field and garrison artillery batteries and engineering, submarine mining and electric engineering companies, while the infantry now consisted of four battalions of the Australian Infantry Regiment. New South Wales was to contribute the 1st and 2nd Light Horse Brigades and the 1st Infantry Brigade to the putative field force. Other, less populous, states combined their units into composite brigades in a manner to be repeated in the AIF later. Thus, the 3rd Light Horse Brigade was drawn from Victoria, but the 4th was made up of Victorian and Tasmanian units, the 5th came from Queensland and the 6th combined men from South and Western Australia. The re-organisation with its emphasis on mounted units was resented in many rural communities, because while citizen soldiering was a popular activity most men lacked the resources to own and maintain a horse, and the disbandment of existing infantry units left these men with nowhere to go.

After Hutton returned to Britain in 1904 his position was abolished and the control of the forces was vested in the Military Board, comprising three military officers and two civilians including the minister. As in Canada with the formation of the Militia Council after the stormy Dundonald period, this dispensed with potentially troublesome senior British officers attempting to exercise command independent of the minister and the government, and in September 1906 the new post of Inspector General, the senior position in the military forces, was occupied by an Australian, Major General J. C. Hoad.

Naval developments figured more largely in the years immediately after Federation, although initially there was no call to change the system of naval defence then in existence. This was based on the previous colonial arrangements derived from agreements reached in 1887. The Royal Navy provided the imperial squadron which was the first line of defence, together with an auxiliary squadron of third-class vessels partly paid for by the colonies and not liable for service outside Australian waters without colonial agreement, although, as we have seen, forces had been detached from the Australia Station in 1900 to take part in the international effort to suppress the Boxer uprising in China. The last tier of naval defence was provided by the colonies' own fleets, used mainly for harbour protection. These latter vessels had little capability and were often manned by nucleus crews.

The 1887 Agreement was due to expire, and it was the process of renegotiation during the Colonial Conference of 1902 which led to the Naval Agreement of 1903 and which brought matters of naval defence to public and government attention. The naval subsidy paid to Britain was unpopular with Australians, since it bought neither ownership nor even control of the fleet units whose costs it helped defray. Equally, there was little likelihood in the financial climate which existed at the turn of the century that the Commonwealth would establish a fleet of its own, and in any case the naval doctrine of fleet concentration and blue-water strategy predisposed the Admiralty to oppose the acquisition of independent squadrons by the dominions. The Australian delegates to the Colonial Conference, Barton and Forrest, nonetheless extracted some important concessions under the new agreement; Australian seamen were to receive local training on one active warship and three drillships as part of the Royal Naval Reserve and, although the subsidy was increased to £200 000, it carried with it the stationing of more modern warships in Australian waters. On the other hand, the distinction between the Auxiliary and imperial squadrons was abolished. Henceforth the ships of the Australia Station would join with vessels on the China and East Indies Stations in dealing with threats anywhere within the boundaries of the three. This meant that vessels could be removed from Australian waters without the agreement of – indeed in the face of objections from – the Commonwealth.

The new agreement was heavily criticised in Australia during the ratification debate in the parliament, both because of the increased subsidy and the dilution of control over the old Auxiliary Squadron. It would be wrong to assume, however, that there was a burning urgency to establish an Australian fleet at this time. Navalist views, like militarist ones, were rare in the early parliament. Although the Labor Party adopted a policy for the acquisition and development of an Australian-owned and controlled navy after the ratification debate in mid-1903, J. C. Watson, leader of the parliamentary party, was on record as stating that the costs of such a move were prohibitive and W. M. Hughes, a leading advocate of compulsory training, favoured renewal of the agreement in the circumstances then pertaining. Forrest's own view was that the acquisition of a navy was impractical 'under existing conditions', and he and Barton negotiated a renewal on the basis of what they believed both people and parliament would tolerate in the light of earlier debates over defence expenditure. They may have misjudged this slightly, at least with regard to the politicians, but equally they would not have persuaded the Admiralty at this stage to break with the doctrine of a single fleet under a unified command – 'one fleet one Empire'. Changing circumstances in both the Pacific and the Atlantic would help to bring that about.

Centralised machinery for the naval forces was supplied on the proclamation of the Defence Act in March 1904, and command of the force was given to Captain W. R. Creswell, formerly the naval Commandant in Queensland and an early exponent of an independent naval force for the Commonwealth. This attitude of mind, together with the fact that he had once been an officer of the Royal Navy, led the Admiralty to regard him with deep suspicion as some form of class traitor. We have noted that Hutton failed to have him brought under the authority of the GOC, and when that position was abolished Creswell was appointed to the Council of Defence as principal naval adviser. He also headed the three-member Naval Board of Administration when that body was constituted in January 1905. This did not mean that his views held sway automatically. In fact Forrest's later successor, J. W. McCay, was as impervious to navalist arguments as his predecessor, and for many of the same reasons.

It is probable that the lack of urgency in defence matters would have persisted but for the intervention of external events favourable to the cause of heightened defence preparedness, and their skilful exploitation by shrewd and ambitious men, principally but not exclusively in the parliament. First among these was the great Japanese naval victory over the Russians at Tsushima in July 1905, closely followed by the return to power of Alfred Deakin. Deakin had been one of those dissatisfied with the increased naval subsidy, and in June 1905 had declared his concern publicly at the indifference expressed on defence. Three months later a group of prominent citizens led by W. M. Hughes had met in Sydney and formed the National Defence League, modelled on the National Service League in Britain. From then until the outbreak of war in 1914, defence issues were to assume an importance which they had not enjoyed previously and which arguably they would not enjoy again in any comparable period of peace. Although it introduces a measure of artificiality, it is best to deal with developments in naval and military policy consecutively since up to a point they involved separate issues, and different personalities.

Creswell had pressed his scheme for an Australian flotilla of destroyers and torpedo boats upon the short-lived Labor ministry of J. C. Watson in 1904, but the move proved abortive. However the ALP endorsed much of Deakin's stand on the issue in the following three years and this, together with the arrogant and short-sighted rejection of legitimately expressed Australian concerns by both the Admiralty and the Committee of Imperial Defence, greatly strengthened Deakin's hand. When the Committee's report on Australian defence in July 1906 rejected Creswell's proposals as 'an imperfect conception of the requirements of naval strategy', Deakin commended the scheme to the parliament and announced the Commonwealth's intention to purchase twelve vessels over three years as an experiment. At the 1907 Colonial Conference Deakin appeared to gain British agreement to the establishment of a local navy, although one based on submarines rather than destroyers. Before the policy was implemented, Deakin left office but not before he had stirred up intense Australian feeling on the fleet issue by inviting the American Great White Fleet to visit Australian ports. Not only did the visit of sixteen battleships and auxiliary vessels produce unexpected exhibitions of enthusiasm in the public, but the manner of the invitation – delivered direct to the United States government and not through accepted Colonial Office 'channels' in London – served notice on the British government that the Australians were serious on the naval issue.

Government passed to the Labor ministry of Andrew Fisher, and he ordered the adoption of Creswell's destroyer plan and even placed the first orders in February 1909. External events again intervened, this time in the form of the 'Dreadnought crisis' which was prompted by the revelation to an alarmed public in Britain that the Germans were building in order to contest naval mastery with the Royal Navy. Fisher came under pressure to follow the leads of Canada and New Zealand in offering to meet the costs of building additional battleships for the Royal Navy; the prime minister argued in turn that the best contribution Australia could make was to maintain a program of Australian naval expansion. Fisher lost office on this issue, among others, to the 'Fusion' government of Deakin and Joseph Cook, who promptly offered the British a dreadnought 'or its equivalent'. Of much greater significance was the furor in Britain occasioned by the naval scare, which led to an official inquiry into the Board of Admiralty in April–July 1909 and which greatly weakened opposition to the building of dominion fleets. At the Imperial Conference in August the British suggested an Australian fleet of four cruisers (one armoured), six destroyers, three submarines and auxiliaries. Creswell fought for his original destroyer proposal, but it was clear that the Admiralty proposal would be accepted, not least when the British offered a 'reverse subsidy' of £250 000 per annum to cushion the initial outlays of £3 700 000 and the annual costs of £750 000. Indeed it was a clever move, because the dominion advocates of a national navy could not decline the suggestion or the offer, and Britain preserved its blue-water doctrine through the arrangements agreed for control of the fleet in the event of hostilities. The scheme was funded through the Naval Loan Bill, passed through the Australian parliament in November the same year, and orders for the cruisers were placed with British shipyards the following month.

The results of all this were less impressive than they seemed. The flag-ship of the fleet, an Indefatigable-class battle cruiser named *Australia*, was an inferior vessel although quite formidable in terms of the naval forces operating in the Pacific. Creswell's scheme for local defence went by the board and the creation of a fleet unit – 'a navy within a navy, a logical outcome for a nation within a nation' as a later Defence Minister,

Senator George Pearce (1910–13, 1914–21), described it – led to a distorted force structure and ensured that the Royal Australian Navy (as it became in July 1911) would be an unbalanced force incapable of independent action in other than limited circumstances. In 1910 Pearce invited Admiral Sir Reginald Henderson to report on the future direction of the RAN, in the manner which Lord Kitchener had done recently for the military forces. This report, presented in March 1911, advocated an Australian blue-water navy of impressive and entirely unattainable size and power given the budgetary constraints of the Commonwealth. Most of it was shelved, but as a result of Henderson's deliberations the Naval Board was reconstituted with five members, three of them naval officers, under the chairmanship of the Minister for Defence.

The 1911 Imperial Conference formalised the arrangements for British command and control of the RAN in wartime and laid down principles of standardisation for the smaller fleet, which lacked important infrastructure and for this reason also could not act independently of the Royal Navy. By 1913, when the first ships of the RAN entered Sydney Harbour, the flagship and two of the cruisers had been commissioned, and half of the planned destroyers; a third cruiser and two destroyers were under construction at the naval dockyard at Cockatoo Island in Sydney and two E-class submarines were being built in Britain. Australia was the only dominion to undertake its own naval defence before the Great War. New Zealand could not afford to do so and preferred to pay for and maintain another Indefatigable-class ship, the battle cruiser *New Zealand*, while the Canadians were unable and unwilling to resolve the problems posed by the need for a two-ocean navy. Empire loyalty and nascent nationalist feeling were not contradictory and these, together with growing feelings of insecurity with regard to Japan, led the Commonwealth to adopt an expensive and, in the opening months of the Great War, highly successful naval defence strategy. In the longer term, the desirability of creating a navy which could function properly only as part of another is not self-evident.

The development of the Australian Military Forces went in quite different directions from the RAN. There was a widespread and entirely mistaken belief that the Boer War had demonstrated the suitability, even superiority, of what one British critic derided as 'the gospel of gallop-and-shoot [which] ignored organisation and ... discipline' and which produced a soldier who was assumed to be 'a match for an indefinite number of the best trained soldiers of any nation'. This had been clear in the original debate on the Defence Bill, when King O'Malley and others had dismissed the need for military training and preparation as wasteful and had commended 'a small skeleton army with a native

Australian de Wet as Commandant' as being adequate to the needs of the nation. Virtually alone among this chorus of military narcissism had been W. M. Hughes, already advocating compulsory military service along the Swiss model and who might be characterised at this time as 'a sort of mad Mahdi of mass mobilisation'. Hughes' motivation was not militaristic; his suspicion of permanent standing forces conformed with good socialist principle. He saw universal service as a means of avoiding the propagation of militarism and the threat that armed forces might be used against the workers, while providing for the defence of the nation with minimal disruption to business and civil life. Once again external developments, not least the Japanese victory over the Russians, lent added force to a position which had not enjoyed wide support, so that by the fourth federal conference of the Labor Party in 1908 the motion in favour of compulsory military training was adopted as party policy.

Much of the agitation for a scheme of universal training had come from Hughes' National Defence League. Although never a mass organisation, it enjoyed considerable influence and enrolled prominent citizens from all sides of politics as well as leaders from the universities, the churches, financial and commercial institutions and the citizen military forces themselves. It disbanded in 1910, its job done, by which time it had twenty-one branches and a membership of perhaps 1600. It published a journal, *The Call*, to spread the message that the defence of Australia was 'the duty of all' and lobbied parliamentarians, publishing a list of seventy-nine candidates for the April 1910 election who were fit to be endorsed by virtue of the soundness of their views on the question of compulsory training. It is interesting to note also that the National Defence League derived much of its literature from the National Defence Association in Britain, but whereas the views of the NDL were to prevail in Australia, the outcome in Britain was quite different. In the British case, the need for a reserve force to supplement the regular army resulted in the creation in 1907 of the Territorial Force (afterwards the Territorial Army).

The idea of conscription aroused very little opposition in the parliamentary arena; Deakin had announced in 1907 that his government would introduce a Bill for the scheme, which duly followed in September the following year. The government fell before it could be enacted, but once the ALP had adopted it as party policy the passage of such measures was virtually assured. When the 'Fusion' ministry of the Deakin–Cook government took office the relevant amendments to the Defence Act were passed, providing for the compulsory training of boys aged twelve to eighteen and for annual training with the citizen forces of young men aged eighteen to twenty. The change in attitude in the course of the decade is well illustrated by the Minister for Defence,

Joseph Cook, who, in introducing the amendments to parliament on 21 September 1909, noted:

> We have no modern defence organisation, practically speaking, in Australia today; and the sooner we set about creating a proper organisation, the better it will be for our self-respect, and for the safety of our country ... We propose to continue the existing organisation of the militia, and to make it our first or striking line – to equip and make it fully ready to march against the enemy at war strength, ready to meet any emergency that may arise.

The 'paramount duty' facing them was no longer efficiency in the interests of economy, but 'to be adequately prepared, and to recognise all the contingencies consequent upon our being part of a world-wide Empire'. The move towards compulsion was to change the nature of part-time soldiering in Australia, but that too was perceived as an advance, at least among many in parliament, although the view was not necessarily shared by members of existing citizens' units.

Seeking professional scrutiny, and approval, of the scheme, the government invited Field Marshal Lord Kitchener, the hero of Khartoum, to inspect Australia's defences and advise on the system best suited to Australia's needs. In a seven-week visit commencing in December 1909 and culminating in a lengthy memorandum in February the following year, Kitchener visited each state to inspect such forces as existed, produced by the country which had sent 'so many fine fellows during the South African War'. His report allowed that considerations of time and space were important to any defence scheme in Australia and New Zealand, and that the Royal Navy might 'for a moment' find itself unable to discharge the defence of the Pacific dominions. Australia therefore should build its forces so as to compel the enemy to attempt an invasion 'on such a scale as to be unable to evade our naval forces'. This called for a force of 80 000 soldiers organised into eighty-four battalions of infantry, twenty-eight regiments of light horse, forty-nine field batteries and seven heavy batteries totalling 224 guns, and communication, field engineer and departmental troops in proportion. He confirmed Hutton's arguments, calling for the provision of a mobile striking force and garrison units to secure the ports and major centres from attack, and while endorsing the system of compulsory training suggested that the period of liability for service be extended to the age of twenty-five, which was duly incorporated in the legislation in 1910. And *pace* Hutton, he reminded his Australian readers that 'the best defence is generally by taking the offensive'.

Although Hughes was the advocate of the scheme and Kitchener had given it his blessing, the real architect was Colonel J. G. Legge, who worked closely with the minister (successively Ewing, 1907–08 and

Pearce) to ensure that the administrative and organisational measures were satisfactorily worked out. Conscription was not a British characteristic and was not adopted in Britain itself as part of the package of reforms introduced by Haldane. Other changes brought about in Britain were reflected in Australia, not least the creation of a General Staff for the British Army. At the 1907 Imperial Conference the War Office had announced the creation of the Imperial General Staff, designed to coordinate the defence of Britain and the empire and with sections based on the military staffs of the respective dominion forces. Australia accepted the proposal, although Canada did not, and the Military Board was reorganised to facilitate the creation of a general staff organisation in conformity with British wishes in January 1909. Until 1963 the newly created post of Chief of the General Staff carried with it also the title of head of the Australian section of the Imperial General Staff. Once again, however, there were differences from the British model in that the staff organisation in Australia drew on officers who lacked formal staff training. In order to meet the demands for more and better-trained officers which these changes brought, the government set up the Royal Military College at Duntroon, a former pastoral lease outside the new national capital, Canberra, in June 1911. On Kitchener's recommendation, RMC did not follow the British model provided by Sandhurst and Woolwich, however, but followed that of the United States Military Academy at West Point which had served as the model for the Canadian Royal Military College, Kingston, and which Kitchener thought more appropriate to the needs of the dominion forces.

Compulsory military training or 'boy conscription' was Australia's first experience of national service, and the belief has long been current that it was resisted vigorously by those caught up in it. In part, this is the result of the projection backwards of attitudes in 1916–17 and later, themselves occasioned by quite different proposals in quite different circumstances. There was a significant pattern of non-compliance, illustrated by the 27 749 prosecutions under the Defence Act in 1911–13, which culminated in 5732 boys serving terms of detention or imprisonment. These figures need to be seen in perspective, which reveals that the ratio of prosecutions to those registered for training was quite low, something like 2 per cent of the total each year, added to which many of those prosecuted were persistent offenders, and further that many of the prosecutions were for minor infringements of the regulations not in themselves symptomatic of an attempt to buck the system. In 1911, 155 000 youths were registered, of whom 92 000 were in training, and roughly 20 000 were added to these figures in each year until the outbreak of war. There is evidence to suggest that the populace

as a whole, many of whom of course were untouched by the requirements to train, were in favour of the scheme; this is consistent with a
belief in the egalitarian outlook of Australians, and with a strain of
authoritarianism which also runs through the national character
(demonstrated in other spheres of national life by measures such as
compulsory voting and 'closed shop' trade unionism). It is consistent
too with the social and cultural expectations of the day.

The impact of the scheme upon the military forces cannot be
doubted. In three years the size of the militia increased by 50 per cent,
enabling the government to increase the number of units set forth in
Kitchener's memorandum. To meet the expanding needs of the force,
the government set up defence factories to produce small arms and
munitions, clothing and harness. By 1914 the defence appropriation
stood at £3 000 000. In 1915 there was a short-term suspension of
compulsory training while the demands of the AIF were met from
existing resources, but the scheme continued with modifications until
suspended by a new Labor government in 1929, one embittered enough
by Hughes' actions in the Great War to reject his handiwork. The real
test of the scheme lay in the war itself, in which perhaps 15 per cent of
the AIF were former 'boy soldiers'. Its contribution to the fighting
effectiveness of that force is unquantifiable but, however small in
proportional terms, the scheme must have had some influence. But
because the army in 1914 was largely made up of men aged between
nineteen and twenty-one, and because of the provisions of the Defence
Act, one unintended fruit of compulsory training was the decision to
recruit the AIF on the basis of voluntary enlistment.

The scheme was probably significant also for the opportunities it gave
to citizen officers to train and command formed bodies of men. The
education and training of such officers was the responsibility of the
citizen forces in each state; for most of the period before the 1950s there
was no Australian journal of the military art (the *Commonwealth Military
Journal*, founded only in 1911, ceased publication in 1916), and no
military education system other than Duntroon, which produced its first
graduates only in 1914, although there were United Service Institutions
on the British model in Sydney and Melbourne at which the interested
officer might read and discuss current military problems and the
military literature from overseas. Citizen officers could be as indolent or
as industrious in the pursuit of their part-time soldiering as they or their
seniors chose. Some were useless, and were shown up quickly in the first
actions of the war in 1915. Others, like Hobbs and Monash, who would
rise to the very top of the AIF in the coming war, applied themselves
diligently to the serious study of the military arts and sciences – more
seriously, in fact, than some of their regular British contemporaries.

Professional opportunities were almost as limited for the regulars, although the possibility existed of attending the staff colleges at either Camberley or Quetta. Brudenell White was the first Australian to attend the Camberley course, in 1906–7. Tom Blamey, who had given away school-teaching in 1906 to take a commission in the Instructional Corps, attended the Quetta course in 1912–13. But only a handful of officers had received regular staff training in this manner by 1914.

As noted already, successive Australian governments in this period had grappled with British desires for the establishment of some scheme of mutual assistance within the empire in the event of a great power war, and the creation of the general staff was part of this. In general the dominions, and especially Canada, had resisted any measures which carried the implication of central direction from London, but in the preparations for the 1911 Imperial Conference Lord Esher, a member of the Committee of Imperial Defence, sought to replace the 'pious aspirations' and 'vague generalities' which governed empire defence relations with a solution to 'the vital problem of the means and methods by which all portions of the Empire are instantaneously to cooperate in a scheme of common defence in the event of the Empire being threatened by a combination of hostile powers'. The British government was clear that the dominions had no option but to be parties to any British commitment to war, but equally clear that the provision of any naval and military forces outside their own territories was a matter for decision by individual dominion governments. In the defence discussions at the 1911 conference Pearce made it plain that while in the event of war many Australians would undoubtedly volunteer for service overseas, the Australian government could and would agree to contingency planning only, and with this the British had to be satisfied (as, indeed, they seem to have been).

A matter of months before the war's outbreak, the Australian forces were again inspected by a senior British officer, this time the Commander-in-Chief in the Mediterranean and Inspector General of Overseas Forces, General Sir Ian Hamilton. He was critical of the system, which he thought entirely suited to peacetime conditions but unlikely to withstand the demands of war by more than a few weeks, but complimentary about the qualities of the soldiers he inspected and reviewed:

> The best assets of the Australian land forces . . . are to be found in the natural soldierlike spirit, in the intelligence, and in the wiry and athletic frames of the bulk of the rank and file . . . Patriotism, keenness, study and careful instruction, strain and struggle at the heels of practical experience and habits of discipline, but rarely quite catch them up.

He thought that peacetime militia soldiers would always lack self-confidence when faced in the field with professional regular forces, and was critical also of the command arrangements and of many of the officers. But his final observations about discipline, and the relations between officers and men, prefigure the complaints to be made by British soldiers in the coming war, and perhaps tell us something about those qualities of the Australian soldier which essentially do not change. After noting that the examples of indiscipline which allegedly had been a trait of the Australians in South Africa were not exhibited by the forces he saw, he added that nonetheless '[m]anifestations of any feeling, but more especially of feelings of respect, are discountenanced under the unwritten code of Australian conduct. The private soldier does not clearly understand that what an officer *is*, is one thing, and that what he *stands for* is another, and, militarily speaking, the significant thing'. He would change his opinion at the Dardanelles.

The years between Federation and the Great War provide little support for the notion that Australia lacked any semblance of a defence policy until the Second World War, although there is less evidence for the contention that successive Commonwealth governments in this period were pursuing clearly defined and expressed Australian interests. The demands of nation and empire did not appear to conflict in the hearts and minds of this generation of 'independent Austral Britons', for whom there was no contradiction between the sense of an identity as Australians and a wider loyalty caught up in a sense of empire nationalism. Self-reliance in defence matters increased rapidly after 1905, but largely in order that Australia might play a greater part in the defence efforts of the empire; the creation of an independent navy was unique among the self-governing dominions, yet it was created in such a way that it could operate effectively only as part of the Royal Navy. Defence was seen by Deakin as a means of improving Australia's standing in the councils of the empire and of breaking down colonial parochialism, by which he meant not relations between the former colonies and the metropolitan power but relations between the six former colonies themselves; a means of breaking down the divisions between 'modern national and the older colonial sentiment'. The latter goal at least was to be enhanced by participation in the Great War.

CHAPTER 5

The Great War, 1914–1918

Some of the central myths in Australian history have their genesis in the Great War. In the late nineteenth century, Australians had bewailed the lack of a martial tradition in their country, convinced that only when a nation and a people had shed its blood and treasure in a great conflict of arms had it truly passed the test of nationhood. This crude mixture of social Darwinism and British racial propaganda was a powerful idea by no means confined to the Australian colonies, but the vision of warrior heroes which it evoked was sadly out of tune with the methods and consequences of modern industrial warfare.

Australia was a very long way from the theatre of war in 1914, and although Australians followed the gathering crisis in Europe in their newspapers their attention in July and August was focused more closely upon the constitutional crisis in Ireland, which threatened to spill over into civil war, and on the election for the federal parliament scheduled for 5 September. The election campaign allowed politicians a public forum for declarations of loyal support, and these were readily forthcoming. On 29 July the governments of the dominions had been advised by London that war was imminent, and when New Zealand offered a contingent of troops the next day, matched by the Canadians on 31 July, Australian politicians quickly followed suit. Foremost among them was the leader of the Opposition Labor Party, Andrew Fisher, whose memorable phrase promising to back Britain to the 'last man and last shilling' might be thought ominously prescient by the war's end. Preliminary mobilisation was undertaken, with the Australian Squadron ordered to Sydney for coaling. A mobilisation plan for the provision of a joint Australian–New Zealand division for overseas service had existed for several years, but the prime minister, Sir Joseph Cook, was determined that the Australian offer should try to match that of Canada, at that time erroneously reported to be 30 000 troops. Accordingly, the Cabinet decided that a force of 20 000 men should be sent from Australia for service wherever the British desired, and that the RAN should be placed under Admiralty control, which conformed with the agreements arrived at during the 1911 Imperial Conference. The troop offer was announced at once, and on 6 August the British government cabled its acceptance and requested that the force be made available as soon as possible.

The manner in which the dominions raised their forces differed from one to the other. The careful mobilisation plans which had existed in Canada for some years were carelessly overthrown by the Minister for Militia, Major General the Honourable Sir Sam Hughes, in a characteristic gesture combining energy and marked eccentricity. The Canadian Expeditionary Force was raised by voluntary enlistment, the ties between the numbered infantry battalions of the CEF and the militia regiments which provided the recruiting base for the force being tenuous at best. In New Zealand, the infantry and mounted rifles brigades sent in the first contingent were raised from cadres of volunteers drawn from the existing battalions, batteries and other units of the militia, thus maintaining a clear link between the force overseas and the home service army. In Australia the Defence Act precluded the dispatch of any but volunteers for overseas service, and the compulsory training scheme had seen the militia manned almost exclusively by young men of eighteen to twenty-one years of age. Accordingly the contingent, designated the Australian Imperial Force or AIF, was raised by voluntary enlistment from the whole population. Recruitment began on 10 August for an infantry division and a light horse brigade, to sail for the war in just six weeks.

A number of command appointments were made at this time. The Chief of the General Staff, Brigadier General J. M. Gordon, a British officer whose term of office had expired, was replaced by Colonel J. G. Legge, an Australian officer at that time on attachment at the War Office in London. A former CGS, and since 1 July the Inspector General of the Australian Military Forces, Brigadier General William Throsby Bridges, was appointed GOC of the AIF. As his chief of staff he selected one of the brightest lights in army headquarters, Major C. B. B. White, then Director of Military Operations. The permanent head of the Defence Department, Commander Samuel Pethebridge, was out of the country when war was declared and his position was filled by the chief clerk, Thomas Trumble, pending his return. Matters of censorship were also brought under control; formally a responsibility of the CGS, the censorship of all cable and wireless traffic was delegated to Colonel the Honourable J. W. McCay, former Minister for Defence and an officer in the militia. When he was given a command in the new force, his place as deputy chief censor was taken by Colonel John Monash, who held the post briefly before he, too, was given a brigade command.

That same physical isolation from theatres of war which has usually been Australia's great defence against direct attack has also been a complicating factor in dispatching troops overseas, and so it proved in 1914. In opposing the creation of an Australian navy the Admiralty had argued, in keeping with the dominant strategic ideas of the American naval theorist Alfred Thayer Mahan, that naval security lay in the battle of great fleets which would take place in the Atlantic and North Sea, and that the diversion of resources to a naval force in Australian waters was not a means of providing additional security but in fact a diminution of overall naval strength. The existence of the German Pacific Squadron and the fear that the obsolescent vessels on the China and East Indies stations would be outclassed by the powerful modern cruisers *Scharnhorst* and *Gneisenau* had induced the Australian government to keep the battle cruiser *Australia* in home waters. The Australian Naval Board and the commander of the Australian Squadron, Admiral Sir George Patey, argued that the first duty of that squadron was to find and eliminate the German Pacific Squadron, but the Admiralty vetoed this proposal, preferring that the ships of the Australian Squadron be available to escort the forces dispatched to occupy the German Pacific colonies.

Germany had come late to great power status, and its colonial possessions were few and scattered, confined largely to eastern and southern Africa and the island chains of the Pacific. It was these latter which were of greatest strategic value, especially in terms of a naval conflict. By erecting radio stations on these islands, the Germans had created an important strategic asset which enabled them not only to control their own warships across the great expanse of the Pacific and Indian oceans, but also to monitor and intercept radio traffic from the ships of their opponents and thus set their own ships upon inviting targets or provide them with recent intelligence on the movements of allied warships. The elimination of this radio network was an important task, and on 6 August the Admiralty asked the Australian and New Zealand governments to embark upon it 'as a great and urgent Imperial service'.

Radio traffic from the German Squadron had been monitored in Australia at the war's outbreak, but no-one knew exactly where the enemy were, although they were suspected of hiding out in the excellent natural harbour at Rabaul, the capital of German New Guinea. This was searched by ships of the Australian Squadron on 11 August, but without result. In fact, the German Squadron was heading across the Pacific and into the Atlantic by way of Cape Horn. It surprised and sank a British force off Coronel on 1 November, before itself being surprised and destroyed by a powerful cruiser force in the Battle of the Falklands on 8 December. It was resolved however to seize German territory in the Pacific, with the New Zealanders mounting an expedition against German Samoa while the Australians were to occupy Nauru, the Carolines, and German New Guinea.

Virtually Legge's first task as CGS was to oversee the formation of the Australian Naval and Military Expeditionary Force (AN&MEF), allotted the task of capturing German New Guinea. Command of the force was given to Colonel William Holmes, a citizen force officer commanding the 6th Brigade in New South Wales and secretary of the Sydney Water Board. It comprised a battalion of infantry enlisted in Sydney, a 500-strong naval landing party recruited from naval reservists and ex-seamen, and part of a battalion of the citizen forces drawn from Queensland, which had been sent to garrison Thursday Island on the outbreak of war and 500 of whose rank and file now volunteered to serve outside Australia. The capital ships from Patey's squadron were diverted from their search for the enemy cruisers and assigned as escorts, first to the New Zealand force which seized Samoa on 30 August. On 23 August the Japanese entered the war on Britain's side, immediately commencing operations against German forces in China and greatly augmenting allied naval strength in the Pacific. The AN&MEF sailed from Sydney on 19 August; it waited at Port Moresby for escorts from Patey's squadron, and while there Holmes decided to leave the Queensland militia unit behind since its young soldiers were poorly equipped and largely untrained. Accompanied by the cruiser *Sydney* and *Australia*, the force reached Rabaul on 11 September, which was occupied the next day after some minor fighting against the small German garrison. In truth, the Germans had made few preparations to turn their colony into a major military stronghold; their forces in the area were mostly native constabulary, with a few white officers and NCOs. Although they held out in the interior for a number of days, resistance was quite useless and on 17 September terms of surrender were signed, to come into effect on the 21st. Forty white soldiers and 110 indigeneous peoples surrendered and Holmes set about creating an administration which was to last, barring the period of Japanese occupation after 1942, until independence was granted to New Guinea in 1975. Total casualties incurred in the seizure of what became Australia's principal colony were two officers and four men killed and one officer and three men wounded. Although light, the proportion of the losses indicates the closeness of the combat. The assaulting force prevailed not least because their unexpected ability to fight in close country, and their resultant outflanking of the German positions, unnerved their opponents.

At home, the first contingent of the AIF was being recruited in an astonishingly short space of time, eloquent testimony to the near-unanimity of viewpoint within the Australian community which regarded the war as just and service in it as both obligation and privilege. To enlist, men needed to be between eighteen and thirty-five, with a minimum height of five foot six inches and a chest measurement of thirty-four inches. At least half the force was to be made up of men aged twenty years or over who were serving in the militia. The rest of the force would be drawn from former militiamen or men with other relevant war service. The medical standards at this stage were exacting, and men were rejected for having filled teeth. By the end of August the force had been raised: 624 officers and 17 351 men in the three infantry brigades and divisional units, 104 officers and 2122 men in the light horse brigade, and 153 officers and 272 other ranks specially chosen and filling various specialist appointments, for a grand total of 881 officers and 19 745 other ranks. The two most populous states, New South Wales and Victoria, provided the 1st and 2nd Brigades respectively, while the four 'outer' states fielded the 3rd. The 1st Light Horse Brigade had regiments from New South Wales, Queensland, and a composite unit from South Australia and Tasmania. In general, the composition of the AIF as a whole was to reflect this balance between the states.

Bridges and White chose their brigade and artillery commanders and principal staff officers, largely without reference to Legge or army headquarters, drawing on a mix of militia officers, some with service in South Africa, and serving or ex-British regulars. There were no graduates of the new RMC in such posts because the first class graduated only in August 1914, and early at that in order to provide junior staff and regimental officers for the 1st Division. The second class also graduated early, in November, in order to fill the same function for the later contingents which sailed at the beginning of 1915. The brigade commands went to Colonels H. N. MacLaurin and J. W. McCay (the former Minister for Defence), both militia officers, and E. G. Sinclair-McLagan, a British regular. Command of the light horse brigade went to Colonel H. G. Chauvel, who had extensive experience in South Africa and who had accepted a regular commission in 1896 after a period in the Queensland colonial militia. The chief gunner was Colonel Talbot Hobbs, another militia officer, while the head of the medical service was Colonel N. R. Howse, VC, who had already taken part in the expedition to New Guinea. The brigadiers then chose their unit commanders, who picked their own subordinate officers except where they had regulars posted in to specialist and administrative posts such as machine gun officer or adjutant. Some of the NCOs had previous militia service or were former

British regulars. In a move which reflected the progressive nature of much Australian industrial and social legislation at the turn of the century, it was decided that the pay of a private soldier should equal the wage of the average worker, resulting in his being the best-paid soldier of the war at a rate of six shillings a day; hence the tag 'six bob a day tourists'.

All sorts of claims have been made about the 'nature' of the AIF, about its ethos, effectiveness and the basis of its recruitment. Bean believed that the best soldiers came from the 'outer' states, because there the values of the bush were closest to everyday life and the inhabitants were inured to hardship. But he also held that the values of the bush permeated the towns and cities, thus getting around the problem posed for his thesis by the simple fact that Australia was one of the most highly urbanised countries on earth in 1914, and that the majority of enlistments came from the cities and towns. To be fair, Bean never stated that the bush was the only factor in the AIF's effectiveness and image, and he thought that the open and democratic nature of dominion society in general and Australian society in particular accounted far more for the virtues and qualities which he singled out for praise. But his frequent use of bush and rural imagery in the official history tends to leave an impression of the importance of the 'direct physical influence' of rural life on the character of the AIF. And his view on the quality of 'outer' states soldiers is not sustained by evidence, nor is it sustainable.

In so far as it can be generalised from the available evidence, the 'profile' of the AIF in terms of birthplace, occupation, marital status, age and religion was as follows: at least 21 per cent were born in Britain or elsewhere outside Australia; of those born here 55 per cent came from the two most populous states. Twenty-one per cent were engaged in primary production, but 41 per cent were employed in industry, transport and commerce, while 10 per cent were in clerical or professional callings. That left 22 per cent who were labourers and another 10 per cent whose trade or calling was not stated. In keeping with the enlistment requirements of the early part of the war, over 80 per cent were single. Again not surprisingly, 73 per cent were of prime military age, that is between eighteen and twenty-nine years; 20 per cent were in their thirties, with the balance made up of overage and a few underage recruits (the popular image of large numbers of very young men lying about their age in order to enlist is a myth. It was much more common for older men to put their age down in order to meet the eligibility criteria). Anglicans accounted for nearly half the total. Other Protestant denominations added a further 29 per cent and Catholics 20 per cent, in rough proportion to their percentage in the population as a whole. At one time or another 17 per cent of the total would be NCOs, and 5 per cent would be commissioned.

Bean asserted, rightly, that the most important factor in the training, discipline and effectiveness of a unit is the quality of its officers. As part of his thesis about the democratic nature of the AIF, he pointed to the selection of officers from the ranks and linked military effectiveness to this policy. But as already noted, at least initially officers were not appointed from the ranks, and in fact it was not until after January 1915 that the only point of entry to the AIF became enlistment in the ranks. Even then, this did not apply to members of the Staff Corps, who continued to be sent to units as they graduated from Duntroon, although the total numbers involved here were very small. And thereafter, as Bean noted, selection from the ranks for officer training was influenced by factors such as education and manners. When the AIF was expanded and reorganised at the beginning of 1916, the commanders of the 1st and 4th Infantry Brigades drew most of their junior officer replacements from the light horse, with a higher proportion of Greater Public School men in its ranks, rather than from their own units. There do not appear to have been many officers from labouring backgrounds, nor many Catholics either.

It remains a fact, however, that the majority of officers in the AIF enlisted originally as private soldiers. By the end of the war there were plenty of officers who sported an MM or DCM (decorations restricted to other ranks), alongside their MC or DSO (decorations awarded to officers). Probably the majority of company and battalion commanders in 1918 had risen from the ranks. Staff Corps officers remained frequently in staff and specialist postings and were denied promotion beyond the rank of major and the opportunity to command units, although a few did so unofficially in the exigencies of battle. With the remarkable expansion of the AIF, especially in 1916, and with the heavy attrition among officers and NCOs, such a commissioning policy is hardly surprising and it mirrored practice in the British Army which, contrary to popular belief, drew increasingly upon short service commissions from the ranks as the war went on.

It was a sound policy also given the small base of officers on which the AIF could draw at the war's beginning, and the variable quality of that base. Some of those who embarked for overseas were too old for active service, and others were unfit in a variety of ways. Some units had appalling problems with incompetent officers who had been selected for posts on the basis of their social standing or long service in one or other militia unit, and a goodly number were sent home in 1915 or, if merely physically unfit for the demands of modern war, were sent to the

Table 5.1 Net enlistments in the AIF, 1914–18

Year	Enlistments
1914	52 561
1915	165 912
1916	124 355
1917	45 101
1918	28 883

Source: Ernest Scott, *Australia During the War*, Sydney, 1936.

rear areas to run lines of communication units. The haste with which the AIF was raised and dispatched overseas showed itself not only in the lack of training which units had received, but in the sometimes poor personnel selection which accompanied it.

So massive was the response to the calls for recruits that the government was able to inform the British that a further contingent comprising first reinforcements (3237), two light horse brigades (about 4000), a fourth infantry brigade (4500) and assorted medical and support troops (about 2000) would be dispatched. The first convoy containing the 1st Division left the rendezvous in Australian waters at Albany on 1 November, accompanied by ten transports carrying the first contingents of the New Zealand Expeditionary Force (NZEF) and escorted by the British cruiser *Minotaur*, *Australia* and *Sydney*, and the Japanese cruiser *Ibuki*. The departure had been delayed several times because of fear that the German Squadron might intercept the convoy, and it was only when the enemy ships were reported near Papeete on 30 September and the escorts were called back from searching for them, at the insistence of the New Zealand government, that the convoy sailed. The concerns of the New Zealanders were borne out when in the early morning of 9 November the convoy was alerted to the presence of the German cruiser *Emden* off Cocos Island. *Sydney* was dispatched to deal with the threat. Its heavier guns, newer and more powerful engines, and some inspired seamanship told in its favour. An engagement lasting just twenty-five minutes ended with the celebrated signal, '*Emden* beached and done for'. With the older cruiser *Konigsberg* sheltering in East African waters and unable to emerge, the German threat in the Indian and Pacific oceans had been neutralised. The convoy sailed to Ceylon and thence to Egypt. The Australian warships were ordered to the Atlantic and then to join the Grand Fleet where *Australia* became flagship of the Second Battle Cruiser Squadron, only to miss the Battle of Jutland because of a collision with *New Zealand* a month earlier. For the rest of the war the ships of the RAN would operate as part of Royal Navy flotillas and in accordance with Admiralty doctrine, operating against the German High Seas Fleet and the submarine menace. But the performance against German warships and installations in the Pacific in the first months of the war confirmed the wisdom of Deakin and others who had argued for Australian control of an Australian navy.

It had been intended that the Australian and New Zealand forces would proceed to England for training and then depart for the Western Front, as the Canadians had done. When the convoy reached the Suez Canal at the end of November orders were received to disembark the troops in Egypt to assist in the defence of the canal against the Turks, who had entered the war on Germany's side on 29 October. The two forces were to be formed into a corps, the Australian and New Zealand Army Corps or ANZAC, command of which was vested in a British officer, Lieutenant General W. R. Birdwood. It was always intended that the troops should go to the Western Front eventually, but the pressure on accommodation and equipment in the great training areas on Salisbury Plain precluded the arrival of any more troops in England that winter, and so the Anzac Corps remained in Egypt.

The period between the arrival in Egypt and the embarkation for Gallipoli was marked by training and reorganisation. Later contingents arrived from Australia, and the 4th Brigade was joined with the two New Zealand brigades and the 1st Light Horse Brigade to form the New Zealand and Australian Division, known as the NZ&A, under Major General Alexander Godley who commanded the NZEF. Godley was another of those imperial officers who had commanded and reorganised the dominion and colonial forces of the late Victorian and Edwardian eras, in his case in New Zealand. He was an able administrator although not a success as a senior field commander, and his austere character earned him considerable hatred from his New Zealanders in the course of the war for what many of them felt was his lack of concern with their well-being and a perceived disregard for the casualties they incurred. This did not do him justice, but then reputations were among the many casualties of the war.

The period in Egypt was a useful one, in which the units and formations 'shook down', but too much should not be made of it. The training was of the standard British prewar pattern. Nothing of the developments in warfare imposed rapidly by action in France and Belgium had permeated through to the forces in Egypt, nor had any of the advances in the materials of war – bombs, periscopes, and the heightened use of the machine gun. The 1st Division never got to the stage of divisional manoeuvres, although in the context of what awaited them on Gallipoli this did not matter much. Godley's formation reached the stage of mounting field days, but the toughening of the troops did not make up for the lack of experience of the junior – and many of the more senior – officers, nor rectify weaknesses in staff work. Bean stated that some observers thought the 1st Division one of the best prepared ever to take the field; there is little evidence for this contention, and it seems more likely that, for all the courage of its soldiers, the 1st Division was probably the worst-trained formation ever sent from Australia's shores. In February 1915 the Turks made the first attempt to attack the Canal Zone. They were beaten off with heavy losses in a series of short actions in which the Australians were not engaged.

The Gallipoli campaign remains one of the most contentious in modern British history. Arguments still rage over the role and responsibility of Winston Churchill, the campaign's chances of success, its strategic and tactical shortcomings. Its intentions were clear enough: to knock Turkey out of the war, and bring the Balkan states in on the allied side and, with their armies, advance on Austria–Hungary along the Danube. Opening the straits to enable shipping and supplies to reach the Russians' southern ports while allowing them an egress for their wheat shipments which in turn would provide them with desperately needed foreign exchange, and safeguarding the imperial line of communications to India, were important, though secondary, strategic aims. Taken together, their realisation promised to transform the war. But the execution of the concept was hopelessly faulty, an unintended result perhaps of the ease with which the Turkish assault upon the Canal Zone had been repulsed and which had suggested that the Turks were a less than formidable military force.

The early stages of the campaign are well known: the failure of the navy to force the Narrows, hung up on the Turkish minefields and losing six capital ships in a day and warning the Turks of allied intentions. The decision was taken to stage a landing, clear the shore on either side of the straits of the enemy and open the waterways to the navy which would then progress to Constantinople to receive the Turkish surrender. General Sir Ian Hamilton was given command of the Mediterranean Expeditionary Force, and a use was found now for the thousands of Australian and New Zealand troops who had been stuck in Egypt waiting to embark for the 'real' war in France, and who had been making a considerable nuisance of themselves in the bazaars, bars and brothels of Cairo. For Australians and New Zealanders the ANZAC role in the campaign has always been central, but they were outnumbered always by the British, Indian and French contingents and the role planned for them in the initial stages was a subordinate one, in keeping with the expectations held by British regulars in regard to untried troops.

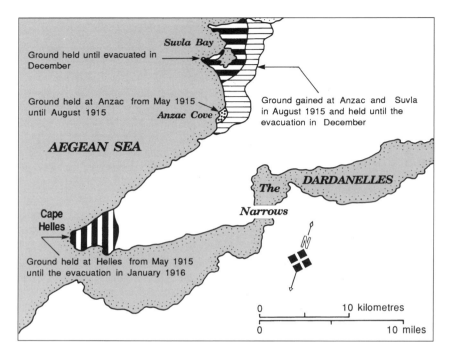

Map 6a   Gallipoli and the Dardanelles

The course of the campaign falls naturally into four stages. The first, the landing of the 3rd Brigade in the early hours of 25 April, involved the initial assault upon the Turks which was contained thanks to the reinforcements which had arrived since the first naval attacks in February and their determined tactical and strategic direction by Mustapha Kemal. The second stage, which ran from May to August, involved the consolidation and expansion of the lodgement area. The third, during the month of August, saw the forces at Anzac Cove take the leading part in a major offensive effort to break the deadlock in concert with the landing further north at Suvla Bay of a New Army formation, IX Corps and, when this failed with heavy losses, involved the Anzacs in some further straightening of the lines at Hill 60. The fourth and final stage lasted from September until the evacuation in mid-December, when it had become clear that the forces involved were exhausted and incapable of further sustained offensive activity.

The overwhelming impression of the conduct of operations at Gallipoli is one of mismanagement, but inexperience also played a large part. The landing itself was mishandled. The battalions in the lead brigade were put ashore a mile from their intended position, almost certainly due to navigational error on the part of a midshipman in one of the leading tows (and not to any vagaries of the current). Instead of advancing across relatively open country – which, as it turned out, was well defended by the enemy and provided them with open fields of fire across the beach – the Australians found themselves on a narrow beach which quickly rose in steep and rugged hillsides covered with thick scrub, swept by Turkish fire from the heights above. In his official dispatch of 8 May 1915, Birdwood described how the landing force faced

> a hill covered with dense scrub with ravines running everywhere and in places quite precipitous. Every ridge had been thoroughly entrenched by the Turks, and it was against this position they hurled themselves with the utmost determination, and with complete success. So vigorous was their onslaught that the Turks were unable to stand before it, and fled from ridge to ridge pursued by the Australian infantry.

But he admitted in a private report to Hamilton on 28 April that 'we have lost a great many officers, and this has naturally led to much trouble, while the country we have had to fight over is so absolutely different to what the men have been accustomed to or trained to, that [sic] they should have done as they have is I think tremendously to their credit'.

Their inexperience was probably their saving for, undaunted by the tactical problems posed, the platoons and companies charged forward and seized the enemy-held positions above and continued through to the second and even the third ridgeline beyond. 'A brief pause on the beach to fix Bayonets', wrote Major A. H. Darnell of the Fifth Battalion,

> and ... swearing and cheering we charged up a hill so steep in places we could only just scramble up. No firing all Bayonet work. Clean over a machine gun we went, men dropped all round me, it was mad, wild, thrilling ... not till I was near the top of the hill did I realise that in the excitement I hadn't even drawn my revolver.

In some cases this was to represent the furthest advance inland in the whole of the campaign, and it was not sustained beyond the first day. Disorganisation among the troops and staffs and the clear realisation that the enemy's defensive positions would not be turned led Birdwood and Bridges to request that the force be evacuated that night. Conventional military wisdom states that the only operation of war more difficult than an opposed seaborne landing is an evacuation while in contact with the enemy. Hamilton told them, wisely, that there was nothing for it but to 'dig, dig, dig, until you are safe'. And so the great

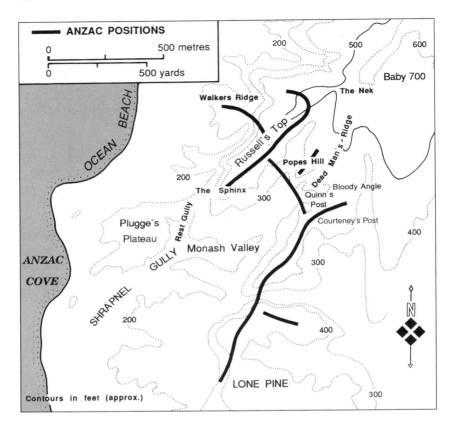

Map 6b Anzac Cove, May–December 1915

manoeuvre to open the straits degenerated into positional warfare within the first twenty-four hours.

The Anzacs were not equipped for what followed. There was a complete absence of trench and engineering stores, and for the first weeks the trenches and posts were shallow scrapes protected by sandbags and covered by Turkish fire from several directions. In places like Quinn's, Steele's and Courteney's Posts the two sides were only yards apart, and this remained the case throughout the campaign. Conditions improved gradually with the arrival of wire and timber supports from Egypt, so that by August the trenches and tunnels were deep and had overhead cover against Turkish bombing, but all construction and fortification work was carried out at night and under constant Turkish fire. Indeed one of the distinguishing features of Anzac Cove was that the entire position, right down to the beach, was able to be brought under fire by the Turks. Colonel MacLaurin and his brigade major were killed by a sniper on 27 April; Bridges himself was mortally wounded in this manner on 15 May, and died soon after. Disease was an even greater problem than enemy fire. Flies and lice spread dysentery, enteric fever and paratyphoid, while the monotonous, irregular and insufficient diet assisted the spread of disease. By the end of July 200 men a day were being evacuated sick. In further evidence of gross mismanagement, the medical evacuation system was overwhelmed and men died waiting to be taken to hospitals; in Egypt, the Australian base hospitals were swamped by the influx of casualties, and in the early weeks were seriously overcrowded.

Losses from disease and enemy action, especially after the large Turkish attacks on 19 May, posed serious reinforcement problems. In the middle of May the light horse regiments, without their horses, were shipped to Anzac as replacements. A light horse unit was not as large as an infantry battalion and, in addition, had to leave behind one-quarter of unit strength to act as horse handlers. Throughout the campaign, unit and brigade commanders complained to their superiors about the manpower problem which they faced when holding trenchlines with handfuls of men. Part of the problem lay in the evacuation and reinforcement system itself, since once a man was evacuated from the Peninsula it proved very hard to get him back to his unit once fit because of the breakdown in administration. The 3rd Light Horse Brigade reported on 28 July that 21 per cent of its strength was in hospital sick; by 30 August the Fifth Light Horse Regiment mustered just 200 effectives of whom only 141 were 'bayonets' in the line. By 20 August the brigade as a whole had only 907 all ranks, having lost 1263 men from all causes and receiving only 498 reinforcements. By late September the brigade held 500–600 yards of trench with just 400 men which, while adequate as a holding force, left nothing in reserve. Of the 1900 or so who had landed in May, only 130 other ranks were still serving on Gallipoli at the evacuation, and only one original officer, the brigade major.

Inadequacies in training and equipment showed up also. The artillery had been raised on an establishment which permitted fewer guns per battery than its British equivalents, nine four-gun batteries per division instead of fifteen, with the result that the Australian units were undergunned. In any case, the exigencies of trench warfare demanded howitzers, of which the Australians in the beginning had none, and the supply of these artillery pieces was always problematic because production in Britain could not meet the demands of all fronts and the BEF in France received first priority. Supplies of ammunition for such guns as the Anzacs possessed were often short and the quality of the ammunition was poor, with a high percentage of duds and defective rounds which posed a greater danger to the gun crews than to the enemy. Bomb factories were set up to manufacture grenades from ration tins, old iron and rifle ammunition.

The lack of training and the poor quality of the staff work were shown up in the major offensives launched in August. The night approach march attempted by Monash's 4th Brigade was hopelessly over-ambitious for tired men in poor health who lacked the necessary training in night operations; the troops got lost, failed to reach their starting positions on time, and took heavy casualties when exposed to Turkish fire in daylight. The infamous charge at The Nek was a prime example of the breakdown in communications between the front line and the brigade staff; it should not have proceeded after the first two lines were shot down. But this was a case of inexperience as much as anything else, as Bean himself noted when he declared that such an operation would not have been undertaken at all later in the war, a clear admission that the Australians still lacked experience in judging and handling tactical situations. The assault on Lone Pine, intended to draw Turkish reserves away from the New Zealand attack on Chunuk Bair to the north, was declared a success, but at the cost of most of the surviving 1st Brigade – the Australians lost eighty officers and 2197 men from six battalions, and in some units every officer was killed or wounded. But the Anzacs were being asked to achieve the impossible in any case, and it is not clear that more proficient staff work would have altered the final result in any of these actions.

Strategically, the failure of the August offensive emphasised the inability of the allies to force a decision. Hamilton was sacked and replaced by Lieutenant General Sir Charles Monro, who had recently commanded the Third Army in France and who believed in any case that the main British effort should be made there. Lord Kitchener made an inspection of the positions in mid-November, and concurred in the recommendation that the forces be evacuated and the theatre abandoned. In what was easily the best planned operation of the entire campaign the Australians were evacuated from Anzac in stages, the whole completed without a single casualty on the night of 19–20 December. Total Australian casualties in the Mediterranean Expeditionary Force were 26 111 – 1007 officers and 25 104 other ranks. Of these, 362 officers and 7779 men were killed in action, died of wounds or succumbed to disease. The only result of any strategic value was that the Turks too had suffered heavily; unlike the allies at this stage, they could not replace their greater losses so easily.

The Australians and New Zealanders returned to Egypt to rest, retrain and re-equip, and absorb the necessary reinforcements who were waiting in the depots and holding units outside Cairo. The AIF now underwent a period of considerable reorganisation. Administrative procedures were formalised also. Until his death, Bridges had commanded both the 1st Division and the AIF as a whole. He had been responsible to the Australian government for all matters of internal discipline and administration, promotion, organisation and training, while the general direction of the campaigns and higher formations in which they served remained with the British. Legge had been dispatched from Australia to take over this role after Bridges was killed, and for short intervals during the campaign he and Godley exercised this function alternately. After the evacuation the Australian government appointed Birdwood to command of the AIF as a whole, an arrangement which was to last for the rest of the war. As his chief of staff and principal adviser Birdwood took Brudenell White, who had fulfilled the role for Bridges.

In May and June the news of Gallipoli had led to a renewed surge of enlistments in Australia, and in July 1915 the new battalions which were arriving in Egypt were formed into a second infantry division, organised and then commanded on Gallipoli by Legge. In the last weeks of the campaign those men who would have proceeded on to their units were stopped when the decision was made to evacuate, and by the beginning of 1916 there were 20 000 men in the depots even after a further 10 000 had proceeded to Lemnos to reinforce existing units taken off Gallipoli. And more men were arriving all the time. Between May and September 1915 over 100 000 men enlisted in Australia, over 36 000 in July alone.

Political changes in Australia had brought William Morris Hughes to the prime ministership in October 1915, and this was to have an enormous bearing upon manpower issues and domestic politics in Australia for the rest of the war. We have seen how Hughes had been the leading campaigner in parliament after Federation for the implementation of compulsory military training, and the authoritarian streak in his nature was to be given full rein by the demands of a great industrial war. One of his first acts as prime minister was to conduct a War Census of eligible manpower in Australia under the wide-ranging terms of the *War Precautions Act 1914*, which he had seen through parliament at war's outbreak while serving as Attorney-General in Fisher's ministry. The census 'revealed' that there were 215 000 fit men of military age and without dependents still in Australia, and on this basis the government decided that as well as fielding the 9500 men per month needed as reinforcements for the units already overseas, it would raise and dispatch a force of 50 000 more men organised into thirty-six battalions.

The War Office accepted the offer (with alacrity), indicating that it would prefer three complete divisions properly organised.

While this was being decided, Godley had recommended in January 1916 that the reinforcements in Egypt be used to expand the New Zealand brigades into a New Zealand division, and that the Australians be expanded from two divisions to four, the whole to be formed into two Anzac Corps augmented by a further Australian division when the promised additional men arrived from Australia. Broadly, this was what happened – Birdwood backed the scheme enthusiastically, in the hope that the War Office would then agree to the creation of an Australian and New Zealand Army, presumably with himself at its head. He suggested also that the additional Australian division be formed in Australia before departing overseas, a proposal which was adopted with the creation of the 3rd Division. In Egypt, the Mounted Rifles and Light Horse Brigades were formed into an Anzac Mounted Division and the light horse began the first systematic training in mounted infantry doctrine which they had received since leaving Australia. To effect the expansion of the AIF, Birdwood ordered that existing battalions would be split, with a cadre from one veteran unit being used to create a new one and the two then being made up to strength by the addition of reinforcements. Thus the battalions of the 1st and 2nd Brigades were used to create the 14th and 15th Brigades of the 5th Division, while the 3rd and 4th Brigades helped form the 12th and 13th Brigades in the 4th Division. A reconstituted 4th Brigade was allotted then to the 4th Division, the 8th Brigade to the 5th Division, and four divisions were activated from two. The 2nd Division was left intact since, despite its experience on Gallipoli, it had never completed its organisation or training. The expansion had the effect of spreading experience evenly throughout the AIF, but it spread the strain also. There was thus no concentration of experience or exhaustion within the AIF, a feature which the New Zealanders were to appreciate late in 1916 when they reorganised their own brigades to break up the concentration of Gallipoli veterans in the 1st Brigade; after two years hard campaigning this feature was no longer an asset.

The expansion of the AIF created opportunities anew. Battalion commanders on Gallipoli were given command of brigades. Young company commanders, often in their early twenties, found themselves as COs of battalions, and there was a similar promotion of NCOs and junior officers. Birdwood tried to give the new divisional commands to officers of the British and Indian armies, but the Australian government argued the case for Australian commanders. Monash was to command the 3rd Division when it arrived from Australia, McCay was given the 5th Division, while the 4th went to an Indian Army officer (like Birdwood),

Major General H. V. Cox. Legge continued in command of the 2nd Division while the veteran 1st Division was commanded by the capable and well-liked British general, H. B. Walker, who would retain his command until 1918. The Anzac Mounted went to Chauvel, who had done so well on Gallipoli leading the 1st Light Horse Brigade. I Anzac Corps (1st and 2nd Australian and the New Zealand Divisions) was commanded by Birdwood, II Anzac Corps (4th and 5th Australian Divisions) was given to Godley.

On 13 March the first Australian units of I Anzac Corps left for France and the Western Front. This came as no great surprise, as it had been assumed for some time that the infantry divisions at least would be sent to fight the Germans. Indeed, in the months immediately after the evacuation the troop strength in Egypt diminished rapidly as forces were reallocated to the main British theatre of the war. The men had still received little training in techniques of trench warfare, and the artillery situation in I Anzac had been improved only by stripping II Anzac of its guns in order to bring the establishments of the former up to strength. In recognition of the changing demands to be made upon them, pioneer battalions, trench mortar batteries and machine gun companies had been added to each division. I Anzac was put into the line in a 'nursery' sector south of Armentieres on 7 April. The Australians' introduction to war on the Western Front had finally begun.

War in the Middle East was a poor preparation for the Western Front. However desperate conditions on Gallipoli had seemed, life in the rat-infested and waterlogged trenches of southern Belgium and northern France was often infinitely worse. Of course, there were elements of their service on the Western Front which were a distinct improvement; a greatly expanded and more efficient medical and casualty evacuation system, the (reasonably) regular provision of hot meals and fresh food, the availability of leave both in the rear areas – which were populated still by civilians in contravention of regulations and French law – and further back among the comforts of Paris or even England itself. But many other features were terribly new. Gas, aircraft, flame-throwers, great defensive belts of barbed wire, batteries of machine guns, and above all the incredible concentrations of artillery and the weight of shell fired by them, had been absent on Gallipoli. The Germans were a more skilful and deadly opponent than the Turk, which perhaps accounts in part for the hatred with which many Australians regarded them. In the long term the Australians, like the Canadians, New Zealanders and British, were to dominate the enemy in any positions they occupied, but this was a slow process and in 1916 and 1917 the AIF had cause to understand why many observers regarded the Germans as the most formidable army in the world.

Again in contrast to the Middle East, in France the AIF was a small force subsumed within a much larger one. On Gallipoli, Birdwood had been almost an independent commander. In France in 1916 the Anzac Corps were just two among eighteen in five British armies which comprised forty-four infantry and five cavalry divisions. Far more than before, the Australians were now an integral part of the great army fielded by Britain and its empire, with all which this might entail. On the one hand, it meant that the fruits of experience were passed quickly to the new arrivals. Officers and NCOs were detached to schools for instruction in gas warfare, machine guns, sniping, bombing, and the use of the trench mortar. As Bean himself noted, '[a]s in Roman, and even Persian, times the efficiency of armies depended upon elaborate schooling', the previous lack of which began to be made up. In common with all the dominion forces, the 'teeth to tail' ratio in the AIF was very high, the vast majority of the force being made up of combat and combat direct support units. For logistic and much higher administrative support the Australians, like the Canadians, relied upon the British. Contrary to popular belief about British attitudes towards the Dominion forces, the British army in fact went out of its way to ensure that the administrative and logistic requirements of the Anzac Corps were met quickly and fully. Where deficiencies continued to exist in these areas, they usually reflected shortages and problems which were shared across the empire armies generally. Grouped within British formations, and in keeping with British doctrine, the Anzac Corps were also supplied with tanks and heavy artillery from British resources, and British staff officers filled some of the technical and specialist posts on their headquarters which the Australians lacked the resources to supply themselves. Back in England an AIF administrative network of depots, training and convalescence units was established, controlled from AIF Headquarters in Horseferry Road, London, which was housed in a former Wesleyan Training Institute.

The Australians avoided the awful first day on the Somme, but were drawn into Haig's great offensive within three weeks of its commencement. The 5th Division, newly arrived with II Anzac from Egypt, suffered 5533 casualties in a single twenty-four-hour period in an ill-prepared feint attack near Fromelles. Assigned the task of taking German positions around Pozières in mid-July, where British formations earlier had failed, the Australians in I Anzac suffered 17 000 casualties but attained their objectives, which were limited in any case. This first experience of war on the Western Front was unnerving to many. 'Heavy firing all morning – simply murder', recorded Sergeant L. R. Elvin of the 1st Battalion at Pozières. 'Expecting death every second. Twenty-three men smothered in one trench. Dead and dying everywhere. Some simply blown to pieces. Shells falling like hail during a storm'. And Lieutenant K. S. Anderson of the 22nd Battalion, killed a few days later, noted the relief when the barrage lifted: 'half dazed, we climb from the trenches and make a wild rush to get away while we have the chance'. Taken out of the line, the AIF was recommitted later in the year in a series of grinding attacks around Flers, in which high casualties were exchanged for small gains in ground.

The Australians' attacks in 1916, like the offensives of which they were part, were failures. The blame at Fromelles should be apportioned equally between the divisional commander, McCay, and Lieutenant General Sir Richard Haking, the commander of the British XI Corps to which the Australians were attached. The Germans had been warned of the impending assault by the pre-registration of the British guns, but the bombardment of the enemy trenches in support of the attack was neither intense nor efficient. German machine guns continued to fire at the attacking force throughout the bombardment, and casualties among the Australians were heavy from the moment they advanced. The troops were raw, but their objectives had been hastily assigned and poorly thought out, since this was intended as a feint only, and McCay ordered his men to abandon the enemy trenches once they had cleared them, instead of consolidating against the inevitable German counter-attack which followed. Haking thought the attack had done the division 'a great deal of good'.

At Pozières on 23 July the 1st Division succeeded in taking the German positions with minimal loss, thanks to Walker's greater experience as a divisional commander and a better plan, for which he too was responsible. Unlike McCay, he insisted on being given more time to plan his assault, and the commander of the Reserve Army, General Sir Hubert Gough, gave way. Once the Germans had recovered, they subjected the Australians to an intense artillery bombardment and, by the time they were relieved by Legge's 2nd Division, the 1st Division had suffered 5286 casualties. Legge lacked experience and, acceding to pressure for rapid results from Gough, launched an ill-timed attack on 29 July which failed for the further cost of 3500 casualties. Legge was unlucky, because the enemy detected the brigades while they were forming up on the start lines and the Australians were subjected to another heavy artillery bombardment and the relentless attention of the enemy machine guns. Going in again on 4 August, Legge's division took all its objectives but by the time they were relieved had suffered 6846 casualties. Legge himself was relieved not long after, as was McCay. The 4th Division completed the Australians' immersion in the 1916 offensive, losing 4649 men in the assaults on Mouquet Farm in mid-August, again under Gough's prodding. Again, the attacking force was

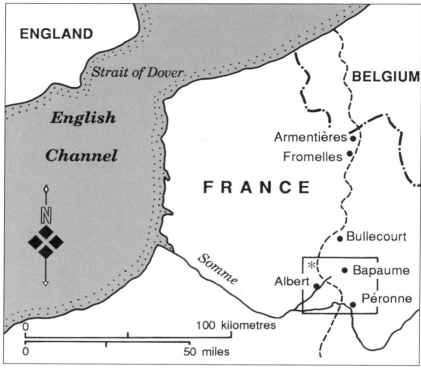

* See Map 7b for enlargement

Map 7a   Western Front 1916

subjected to heavy artillery bombardment, this time from three sides of the salient which had formed around Pozières. In all cases, the assaults were launched on a frontage of a mile or less, enabling the Germans to concentrate their efforts against the attackers. In forty-five days on the Somme the AIF lost 23 000 men in an area 'more densely sown with Australian sacrifice than any other place on earth', to borrow Bean's inimitable phrasing.

Several things emerged from this awful experience. The first was the widespread distrust of British higher command which permeated virtually all ranks. The hostility extended to Birdwood for a time, who many held had not protested vigorously enough against operations which had little chance of success. In this respect, Legge's sacking had something of the scapegoat about it. The second was that the Australians put the experience to good use and began to learn from their mistakes, in particular the value of careful preparation before an

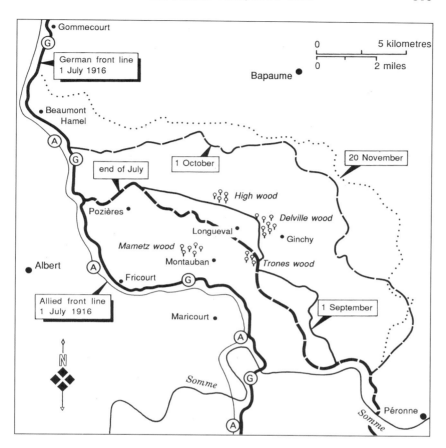

Map 7b The Somme 1916

attack. But third, it should be clear that Australian generals were as good at killing Australian troops as were British generals, at least in this period, and that even successful operations like Walker's brought with them a heavy casualty bill. This latter point was perhaps the most important single lesson of the Western Front, that even successful battles were costly. As the French general, Mangin, pointed out, 'whatever you do, you lose a lot of men'.

The fighting in 1917 involved operations against the Hindenburg Line and Haig's great offensive at Ypres in the north. The Australians' experience on the Hindenburg line at Bullecourt in April and May was in many respects a re-run of the previous year, once again as part of

Gough's Fifth (formerly Reserve) Army. The Germans had fortified entire villages as part of their new defensive lines, and poorly coordinated and unsupported assaults upon heavily defended positions were repulsed with heavy casualties. In the attack on 11 April the assault was launched against a re-entrant in the enemy line, and the attacking brigades were caught in enfilade from positions which their supporting artillery had failed to neutralise. The 4th Brigade alone suffered 2339 casualties out of 3000 men engaged. In the second attempt on 3 May, the assaulting brigades attacked in exactly the same manner and over the same ground. Despite heavy losses, the initial assault took and held part of the Germans' first trench line, but it was several days before the positions in Bullecourt itself were taken at a total cost of 7000 casualties. The failure of the first attempt in April may be laid squarely at Gough's door: he had ordered the attack despite the failure of the artillery to cut the great belts of wire in front of the German positions, and against all evidence maintained that the Germans were in fact abandoning their defences. The heavy casualties from the second attack in May were the result of poor planning and coordination on the part of Birdwood and White, not least by staging the second attack in the same manner as the first and over the same ground.

The 3rd Division arrived in France in February and, with the 4th Division, took part in the assault upon Messines in June as part of Godley's II Anzac Corps in Plumer's Second Army. Plumer was a methodical planner careful with the lives of his soldiers, and Messines is regarded usually as one of the great set-piece victories of the war. Over 2200 guns fired three and a half million shells in the bombardment of a salient eight miles by six, and the assault was preceded by the detonation of nineteen large mines tunnelled under the German positions. Despite its success, the relatively limited gain in territory cost 26000 British casualties, of which II Anzac incurred almost half the total. The second half of 1917 saw Haig renew the offensive to the north, around Ypres, in order to take pressure off the French, by then in serious disarray, and in fulfilment of a long-intended plan to turn the German flank in the north along the Channel coast. After some modest early successes in favourable conditions, the skies opened and the great offensive ground to a halt in an ocean of mud. Conditions were wretched, as Lieutenant F. R. Fischer, a Gallipoli veteran of the 6th Battalion, recorded in a letter: 'some of our chaps were on outpost for 36 hrs at a stretch during which time it rained incessantly, they never had the slightest covering & were [always] either standing or sitting in water'. Gunner A. G. Barrett in the 12th Field Artillery Battery noted laconically merely that 'Belgian mud is incomprehensible to anyone who has not experienced it'. GHQ persisted with the attacks, and Haig's armies slithered forward with excruciating slowness, once again exchanging casualties for tiny gains in territory. The Australian divisions made successful assaults at Polygon Wood, Menin Road and Broodeseinde Ridge, but again, success was expensive. A further 38 000 casualties were incurred in the Passchendaele offensive for a total of 55 000 for the year.

In the course of 1916–17 the AIF consolidated a reputation for reliability and competence. When Haig was asked about discipline problems among the Australians he is supposed to have replied that the Australians were well disciplined because they always attacked when they were told to. His attitude to 'wayward colonials' epitomised by his criticism to White in 1916 – 'you are not fighting Bashi Bazouks now!' – had changed somewhat by 1917, influenced by an appreciation of the quality of all the dominion divisions. It is clear equally that he held Monash in very high regard, dating from the time when the latter was a divisional commander. But the Australian divisions were no more able to break the deadlock in the trenches than were the British or French.

On 1 November 1917 the five divisions were grouped into an Australian Corps. It was commanded by Birdwood initially until he was promoted in Gough's stead to command of the Fifth Army after the German offensives in March, and Monash was placed in command of the corps in May. The formation of an Australian Corps met a widespread desire which had been voiced first at the beginning of 1916, and at the same time as it received an Australian commander the command of the divisions was nationalised also. Walker and Smyth were replaced by Glasgow and Rosenthal in the 1st and 2nd Divisions, Hobbs retained the 5th Division, and Monash's 3rd Division went to Gellibrand. Although he was a British officer, Sinclair-MacLagan continued to command the 4th Division; as a member of the staff at RMC since its inception, and having joined the AIF in 1914, he doubtless counted as an Australian. Birdwood took White with him to his new HQ, and Monash selected Brigadier General T. A. Blamey as his chief of staff. White still exercised some influence, however, because Birdwood retained administrative command of the AIF.

The whole question of the formation and command of an Australian army in France is an interesting one. The Canadians had insisted upon the formation of a Canadian Corps as soon as two Canadian divisions were fielded in 1915. What is more, throughout the war the Canadian government exercised close control over the administration and command of its forces in France and England through the appointment of a cabinet minister in London to the Canadian Overseas Ministry; this close oversight did not, however, extend to control over the operational deployment of the Canadian Corps. They were generally fortunate in their commanders. The first, Lieutenant General Sir Richard Alderson,

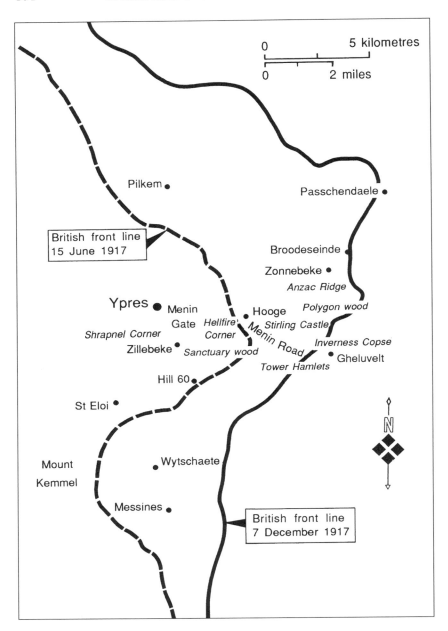

Map 8   Western Front 1917

was a competent officer who fell foul of the political machinations of the Canadian Minister for Militia, Sam Hughes. His replacement, General Sir Julian Byng, was both a talented commander and convinced that his most important task was to nationalise the Canadian Corps so that his successor, and as many of his subordinates as possible, would be Canadian. In June 1917, the Canadian Corps received a Canadian commander, albeit at British nomination, Lieutenant General Sir Arthur Currie. The contrast with Birdwood and the AIF is worth pondering. Bean states that Birdwood had to be persuaded to give up the corps command in the interests of promoting Australians, and it is clear that he did little to press the claims of Australians for positions on the staff of British formations although he was quick to place British officers on Australian staffs. It is true that earlier in the war there were insufficient numbers of trained Australian staff officers to go round, but Birdwood also resisted moves to attach Australians to British formations as staff learners, realistically the only way in which such a shortage would be overcome, although Chauvel among others strongly urged him to do so. His declarations of empathy notwithstanding, it is difficult to avoid the conclusion that Birdwood regarded his command of the AIF largely in careerist terms and his shortcomings as a corps commander, both on Gallipoli and in France in 1916–17, together merit far greater censure than customarily he has received. In many respects he was a poor choice as commander of a national force drawn from what the Canadian historian Desmond Morton has characterised as a 'junior but sovereign ally'.

Pulled out of the line for necessary rest and refitting, the Australian divisions missed the great German offensive which Hindenburg and Ludendorff unleashed in the west on 21 March 1918. Put back in the line before Amiens in April, the Australians helped to blunt an offensive which was running out of steam in any case. In the hiatus which then occurred between April and July, as both sides recovered from their tremendous exertions, the Australians made significant gains of ground by use of 'peaceful penetration'. Termed 'minor aggression' by Monash, this showed the Australian use of small-unit tactics at its very best, reliant for success upon the skill and initiative of junior leaders and the fighting ability of all ranks. Ground was gained and prisoners taken without any special organised effort, and with minimal casualties. Such methods, however, do not win wars, or battles, and Rawlinson used the Australian Corps in the opening round of the great offensive which brought victory in 1918, initially at Hamel on 4 July in a well-planned action which attained all its objectives in less than two hours. Monash described it, with characteristic modesty, as 'a brilliant success'.

Together with the stronger Canadian Corps, the Australians were heavily engaged in the battle of Amiens on 8 August – 'the black day of the German army' according to Ludendorff – and took a leading part in the series of advances which followed from then until the Australian Corps was withdrawn from the line for rest in October. An NCO of the 14th Battalion, killed in the last weeks of the war, thought this period of the war 'was much more to our liking than anything previously'. An officer in the 15th Battalion, Lieutenant H. V. Chedgey, agreed that 'this style of warfare suits us better and the men are keen . . . We fight in open fields, among hedges and farm houses and dig trenches all over the country. We have got right away from fixed trench warfare'. The deadlock on the Western Front had indeed given way to open warfare, brought about by the development of appropriate tactics in the British armies, the greater weight of artillery brought against German defences and the more efficient handling of the guns, and the weakening and demoralisation in the German Army.

Results were commensurate with the effort made; 29 144 prisoners, 338 guns, 116 towns and villages liberated, for 21 243 casualties, one-quarter of whom were killed. By 1918 the experiences of poor planning, incompetent staff work and unsympathetic British generals were behind them. Staff work in the Australian Corps under Monash was rated highly by all who observed it, and he was given greater leeway in planning his operations than Birdwood had ever enjoyed (arguably no bad thing in itself, since Birdwood's tactical acumen was sadly deficient). But the troops were worked to the limit, and by 5 October the Australians had been pulled out of the line for a rest, at Hughes' insistence. Some men who had served from the beginning had already availed themselves of the 'Anzac leave' offered by the government, and were departing for Australia. The war ended before the corps could return to the line, although some artillery units remained in action in support of American and British formations until early November, and the squadrons of the Australian Flying Corps were in action till the end.

Much has been made of the ethos of the AIF, its undoubted quality as a military formation explained variously by references to its volunteer nature, the influence of the bush, and the often undefined quality of 'mateship'. In military terms, this latter explanation is a rational one. Virtually all modern armies recognise the importance of small-unit identity and group cohesion as the cement which binds the building blocks of units and sub-units together in the face of the awful demands of the modern battlefield. That the Australians displayed this is not in dispute, and forms part of that complex process by which the morale of armies is both built and then sustained. For all the claims made subsequently, however, it must be understood equally that it was not a phenomenon confined to the AIF. Canadian and New Zealand commentators lay claim to similar qualities among their own troops, and it is clear that the German, British and American armies displayed it

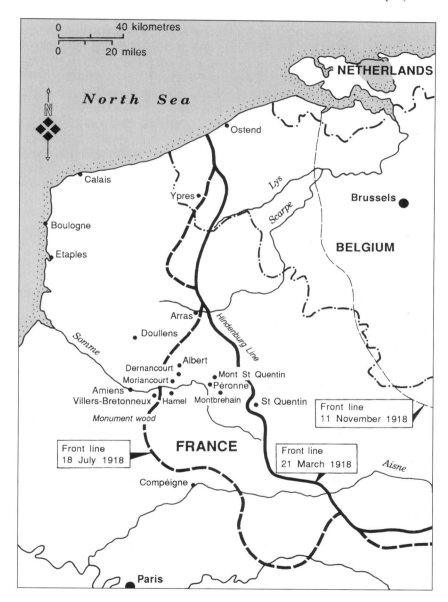

Map 9 Western Front 1918

also, both in this and the following world war, although they identified
it by different names. Equally, volunteer status by itself conferred no
special military qualities. The British soldiers who advanced at the
Somme on 1 July 1916 were all either regulars or 'Kitchener' volunteers.
The status of their enlistment availed them nothing in the face of
German artillery and machine gun fire and uncut belts of barbed wire.
What made the difference in 1918 was the increased effectiveness of the
fire-support given to the troops. This took the form of increased
numbers of Lewis guns per platoon, and more and better artillery.
Individual skill and morale were no substitute for fire and movement.
And the AIF had no monopoly on the latter.

When all claims of national uniqueness are left aside, the only real
feature distinguishing the AIF from the forces around it was the simple
fact that the voluntary nature of its enlistment remained unchanged
throughout the war, alone of all the combatant nations (save the South
Africans, whose contribution to the Western Front was a single brigade).
The penalty exacted by the volunteer system was paid by the men
themselves. The drying up of reinforcements in 1918 led to under-
strength units which were required nonetheless to perform the same
tactical tasks as if they were at full establishment. The shortages in
manpower were compensated as far as possible through the provision of
additional artillery and the issuing of an increased number of Lewis
guns per platoon to provide greater mobile fire support, but it also
meant that increasingly the divisions were built up by men returning
from the hospitals and convalescence depots in England. As Bean
observed, in the circumstances of the Western Front the old soldier was
not always the best soldier; one nameless member of the AIF earned the
distinction of being wounded no fewer than seven times in the course
of his service and there were literally some thousands of men wounded
three and four times.

By the end of 1917 the allies were facing severe manpower shortages.
The Australian Corps had been formed in part as a means of staving off
the disbandment of the weakened 4th Division, which acted as a 'depot'
formation for the others on a rotating basis henceforth. A planned 6th
Division had been broken up and its men distributed in drafts among
the rest after the heavy casualties sustained in the second half of 1917.
(The Canadians likewise disbanded a planned 5th Division while the
New Zealanders, who had resisted pressure from the War Office to raise
a second division, broke up the 4th Brigade which had seen the New
Zealand Division functioning as the only four-brigade formation in the
British armies.) But the AIF did not adopt the British expedient of
reducing the number of battalions in the brigades from four to three,
although AIF Headquarters did disband individual units, distributing
their men among the remaining battalions. The effort of maintaining a

field force of approximately 117 000 men in France was becoming too great for Australia to bear.

The voluntary system in fact had shown signs of falling off in late 1915, and Hughes had the solution to hand – conscription. The appalling losses in July 1916 merely underlined the urgency of the situation. Hughes visited Britain in the first half of the year, sitting in on the deliberations of the Cabinet, and probably became convinced of the need for conscription for overseas service while there. The voluntary system had failed in Britain and, after considerable and agonising debate and the clear failure of the Derby Plan to stimulate voluntary enlistment, a conscription Bill was introduced into the British parliament in January. The flow of volunteers was tailing off in Canada and New Zealand also. Hughes was aware of all this when he returned to Australia from London on 31 July.

Hughes had long been a passionate advocate of compulsory service, and saw no contradiction between conscription and socialist principle. Fisher had been opposed to the idea, fearing that it would undermine the social cohesion necessary for the prosecution of the war effort; in what may be thought a contradiction, he had warned too against creating the impression that the burdens of the war were being borne unequally. To Hughes' own inclinations were added the pressures from London. In mid-August he received a number of cables from AIF Headquarters suggesting that two light horse regiments and all excess reinforcements in the Middle East be sent to France as a means of avoiding the disbandment of the 3rd Division, a step which had been recommended by the British War Council. This proposal was not countenanced because of the critical role which the mounted units were playing in Palestine, but on 24 August the British government advised that drafts would have to be drawn from the 3rd Division and that the monthly rate of reinforcements would need to be increased to 16 500 a month for three months in order to keep the 3rd Division in being. The government agreed to this heavy increase in the reinforcement rate, although the total enlistments for the months of June to August had been only 16 689. Senator George Pearce, the Minister for Defence, announced to the parliament that the voluntary system could no longer be relied on, and Hughes decided that the question of whether or not to conscript single men without dependants would be put to the electorate under the terms of the Conscription Referendum Bill. (Strictly speaking it was a plebiscite, not a referendum, since no constitutional issue was in question, but the word 'referendum' was used at the time and has remained the accepted nomenclature.)

Hughes had the power to impose conscription by gazetted regulation under the War Precautions Act, provided that it was approved by both houses of parliament, but there was no chance of this happening in the

Senate. Many in the Labor Party were opposed irrevocably, and Hughes and his supporters were expelled from the New South Wales branch of the party on 4 September after the State Executive rejected the proposal overwhelmingly. The nation was to vote (compulsorily, in keeping with earlier legislative provision) on 28 October 1916, and in the intervening two months the tone of the political debate degenerated rapidly. To the fundamental questions of societal obligation and free will were added a number of irrelevant ones which nonetheless increased the passion with which the debate was conducted while effectively obscuring the issues. Foremost amongst them, with appeal to differing sections of the electorate, was the Easter Rising in Dublin six months earlier. The extent to which this influenced the vote is impossible to quantify, but the public antagonism over the conscription issue between Hughes and the Catholic Coadjutor Archbishop of Melbourne, Daniel Mannix, and the hysterical imputations of disloyalty thrown at the Irish-Catholic working-class electorate must have predisposed that electorate to cast their vote against the government's proposal. Of even greater importance was the government's ham-fisted call-up of all men between twenty-one and thirty-five for home service at the beginning of October, using powers under the Defence Act. This move seemed merely to confirm the views of those who regarded Hughes' proposal as unbridled militarism. The proposal was defeated by 1 160 033 votes to 1 087 557, with three states voting 'no' absolutely. The soldiers' vote, which Hughes had hoped to use as a propaganda ploy to influence the vote at home, was in favour by only a slim majority of 12 000 votes.

Two major consequences of the referendum were that voluntary recruiting declined even further, and the Labor Party split. Another long-term legacy of considerable significance was the creation of a tradition of opposition to the use of conscripts on overseas service. As late as the Vietnam War this emotional commitment still flourished in Labor ranks. The immediate impact on the Labor Party had been catastrophic. On 4 December the federal party voted to expel all members who supported conscription for overseas service, following the lead of most of the state branches. Hughes and twenty-six supporters had already walked out of the federal parliamentary caucus, and did a deal with the opposition Liberal Party to form a National Labor government in coalition. A major effort was made to revamp the recruitment system, which yielded some fruit but was still insufficient to meet the demands of the front in view of the heavy casualties incurred in 1917. Limited numbers of enemy aliens and citizens of German extraction were interned, the sectarian issue continued to simmer, and the year saw widespread industrial disputes and a major strike in New South Wales which began with the railways and soon spread to the waterfront and other areas. Censorship was imposed rigorously and often ineptly, and Hughes again confirmed the views of his opponents with the suppression of the Industrial Workers of the World and the gaoling of twelve members in New South Wales on charges of sedition and sabotage, allegedly for planning to burn down Sydney. In the course of 1917 the Australian war effort was in danger of becoming unhinged and the political climate at times bordered on the hysterical.

New Zealand had already enacted conscription in late 1916, the Canadians did the same in August 1917 after a debate as bitter as that which occurred in Australia, and the United States had introduced the draft for overseas service upon entry into the war in April. On 7 November Hughes announced that the question of conscription for the AIF would be put to the people again, on 20 December. Reinforcements were needed at a rate of 7000 per month, and Hughes made it clear that he would not continue to govern unless the proposal was passed. An even more bitterly divisive debate ensued, one unintended consequence of which was the creation of a federal law enforcement agency – the Commonwealth Police – following an incident at Warwick, Queensland, in which the prime minister was pelted with eggs. The proposal was again lost, this time by 1 181 747 to 1 015 159, and four states voted against absolutely. Once again the issues became confused, not least because no-one seemed able to agree on just what level of reinforcement the AIF required to remain a viable force. Once again, the soldiers voted in favour, but by a margin of less than ten thousand. Following the result Hughes received a vote of confidence from his Nationalist Party colleagues and, with the assent of the Governor-General, then resumed office at the head of the same ministry as before. The parliamentary Labor Party protested, to no avail.

There is no monocausal explanation for the defeat of conscription in 1916–17. Sectarian and class issues were important, but there were significant exceptions within the Protestant and Catholic churches to the general pattern of 'pro' and 'anti' positions which they adopted, and the working-class vote was similarly divided. Mannix was distrusted by some of his fellow bishops while enjoying considerable support among the laity, and his prominence and influence within the 'anti' movement may be explained as much by the attention which Hughes focused upon him as by any judgements and activities of his own. The female vote was obviously important, but for every mother who wished to keep her son at home there may have been another who wished to see hers reinforced in France. The pacifist tradition on the left and the bitterness felt within the industrial wing of the labour movement explain the form which the 'anti' case took, but do not explain why people voted in a particular manner. It is clear, for example, that many traditionally conservative voters must have deserted their formal allegiances for the purpose of the referenda, since between the two campaigns they returned the Nationalist governments in New South Wales and federally with increased majorities. Significantly, the federal election in May 1917 was fought on the conduct of the war effort and in terms of a promise from Hughes that the return of his government would not bring with it the imposition of conscription. It is sometimes supposed (erroneously) that the soldiers voted against conscription; we have no way of knowing for certain how the AIF voted on a unit or theatre basis, but it is generally assumed that the divisions in France voted against while the AIF in the Middle East, where conditions were less extreme and casualties far lower, joined those in the base areas in voting 'yes'. What is clear is that neither side had a monopoly on the moral high ground in the issue, and some weight should be given to self-interest among the 'anti' vote, especially among males in Australia of military age. The results, especially the second one, are evidence of the war-weariness, disillusionment and division which permeated large sections of Australian society by the last full year of the war. Recruiting in 1918 dropped to around 2500 per month.

For most of the war the Australian government had absolutely no say in its conduct. But with no end in sight and with the intention of strengthening Britain's voice in allied councils, in 1917–18 Lloyd George chose to expand the War Cabinet to allow imperial representation. This extension of the War Cabinet came about as a result of the gathering of dominion premiers for the Imperial Conference in March 1917, although Hughes did not attend because of the domestic political situation in Australia. The Imperial War Cabinet included representatives from India as well as the self-governing dominions, but the inaugural sessions in 1917 achieved little. It reconvened in June 1918, this time with Hughes in attendance, and discussed not only the wider conduct of the war, but also the British war effort and the conduct of operations on the Western Front by the British High Command. Its actual influence in such matters is problematic. The role played by the empire representatives at this stage of the war laid the basis for separate empire representation at the Peace Conference in Paris the following year, although even there it may be doubted whether the dominion premiers achieved anything which ran contrary to Lloyd George's wishes. Attempts to replicate it in the Second World War were unsuccessful in the face of Churchill's total opposition.

The AIF in the Middle East had continued operations in the war against Turkey after the infantry divisions were shipped to France, and made a major contribution to the course and outcome of the campaign. After Sinai and the Canal Zone had been secured in operations at the

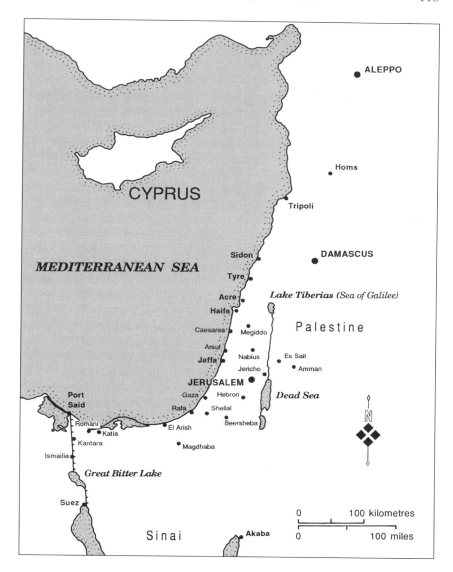

Map 10   Theatre of operations, Sinai and Palestine, 1916–18

end of 1916, the Egyptian Expeditionary Force had commenced the offensive into Palestine, only to receive several checks before Gaza. Chauvel was appointed to command the Desert Mounted Corps in June 1917, becoming the first Australian corps commander, although not of an Australian Corps since the Desert Mounted Corps contained New Zealand, Indian and British Yeomanry regiments as well as Australian light horse. Gaza was captured at the beginning of November after the mounted charge of the light horse at Beersheba, and this success unlocked the whole Turkish defensive position in southern Palestine. Jerusalem was captured on 9 December, as a Christmas present to the British people as Lloyd George had requested. Offensive operations resumed in February 1918 after the winter rains, and in a series of moves the allied army pushed into Syria and Lebanon, driving the collapsing Turkish armies before it and capturing Damascus on 1 October and Aleppo on the 26th. The Turks sued for an armistice on 30 October, bringing the war in this theatre to an end.

Casualties in the Middle East were far lighter than in France: ninety-six officers and 1278 other ranks dead from all causes, and 416 officers and 4435 other ranks total battle casualties. Alone of the British theatres of war, the fighting in Sinai and Palestine allowed a large role for mounted troops, and the Australians and New Zealanders in the Australian Mounted and Anzac Mounted Divisions provided the bulk of the mounted troops in the EEF. The campaign proved the continuing importance of mobility – though not necessarily of cavalry – to modern war and allowed full scope for the mounted infantry skills at which the dominion horsemen excelled. It is important to remember that the light horse was employed largely in its proper role as mounted infantry, and not as cavalry, the mounted charge at Beersheba notwithstanding. The charge was not the first occasion on which the light horse had assaulted an enemy position on horseback – the 10th Light Horse did just that at Magdhaba in December 1916 – but the tactic was not well suited to modern war and several Yeomanry regiments which sought to emulate it early in 1918 were shot to pieces by the Turks. The terrain and climate imposed as great a strain upon the troops as did the enemy, and lack of water and the difficulties of maintaining logistic supply lines influenced the planning of operations as significantly as the moves and intentions of the enemy. Conditions were often primitive and medical evacuation difficult, as shown by the fact that as many Australians died of wounds (337) as died of disease (343).

Men of the Australian Flying Corps operated in both France and the Middle East. Organised into four squadrons, the AFC remained part of the AIF for the war's duration even though Australian military aviation had its origins before 1914. Although small, the preservation of an identity as a separate national force was important, and unusual. Thousands of Canadians flew for the Royal Flying Corps, Royal Naval Air Service and Royal Air Force between 1914 and 1918, but almost entirely as aircrew in British squadrons. Although one-quarter of the RAF was

Canadian by the war's end, as were many of the leading aces, the Canadians did not gain the benefit of command and administrative experience which might have accrued to them otherwise from an independent air service and which would be an asset after the war. A total of 460 officers and 2234 other ranks served in the AFC in the course of the war, while about 200 more served as aircrew in the British services.

By the end of the war Australia had enlisted 416 809 men in total, a staggering effort for a country of approximately 4 million people. Over half the eligible white male population enlisted, and 80 per cent of these served overseas, mostly in France. Nearly 20 per cent were killed and a further 45 per cent were wounded. Proportionate to population, the Australian casualty rate was the highest of the war save only that of New Zealand. More than 210 000 men served in the infantry and more than 30 000 in the light horse, figures which explain this high proportional casualty rate. The price paid by Australia in the Great War stands at 58 961 dead from all causes, 4098 missing and prisoners of war, 166 811 battle casualties, 87 865 sick, and 218 from causes not specified.

At the armistice there were 95 951 men in France, 17 255 with the EEF, and a further 58 365 in depots, bases and hospitals in Britain. War

Table 5.2 Casualties in the AIF, 1914–18

Casualties	British Expeditionary Force	United Kingdom	Egyptian Expeditionary Force	Mediterranean Expeditionary Force	Total
Total deaths					
Officers	2 261	107	96	362	2 826
Other ranks	44 058	2 191	1 278	7 779	55 306
Wounded					
Officers	4 778	–	304	639	5 721
Other ranks	109 654	1	3 047	17 261	129 963
Gassed					
Officers	583	–	–	–	583
Other ranks	15 904	–	–	–	15 904
Prisoners of war					
Officers	148	–	16	6	170
Other ranks	3 713	–	110	64	3 887
Total battle Casualties					
Officers	7 770	107	416	1 007	9 300
Other ranks	173 329	2 192	4 435	25 104	205 060

Source: Australian Imperial Forces, 1914–1920: Data, Canberra, 1972.

Table 5.3 Comparative casualties, 1914–18

Country	Total deaths	Total mobilsed	per 1000 mobilised	per 1000 population
UK	723 000	6 147 000	118	16
Canada	61 000	629 000	97	8
Australia	60 000	413 000	145	12
New Zealand	16 000	129 000	124	15
South Africa	7 000	136 000	51	1
India	54 000	953 000	57	0
All allies	5 421 000	45 001 000	120	7

Source: Ernest Scott, *Australia During the War*, Sydney, 1936, and J. M. Winter, *The Great War and the British People*, London, 1985.

expenditure in 1917–18 was £66 742 350, for the war as a whole £376 993 052. This cost was met by a mixture of loans (£262 507 829) and normal revenue (£71 087 125). Logistic and other needs of the troops were met by the British on a capitation system at a cost of £43 398 098, the basis of Australia's sizeable postwar foreign debt. (In 1918–19 the interest alone on these payments was £3 430 000.) Added to this was the total ordinary defence expenditure, which in that year amounted to £3 922 855. In 1918 the citizen forces in Australia mustered 105 204 citizen soldiers, as well as 90 000 senior cadets, in a total ground force of 202 423 not counting the rifle clubs and excluding the AIF!

At the war's outset the Australian economy had been small and heavily dependent on agricultural and mineral exports. Standards of living were high, in keeping with the progressive nature of much early industrial and social welfare legislation. The war had no very great impact upon the economy, although it did begin the process by which it was to diversify and become more complex during and after the Second World War. Receipts from income tax jumped significantly, as did the

Table 5.4 Empire casualties as a proportion of forces fielded, 1914–18

Country	All casualties	Total embarkations	Percentage
UK	2 535 424	c. 5 000 000	50.71
Canada	210 000	422 405	49.74
Australia	215 585	331 781	64.98
New Zealand	58 526	98 950	59.01
India	140 015	1 096 013	12.77

Source: Ernest Scott, *Australia During the War*, Sydney, 1936, and J. M. Winter, *The Great War and the British People*, London, 1985.

Table 5.5 Wartime defence expenditure, 1914–19 (£)

Financial Year	Total expenditure (ordinary)	Buildings and sites	War expenditure	Total
1914–15	4 568 321	–	15 111 335	19 679 656
1915–16	5 072 183	–	41 201 946	46 274 129
1916–17	4 830 664	–	61 535 891	66 366 555
1917–18	3 922 855	115 700	66 742 350	70 780 905
1918–19	4 495 243	321 500	100 044 411	104 861 154

Source: *Australian Year Book*, No. 12, 1919.

rate of overseas borrowing by both the state and federal governments. But the war had less direct economic impact in Australia than either the depression of the 1890s or that of the 1930s. Nor did the war have a great impact upon the role and position of Australian women (unlike in Britain, where they had not yet achieved the vote), although the experiences of individual women were highly varied depending on their class, political awareness, and direct or indirect involvement with the AIF either as nurses (at least 2229 served overseas) or as sisters, mothers and wives.

The war in Europe ended abruptly, and the sudden advent of peace left many of the soldiers disoriented. Contemporary accounts record little rejoicing among those at the front. The war had gone on for too long, too many men had been killed, for any sense of exaltation or jubilation. The AIF took no part in the army of occupation which entered Germany, although Canadians and New Zealanders were included, because Hughes insisted on their early repatriation. The return of the AIF was overseen by Monash in Britain, and by Chauvel in Cairo on a 'first come, first go' basis. Within a year of the end of the war, the AIF had gradually faded away as quotas of men returned to Australia by the shipload. A few had not seen enough fighting, or perhaps had seen too much, and delayed their return by enlisting in the British forces fighting in Russia against the Bolsheviks. They confirmed the Australians' reputation for audacity and courage, winning the only Victoria Crosses of the campaign, but the dominion governments had refused flatly to supply forces for quixotic intervention in the Russian Civil War, and the approximately 120 Australians who went were back in Britain before the end of 1919. Units of the light horse were used to help suppress the Egyptian nationalist revolt in the first half of the year, before continuing with their repatriation. In such manner men continued to die after the end of the European war, although more often from the ravages of the influenza epidemic which scoured the world in 1918–19, and which carried off more victims world-wide than had the war itself

The Great War had been greeted with such optimism and rejoicing in Australia in 1914 that the vastly more sombre mood in 1918 was inevitable. The costs of the war continued to be felt long after, not least in the size of the pension payments to disabled soldiers and the dependants of those who had not returned. In 1921 there were 222 537 recipients of such payments, 252 609 in 1926, to peak at 283 322 in 1931; to 1934 the total cost had reached £831 280 947. Efforts to compensate those who returned and to create 'a land fit for heroes', through the soldier settlement schemes, for example, were a less than resounding success. Most Australians, who had not experienced the war directly, wished only to forget it, and to put behind them the shortages and 'sufferings' which the home front had endured in the last two years of the conflict. The political mood of the country was soured, although Hughes remained in office until February 1923. After the short-lived postwar boom came economic recession and a widespread feeling that the war had been in vain, a view which gained added currency in some quarters as the 1920s progressed. And the Australian landscape was transformed as every town and city raised stone monuments to its dead; monuments which, with their long lists of carved names, give a clear and poignant indication of the cost of this war.

CHAPTER 6

The Inter-war Years, 1919–1939

The years between the two world wars were a depressing period in the history of Australian military and defence policy. As is so often the case, the triumphant end of a major war led to a widespread running-down of the machinery of national defence, while an understandable revulsion from war brought about by the casualty lists of the Western Front meant that governments saw few votes in defence issues. As before the Great War, Australia did not act independently on defence and foreign policy issues in the 1920s and 1930s and remained firmly within the alliance system of imperial defence. The benefits which this might have brought were squandered by a generation of conservative politicians who used the theory of imperial defence as an excuse for doing little or nothing to maintain and develop Australia's own forces, aided and abetted by a Labor Party which professed a belief in collective security through the League of Nations but which opposed any measures which might create military forces capable of implementing it. Neither side was unique in its delusions: the same sorry story of inter-war failure was repeated in most of the Western democracies.

The cost of participation in the war was to be measured not only in terms of Hughes' 60 000 dead. Defence expenditure by the Commonwealth jumped from just £4 752 000 in the financial year 1913–14 to a wartime high of £66 690 000 in 1918–19, £62 600 000 of which comprised war expenditure. Not only did the volunteers of the AIF seek demobilisation, the government sought it too in order to rein back the heavy military expenditure of the war years. More than that, in the optimism of the early postwar years, they sought to reduce further the strengths of the permanent military and naval establishments in the belief that there would not be another war.

The defeat of imperial Germany in November 1918 was followed in quick succession by the peace conference at Versailles. The presence of delegates from the dominions at the Paris peace conference was striking evidence of the evolving status of those same dominions, and of the changing relationship between them and the metropolitan power in London. The dominion prime ministers were accompanied by their advisers, who also had the right to attend sessions in the manner of their British colleagues in the secretariat. The empire delegation did not maintain a unified view, nor indeed did it possess unified aims. Hughes was one of the hard-liners at the conference, but his success in obtaining the 'C' class mandates over former German territories in the south Pacific, especially New Guinea, and the rejection of the Japanese-sponsored racial equality clause, owed as much to the general indifference of the European delegations to matters in the Pacific region as they did to the skills and obstinacy of Hughes himself. In terms of Australian military policy, the conference marked the end of one chapter, while the acquisition of New Guinea would pose additional burdens for military planners in Melbourne.

The increase in anti-war and anti-military feeling in Australia which became apparent even before the war had ended manifested itself strongly in the Labor Party, or at least in that part of it remaining after Hughes had formed the Nationalist government in 1917. In June 1918 the conference of the New South Wales branch had passed a number of recommendations aimed at ending the compulsory citizen training scheme which Labor itself had introduced in 1910. Proposals barring the government from raising forces for overseas service or participating in overseas wars without 'a decision of the people' were a reaction bred in the bitter divisions of the conscription referenda, while calls for the recognition of the principle of electing officers were fantasies owing not a little to recent events in Russia. The anti-military and anti-conscription zeal was maintained, however, and when Labor returned to power in 1929 the compulsory training scheme was abolished and the army organised on a voluntary basis with a reduced establishment.

In January 1920 the Minister for Defence, Senator George Pearce, convened a conference of senior officers to advise on the future organisation of Australian defence. The members of the conference were Generals Chauvel, Monash, McCay, Hobbs, White and Legge, and they met in Melbourne from 2 January 1920, reporting to the minister on 6 February. The report identified Japan as the 'only potential and probable enemy', a judgement little changed from pre-war thinking but no less prescient for that. Australia should adopt a scheme which would make all its resources and manpower available quickly should a threat develop and, while the first line of defence should be 'devoted to contributing in full our share of an adequate Far Eastern Fleet', Australia should also 'maintain an Army capable of preventing an enemy from obtaining a decision on shore . . . and it is essential that the Military Force, like the Naval Force, be the maximum obtainable'. To this end, the generals estimated that the nation could provide a field force of two cavalry and four infantry divisions, three mixed brigades for local defence, plus the necessary army, corps and supporting troops with a total war establishment of 270 000. About half this number would be maintained in peace by compulsory enlistment in the militia, which itself was to be reorganised along the lines of the AIF and to adopt the designations of AIF units.

The AIF ceased to exist officially on 1 April 1921 and the new organisation came into force on 1 May. But although the recommendations of the conference of generals were accepted by the government, they were not to reach full implementation or receive acceptance from the wider public. The government was under pressure to reduce defence expenditure and pursue programs for national development. Both the navy and the nascent air force were competing with the army for funds. In February 1922, before the new scheme had functioned for a single year, the government used the successful conclusion of the Washington Conference as justification to reduce spending on the services. The compulsory training scheme was maintained, but confined to populous areas which, in effect, meant the end of the scheme in rural Australia. The decision was reinforced by the abolition of training camps in 1922 through lack of funds. The strength of the militia declined from 127 000 in 1921 to 37 000 in 1922. The divisional structure was retained at the insistence of Chauvel, now Chief of the General Staff, but the organisation was reduced to a nucleus force, which was an optimistic way of describing an army of skeleton units which assembled for only a few days of continuous training each year.

The role of the Army was being confined to local defence against small raiding parties, 'the minor scale of attack', a limited role which the army was disinclined to accept. In 1924 the Council of Defence agreed that army expenditure would be geared towards the training of commanders and staffs, the purchase of essential equipment, and the training of the rank and file, in that order. In reality, the training of regular officers was particularly hard, for there were few opportunities to gain regimental experience or advance professional education, while promotion prospects stalled completely. The government had retrenched seventy-eight of the 300 regular officers of the Permanent Military Forces in 1922, and others left of their own volition, either resigning or transferring into the British or Indian armies. Chauvel's own sons followed this latter path in the early 1930s. The army was

forced to concentrate on 'essentials', for which purpose it was allotted
£1.5 million over five years under the 'Five Years Development Programme' introduced by the Bruce–Page government in 1924. The RAN
and the development of the naval base at Singapore attracted the lion's
share of attention and finances.

The Singapore strategy, with the construction of the naval base at
Singapore and the attendant role of the Pacific dominions in imperial
defence, dominated Australian defence thinking for most of the inter-
war period. It did not develop in a vacuum, but as a result of the
termination of the Anglo-Japanese Naval Treaty in 1921, against the
wishes of the Australian and New Zealand governments, and of
the Washington Treaty limiting naval armaments. The latter established
a ratio of capital ships and aircraft carriers between the three main
powers of 5:5:3, and had implications for lesser powers such as Australia.
The future direction of Australian policy was formulated at the Imperial
Conference of 1923. The Washington Conference in 1921 was the
formal expression of widely felt desires for disarmament, which were
themselves fuelled by popular expectations of its likely outcome. At the
Imperial Conference two years later the representatives of empire
agreed on the need for renewed defence efforts, and for common
principles on which it was to be organised. The change had come about
as a result of the Chanak crisis of 1922, when Britain had appeared on
the brink of war with Turkey as a consequence of the Graeco-Turkish
War, and had sought dominion forces should war eventuate. The crisis
demonstrated both that the potential for international conflict had in
no way lessened as a result of the Great War, and that the principles of
consultation between Britain and the dominions which had been
established in 1921 had failed at their first test, since the British
government had publicly assumed dominion support without dominion
concurrence. The empire had come close to war, and the Australian
government had found itself committed to supporting Britain without
the opportunity to present its views on the international situation.

Doubts were expressed about the concept of a base at Singapore even
before construction commenced. In 1921 the Australian Chief of Naval
Staff, Rear Admiral Sir Edmund Grant, had argued that a base at Sydney
made more sense if the purpose of the exercise was to defend Australia.
In 1923 the prime minister, Stanley Melbourne Bruce, also had some
questions for the British government concerning the siting and completion of the proposed base facilities. Leo Amery, First Lord of the
Admiralty, pointed out that while Sydney indeed was the best location
for a fleet base to defend Australia, it did not meet the needs of
protecting the Indian Ocean shipping routes. The base would be large
enough to accommodate the Main Fleet and, in the normal course of

events, a small Far Eastern Fleet would be stationed there permanently. In any case, Amery clearly regarded geography as the base's best defence, since the distance between the Japanese home islands and Singapore clearly precluded the dispatch of an expeditionary force against it, and the base at Hong Kong would act as a forward defensive position. The fatuousness of this piece of strategic reasoning was exposed in 1941 when the hopelessly outclassed defences of Hong Kong fell within days of the outbreak of war, and the Japanese used forward positions in French Indochina from which to launch their assault upon Malaya – a distance of just 195 miles from Kota Bharu and 430 miles from Singapore itself.

Amery's arguments proved sufficient to convince Bruce, although quite why is unclear. In one of the most unfortunate statements of prime ministerial judgement ever, Bruce observed at the Conference that while he 'was not quite as clear as I should like to be as to how the protection of Singapore is to be assured, I am clear on this point, that apparently it can be done'. The efficacy of the Singapore concept relied upon the automatic transfer of a powerful British fleet in the event of war in the Far East. Even at the 1923 Conference the South African prime minister, General Jan Christian Smuts, had voiced doubts about the whole idea, and these doubts were repeated periodically by senior Australian Army throughout the inter-war period. The weakness of the scheme was obvious, and was a variant on the old German fear of a war on two fronts. If Britain was at war in Europe, the frail resources of the Royal Navy would be required in the North Sea and the Mediterranean; there would be nothing to spare for dispatch to the Pacific should Japan choose to exploit the opportunity which a war in Europe presented.

Successive Australian governments understood that the Japanese presented a threat to Australian security. The only plan devised to meet this threat was reliance upon the Singapore naval base. Even this might have been explicable had the construction of the vaunted base facilities proceeded quickly and efficiently. It did not. In 1924 the short-lived British Labour government of Ramsay MacDonald cancelled the original scheme for a naval dockyard 'as an earnest of our good faith' and belief in international cooperation and arms limitations. The Conservative government of Stanley Baldwin, which won the election in October the same year, decided to persist with the scheme, but reduced its scope and cost. Delays in the construction work prompted the Australian government to embark upon a five-year naval construction program and to announce at the Imperial Conference in 1926 that, as a result, Australia's contribution would be in the form of ships of the RAN, and that no further financial contributions to the costs of construction would be made. The Straits Settlements, Malaya, Hong Kong and New Zealand continued to furnish financial assistance, but the amounts involved were never large.

By 1928 the Baldwin government too felt the need for economy, and expenditure on the defences for the naval facilities was postponed. The second MacDonald Labour administration again slowed the construction work in 1929–30 and once more placed its faith in international agreements, this time in another proposed naval disarmament conference to be held in Washington. In any case the Australian Labor government of J. H. Scullin had again scaled down its own financial contributions as an economy measure. Japanese aggression in China in 1931–32 caused the work to be accelerated, but even as the base neared completion the inability of the Royal Navy to operate simultaneously in home and Far Eastern waters was being stated clearly. At the 1937 Imperial Conference, the last before the war, the British chiefs of staff sub-committee noted that the strength of any fleet sent to the Far East 'must be governed by consideration of our home requirements'. Britain must keep 'sufficient strength in home waters to neutralise the German Fleet'. The great naval dockyard at Singapore was opened on 14 February 1938; the fleet to occupy it did not exist.

Reliance upon Singapore had two consequences for Australian defence in this period; it led to unreasoned reliance upon a flawed strategy, and it skewed the development of Australia's own forces. Australian politicians answered criticism of defence planning by pointing out, as Bruce had in 1926, that Australian expenditure on defence worked out at 27s. 2d. per annum per head of population, and was exceeded only by the British themselves among the rest of the empire. This was perfectly true, but of greater significance was the breakdown of that expenditure. Of the 27s. 2d., the navy received 17s. 2d., the army 5s. 2d., the air force 2s. 8d., while just 2s. 2d. was spent on munitions supply. To approach the issue from a different perspective, consider the case for coastal fortification. Little had been done with this perennial problem since the Kitchener recommendations in 1910. In 1926 the Military Board reported on a memorandum from the Committee of Imperial Defence which recommended a five-year program at a cost of £2 795 000. The Military Board proposed an expanded scheme of coastal rearmament, noting that the Committee's report provided 'for naval requirements only ... on the assumption that the British Main Fleet will arrive at Singapore within six weeks of the outbreak of war'. The proposal, to cost £3 900 000 over five years, was passed to the Council of Defence and rejected on financial grounds. A greatly reduced scheme for the protection of key naval installations only was then offered, and was deferred until 1929, again on grounds of cost. Little was done in this area until the middle of the following decade.

The condition of the individual Australian services was equally bleak, especially for the nascent air force and the army, whose development during the 1920s and 1930s was not coordinated with that of the RAN or with the Singapore strategy. The navy was the service affected least adversely by government policy in this period, but it achieved this at the cost of an independent role and even identity as a service, so totally was it subsumed to the needs, direction and philosophy of its British sister service. On the one hand this made sense since, as the Secretary of the Naval Board pointed out in 1936, 'a small and isolated navy is never efficient and it is a most valuable aspect of Imperial Naval cooperation that the Commonwealth is able to obtain, without cost, the fruits of substantial expenditure by the Imperial Authorities'. Admiral Lord Jellicoe had pointed to the need for close collaboration with the Royal Navy in his report submitted to the Governor-General in August 1919. But Jellicoe had also urged the creation of a large Far Eastern Imperial Fleet for the defence of the Pacific dominions and the empire in the Far East and, as noted above, this level of naval defence capability actually declined between the wars.

At the conclusion of hostilities in 1918 the RAN comprised twenty-six vessels and six submarines, and all were concentrated in Australian waters for review by the Prince of Wales in May 1920. The postwar reduction of the fleet commenced the following September, accompanied by stringent economies in the training program and steaming time. Then followed the Washington Naval Treaty limiting the size and numbers of naval armaments. In 1922–23 the navy was required to accept a reduction of £500 000 in annual expenditure, the placing of some ships in reserve, and restrictions in Citizen Force training. Most significantly, the submarine force was paid off, the submarine depot in Geelong closed, and the battle cruiser *Australia* was sunk outside Sydney Heads on 12 April 1924 in compliance with the Washington Treaty formula.

This reduction in the naval establishment did not last long. Following the decision to cancel the dockyard at Singapore in March 1924, the Bruce government announced a naval expansion program as part of a five-year defence development effort. The RAN was the chief beneficiary. The light cruisers *Sydney* and *Melbourne*, which had reached their age limit in 1923, were to be replaced by new 10 000-ton cruisers to be constructed in Britain. Two ocean-going submarines were to be constructed, also in Britain, and provision was made onshore for five 8000-ton oil tanks and the stockpiling of 32 000 tons of fuel. In order to maintain the dockyard capacity at Sydney's Cockatoo Island, the government commissioned construction of a seaplane carrier there. This level of activity, at a cost of £6 250 000, led Bruce to announce the suspension of financial contributions to the cost of construction at Singapore in 1926.

By the end of the five-year development program, in 1929, the cruisers *Australia* and *Canberra*, the submarines *Otway* and *Oxley*, and the seaplane carrier *Albatross* had been added to the fleet. The old cruisers were scrapped the same year while the cruiser *Brisbane* was placed in reserve, where she remained until disposed of in 1935. The six River-class destroyers placed in reserve in 1922 continued to be held there. The sea-going establishment had increased by 581 as compared with 1923–24, there had been an increase in the strength of the Citizen Force, and the oil fuelling base at Darwin had been established. The development of a modern fleet now received a check with the advent of the Depression and the Scullin Labor government.

The abolition of compulsory military training had some effect upon the composition of the Naval Reserve, cutting the number of ratings from 6919 to 4797 in a single year. More serious was the cut of £326 368 imposed on the navy for the financial year 1930–31. The submarines were paid off into reserve, and in 1932 were paid off altogether and presented – gratis – to the Royal Navy for recommissioning as RN boats. The River-class destroyers were scrapped as a cost-cutting measure as was the fleet collier, since there were now no coal-burning ships left in the fleet. The strength of the permanent forces again was reduced, and the gains of recent years obliterated at a stroke.

The cycle of retrenchment and rearmament which characterised the inter-war decades now asserted itself. Events in the Far East and the generally low level of the empire's defences led the British government to abandon the 'Ten Year Rule', which posited no perceivable threat for that length of time, in March 1932. German withdrawal from the Disarmament Conference in October 1933 and the notice of withdrawal served on the League of Nations the same year contributed to unease at the drift in international relations. The change of government in Australia in 1932 completed the process as far as Australian policy was concerned. The Defence Estimates for 1933–34 noted the 'urgent need for certain extensions' of defence activity and, in the naval sphere, allocated £280 000 for naval construction at Cockatoo Island. A flotilla leader and four destroyers were added, and surveying work on the Barrier reef resumed. In April 1934 the government announced the intention to acquire a modern cruiser, *Sydney*, and to build a second sloop at Cockatoo Island.

This marked the commencement of a three-year program of enhancement of naval defence. Following the completion of this program a second was embarked upon immediately, with £8 783 070 allocated for defence as a whole in 1936–37 alone. The estimates for the following year provided for increased armour in the two modern cruisers and the commissioning of ships currently in reserve. The steady deterioration in the world scene, with the Japanese invasion of China in 1937 and the abrogation of the London Naval Treaty in March 1938, led the Australian government to accelerate naval rearmament in April. A new three-year program would allow for £43 000 000 in defence expenditure, including the acquisition of two more cruisers of the Leander class to arrive by 1939, two additional sloops to be constructed at Cockatoo Island, and the building of modern Tribal-class destroyers in Australia, the first two of which were ordered in January the following year. When war broke out in September, Australia possessed a small fleet of six cruisers, five destroyers and two sloops. While the war remained confined to Europe, the size of the RAN was just adequate to the tasks assigned to it.

But *Canberra* lacked modern high-angle armament for defence against air attack, *Adelaide* had been decommissioned in 1939 because of crew shortages (and had reached replacement age in any case), the navy lacked the capacity to service its vessels, and most naval armaments were still imported from Britain. The existing destroyer flotilla, comprising *Stuart* and the 'V' and 'W' class vessels *Voyager, Vendetta, Vampire,* and *Waterhen,* had all been built in 1917–18 and were described accurately by one contemporary observer in 1939 as 'ancient warriors'. Although armed with four 4-inch guns and six 21-inch torpedo tubes, they too were vulnerable to attack from the air. *Vampire* was lost in the Bay of Bengal to Japanese aircraft in April 1942, and *Waterhen* was sunk by German planes on the Tobruk ferry run in June 1941. As well as the loss of *Sydney* in disputed circumstances in November 1941, Australian ships suffered heavily at the hands of the more advanced and better handled fleet of the Imperial Japanese Navy. The sloop *Yarra* was sunk in the Java Sea in March 1942, *Canberra* went down in the disastrous Battle of Savo Island during the Solomons campaign in August the same year, *Voyager* was lost off Timor in September, *Perth* and the USS *Houston* were sunk in a hotly fought surface action in the Java Sea in March 1942 with the loss of half the ship's complement. The RAN, spread too thinly and assigned too many tasks, was to be handled very roughly by the Japanese.

Like the RAN, the Australian Flying Corps (AFC) emerged from the Great War with a record of individual gallantry and professional competence, but the AFC was part of the AIF and lacked a separate identity as a service. As with the RAF, so the nascent Australian aerial service had to resist the attempts of the army and navy to subordinate it to their needs and organisational and doctrinal assumptions. The decision of the Defence Council in January 1919 to establish a joint air service for both the existing services reflected this. In June that year the British offered a gift of 100 aircraft to each of the dominions interested in forming air forces, which offer was accepted, but in January 1920 the Air Board was still planning Australia's service aircraft requirements to include 297 aircraft for naval aviation purposes, including eleven flying boat squadrons.

The formation of the RAAF was owed to the enthusiasm of Hughes – a self-confessed 'fanatic' in his belief in the value of aviation – the support of leading parliamentary figures such as the Treasurer, Sir Joseph Cook, and the Minister for Defence, George Pearce, and the efforts of a small group of officers from both services who had served with the RFC and AFC during the war. Prominent amongst the latter were Lieutenant Colonel Richard Williams and Major S. J. Goble. A factor of equal importance was the desire to develop a civil aviation capacity in Australia. The passage of the Air Navigation Act through the Senate in November 1920 was an important step in the formation of the air force for, while it related entirely to civil aviation, it was seen as contributing to the economic attractiveness of an Australian air force. As was to be the pattern throughout the 1920s and 1930s, a clear inter-relationship was seen between civil and service flying. The RAAF was to fulfill certain civil functions, such as aerial route surveying and the pioneering of air mail services, while there was an interchange between civil and military pilots. Men like Brearley and Fysh, who went on to set up WA Airways and Qantas, were former air force pilots.

Williams more than any other individual deserves the credit for founding the RAAF as an independent service. It was his extensive memorandum of 1920 which gave direction to the newly constituted Air Board, and at his insistence that body recommended to the Air Council in February 1921 that the Australian Air Force be formed on 31 March that same year. (It received the Royal prefix in July 1921.) The RAAF came into being with a strength of twenty-one officers and 130 other ranks, the 128 machines presented as a gift by the British government, and a further thirty-six aircraft. The air force lacked statutory foun-dation until September 1923, however, because of Labor opposition to the legislative incorporation of the imperial Air Force Act. The objec-tion was based upon the Act's definition of active service, which implied the availability of the air force for deployment outside Australia. (This view presaged the later position of the ALP in the 1930s, which viewed the RAAF solely as a home defence force, a view which suggested a mis-understanding of the nature of air power but which in any case became confused in the wider arguments over imperial versus national commitments.) The government, however, amended its stand in order to pass the legislation so that the provisions of the British *Army Act 1881*, which also covered the RAF, did not apply to the new Australian service.

For some years, permanent officers were trained at the Royal Military College, Duntroon, where from 1928 four graduates from each course were commissioned into the RAAF. Despite the prominence of Australian aviators such as Ulm, Smith and Hinkler in setting new aviation records for distance and endurance flying in this period, the RAAF remained small throughout the 1920s. The total inter-war air force budget allocation was just £13 116 041 from a total in excess of £124 000 000, and by 1928 the service was still flying aircraft which had been designed and built during the Great War. At this point in its development the government sought the advice of an imperial officer in deciding upon the future direction of the service.

It is a curious feature of the inter-war period that recourse was had so frequently to the services and advice of British officers, despite the availability of local talent and with no apparent recognition that officers of the imperial services might see their duty as being to further the interests of the metropolitan power in London rather than the government in Australia. Hutton and Birdwood had been imperial officers with imperial interests; this trend continued, and the advice which the Australian government received on, for example, the establishment of the Singapore base was at variance with the views of many Australian officers – especially in the army – and vitiated attempts to provide for the defence of Australia from Australian resources. The habit of appointing the head of a service from the ranks of the imperial forces – as happened routinely with the RAN in this period and was to occur with the RAAF on the outbreak of war in 1939 – meant that senior officers of the Australian forces missed out on experience of the highest levels of command which would be so necessary with any expansion of the small regular establishments upon the outbreak of war. None of this was the fault of the British officers concerned, who took their opportunities where they found them and who, in some circumstances, backed the views of their Australian counterparts in recognition that Australian interests should be decided by Australians. Government was generally less quick to see the point.

The review of the RAAF was conducted by Air Marshal Sir John Salmond. The government gave him a wide-ranging brief, and his report covered the organisation, training, administration and general policy of the service. It was submitted on 20 September 1928 and, while sympathetic to the problems of the small service, was critical of the obsolete machines, reliance upon Citizen Air Force (CAF) units which did not receive sufficient flying time to maintain efficiency, poor conditions of service and very high accident rates which had led to some spectacular crashes and a number of deaths among flight crew. Only two squadrons were designed to undertake operations in cooperation with the army and navy, but neither was fit to do so because of obsolete machines, the absence of reserve equipment and the low standard of training in these units, two-thirds of whose personnel were CAF men. Salmond recommended improved conditions of service, changes to the training of officers, the establishment and complete equipping of new units, the further development of domestic air routes and the continued close cooperation between military and civil aviation.

Steps were taken to provide the RAAF with more modern aircraft early in 1929 when six Bristol Bulldog single-seater fighters were ordered, but the great problem facing any implementation of the Salmond 'plan' for the RAAF was the background of financial stringency facing the Australian government. This, coupled with the Bruce government's belief that the navy formed the first line of Australia's defence, meant that the Salmond report would be acted upon only within the confines of existing budgetary allocations, and with no room for expansion. The advent of a Labor government late in 1929 brought new pressures upon the air force. Although the ALP's defence policy placed greater emphasis upon air defence, suggestions came from the army and navy that in the interests of economy the air force should again be split and its functions, equipment and personnel hived off to the other two services. This threat to its existence as a separate service was beaten back during a Defence Department review in June 1930, but the RAAF was no more immune from the savage budgetary cuts which took place than were the army or navy. When Scullin took over the Treasury portfolio as well in July that year he announced that the RAAF was to be reduced by three officers arid thirty-seven other ranks (from an establishment of just 104 and 782 respectively) but that, since the service had been working beneath establishment for some time, no dismissals or retrenchments were necessary.

The worsening international situation throughout the 1930s had its airpower dimension, epitomised by the official reconstitution of the German Air Force in March 1935, which prompted the British government to increase the strength of the RAF by, amongst other measures, attempting to recruit pilots and technical crew in Australia. The Australian Chief of the Air Staff, Air Commodore Williams, recommended instead that the existing practice of training pilots in Australia for the RAF be maintained, not least because this permitted the RAAF a larger establishment and established a credit in London in terms of payments which could then be used to purchase aircraft.

After 1935 the first serious steps were taken to set up an aircraft industry in Australia under the initial guidance of Essington Lewis of

BHP, steps which led to the formation of the Commonwealth Aircraft Corporation in October 1936. Equal credit for this step should be given to the Minister for Defence, Archdale Parkhill, although the attempt to establish an indigenous manufacturing capability was beset by problems, not least the conflict over whether to manufacture British or American models under license in Australia, a debate finally decided in favour of an American aircraft which, after modification, became the ill-starred Wirraway. Of equal importance was Parkhill's announcement in January 1936 that new squadrons and aircraft depots would be established, bringing with them an increase in personnel of 563. But attempts to build up the RAAF were hampered by the RAF expansion program alluded to earlier, for although Australia had placed orders for £1 700 000 worth of new aircraft by March 1936, British industrial production was entirely absorbed in meeting the needs of the British service.

As with the RAN, the lead-up to war saw considerable efforts to make good the deficiencies in the air force brought about by years of neglect. In 1938 the RAAF received £12 500 500 in the defence appropriations and priority over the army in defence planning. Efforts were made to increase the strength of the service and the number of squadrons. Another review was carried out by another imperial officer, this time Marshal of the Royal Air Force Sir Edward Ellington, recently retired as CAS. His report was released in August 1938, and contained significant criticisms of the aircraft with which the RAAF was equipped, especially the Wirraway. The greatest distinction of this locally produced aircraft was that it was locally produced, for it was already obsolescent in 1939. Extravagant claims were made on its behalf, probably in order to convince the critics of the value of a local aircraft industry, but that this should have been necessary is in itself an indictment of air policy in the 1930s. Ellington made other criticisms, levelled at under-strength squadrons, the continuing incidence of service flying accidents (which was worse than the RAF), and the need for improved flying training and flying discipline. RAAF squadrons lacked the advanced training in armaments and air navigation, for example, which were standard in the RAF.

At the outbreak of war the RAAF disposed of eighty-two Ansons, fifty-four Demons, seven Wirraways and twenty-one Seagulls in thirteen squadrons, most of them based in south-east Australia. The Demon was a biplane fighter-bomber first delivered in 1935; the Seagull was an amphibian which had entered service in 1935–36 and was due to be replaced by the Sunderland. Ansons were operated as bombers, but were civilian aircraft essentially and were unarmed and obsolescent in any case. Beauforts were on order from Britain together with Hudson bombers from the United States, but both were obsolescent and neither had arrived by September 1939. The Wirraway notwithstanding, there were no modern fighter aircraft in service with the RAAF at the war's outbreak. The secrets of radar were not revealed to the dominions until February 1939, although British research into radar had been undertaken since 1935. As a result all three services in Australia were in general ignorance of the use and potential of this remarkable development. It is almost needless to add that nothing had been done as a result to create an integrated air defence system.

Neither ALP nor conservative governments saw a primary role for the army in the defence of Australia. Until the outbreak of war in 1939 its share of the defence budget consistently was less than the navy's, despite the fact that in the event of war the RAN would revert to the control of the Admiralty and might find its fleet units operating far from Australian waters (as happened in fact in 1939). Australian thinking on imperial defence was primarily navalist while the ALP was hostile to standing armies, an attitude formed from a heady mix of the anti-conscription campaigns of 1916–17, the activities of the New Guard in the early 1930s, and traditional collective attitudes which harked back to Cromwell and the New South Wales Corps.

The Army's political activities in this period, real and assumed, have been the subject of much comment and speculation. Unquestionably, clandestine paramilitary organisations existed in the 1920s and 1930s, intended to forestall 'Red' revolution or social and economic reform agendas of the kind associated with Jack Lang in New South Wales and E. G. Theodore in Queensland. Such groups went by various names: the League of National Security, the Old Guard, the White Army. Their leadership was drawn from prominent conservative figures and included senior officers in the Army such as Generals Charles Rosenthal and T. A. Blamey, but not the first postwar Chief of the General Staff, General C. B. B. White (although this is sometimes alleged). Little evidence exists to link regular officers with these groups; when one commanding officer of a Sydney-based unit invited the New Guard's Eric Campbell and Francis De Groot to a mess function and permitted them to address the soldiers, he was removed from his command by a board of inquiry and transferred to the Unattached List, effectively ending his military career. Most of those so associated came from the citizen forces, or had been officers in the AIF. In this latter category were many of the leaders of the New Guard movement, formed to oppose Lang at the height of the Depression. Many of its men had been soldiers in the AIF, but the New Guard proved a short-lived phenomenon, its decline and demise following closely on that of Lang's premiership. Such organisations were reactionary, in the case of the

New Guard even proto-fascist. Their existence suggests how deeply the domestic divisions of the war years had scarred public life in Australia, while the numbers of returned men in their ranks served to emphasise further the schism between those who had gone to the war, and the rest.

The increasing political polarisation of the 1930s found other Australians prepared to take up arms for a cause – in Spain. The internal militarist–fascist challenge to the Spanish Republic, which began with the revolt of General Franco in 1936, quickly became a testing ground; a dress rehearsal for the much greater conflict which many increasingly feared. About forty Australians actually fought in Spain as part of the International Brigades (and one conservative Catholic enlisted to fight with Franco). Another twenty or so went as non-combatants – nurses, drivers, etc. The unions and parties of the Left subscribed £17 000 through the Spanish Relief Committee, and the conflict of ideas and positions was fought out in town halls, lecture theatres and workplaces between those of the Left and those who were not; between those who believed Spain presented both an opportunity and a duty to stop fascism, and those who held that Communism and the International were the greater threat. The Australian government maintained a policy of 'strict neutrality and non-interference' in common with the other Western powers, which materially aided the fascist cause since Germany and Italy felt themselves under no such inhibition.

The basis of army strategic planning in the inter-war years was the defence of the Australian mainland against invasion. This placed the army squarely in opposition to the prevailing dogmas of imperial defence and the Singapore strategy, with their heavy emphasis upon maritime defence. The army never convinced the navy or the government of the likelihood of invasion or of the need to devote resources to the preparation of defensive measures, but nevertheless planned for the defence of continental Australia. By 1929 a small planning staff had drafted an appreciation of the measures required in the event of invasion, which envisaged the concentration of two corps in the Sydney–Newcastle area with a major supply base at Albury, leaving small forces in the other state capitals for defence against enemy raiding parties. Although the Defence Committee agreed in 1928 that a war with Japan would involve a threat to Australia on the scale of at least three divisions, the RAN, and through it the government, refused to concede that such a force could invade Australia because the operations of the Royal Navy in Singapore would preclude it. In 1932 the Scullin government confirmed that the role of the army was the defence of ports and harbours against raids and the provision of an expeditionary force of one division within three months of the outbreak of war. This latter requirement was met by Plan 401, first devised in 1922 during the

Chanak crisis and in fact used to raise the 6th Division of the AIF in 1939. Planning for an enemy invasion received little further official attention until the defence build-up of the late 1930s.

The suspension of compulsory military training in 1929 dealt the army a further blow. There had been some opposition to the scheme in the course of the previous decade from groups like the Australian Peace Alliance, and from more representative groups within the Catholic church. As noted earlier, the ALP had adopted a clause in its manifesto in 1919 which vowed to repeal the scheme when the party gained office, and within a week of assuming power in October 1929 the Scullin government announced its suspension. In its place a new system was formulated which stressed a volunteer army based upon the recruitment of a part-time militia. The strength of the army fell from 47 931 to 27 454 in a single year. Recruiting for the militia commenced in January 1930 and, under the circumstances, results were relatively good. The old scheme had been abolished without warning or debate in the parliament, and this led to a degree of administrative confusion within the service. Members of the old Citizens Force were encouraged to stay on, and clearly some did so. This was even more remarkable given that there was no prospect of training camps being held in the near future, and the need to take time out from paid employment in order to fulfill such training obligations as existed imposed further hardship as the Depression worsened.

The promising start, however, was not maintained for long. The militia was intended to be a nucleus force. It was based upon the five divisions of the old AIF, although there were some reductions in the overall number of units. There was also a senior cadet force, aged between fourteen and seventeen, with a proposed establishment of 7000. Training times were inadequate, the men being required to attend only six days' continuous training in camp and six separate days' home training each year. Units were often under strength, sometimes by as much as 40 per cent, which further reduced the value of the instruction. It made it particularly hard to train the officers, of whom there were never enough in any case. The intention, expressed in 1929, that the militia would be equipped with modern weapons and equipment was never fulfilled.

Units used the surplus equipment brought back to Australia by the AIF in 1919, much of it obsolete or worn out. Mortars used were of 1914–18 vintage, and the new Bren light machine gun had not been introduced in September 1939, although parts for it had been made available. There was no modern signals equipment, anti-aircraft equipment, or fire control systems. The artillery brigades of the militia were equipped with two batteries of 18-pounders and one battery of 4.5-inch howitzers. This too was Great War technology. The 4.5-inch howitzer had a maximum range of 6000 metres while the 18-pounder in its final variant could achieve 9970 metres with improved ammunition, but greater range and shell weight would be needed, and would require a new gun. The quick-firing 25-pounder, developed in Britain and with a range of 12 250 metres, was available before the war's outbreak, and it was intended to equip the artillery regiments of the 6th Division with two 12-gun batteries since the 25-pounder could do the work of both gun and howitzer. The AIF regiments were not fully equipped with the new gun until 1941. For the anti-tank role the Australian army was supplied with the hopelessly inadequate 2-pounder, which failed dismally against light German armour in France in 1940 and in North Africa and Greece in 1941.

The major advance in equipment and doctrine in the inter-war period involved the tank and the evolving theories of mechanised and armoured warfare. A single subaltern and one warrant officer were sent to Britain in 1926–27 to undergo armoured training, and an Australian Tank Corps was gazetted into existence in 1927 to function as a cadre for a CMF unit and with its headquarters at the Small Arms School at Randwick. It mustered one operational tank for demonstration and training purposes with the small regular cadre at the school. Despite the Depression, some attempts were made to convert light horse units of the CMF to armoured cars, but these too suffered from inadequate and 'experimental' equipment, funding deficiencies and conservative resistance to change. No attempt at large-scale conversion of mounted units was made until well after the coming of war. (This was the case in Britain also with the conversion of the Territorial Army.) The Australian General Staff tried hard to stay in touch with the major developments in this area, although a staff position as GSO II (Mechanisation and Armoured Fighting Vehicles) was created at Army Headquarters only in May 1939. A major's posting, it carried little influence until after the war's outbreak. The major concession to advances in the field was the addition of a mechanised cavalry unit to the 6th Division for mobile reconnaissance, although initially it was suggested that a unit of light horse be sent. It was equipped with carriers and light tanks armed with Brens and belt-fed .303 calibre machine guns.

The declining recruitment levels occasioned by the deepening of the Depression prompted the government of Joseph Lyons to call conferences of militia commanding officers in each state in 1932. Dissatisfaction was expressed about the dropping of compulsory training, but there was no chance of its reintroduction while the economic situation remained grim. Suggestions were made concerning pay and allowances, training, equipment and facilities, all of which required increased levels of expenditure also. The likelihood of either occurring was remote, with the result that there was little change in the condition of the militia in the years immediately following. Even when the economic situation began to improve after 1933, the increase in the defence appropriation went to the RAN. As one Opposition member commented during the debate on the Supply Bill in that year, the army was 'such a small force that it may be whittled away even by discussion'. Such wry observations aside, it was not possible to train an adequate force with the financial and equipment policies then pursued.

Even the army benefited from the increased emphasis upon defence which took place after 1935. In January 1936 the Military Board was instructed to plan for an increase in militia strength to 35 000, the figure originally aimed at in 1929. In 1935 the army vote was still less than it had been in 1928, but thereafter it increased steadily if undramatically. An increase in strength meant an increase in expenditure outlay. In 1935–36 the army received £1 810 751, and this increased to £4 388 597 in the last year before the outbreak of war. In 1938 the government announced a doubling in the militia's strength, the stockpiling of equipment and ammunition reserves, and a modest increase in the establishment of the permanent forces. All this was too little too late, and the 6th Division of the AIF went overseas in 1939 with inadequate stocks of inadequate equipment, while the militia was in no way a fighting force able to face the demands of modern war. Indeed it is doubtful if it met the standards of the armies of 1918.

The army was now less prone to seek the services of senior imperial officers. This was because the fighting record of the AIF and the number of experienced officers which that force produced meant that there was no shortage of senior Australian officers able to advise the government, while the subsidiary role assigned to it under the Singapore strategy meant that there was less need to coordinate army planning closely with the British. Throughout the inter-war years the CGS was an Australian. In 1938, however, the post of Inspector General was revived, and Major General E. K. Squires of the Royal Engineers was appointed with the rank of Lieutenant General. His first (and only) report was submitted in December 1938. Squires had no experience of Australian conditions, but was fortunate to have as his assistant Lieutenant Colonel S. F. Rowell, one of the brightest and best of that generation of Staff Corps officers. His three most important recommendations concerned the provision of permanent force field units, the command system, and the Staff Corps.

To date, the permanent force had always been very small. It comprised the Australian Instructional Corps, formed in 1921 as a successor to the old Administrative and Instructional (A&I) Staff, the Staff Corps, and the small units of engineers, gunners, medical, ordnance and service staffs permitted under the Defence Act. Squires called for the creation of permanent field units to provide a force of adequately trained men from the commencement of hostilities and available to guard vital points. They would also be available to stiffen the militia in war and contribute to its training in peace. The report recommended an establishment of between 8000 and 10 000 men in units spread across the country. Only one such unit was established before the outbreak of war, the Darwin Mobile Force, which was created in 1938 to provide a garrison for the new naval station. True to the Defence Act, the rank and file had to be enlisted as artillerymen and wear the RAA badge, even though they were infantrymen, because the Act made no provision for regular infantry units.

The second and less radical departure from existing practice concerned the higher organisation of the army. The existing organisation was predicated on a system of district bases, each approximating to one of the states. This was replaced in October 1939 with four new regional commands; Northern (Queensland), Eastern (New South Wales), Southern (Victoria, South Australia, Tasmania), and Western (Western Australia), together with an independent garrison at Darwin designated 7 Military District. Each command would be responsible for the training and operations of units and formations within that command, and Army Headquarters would deal with the Command Headquarters in all matters affecting those units and formations rather than directly with the units themselves, as had been the practice previously.

The Staff Corps had languished since the end of the Great War. By 1938 it comprised principally those officers who graduated from the Royal Military College, Duntroon, and was intended to provide the army with professional officers trained in staff duties and the organisational and administrative qualifications needed in modern armies. Squires found much to criticise. While declining to make specific recommendations, he singled out pay, conditions, retirement ages and promotion prospects as important areas in which deficiencies needed to be addressed in order to attract 'young men of the highest capabilities and characters' to compete for selection. This was not altogether fair to existing members of the Staff Corps, many of whom distinguished themselves in the next war. Unquestionably, however, the years between the wars saw an erosion of morale and professional capabilities as a result of hopelessly inadequate funding, stalled promotion, and general neglect. Young officers who had served in France as captains and majors were still acting as unit adjutants to the militia ten years later. Horace Robertson had graduated in 1914, was a major in 1916, but did not gain his lieutenant colonelcy until 1935. There were few opportunities to exercise with bodies of troops, and pay and conditions fell behind those of their civilian counterparts. Some left, either to transfer into the British and Indian armies or to gain employment in civilian life. Many more stayed, unable to leave because of economic conditions and the lack of training or funds to help them start over again. Among future generals, the young John Wilton went to the Indian Army upon graduation in 1932 because there were no vacancies in Australia. George Wootten, a divisional commander in 1945, left altogether and became a solicitor. Syd Rowell, a future CGS, thought of leaving but, like George Vasey, who was to command a division in New Guinea, had neither private capital nor professional civilian skills to fall back on. Some of the best soldiers Australia has produced simply marked time for two decades.

When war came in September 1939 Australia was no better prepared than it had been in 1914. In some respects things were worse. None of the services had yet reached the equipment and manpower targets set for them, which was not surprising since the programs under which these were to be achieved still had several years to run. The country was tied to a strategy based on Singapore which would not work in the only circumstances in which it was likely to be called upon, namely a war in both hemispheres simultaneously. The RAN was able to work efficiently as part of the Royal Navy, but could not offset the lack of British naval strength in the Pacific. The ability to integrate with the RN also served to conceal the fact that the RAN was neither a big enough nor a sufficiently balanced force to act independently in the event of a threat to Australia's north. The RAAF entered the war with obsolete aircraft, while the country still lacked the capacity to produce sufficient numbers of modern aircraft itself. The signing of the Empire Air Training agreement after the outbreak of war added greater problems still, and deprived the air force in Australia of thousands of excellent potential aircrew. The army also lacked modern equipment. Its task was to be complicated by the existence of two armies, the existing militia and the soon-to-be recruited volunteers of the 2nd AIF. The tensions thus created manifested themselves fully only after the beginning of the war in the Pacific, but they were to cause Australian planners and generals endless difficulties.

For most of the inter-war period, it is clear that little or nothing was done to increase the government's ability to carry out its military responsibilities, and the hurried rearmament measures adopted after 1935, and especially after 1937, in no way made up for the years of neglect. The demands of modern industrial warfare required well-trained, equipped and balanced armed forces, and these are not created overnight. Australian governments of both persuasions chose to believe that another major war would not occur, or that if it did someone else would fight it on our behalf. It could be argued that the optimism of the 1920s, with successful moves in the field of naval disarmament, justified the government's concentration upon issues other than defence. This cannot be sustained to justify the lack of urgency in the 1930s, by which time it was too late to make up lost ground without a crash program of rearmament which even then the Australian government would not countenance fully, and which relied in any case upon supplies from Britain which were not forthcoming in light of Britain's own desperate attempt to rectify a similar situation. It is not merely hindsight to judge the conduct of defence and military policy in this period as deficient, a deficiency shared in all the democracies and the consequences of which were soon to be made clear.

CHAPTER 7

The Second World War, 1939–1941

Australia was not prepared for war in 1939. It was not much better prepared when the war came to Australia's shores at the beginning of 1942. In between, the country raised four infantry divisions and assorted corps and army troops and sent them overseas, three to the Middle East and one split between Malaya and the islands to the near north. Ships of the RAN operated in the Atlantic and Mediterranean in concert with the Royal Navy. Under the Empire Air Training Scheme (known also as the British Commonwealth Air Training Plan), thousands of young men were 'surrendered' to the control of the RAF, and fought their war in the skies of Germany in the strategic air offensive. Meanwhile the air defences at home were in a pitiful state, and remained that way until after the entry into the war of the Japanese and the Americans.

As part of the hurried preparations for the war which everyone felt was imminent, in early 1939 the government had produced the *Commonwealth War Book*. This gave the administrative and organisational details necessary for coordinating the transition of civil government from peace to war, on the basis that such a war would require the mobilisation of all national resources in waging it. It was published without chapters on either manpower or supply. Some government departments were closely involved in its production; others played little part. Its chapters on the economic base of the war effort were out of date, and it had little to say about the mobilisation of the civilian community or the inevitable reliance of the armed forces upon that community. Like so much else in the lead-up to war, it was a necessary measure amateurishly applied.

Australia's declaration of war against Germany was made by the prime minister, Menzies, without debate in the parliament or recourse to Cabinet. The proposition that the dominions were bound to follow the

United Kingdom automatically into a state of war was not disputed when parliament met three days later, on 6 September. The Australian Labor Party was concerned that there should be no conscription for overseas service, an option which the government never seriously considered. The Opposition was also concerned that troops should not be sent outside Australia, and here the two sides divided. This arose not through any anti-imperial sentiment on the part of the Labor Party, but from a desire to fulfill one of the primary tenets of imperial defence, namely that each part of the empire accepted responsibility for local defence. Given the appallingly run-down state of local defences and the growing suspicion in some circles that Britain would be unable to fulfill the pledge of Singapore, it seemed sensible to retain men and equipment in Australia against the possibility of Japanese aggression in the Pacific. For the first two years of the war, however, Australia concentrated its military effort in overseas theatres against the Germans, Italians and Vichy French in Europe and North Africa.

Later generations may ponder the phenomenon of thousands of Australians and New Zealanders volunteering 'for service half a world away', and the willingness to send forces to Europe in 1939–40 has prompted speculation about an expeditionary force mentality. Menzies' endorsement of this course of action is seen as further confirmation of his uncritical willingness to further imperial interests at the expense of local ones. Such critics overlook the delays he imposed on the dispatch of troops while he sought assurances from London over possible Japanese intentions. While aspects of government policy deserve censure (especially in relation to the Empire Air Training Scheme), overall it must be remembered that in 1939 the Japanese had not attacked in the Pacific and gave signs of becoming bogged still further in the war in China, and that the threat posed by Hitler was real. It was unthinkable in any case that a homogeneous Anglocentric society like Australia would stand by and allow Britain to face the German onslaught alone, nor should it be thought that a British defeat did not pose serious economic and strategic dangers for the dominions and the empire as a whole. Menzies was never the uncritical Anglophile of later caricature, and on several occasions between 1939 and 1941 drew attention publicly to the fact that Britain's 'Far East' was Australia's 'near North' with all that implied.

Hesitant steps towards a war footing had been made in the days before the declaration of war. The government had been warned on 24 August by the British that war was imminent, and had ordered the ridiculously small cadre of the permanent forces to man coastal defences in all military districts on 2 September. On 5 September the militia was called up 10 000 at a time to provide relays of guards on selected points, but was to serve for just sixteen days at a time. On 15 September it was announced that the whole of the militia would be called up, in two drafts of 40 000, for one month's continuous training, but the suspension of compulsory training imposed by Scullin in 1929 was not lifted until 1 January 1940. In New Zealand the government had already announced its decision to raise a force for overseas service, while in Britain conscription had been brought in well before hostilities commenced, in April 1939. The Australian government still behaved with the lack of urgency and sense of purpose of the inter-war years. In parliament on 17 September the Minister for the Army, G. A. Street, announced that the first priority was to give more training to the militia.

Two days earlier the government had declared that a division would be raised for overseas service, but it was to be raised outside the existing militia structure and on a voluntary basis. While it was expected that most of the volunteers would have a militia background, it was also argued that the raising of the force should not set back the training of militia units. As a result, a decision was taken that half the vacancies in the division would be reserved for militiamen, one-quarter for those with previous service in such units, and just one-quarter for men from country districts where there had been no militia training since the early 1920s. From the beginning, government spokesmen seemed intent to 'talk down' enlistment by militia men into the first division of the 2nd AIF. In mid-October, Street observed in a broadcast that the burden of enlistment would fall most heavily upon 'men of the militia, their wives and families and employers', and spoke of serious problems caused by 'the withdrawal of militiamen from industry'. Neither sentiment was calculated to boost recruitment. Nor was the system of restricted occupations overseen by manpower officials at each place of enlistment. This concern with the impact of recruitment upon the economy would make more sense had these restrictions been devised with Australian conditions in mind, but in fact the government merely borrowed the categories of restricted occupations which applied in Britain, without apparent concern for their relevance here.

The restrictions were such, recalled Major General Clive Steele, that 'they prevented everybody joining the AIF except, as I remember it, stockbrokers and certain classes of unemployed. Professional soldiers were debarred from enlisting. Under these circumstances only the ultra-loyal, many of whom are stated to have enlisted under an assumed name or calling, were available'. Many men did lie about their employment, and some lied about their age. This gave rise to a belief that the volunteers of the 6th Division were 'economic conscripts' and 'six bob a day murderers' in the parlance of the time. In addition, some of the unemployed stated their usual occupations on their attestation forms, so that a statistical breakdown of occupations at enlistment would not necessarily enlighten on this point. Gavin Long states that of 14 953 men chosen at random from those who enlisted in 1939, just 200 claimed to be unemployed. Slightly less than half of the total group was aged between twenty and twenty-four years of age, but 116 of them were under the legal age of twenty, and 732 were over thirty-five. Again, men lied about their previous war service and military experience in order to enlist, and some were picked up only when they sported their First World War medal ribbons on their uniforms after their convoys sailed for overseas. The proportion of such veterans was probably higher in non-combat arms and services, such as the medical and signal services, and some medical problems were experienced in North Africa with over-aged men who could not withstand the strains of active service in combat arms.

Although the militia had been intended to provide half of the 20 000 men for the 6th Division, its proportional enlistment fell well below this. Some militia officers discouraged their men from volunteering, aided by a Military Board instruction that militiamen whose departure would weaken the unit were not allowed to enlist. Some units lost hardly any of their members to the initial drafts for the AIF; in cases where militia officers were appointed to commands, many members of their units followed them, preserving the regional affiliations between some AIF battalions and their notional militia counterparts. Less than one-quarter of the force came from the militia in the end, not only because of obstruction on the part of some militia unit commanders but because of the failure of the government to inspire voluntary enlistment and the unattractive prospect of relinquishing paid employment to join a force which might go no further afield than Singapore. In this context it was not without significance that rates of pay in the AIF were lower than in the militia.

From the beginning, therefore, Australia followed a policy of maintaining two armies, one volunteer and eligible for overseas service anywhere in the world, the other militia and ineligible for service outside Australia. This was a short-sighted policy which caused great difficulty after the beginning of the war in the Pacific. But in addition to the strains imposed by this policy, there were other tensions within the army caused by rivalry between the officers of the Staff Corps and those of the citizen forces. Such animosity had simmered throughout the 1930s and occasionally came into public view, as when Major General Gordon Bennett wrote a series of newspaper articles in 1937–38 complete with sneering references to the alleged inability of Staff Corps officers. The tensions heightened at the outbreak of war and continued to manifest themselves until after 1945. At times, it might be wondered whether some of Australia's senior officers ever put as much energy into fighting the Germans and Japanese as they did into quarrelling with one another.

The majority of commands in the new division went to militia officers – which served merely to fuel the antagonism. Indeed, Menzies went so far as to announce that all operational commands would be filled by citizen soldiers. But Lieutenant General Sir Thomas Blamey, who had been selected to command the AIF, did not concur in this (if, indeed, he was consulted), and over the course of the war the Staff Corps filled almost as many of the senior command positions as the others. But they remained under-represented at the level of unit command, a situation which affected the junior members of the Staff Corps more than their seniors. Unlike 1914, no effort was made to bring forward the graduation of current classes at RMC Duntroon in order to staff the new units and formations. Of the thirty-seven graduates of the class of 1939, only four were appointed to positions in the 6th Division.

The British government was keen that the Australian division should proceed overseas as soon as possible, and the British chiefs of staff stressed to the Australian government that there appeared little likelihood of an attack by Japan. The Australian Defence Committee recommended that the 6th Division be sent to Egypt, and that a second division be raised and dispatched to join it, forming an Australian Corps. War Cabinet considered the advice on 15–16 November, but was unable to agree; meanwhile on 20 November the New Zealand government announced that its first contingent was to be sent to Egypt as soon as sufficient shipping was available. On 28 November the Full Cabinet decided that the 6th Division would go to the Middle East, but without artillery. This decision was soon modified to enable one of the three field regiments to take their guns, but both decisions were curious ones since there was enough field artillery in Australia to equip the regiments of seven divisions, and a decision had been taken earlier not to manufacture field guns in Australia presumably because of the surplus already in existence. The decision on the formation of another division was deferred, and approval for the raising of the 7th Division was not forthcoming until February the following year.

The mobilisation of the RAN provided no such difficulties. The navy's establishment was brought up to 10 250 by calling up 4800 reservists and, in the course of September 1939, a number of small vessels were requisitioned to perform as minesweepers while five liners were armed and commissioned as merchant cruisers. The new light cruiser *Perth* was in the Caribbean on the way home from Britain, where it had been commissioned as an Australian ship in June. The Admiralty's request that it be retained on the West Indies Station was agreed to late in

August, on the proviso that the decision be reviewed should Japanese intentions become hostile. A further request on 29 August to have RAN ships begin moving to war stations, including in the Mediterranean, was not agreed to, despite being backed by the acting CNS in Melbourne, Commodore J. W. Durnford, who, like the CNS, Admiral Sir Ragnar Colvin, was a Royal Navy officer. Although New Zealand and India had already placed their fleets at the disposal of the Admiralty, the Australian government stipulated that no units of the RAN were to be taken from the Australia Station without its concurrence. When it became clear that the Japanese did not intend to exploit the outbreak of war in Europe in the immediate future, an Order-in-Council placing all naval ships then in commission at the disposal of the British was signed on 7 November. But in recognition of the continuing unease in regard to Japanese intentions, and the threat posed by the depredations of German raiders, *Perth* was returned to Australian waters in December, and *Sydney* joined the East Indies Station.

Decisions taken with regard to the Royal Australian Air Force illustrated the disagreement within some circles over whether Australia's resources should be placed at the disposal of the empire or whether Australia had a duty to utilise some at least of those resources in its own defence. In fact, of course, inter-war imperial defence thinking had always emphasised that local defence was a dominion responsibility, so that in a sense this argument was no argument at all. But the legacy of neglect of the previous decades, coupled with the policy of a 'war of limited liability' which the Menzies government seemed determined to follow, meant that a large proportion of the relatively meagre forces raised initially would have had to be retained in Australia if the government had embarked seriously upon an upgrading of Australia's own defences, leaving even less to dispatch overseas. There were other considerations at work as well, not least in the characters of Menzies himself and of Bruce, former prime minister and High Commissioner in London since 1933.

One squadron of the RAAF was already in Britain when war was declared, and this was brought up to strength and placed under the command of the RAF's Coastal Command. At the outbreak of war the air force numbered 3000 regulars, 500 men in the Citizen Air Force and 150 officers on the reserve list. On 20 September the government offered a force of four bomber and two fighter squadrons for service with the RAF, at a strength of 3200 all ranks. Together with the squadron being formed to operate out of Port Moresby, this offer represented virtually the whole strength of the RAAF, and left nothing for home defence or reinforcement. The upper echelon of the service was in turmoil as well. Williams had been sacked as CAS after the presentation of the Ellington report, and sent on attachment to the RAF in Britain. This was manifestly unjust, since no individual service officer could be held responsible for the shortcomings of his service which followed inevitably upon the policies of successive governments between the wars, and Ellington himself expressed misgivings over the use to which his report was put. Menzies opted for an RAF officer to succeed Williams and appointed Air Chief Marshal Sir Charles Burnett. The latter was an undistinguished appointment, and matters were exacerbated in December when the acting CAS and old rival of Williams, Air Vice Marshal S. J. Goble, resigned over policy matters related to the implementation of the Empire Air Training Scheme (EATS).

Both Bruce and the Canadian High Commissioner to London, Vincent Massey, claimed to be the originators of the scheme, although the general idea of an empire air force had been around since at least 1936. Bruce suggested to the British that the air training resources of the empire be pooled, that advanced air training be carried out in Canada, and that dominion crews join squadrons formed in Britain. On 26 September the British government urged such a scheme upon the dominions, with additional prompting in Australia from Bruce. On 5 October Menzies agreed, without consulting the Air Board, and a conference was convened in Ottawa to work out the details. Australia was represented by the Minister for Air, J. V. Fairbairn, a former pilot with the Royal Flying Corps. He insisted that at least half the Australians should receive their advanced training in Australia, a sensible move since it involved the basing in Australia of advanced training aircraft with military capabilities. The Canadian schools would take half the monthly intake of 2800 trainees from Canada itself, one-third from Australia, and the rest from Britain and New Zealand. The initial agreement signed in Ottawa on 27 November was to run till 31 March 1943, although in fact it was renewed at a further conference early in 1943.

The offer of an aerial expeditionary force was now withdrawn, since the EATS was expected to meet the needs of the RAF, and existing officers of the RAAF would be needed to administer and train aircrew in the thirty-three training establishments set up in Australia. A total of 9600 aircrew passed out of these schools before going to Canada, while over 15 000 did all their training there before dispatch to Britain. Very few saw service in the Pacific at any time during the war. The scheme was to prove disastrous for the RAAF, for several reasons. It reduced the air force to a training organisation for the RAF, and removed thousands of potential aircrew from utilisation in the defence of Australia. Australia paid most of the costs of initial training, but received no direct benefit from the outlay. Absorption into the empire scheme meant that few

Australians rose to high rank or gained experience in senior command posts, because the policy was to break up the intakes and form 'empire' crews of the various nationalities, while the majority of Australian crew served in British squadrons in any case. Under Article XV of the Ottawa agreement, aircrew were to be identified with their country of origin by the creation within the RAF of distinctive dominion components. Canada insisted on this, and No. 6 Canadian Group was formed in Bomber Command in 1943. (On the debit side, the Canadian Group was slow to receive modern equipment and newer types of aircraft, and early in its existence it suffered severely from inexperience among commanders and crews, which increased the casualty rates.) Eighteen RAAF squadrons were supposed to be formed within the RAF, but only seventeen were ever activated, and these did not contain the majority of Australian aircrew in any case. The Australian government failed signally to exercise control over, or much responsibility for, the thousands of young men sent to fight in the skies of Europe. The surrender of such control negated many of the advances made since 1914 in ensuring the effective control of national forces by the government which fielded those forces.

As already noted, the professional head of the air force was now a British officer. The CNS was a British officer, appointed in 1937, and the next most senior officer in the RAN, the commander of the naval squadron, Admiral Sir Wilfrid Patterson, likewise was from the British service. On the same day that Blamey was appointed to command the AIF, the government announced that Major General Squires would take up the post of CGS, replacing Major General J. D. Lavarack who had been in the job since 1935. Thus within a few months of the outbreak of war, the government's senior military advisers were all British officers. On the civilian side, the government announced the formation of a War Cabinet on 15 September, to comprise the Prime Minister, who was also the Treasurer, the Attorney-General, W. M. Hughes, the Minister for Supply and Development, R. G. Casey, the Minister for Defence, G. A. Street, the Minister for External Affairs and Information, Sir Henry Gullett, and the Minister for Commerce, Senator McLeay. The secretary of the Department of Defence, F. G. Shedden, was also secretary to the War Cabinet, which first met on 27 September.

Menzies had no military experience, other than some service in the pre-1914 militia. Within the War Cabinet, however, Hughes had been prime minister for much of the Great War, while Casey, Street and Gullett all had war service and Street had been a brigadier in the interwar citizen forces. In the wider ministry Fairbairn, Minister for Air, Eric Harrison, Minister for the Interior, and H. B. Collett, Minister for Repatriation in the 1941 Menzies ministry, had served in the Great War also. While not a ministry of all the talents, it was a relatively young ministry with experience of office and, in particular, with some direct experience of war.

At the beginning of 1940, three months into what was to be the greatest war in Australia's history, the description 'business as usual' applied, in a sense, as much to the military preparations for war as to the wider civilian society. The forces were headed by British officers who, Squires excepted, owed a higher loyalty to their parent services in Britain. Some measures were taken to provide for home defence but, as had been the pattern for twenty years, these were ineffectual and half-hearted. The navy had reverted to British control, decisions had been made concerning the air force which were seriously to impair its operational effectiveness for the rest of the war, and the government's contradictory attitude towards the raising of a field force for overseas service perplexed and confused many, soldier and civilian alike. Unquestionably, there was concern about Japanese intentions in the Asia-Pacific region, but it is not merely hindsight to suggest that the time for adequate preparations against the eventuality of war in our own region had rather passed successive governments by, and that the outbreak of war in Europe called for a more determined attitude than in fact prevailed.

Despite this, 100 000 men had volunteered for service overseas by the end of March 1940, 22 000 in the AIF, 7000 in the navy, and a staggering 68 000 who had signed applications to join the air force. In 1940 there were approximately 600 000 men aged between twenty and twenty-nine, so one in six of those considered to be of military age had joined up or registered an intention to do so. Enlistment had tailed off in January and February, after the 6th Division had sailed for Egypt, but picked up dramatically with the announcement in February that the 7th Division would be raised and sent overseas. The raising of the 8th Division was announced in June, and the two divisions were full by July 1940 with a surplus of enlistments of 50 000, sufficient to raise two further divisions if necessary. On 11 July the government suspended recruitment for the AIF, and decided to raise and maintain a home defence force of 250 000 men of non-military age or in reserved occupations, the Volunteer Defence Corps (VDC). In September 1940 the 9th Division was formed, based on two brigades which had been diverted to Britain, while a fifth AIF division, the 1st Australian Armoured Division, was raised in 1941 but was never sent overseas. These later divisions had a higher proportion of regular officers than had the 6th Division, although command of the ill-fated 8th Division went to the cantankerous citizen soldier and inveterate hater of the Staff Corps, Gordon Bennett. Elements of this division were sent to Malaya in February 1941 following a request for

Table 7.1 Net enlistment in all services, 1939–47

Date	RAN	AMF	RAAF	Total
Sept. 1939	7 982	3 432	3 489	14 903
Nov. 1941	19 367	288 100	61 192	368 659
Aug. 1942	22 775	525 678	107 643	656 096
Aug. 1943	32 982	542 570	156 448	732 000
Aug. 1944	35 112	480 077	181 877	697 066
June 1945	40 413	427 076	176 516	644 005
June 1946	19 533	101 272	22 658	143 463
June 1947(a)	11 176	32 192(b)	12 044	55 412

Note: Female enlistment began in 1941, and is included with male
         enlistment after that date.
Source: *Australian Year Book*, No. 37, 1946–47, and Gavin Long (ed.), *Australia
         in the War of 1939–45*, Canberra, 1952–77.
(a)   Date of disbandment of AIF.
(b)   Gross enlistments in the army (AIF, CMF, PMF, Women's Services) to
         June 1947 total 735 781.

reinforcement from the British government the previous October, while
the 9th Division under Major General H. D. Wynter was concentrated in
the Middle East in December 1940.

There was very little interaction between the fighting forces overseas and the Australian home front in the first two years of the war.
There was some internment of enemy aliens, although the numbers
involved were relatively small until after the outbreak of the war against
Japan. The Communist Party was finally banned in June 1940 under
the *National Security (Subversive Associations) Regulations*. The uncritical
parroting of the Comintern line on the 'imperialist' war against Hitler,
with whom Stalin had signed a non-aggression pact, and the efforts by
communist organisations to undermine the war effort, made this an
inevitable step (although it is only fair to add that some members of the
Party were disturbed and bewildered by the sudden change in the Party
line, a foretaste of things to come in 1956 and 1968). But sporting
fixtures and other forms of popular entertainment continued much as
before, and there was little sign of a decrease in consumption of consumer goods. The increase in munitions production was likewise
modest. Steps were taken towards the creation of a war economy,
with the Menzies government introducing exchange controls and the
licensing of foreign trade. A serious coal strike disrupted production in
New South Wales for several months. On the other hand, the bumper
wheat harvest of 1939 was successfully marketed in Britain, although
the British did not need it, were destined not to receive much of it,

and may have agreed to purchase 63 million bushels as a means of helping ensure that Australian troops were dispatched overseas. Before December 1940 only petrol was rationed, although taxation rose sharply. There was still no system of directing and organising manpower according to some central policy; the economy merely 'took up the slack' from the high unemployment of the prewar period.

The strategic direction of the war lay in London, and the Australian government was to record its displeasure over the lack of consultation by the British without being able to do much to alter the situation. Domestically, there were calls for a national government of all parties in emulation of the British, but the ALP declined the offer and fought the federal election of September 1940 in the normal manner. If the purpose of the election was to determine either side's credibility as a wartime administration, it failed, for the electorate returned the United Australia Party to government in coalition with the Country Party and relying on the votes of two independents for its continuing existence. Friction and instability marked the progress of the conservative parties until 7 October 1941, when the Labor Party took office following the defeat of the government in the parliament over the budget.

In domestic politics, then, the first two years of the war were an uninspiring example of Australia's ability to meet the demands of modern war. The conservative parties' performance was not helped by the deaths of three of its ministers, Gullett, Street and Fairbairn, in an air crash in August 1940. All had had military experience, and the able and widely respected Lieutenant General Sir Brudenell White, who had succeeded Squires as CGS on the latter's death, was killed with them. But if inspiring wartime leadership was beyond him, Menzies did take some sensible administrative steps to assist in the prosecution of the war. Not the least of these was the formation of the Advisory War Council (AWC) in October 1940, made up of four ministers and four members of the Opposition and designed to bring the ALP into consultation on war policy and associate them with the decision-making process. Labor maintained the AWC, when it came into office, for the rest of the war. Of even greater significance was the issue of a 'charter' to Blamey which insisted on his right of consultation with his own government in such circumstances as he saw fit, and which provided for the maintenance and recognition by the British of the national integrity of units of the AIF.

Between Poland and Pearl Harbor, the Australian response to the fact of war was a gradual one, and the progression to a full war footing was steady but unhurried. The contrast with the months after the fall of Singapore is marked, and it is the later years of the war which provide the popular image of the Second World War for Australians. For that reason, steps taken early in the war have been dealt with in some detail here. Having looked at the organisational responses in Australia, it is appropriate to examine the early campaigns in which Australian forces were engaged.

The 6th Division was dispatched overseas with little training above the platoon level and equipped with personal weapons only, the intention being to complete training and equipping in the Middle East before the division moved to France, a decision reminiscent of the Great War. Egypt had been chosen as a staging-place because the French were still actively in the war in early 1940 and had large forces in Syria and French North Africa, while the Italians, with forces in Libya and Italian Somaliland, had not yet become belligerents. Later divisions received much of their unit training in Australia before departing for overseas service, and were much better equipped. This was a reaction to the experience of the 6th Division, but it also meant that there was a considerable delay before the remaining Australian divisions reached the theatre of war and were grouped into an Australian Corps. The 6th Division was to fight its first campaign by itself.

The division had been raised on the old AIF establishment, four battalions to a brigade. When the British Army endeavoured to make its manpower go further by reducing its brigades to three battalions each, the Australians followed suit. The 18th Brigade had been diverted to England in any case, so a new brigade, the 19th, was raised from the discarded fourth battalions of existing brigades, and the 6th Division then comprised the 16th, 17th and 19th Brigades. (The 18th later formed part of the 7th Division.) A rigorous training program commenced in Egypt and attempts were made to bring the division's equipment levels up to scratch. The former bore more fruit than the latter. Full divisional exercises mounted in November 1940, however, demonstrated that the various units had not progressed to an even standard, and that the division still lacked important items of equipment. The former weakness was to be confirmed in the early actions of the ensuing campaign, the latter deficiencies were made up from captured Italian equipment after the campaign opened. These included artillery pieces, machine guns, carriers and other vehicles. During exercises, the divisional orders stated that the types of weapons represented by wooden mock-ups might be 'distinguished by different coloured paints'.

That the Australians' first theatre of operations should be North Africa owed more to Hitler than to the decision-making of the government in Canberra. Australian intentions to fight in France like their fathers ended with the fall of France in June 1940 and Mussolini's declaration of war upon the allies. Italian entry into the war posed acute strategic problems for the British. The Italian colonies and recent Italian conquests in the region posed a direct threat to British positions in Egypt and the Sudan and threatened the security of the Canal Zone and the lines of communication with India. Bundled out of France with the loss of all its equipment, the British Army had little to spare for a new theatre in North Africa. For a while, the Australians were to be the mainstay of the ground offensive against the Italians and, later, the Germans in the eastern Mediterranean.

Italy had half a million troops in Libya and Abyssinia (Ethiopia). Not only did they outnumber the British and empire forces in the region, but they required the Commander-in-Chief, Wavell, to fight campaigns in two directions simultaneously, further weakening his small force of 85 000. He received reinforcements late in 1940 in the shape of the 5th Indian Division, which he earmarked for operations in Abyssinia, and the 7th Australian Division, which arrived in November and which was not ready to take part in the Libyan campaign which began the following month. The short and highly successful campaign against the Italians in Libya was fought largely by the 6th Australian Division and the British 7th Armoured Division. The opening phase was fought by the 4th Indian Division, which beat the Italians at Sidi Barrani in December before being sent to Abyssinia to reinforce Indian forces there. The 6th Division was ordered forward to replace it.

The first Australian land campaign of the war was a short and brilliantly fought effort. The 6th Division and its citizen–soldier commander, Major General Iven Mackay, won plaudits all round for its resolute and skilful advance across Libya, taking major Italian positions at Bardia (3 January), the port of Tobruk (22 January), and Benghazi (7 February). Over 40 000 prisoners were taken at Bardia alone, 25 000 more at Tobruk, together with enormous quantities of equipment and munitions. Like any soldiers in virtually any army, the Italians showed that poorly led men with obsolete weapons in general do not acquit themselves well. But despite the large number of prisoners taken, some sections of the Italian army fought well, especially their artillery and machine gunners, and the Australians quickly were disabused of the notion that the enemy would give in without a fight. The resistance offered by some posts at Bardia, for example, was a salutary lesson to the Australians, who lost 130 killed taking the defences.

These early actions were significant for other reasons. Success was important psychologically, for it confirmed in the minds of the troops that they were worthy successors to the old AIF and had passed the test which they had set themselves. The commanders performed well, and many officers were to go on to brigade and divisional commands later in the war. The strains between Staff Corps and militia officers, always just

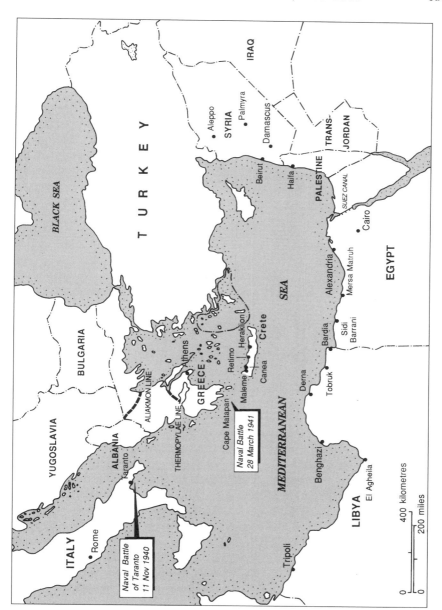

Map 11   Theatre of operations, Mediterranean, 1940–42

beneath the surface, were exacerbated by various incidents and the mutual antipathy which developed between the commanders of the 17th and 19th Brigades and several of the senior staff officers on the divisional headquarters was to last for the rest of the war. Not all officers and units performed as well as others, and problems were identified with poorly trained reinforcements. There were shortcomings in air–ground co-operation, and in precautions against enemy air action. This was less important against the Italians since their air force in the theatre had been virtually wiped out. It was to assume greater importance against the Germans. Finally, great though the Australian contribution had been in this campaign, it could not have been won without the air cover provided by the RAF, the support of British armoured and other units, and the leadership and planning of the British Corps commander, Lieutenant General Richard O'Connor, and his staff. Contrary to popular beliefs about Australian soldiers and British officers, the commanding general of XIII Corps was well regarded by his Australian subordinates.

Fighting in the Western Desert was matched by early action against the Italian Fleet, and Australian naval units played a part in this also. Australian ships had operated in the Mediterranean before the Italian declaration of war on 10 June, contributing units to the Red Sea Force, the 7th Cruiser squadron, and the 10th Destroyer flotilla. The Italians opened naval hostilities with a submarine campaign designed to con-fine the Royal Navy in Alexandria harbour. Within nineteen days they had lost ten submarines, and the mine-fields sown in the harbour approaches were marked and neutralised. Australian ships also took part in ship-to-shore bombardment in support of the ground forces at Bardia. In September, the cruiser *Australia* was involved in the ill-starred expedition to Dakar in Senegal, an attempt to win a foothold for De Gaulle's Free French in French territory from which they might rally support against Vichy. There was considerable criticism of the affair in Britain, though little in Australia, but the Australian government com-plained to Churchill that it had been given no details on the action or the decision to abandon it when the Vichy forces offered unexpectedly stout resistance. The matter was resolved amicably enough, and arose largely because of the weakened position of the Australian government following the 1940 elections. It illustrated the problems of consultation, however, faced by a sovereign government which turned over opera-tional control of its forces to those of another power, and was a foretaste of things to come.

For the first time in its history, the RAN took part in a large fleet action against the Italians in the battle of Calabria on 9 July. While little actual damage was inflicted on either side, it was good experience for unblooded ships' crews, and was the precursor to the first major victory of an Australian ship in the war. On 19 July the cruiser *Sydney* engaged and sank the Italian cruiser *Bartolemeo Colleoni* in a classic ship-to-ship naval action of the type which everyone understood and expected, but which happened less frequently than most people imagined. Minesweeping, patrolling, convoy and supply escort duties and naval gunfire support were more common features of the naval war in the Mediterranean, especially since the Italians avoided fleet action whenever possible, leaving offensive naval activity to their submarines and aircraft. This strategy did not prevent them suffering a major defeat at Taranto in November when Fleet Air Arm aircraft inflicted heavy damage, an action which saw *Sydney* involved in the more commonplace task of convoy interdiction.

The victory in the first Libyan campaign had bundled the Italians all the way back to Tripoli, but was less complete than it first appeared. The Germans could not allow their principal ally to be knocked out of the war so quickly, and were reinforcing the Italians in Libya and, more ominously, Greece. Mussolini had invaded Greece in October, but had been pushed back into Albania by spirited Greek resistance. Hitler resolved to come to his aid, and Wavell was ordered to weaken his army in North Africa in order to supply troops for a Greek campaign. Most of the forces sent to Greece were from the dominions, but the strategic decision-making took place in London, and involved what amounted to the deception of the Australian government and its senior commander in the field, Blamey.

The reasons for intervention in Greece seemed compelling at the time, and had some validity. Greece was the only ally on the European continent still engaged actively in the war against Germany and Italy, and it was unconscionable that it should be over-run without some attempt being made to assist it against the common enemy. Successful German occupation of Greek territory would provide new airfields and maritime bases from which to strike at Malta. Most persuasive of all was the potential for influencing opinion in the United States, where the isolationist lobby still held considerable sway. The abandonment of a small but resolute ally would do nothing to enhance the allies' position in the eyes of those Americans inclined to leave Europe's 'squabbles' to the Europeans.

In the course of 1941 Menzies made the long trip to London to consult with the British government on the course and conduct of the war and in the hope that Churchill could be pursuaded to constitute a war cabinet of dominion leaders of the kind convened by Lloyd George in the last two years of the previous war. On the way he visited Australian troops in the Middle East, and held discussions with Wavell in early February. It was at this time that the proposed Greek campaign was first outlined to him. He concurred with the scheme, although he did not consult with Blamey. He may have believed that Blamey's views had already been sought. They had not, and when Blamey expressed misgivings about the operation and stated that the matter had to be referred to his government, he was told that it had already been discussed with the Australian prime minister. When Menzies reached London he was told that Blamey had been 'consulted' and, although he too appears to have had misgivings about the proposed campaign, Menzies agreed to the dispatch of Australian troops to Greece. The Australian government in Canberra received notice of what was afoot by letter from Blamey only after the decisions had been made and the troops were already embarking.

The Australians were ill-informed and not consulted at the critical stages of the decision-making process. Menzies was lied to, for Blamey had not been 'consulted' in the manner suggested at all. Pressure was placed upon the Australian prime minister for a quick decision in view of the deteriorating situation in the Balkans, which further restricted his opportunities to consult with the Australian commander directly affected. Churchill was not inclined to consult with the government which would provide the bulk of the forces for an operation which many people believed was a forlorn hope. But neither Blamey nor Menzies can escape censure entirely. Blamey should have insisted on the right of direct consultation with his government which was explicit in the charter he was given by that government when the AIF went overseas, the more so because he had serious misgivings about the enterprise to which those troops were being committed. He had been selected for the command because it was felt that he was ideally suited to handle the difficult politico-military problems which he would encounter. He failed the test on this occasion. Menzies should have insisted on receiving Blamey's views directly, and not through the filter of British official opinion. Contrary to popular belief, Menzies stood up to Churchill quite vigorously in the War Cabinet meetings which he attended but he lacked the detailed professional knowledge with which to resist successfully the determined push for a campaign to aid the Greeks.

Both men emerge from the episode with greater credit than Churchill, who seems to have regarded the AIF as being at the disposal of the British, to do with as they, meaning he, saw fit. (In ameliorating this judgement, it might be added that he received confused advice from his senior officials on the ground, the Foreign Secretary, Anthony Eden, and the CIGS, Field Marshal Sir John Dill.) On a wider level, the problem is an old one. There were general allied interests and more specific Australian interests at stake, and the two sometimes clashed. This is a familiar problem in inter-allied relations, especially in an alliance between great and lesser powers. But the duplicity involved on this occasion soured relations and undermined Australian faith in Churchillian reassurances. Future clashes between British military assessments and Australian military advice, such as over the withdrawal of the 9th Division from Tobruk or the diversion of Australian troops to Burma, would be decided in favour of the Australian commander-in-chief. It might be argued that with the Greek campaign Churchill sacrificed the confidence of Australian (and New Zealand) politicians and soldiers for a very short-term advantage.

The Greek campaign was conducted at the same time as the Germans under Rommel renewed the offensive in North Africa. Because of this, the 7th Australian Division was withdrawn from Lustreforce, destined for Greece, and Blamey was left with the 6th Australian and 2nd New Zealand Divisions. The Greeks fought hard and well, but neither they nor their allies were able to withstand the assault of eight German armoured and mechanised divisions, nor did courage compensate for tactical air superiority, which the Germans maintained easily.

The German attack began on 6 April. Allied forces held a line along the Aliakmon River, between the Yugoslav border and central Greece. The Germans pinned the allies by a frontal attack while advancing in their rear into the Florina valley. Outflanked, the allies were forced to retreat, with elements of the Australian division fighting a rearguard action to cover the Greeks' retreat. A new defensive position was established along the Thermopylae line on 19 April, but by this stage it was evident that Greek resistance was beginning to crumble. The Greek forces in Epirus surrendered to the Germans on the 20th, without orders; Athens fell on the 27th. On 19 April Wavell had given orders for the evacuation of British and empire troops, which proceeded over several nights from 25 April. More than 50 000 men were evacuated but 14 000 were left behind, including 2000 Australians. The force lost all its vehicles and heavy weapons, but in all other respects the evacuation was the most successful part of the campaign.

Many of those brought out of Greece were diverted to Crete, where they fought a second short campaign against the highly trained German paratroop division. There were over 30 000 allied troops on the island, but they lacked all heavy equipment and were tired after the fiasco of the previous month. The 10 000 Greek troops evacuated with them were poorly trained and ill equipped, and of little real use. The allies established defensive positions at Suda Bay, Maleme airfield, Retimo and Heraklion, and German assaults were launched on 20 May against the latter three and at Canea, midway between Maleme and Suda Bay. The fighting was intense and lasted several days, but on 26 May Major General Bernard Freyberg, the New Zealand divisional commander in overall command of the defences, informed Wavell that the position was hopeless and over several nights attempts were made to evacuate the force to Egypt. Losses in shipping were heavy due to German air attack, and 12 000 men were left behind, including 3000 Australians. As Rowell wrote years later, 'a forced evacuation is a defeat and ... the British, Australian and New Zealand forces suffered heavy losses in men and material'.

In just three months, the fortunes of the allies in the eastern Mediterranean had been reversed. The naval and air forces were heavily reduced after losses in Greece and Crete, and two of Wavell's best divisions, 6th Australian and 2nd New Zealand, were ruined as fighting forces and would require months of refitting and recuperation. The Germans had suffered 5200 casualties in Greece, and their paratroop division was so badly mauled in Crete that they never attempted a full airborne assault of that kind again. Claims that the reduction of Greece adversely affected the German timetable for Operation Barbarossa, the invasion of the Soviet Union, however, are not supported by evidence. To add further to his difficulties, Wavell was now hard-pressed in North Africa and was scheduled to conduct an invasion of Syria to pre-empt its occupation by the Germans through their Vichy French collaborators.

The Germans and Italians had renewed the offensive in Libya on 31 March, and had soon regained all the territory lost at the beginning of the year. The port of Tobruk was garrisoned by the 9th Australian Division, one brigade of the 7th, and some British units. By 11 April the city was surrounded and cut off from all land access, being resupplied at night from the sea. Local air superiority rested with the Germans but Major General L. J. Morshead, the garrison commander and GOC of the 9th Division, conducted an aggressive defence on the perimeter with a strong emphasis on night patrolling and the denial of 'no man's land' to the enemy, reminiscent of Australian tactics in 1917–18 in France. The enemy made numerous local attacks and took heavy casualties in the process, but failed to induce the garrison to surrender. The Australians participated in the defence of Tobruk for six months of the eight-month siege, being relieved by sea in October, and this was the first legacy of the Greek campaign. Blamey insisted that the AIF be grouped together as stipulated by his charter and, when Morshead reported that the health of the garrison was declining, insisted that the Australians be withdrawn. Auchinleck, Wavell's successor, considered resigning over the issue, but was made to see that in such matters Australian demands, in Blamey's phrase, had to be treated like those of any other sovereign state and ally. Accordingly, by late October the Australian garrison was replaced although one battalion remained until the port was relieved in December. The defence of Tobruk was important, but so too was the state of the AIF. The 6th Division was out of action after the Greek campaign, and operations at Tobruk had cost the Australians over 800 killed and nearly 3000 other casualties. They could not afford to wear down another division by constant operations to the point where it was incapable of further sustained activity especially with the deterioration of affairs in the Pacific. In his insistent position Blamey was supported by the government back in Australia, which had also learnt a few things from the Greek campaign.

While the 9th Division was in Tobruk the remaining brigades of the 7th Division were used in the invasion of Syria, which began on 8 June. A revolt by Iraqi nationalists and German attempts to supply them through Syria provided the strategic rationale for the campaign. The allied force involved included British, Indian and Free French units, but the Australians did most of the fighting and took the bulk of the casualties against 30 000 well-equipped French regulars commanded by General Henri Dentz. Any expectation that the Vichy forces would collapse quickly dissolved in the stiff fighting which ensued before an armistice was signed on 14 July. The invasion in fact was premature, because Hitler was preoccupied with the invasion of Russia and the German General Staff in any case regarded the Middle East theatre as peripheral, and because the Iraqi nationalists had been defeated by 30 May. Tactically the campaign was well managed, but the strategic necessity for it had not been well thought out.

By December the allied position had recovered considerably. The Middle East had been denied to the enemy, and Australian forces had played an important role in that process. Although there were battles still to be fought in North Africa, only the 9th Division would remain to take part in them. With the advent into the war of the Japanese, pressure was applied immediately for the return of Australian troops from the Middle East to take part in the defence of Australia.

The first two full years of the war were an important preparation for the great struggle in the Pacific which was to follow. The three divisions of the AIF had fought Germans, Italians and French and had learnt much about modern industrial warfare in the process. Their leaders had gained valuable experience not only in action but in the vital areas of staff work and administration without which no modern army can long survive. Strong attention was paid to training, both within units and formations and in the processing of reinforcements. The soldiers themselves were beginning to take on some of the features of long-service professionals, and this was a trend which would be accentuated for the rest of the war. The wisdom of defending Australia in the Middle East was shown by the eventual return of three battle-hardened divisions to fight the Japanese, a resource which would not have been available in any other circumstances, perhaps with most serious consequences.

CHAPTER 8

The Second World War, 1942–1945

Japan's entry into the Second World War in December 1941 confirmed the collective strategic and racial fears of several generations of Australians. The Pacific war served also to show up the inability of the British to defend Australia, and the necessity for Australians to defend themselves. Despite two years of war Australia was in no way prepared for the Japanese onslaught when it came, and the legacy of inter-war neglect was paid for by young militiamen, poorly trained and equipped, in New Guinea in 1942. That, in the event, Australia was not invaded and over-run by the Japanese owed nothing to the defence preparations of the preceding twenty years.

Some preparations had been made nonetheless, for as noted earlier the government was mindful of the Japanese threat when making its initial force contributions to the war in Europe and the Mediterranean. Japanese intentions in the region were increasingly plain from the fall of France onwards, even if one discounted the war waged in China from 1931. German occupation of France and the Netherlands raised questions about the control of their colonial possessions in Southeast Asia and the Pacific. The administration of the Netherlands East Indies remained in the allied camp after the fall of the metropolitan government, but the government of French Indochina became a Vichy one, and acceded to Japanese pressure to stop the traffic of war material through Indochinese ports on its way to China. The British also bowed to Japanese wishes and temporarily closed the frontiers between China, Burma and Hong Kong, thus further isolating the embattled Chinese.

Australian apprehension centred upon Singapore and the Malay peninsula. In August 1940 the government sent three squadrons of the RAAF to strengthen the air defences of the island base. In June the British had asked that Australia send a division to Singapore, a request which the Australian government would not meet either by returning the 6th Division or dispatching one of the new formations still in Australia. They maintained this position for several months while an argument was conducted over the strategic priorities of the two theatres; the Australian government felt also that Australian troops were not being raised simply to fulfill garrison tasks. It was intended initially that all four infantry divisions of the AIF would go to the Middle East and form an Australian Corps, and this was still the intention as late as September 1940. Only following an exhaustive review of Singapore's defence capabilities in October did Menzies agree to dispatch troops to Singapore. Even then, he offered only one brigade group of the 8th Division, and stipulated that it was to be relieved later by Indian troops and was then to join the rest of the division in the Mediterranean theatre.

As is now known, 1941 was crucial in the development of Japanese strategy in the Pacific. The American-led embargo on Japanese oil supplies increased the pressure for a strike southwards towards the oilfields of the Netherlands East Indies. The Imperial Japanese Army, militantly anti-communist and xenophobic, favoured a strike northwards, using Manchuria as a base to launch a war against the USSR. Their defeat by the Russians at Nomonhan in 1939 had not dissuaded them, but the signing of a Neutrality Pact with the Soviet Union in April 1941 and the decision in July to favour the strike southwards determined the course of the Pacific war and brought the Japanese into direct conflict with the Dutch, British, Americans and, of course, Australians. Had the Japanese coordinated a northwards strike with the German invasion of the USSR, the outcome of the Second World War might have been very different.

In the months after the October review of Singapore the forces there were increased; two Indian divisions arrived in December and March, while Gordon Bennett's 8th Division headquarters and the 22nd Infantry Brigade arrived in February. The air strength remained low, however, and many of the aircraft types deployed were obsolescent. Also in February, the Australian Chiefs of Staff advised the government that the 8th Division should be retained in the region for the defence of Australia and that in the event of hostilities the islands of Timor and Ambon should become an Australian responsibility. The War Cabinet accepted this, and decided as well to station the 2/22nd Battalion at Rabaul, capital of the mandated territory of New Guinea. The only other forces in New Guinea were a small, part-time unit, the New Guinea Volunteer Rifles, and the dedicated and clandestine organisation of Coastwatchers which had been set up by Naval Intelligence in the 1920s, and which drew upon planters, missionaries and patrol officers with long experience and detailed local knowledge of their areas.

Despite attempts to influence the distribution of forces between the Atlantic and Pacific theatres, the Australian government had no say in the strategic decisions of the Anglo-American alliance as they affected the Far East. In February–March 1941 a top secret Anglo-American conference in Washington resolved on the 'Beat Hitler First' strategy, a decision communicated to Australia unofficially by the naval attaché based there. In May 1941 the Americans had switched part of the Pacific Fleet from Hawaii to the Atlantic at British request, and told the Australians later; Menzies' attempts in London in March to obtain information and reinforcements for Singapore were unsuccessful. The visit to Australian and New Zealand ports in May of an American naval squadron was good for public relations, but it is doubtful if it deterred the Japanese in any way; and fleeting visits were no substitute for the 'fleet to Singapore' which had now shrunk in British planning to an aircraft carrier and a single cruiser, to be dispatched at the outbreak of hostilities. All of this was confirmed at the Arcadia Conference in December 1941–January 1942, and had enormous implications for Australia and the Southwest Pacific, implications which do not seem to have sunk in until well after the Japanese attack.

Menzies returned to Australia in late May 1941. He had pushed hard for British reinforcement in the Far Fast and for a greater Australian share in the flow of information concerning the conduct of the war, largely without success. In June the Cabinet decided to send the 27th Brigade of the 8th Division to join the 22nd Brigade in Singapore. This left the 1st Armoured Division, still forming and without armoured vehicles, and the 23rd Brigade of the 8th Division as the only AIF formations available for the direct defence of Australia and the latter, in any case, was earmarked for Ambon, Timor and Rabaul in the event of hostilities.

Recognition of the increased volume of administration occasioned by a major war had led to the creation of separate service departments of government (Army, Navy, Air) in November 1939. The threat of war close to our shores, and the potential for actual invasion, required further measures. In particular consideration was given to the appointment of a Commander-in-Chief of the Home Forces in April 1941 at the behest of the Minister for the Army, Percy Spender, who thought that while the Chief of the General Staff had all the practical powers for the direction of Australia's defence, 'on psychological grounds affecting both the Military Forces and the general public' a C-in-C ought to be appointed. Among other things, he proposed that this would lead to the abolition of the Military Board of Administration and the transfer of its powers and authority to an individual.

This approach had a number of points in its favour. The task facing the CGS was a large and complex one. He was responsible for the training in Australia of the AIF for both Malaya and the Middle East, but had no operational control over it; he was responsible for its resupply also. He administered the militia and oversaw its training, and had overall responsibility for the army in the defence of Australia. This was too much for one man. The senior officers of the militia were often older men, unfit for active service and out of touch with the developments in warfare since 1918. A younger man with experience of the fighting in the Middle East would galvanise a machine for home defence which still operated slowly and inefficiently. Finally, the antagonism between AIF and militia soldiers might be lessened by bringing them under one command inside Australia. War Cabinet approved Spender's proposal in principle on 9 May, but insisted on maintaining the Military Board and the position of CGS. The army had reservations about the worth of such a set-up, but the government was impressed by the British system in which the GOC-in-C Home Forces functioned alongside the Chief of the Imperial General Staff and the Army Council. In any event, on 5 August the commander of the 6th Division, Major General Sir Iven Mackay, was appointed as GOC-in-C of the Home Forces, effective from 1 September.

The appointment was the last significant act of the Menzies government. His position weakened by the slight majority he enjoyed after the 1940 election, Menzies had been criticised inside and outside the government since his return from overseas. He again invited the Opposition to join an all-party government on 22 August, was rebuffed again and, at a party meeting on 28 August, resigned in favour of the leader of the Country Party, Arthur Fadden. The latter lasted less than a month, the government being defeated on the passage of the Budget when the two independent members of the House of Representatives voted with the ALP. On 3 October the Labor Party took office, and John Curtin became prime minister.

Menzies has received an unsympathetic press as a wartime leader. Much of this stems from hostility to his second period as prime minister after the war. The circumstances of his elevation to that office in 1939 left some bitterness among conservatives also. In general, he did better than he has been given credit for. The deplorable state of Australia's defences was not his fault. He was hoodwinked by the British over the Greek campaign, but then so was Blamey, who should have known better. He stood up to Churchill in the British Cabinet more robustly than Curtin ever tackled MacArthur later, and his failure to extract reinforcements for the Far East was matched by Labor's failures in the same area in 1942. The use of the phrase 'business as usual' was unfortunate, but it is generally overlooked that the other great slogan of the home front effort, 'All in', was of his government's manufacture, not Curtin's as is often assumed. If he was not a great wartime prime minister in the mould of Churchill, he was adequate to the demands made by the war in Europe. Australia could certainly have done worse.

The new Labor government viewed the defence of Australian territory with concern, but had little opportunity to do anything before the Japanese attack on Pearl Harbor which widened the war to truly global dimensions. In the month before the outbreak of war in the Pacific, however, Blamey returned to Australia for meetings with his new political masters. The trip was made at his request, partly at least to head off proposals for reorganising the AIF in the Middle East which he believed would be counter-productive. Leaving Cairo on 2 November, he stopped at Singapore on the way home and met with Gordon Bennett and the senior British officers of Malaya Command. He was unimpressed with the 'Indian garrison' atmosphere of lazy unconcern which he found there, and was equally astounded by the complacency he detected in the Australian population when he reached Melbourne, and said so. He returned to the Middle East in early December, having given Curtin and the Cabinet a chance to assess their most senior field commander. This was a useful opportunity in view of British complaints at the time concerning his 'political' attitude towards orders from his British superiors coupled with requests for his removal which the Australian government had ignored. His visit achieved little else in terms of preparing Australia for the months of crisis and panic which were to follow shortly.

Early on the morning of 8 December Japanese forces established a beachhead at Kota Bahru, while shortly afterwards the main landings were made in 'neutral' Thailand at Singora and Patani. For Australia, the war in the Pacific had begun. The prewar plan for the defence of Malaya, Matador, had precluded British violation of Thai sovereignty unless and until the Japanese attacked. By the time they had done so it was too late to defend Malaya by launching a pre-emptive strike across the border, and the dithering over the question of respect for Thai neutrality hampered the planners and commanders in Singapore. Allied preparations for operations along the border were not well advanced, and the Japanese soon crossed in two columns, advancing down both the east and west coasts of the Malayan peninsula. The inadequate British–Indian forces which stood in their way were soon brushed aside or by-passed.

The fundamental problem in the defence of Malaya involved local air superiority, or the lack of it. After the first day, the Japanese enjoyed the undisputed control of the air; there were only 161 front-line aircraft available to the British at Singapore, and in a single day's action on

8 December one-third of these were rendered unfit for operational use. In the first weeks of the campaign the Japanese XXV Army advanced more than 500 kilometres to the southern states of Johore and Malacca. The forces resisting them were poorly trained and often ill led, and in the case of the 8th Division this weakness existed right at the top. Gordon Bennett proved quarrelsome and uncooperative with his British superior, General A. E. Percival, and his battlefield performance fell well short of his own boastful declarations. Such successes as Australian arms enjoyed, at Gemas on 14–15 January or at Muar four days later, were local victories which merely delayed the Japanese and which were owed to the determination of the battalions involved and the tactical skills of their commanders. The retreat down the Malayan peninsula was a dispiriting, even frightening, affair for those involved. The Japanese manoeuvred almost at will and units found themselves outflanked and cut off with bewildering frequency. In the retreat from Parit via Parit Sulong, units of the Japanese Guards Division got behind the retreating Australians and Indians who, at Bennett's insistence, had not prepared lines of retreat in advance. The able-bodied infiltrated the Japanese road blocks by swimming and wading through the surrounding swamps, but the wounded had to be left behind, and were bayoneted or shot by the advancing Japanese soon after.

As a result of deliberations at the Anglo-American Arcadia Conference in Washington, a new theatre command was created in Southeast Asia even as it was falling to the Japanese advance. Dubbed ABDA – American–British–Dutch–Australian – it took in all the territory from Formosa to northern Australia, including New Guinea, with its western boundary on the Indo-Burmese border. It owed much to American views since it unified command under a single officer, rather than allowing the three services to run their own shows as was the British practice. General Sir Archibald Wavell, recently relieved by Churchill from his command in North Africa, was appointed Commander-in-Chief on 29 December and assumed responsibility almost at once. His directive spoke of defending the 'Malay barrier', but by the beginning of 1942 parts of this were in Japanese hands already, and by the time ABDA was dissolved in February, following the fall of Singapore, virtually the whole area other than Australia had been conceded to the enemy.

On 31 January the Johore Causeway was blown, ineffectually, and the final agony of the Malayan campaign began. The weakness in the Singapore defences lay in the absence of fixed defensive positions on its northern shore, facing Johore. The famous naval guns defending Singapore harbour were not fixed out to sea, contrary to popular belief, but were capable of traversing through 360 degrees. However, they were almost entirely supplied with heavy armour-piercing ammunition for

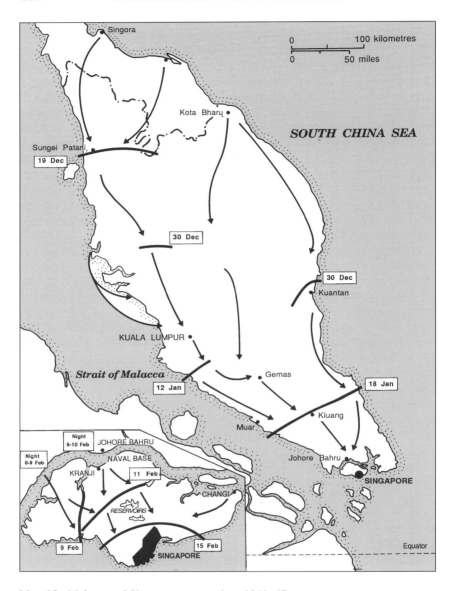

Map 12   Malaya and Singapore campaign, 1941–42

use against enemy ships, and this was of much less use against ground forces (although the impact of their shells was frightening nonetheless, as Japanese accounts attest). Being naval guns, they also had a flat trajectory. The defenders on Singapore numbered over 80 000, but not all were front-line troops and not all of the latter were in good condition. Percival could deploy 266 field guns, seventeen Indian battalions, fourteen British, seven Australian, two Malay and two raised from local volunteers, mostly Europeans. Little use was made of the indigenous population, either in Singapore or Malaya generally. The Japanese commander, Yamashita, had three divisions with which to make the assault.

The Japanese placed thirteen battalions across the strait on the night of 8 February, and drove inland against sporadic resistance. Within two days one-third of the island was in Japanese hands, and panic broke out on the Singapore waterfront as civilians and some soldiers attempted to force their way aboard anything which floated. In a move whose rationale still mystifies, Army Headquarters in Melbourne landed nearly 2000 fresh recruits on Singapore as late as 24 January; they were largely untrained and served simply to fill out the bag of prisoners taken by the enemy. Some also behaved badly in the final hours before the surrender, forcing their way onto boats in the hope of escaping, and descending into bouts of looting, drunkenness and general indiscipline. Some British staff reports subsequently attempted to lay such behaviour entirely at the feet of the Australians, but we can be sure that such indiscipline as there was knew neither age nor nationality. Percival was a humane man and was concerned about the civilian population, which numbered about 1 million people. He was disinclined to follow Churchill's order that he stage a 'last man, last round' defence 'among the ruins of Singapore City'. Yamashita demanded the surrender of the garrison on 11 February. Fighting continued for a further three days until the defence was being conducted in a perimeter around the city itself. At midday on 15 February Percival acceded to the Japanese envoys' requests, and agreed to capitulation.

We now know that Yamashita's lines of supply were badly over-extended and that his men were tired and short of supplies. His per-emptory insistence upon immediate surrender was designed to disguise this fact from his opponents. In sixty-eight days his force of three divisions had conquered Malaya, and took 130 000 British and allied troops prisoner. The Japanese suffered 10 000 casualties in the campaign, evidence that they did not have it all their own way. About 8000 allied troops were killed in the defence of Malaya; 1789 Australians were killed in the campaign overall and a further 1306 wounded. The survivors of the 8th Division, 15 395 strong, went into a captivity the deprivations and brutality of which had little equal anywhere else during the Second World War. The shock of the fall of Singapore, cornerstone of imperial defence in the Far East for nearly twenty years, was immense.

Singapore was not the only disaster to befall allied arms in the early months of the Pacfic war. Hong Kong had fallen on Christmas Eve after a campaign lasting a matter of days. Two battalions of the 8th Division detached for duty at Rabaul and Ambon were overwhelmed in January, many of those captured after the surrender of these areas being murdered by their captors. The third battalion of this brigade, based in Timor, was defeated in February, although the 2/2 Independent Company continued the fight on Timor for months thereafter. The invasion of Java began on 1 March, and the Dutch command surrendered a week later. In Burma the Japanese advance was approaching Rangoon, while on 9 April the investment of American forces on Bataan began, an operation which brought victory in just four days. The final round in the Philippines, the surrender of Corregidor, occurred on 8 May after two assaulting battalions overwhelmed a garrison of 12 000 men following an intense three-week bombardment. On 19 February Darwin suffered its first, and most damaging, air raid.

As the allied theatre of war in the Far East collapsed, desperate attempts were made to stave off the inevitable. The most serious of these from Australia's point of view was the attempt by Britain to divert I Australian Corps, then en route from the Middle East, to prop up the defences of Burma and Java. In fact, a few units were landed in Java on 14–15 February and went into captivity a few weeks later. The old problem of control of Australian forces reasserted itself. Having diverted two transports to Batavia, Wavell wanted the 6th and 7th Divisions sent to Burma. Curtin, with the strong prompting of the CGS, Lieutenant General Vernon Sturdee, argued for the return of these two highly trained, equipped and experienced divisions, and for the 9th Division to be readied for departure from the Middle East also. The Australian government came under strong pressure from both London and Washington to agree to the diversion of the troop convoys, and on 20 February Churchill actually ordered the diversion of these formations to Rangoon without informing either his own War Cabinet or the Australian authorities.

Curtin reacted with anger and vigour, and Churchill was forced to back down on the issue. This perhaps was one of the unintended fruits of the deception over the Greek campaign, but the Australian government was strengthened in its stand by the attitude of the Chiefs of Staff. Sturdee, the only Australian officer of the three, declared that the return of experienced Australian formations was so important to the adequate defence of Australian territory that he would resign unless it was brought about, and in this he was backed by the CNS and CAS who stated that a decision of such fundamental importance to the country's war effort should be made by Australians, and agreed to back Sturdee

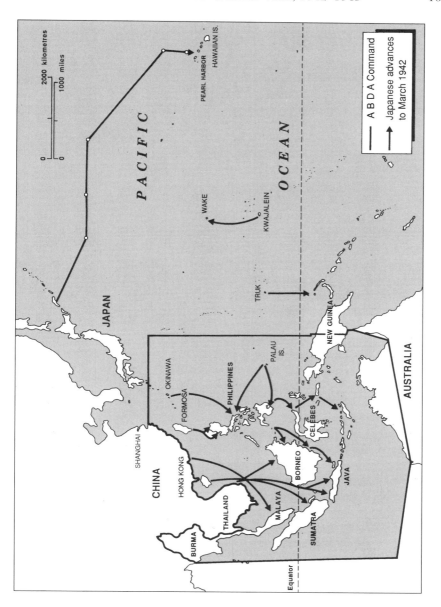

Map 13 Japanese advance in the Pacific to March 1942

whatever his view on the matter. In the event, and as a means of patch-
ing strained relations between London and Canberra, two brigades of
Australians were disembarked in Ceylon until the garrison there could
be reinforced by British units. Rangoon fell on 8 March.

Even as events turned for the worse in the Far East, decisions were
being made in Washington which, in the long term, would result in
the defeat of Japanese aggression. Newly appointed to the War Plans
Division of the War Department, Colonel Dwight Eisenhower recommended to General George Marshall in mid-December 1941 that Australia be developed as a base of operations from which to sustain and
support American efforts in the Philippines. This was followed by a
stream of memoranda organising the US Army Forces in Australia
(USAFIA) and setting up methods of cooperation between American
and allied forces in the South West Pacific. The decisions which flowed
from this were of enormous consequence for the defence of Australia,
although that was not a justification in American eyes. As early as
22 February Eisenhower predicted that 'circumstances are going to pull
us too strongly to the Australian area'. (The circumstances were the fall
of Singapore and the lack of an overall strategy in the South Pacific.
Eisenhower, an advocate of the 'beat Hitler first' strategy, favoured
concentration upon the European theatre.) The Chief of Naval
Operations, Admiral Ernest J. King, put the problem with characteristic
bluntness: Australia and New Zealand should not be allowed to fall to
the Japanese because they were 'white men's countries'. But agreement
over the responsibility for the Pacific area was decided between
Churchill, Roosevelt and their advisers and, although the Australian
government registered its preference for an American commander-in-
chief in the theatre, Roosevelt wrote to Churchill on 18 February that
'the US should take the primary responsibility for ... immediate
reinforcement and maintenance [of SWPA], using Australia as a base'.
On 9 March a proposal was forwarded to the Joint Chiefs of Staff for
the creation of the South West Pacific Area. As was becoming the
pattern in this war, the momentous decisions which affected Australia
were made elsewhere.

Tied up with the creation of SWPA was the appointment of a
commander-in-chief of the Australian army, since with the return of the
AIF the great majority of the available forces were now concentrated
in Australian territory, or the Anzac area as the Australian authorities
continued to think of it for some months. This necessitated the reorganisation of the Australian command structure. Pending Blamey's
return, Lieutenant General Sir John Lavarack, recently commanding I
Australian Corps, was to act as commander-in-chief. Until a supreme
commander was appointed by the Americans, the C-in-C would be

directly responsible to the government for the administration of the army and the exercise of the Defence Act; the Military Board of Administration would go into abeyance for the duration. The existing system of regional commands and bases would be replaced by field armies and lines of communication areas. The position of GOC-in-C Home Forces was abolished also. In Australia, the army at least was being placed on a war footing.

MacArthur arrived in Australia on 17 March to take command of SWPA, having been ordered to leave the Philippines by President Roosevelt. Six days later Blamey arrived in Fremantle, and was handed the letter from Curtin appointing him C-in-C of the Australian Military Forces. While he had been in transit from the Middle East, a number of younger general officers had discussed openly the desirability of retiring all officers over the age of fifty, and promoting young, fit and experienced replacements. This would have included Blamey and many officers of the rank of Major General and above. The so-called 'revolt of the generals' never amounted to anything, and indicated more about the factionalised state of the senior officer corps than anything else. Its targets were Lavarack, the acting Commander-in-Chief, whom some thought would be inclined to tell the politicians what they wanted to hear rather than what they needed to be told; and Gordon Bennett, trusted by virtually no-one after he abandoned his troops at the fall of Singapore and made an unauthorised return to Australia.

The months immediately following the fall of Singapore seemed to carry with them the direct threat of Japanese invasion of Australia. Air raids continued in the north and west, Darwin being hit repeatedly. Australia's forces were incapable of resisting a serious Japanese attempt at lodgement on the Australian mainland; the air force lacked modern aircraft, the navy was too small and unbalanced a force to resist the Imperial Japanese Navy on its own terms, and the army, though large and now with an admixture of experienced AIF formations, could not be moved around the country with any speed. The continuing lack of strategic road and rail networks, especially in the north and west, was another legacy of short-sighted planning in the 1920s and 1930s.

In fact, the Japanese did not intend to mount a direct invasion of Australia. Put simply, the Japanese did not possess the resources in manpower or material to mount such a complex military operation – the whole southern drive had been accomplished by just eleven divisions, and Australian commentators then and now tend to overlook the fact that most of the Japanese Army was committed in China and the home islands throughout the war. Conventional military wisdom dictates that an attacking force must outnumber its opponents by three to one when assaulting defended positions, and throughout the first half of 1942 the Australians enjoyed a numerical advantage along the south-eastern seaboard, which comprised the industrial and population heartland. (It may be objected that the allies had enjoyed numerical superiority at Singapore, but the Japanese understood that a people fighting for its own territory would be a more formidable proposition, and the Japanese forces had enjoyed a local numerical superiority when they launched their assault against Singapore's defences.) April–May saw the arrival of two American infantry divisions, the 41st and 32nd. National Guard formations, they required further training and re-equipping and would perform poorly in their first engagements in New Guinea, but they were the first components of the USAFIA which would grow to 120 000 by September 1943 and which would eventually see over 800 000 US personnel in the South West Pacific Area.

Exaggerated or not, the fear of invasion was real and led to some extraordinary steps, or at least to some extraordinary subsequent allegations. The most important of these concerned the 'Brisbane Line'. As GOC-in-C Home Forces, Mackay had proposed in early February that efforts be concentrated in the vital south-east of Australia. There was no suggestion that the rest of Australia would simply be abandoned, as was later alleged, and had the Japanese sought to establish lodgements at Darwin, Fremantle or Brisbane they would certainly have been resisted, though to what effect is another matter given the deficiencies in Australia's defences overall. It is not clear how far the government believed that invasion was imminent; Curtin seems to have overstated the dangers but this may have been a tactical device designed to jolt Australians out of their complacency, and perhaps also to boost Australia's importance in Washington and London in the hope of attracting more forces to the region. Certainly his famous newspaper article of 27 December 1941, in which he declared the necessity for Australia to 'look to America, free of any pangs as to our traditional links' with the British, might suggest this, but if so it had the opposite effect to that intended, causing considerable irritation in the White House. Equally, it is clear that plans existed for a 'scorched earth' withdrawal in the face of a Japanese invasion.

The Japanese decided in any case merely to isolate Australia through air and naval action and the seizure of New Caledonia, Fiji, and the Solomons. Landings were made in New Guinea also, which increased Australian fears of direct Japanese attack while presenting the enemy with the makings of a logistic dilemma, since prolonged simultaneous efforts in New Guinea against the Australians (later joined by the US Army) and in the Solomons against the US Navy were to prove beyond their capabilities. As noted, Australia had considerable attractions as a base for the American counter-attack against the perimeters of the

Japanese position in Southeast Asia, and Curtin fell in willingly with American plans for the Southwest Pacific Area. His acceptance of MacArthur as the supreme commander of all allied forces in the theatre represented a significant surrender of national sovereignty, made worse by MacArthur's personality and foibles. No Australian or Dutch officers were appointed to head the staff branches of his headquarters, and he made it clear to his subordinate American commanders that, upon arrival, they were to pay their respects to their Australian opposite numbers and then were to have nothing further to do with them. There was never any attempt to form a combined staff and, although Blamey was appointed commander of Allied Land Forces, practical steps taken by MacArthur meant that he exercised no command function over US ground forces. Not all his subordinates shared the Supreme Commander's contemptuous views of the Australians and, since the vast majority of his forces in 1942–43 were Australian and since it was they who would administer the first defeats to the Japanese in New Guinea, Curtin's absolute surrender of control of those forces is deserving of greater censure than it usually attracts.

The relationship between the Australian and American high commands in SWPA was a complex one. MacArthur dealt with Curtin and, by extension, the Australian government as an equal, much as he had dealt with the Philippines government. Regular consultations between the prime minister and the supreme commander were conducted in private, with Shedden in attendance to record the decisions made. The C-in-C of the Australian Military Forces and the government's principal military adviser, Blamey, was excluded, except when his opinion or advice was sought on matters affecting the Australian forces. MacArthur later expressed surprise at the celerity with which Curtin had ceded authority over the Australian military effort to him. He used his influence with the Australian prime minister in his arguments with his superiors in Washington over manpower and equipment priorities for his theatre. Curtin was happy to coordinate his own appeals to Washington with those of MacArthur, especially in the first years of his premiership, as a means of ensuring that London and Washington did not forget Australia's needs as they concentrated upon the defeat of Germany. It is not suggested that MacArthur used Curtin solely for his own ends, but by 1944–45 the benefits in the relationship flowed one way and there is some evidence that towards the end of his life Curtin regretted the degree of control which he had given MacArthur. It was his inexperience in military affairs in the face of the crisis in 1942, matched by that of his government, which had led to this unparalleled situation.

In April 1942 there were 46 000 men of the AIF back from the Middle East and a further 63 000 who had completed their training but not left Australia; to these may be added 280 000 militia and just 33 000 Americans from all services. For most of the rest of the war Australia's main military effort was to be concentrated in the Southwest Pacific, but the early blows against the Japanese were struck by forces of the US Navy's Pacific Area command, under Admiral Chester Nimitz. The inter-relationship between these two theatres, as between their commanders, is important in understanding American strategy for the prosecution of the Pacific war. MacArthur's repeated attempts to have all allied efforts against Japan placed under his command were resisted, successfully, by the Navy and the eventual decision to mount a two-pronged advance against Japan, from SWPA north to the Philippines and westwards across the Pacific by naval carrier task forces, owed much to the inability of Washington to impose one or other solution upon the two services, their theatres and their supreme commanders.

As part of the design to cut communications between Australia and the United States, the Japanese embarked upon the seizure of the southern Solomons and Port Moresby. Moves were afoot also to seize Midway Island in order to bring to battle the American carriers which had escaped the attack on Pearl Harbor. Japanese convoys embarked for Port Moresby from Rabaul on 4 May but were recalled following the carrier engagement in the Coral Sea on 7–8 May. This action was inconclusive in naval terms, but of great significance in stopping the troop convoys. The advance to Port Moresby was now to be overland from lodgements in the north and east of the island, while the Japanese fleet would force the issue at Midway. Unfortunately, the Americans had been reading some of the Japanese codes for months, and were ready for them. In another great carrier battle on 4–5 June the Japanese suffered a strategic defeat and lost four carriers and a heavy cruiser, as well as many aircraft and their highly trained crews. The US Navy would outbuild them and gradually outclass them for the rest of the war, while the planned assaults on New Caledonia, Fiji and Samoa were postponed, for ever as it transpired.

The first Japanese beachheads in New Guinea had been made at Lae and Salamaua in early March. New Guinea was important for the defence in depth which it added to enemy positions in the Netherlands East Indies, as well as for the great base area which the Japanese constructed at Rabaul and which the allies wisely chose never to assault directly. The early fighting in New Guinea was connected again with the campaign in the Solomons, with the Americans on Guadalcanal and the Australians in Papua fighting a mutually supporting campaign against an enemy who had over-reached himself and who was eventually defeated in detail. In May the Japanese began to move inland from Lae, and on 15 May Blamey sent reinforcements to Port Moresby, the first received there since the beginning of the year and which brought the garrison to two militia brigades along with some aircraft and artillery. MacArthur, still pleading for reinforcements from the United States, had been slow to move forces northwards to Buna on the coast where it was intended to establish a forward airfield. Japanese moves south now pre-empted this.

The Japanese landed in the Buna–Gona area on 21–22 July, and within a week had moved inland and seized Kokoda, forcing the Australian defenders there to retreat. The militia was reinforced by AIF units, but this was insufficient to stop the Japanese advance and the withdrawal towards Port Moresby continued. An attempt by the enemy to hook round the Australian defences via Milne Bay in late August was defeated after heavy fighting, but the pressure against the defences along the Kokoda track was maintained. Conditions were appalling and the strain upon the men was enormous. Lieutenant Colonel Ralph Honner who commanded the 39th Battalion, a militia unit, on the Kokoda track at Isurava, wrote of his men that:

> Physically, the pathetically young warriors of the 39th were in poor shape. Worn out by strenuous fighting and exhausting movement, and weakened by lack of food and sleep and shelter, many of them had literally come to a standstill. Practically every day torrential rains fell all through the afternoon and night, cascading into their cheerless weapon-pits and soaking the clothes they wore – the only ones they had. In these they shivered through the long chill vigil of the lonely nights when they were required to stand awake and alert but still and silent.

In desperate circumstances and against heavy odds, the 39th Battalion checked the advancing Japanese through a measured if exacting withdrawal, until replaced by fresh units of the 2nd AIF hurried forward for the purpose. Their reward was to be disbanded later in the year and distributed as reinforcements among other units.

New Guinea Force, as it was now known, continued to receive reinforcements from Australia while MacArthur moved his headquarters from Melbourne to Brisbane to be nearer the fighting, and to keep a closer eye on the course of operations because the continuing enemy pressure in the area was causing alarm in both Washington and Canberra. MacArthur's low opinion of the Australians and his wildly inaccurate notions of the terrain and enemy strength, together with his fear that another losing battle might see him relieved of his command, led him to order Blamey forward to take command in Port Moresby on 23 September. Within days Blamey had relieved the local commander, Rowell, just when his troops had forced the Japanese to retreat and had removed the threat to Port Moresby. Rowell had been Blamey's chief of staff in Greece, and made no great secret of his contempt for his superior thereafter, but the incident was one more example of the extraordinary level of feuding and ill-will between senior Australian officers. There was fault on both sides, but the situation was exacerbated by MacArthur's insistence that Blamey go forward and by Curtin's meek acquiescence. This represented an opportunity missed, in that Rowell's successful operations might have provided the Australian government with a means of stressing Australia's contribution to the anti-Japanese struggle, before the Australian war effort was subsumed in the enormous US military machine. (Churchill had understood this imperative far better when he had pressed Montgomery for a British victory at Alamein before the Americans came in to 'run the war' in Europe.) Rowell was replaced by Lieutenant General 'Ned' Herring, another officer with experience in the Middle East who had been reorganising the defences of Darwin.

The performance of Australian generals in the Second World War is an important subject. The war produced no Monash, although arguably Blamey faced far greater tests at a higher level than his old chief had ever done. But Blamey's reputation was hopelessly compromised for many, both in the army and elsewhere. His record in Greece and his feuds with some of his subordinates were matters of public comment by 1945, while his allegedly Rabelaisian lifestyle and the imputation of scandal which surrounded his period as Police Commissioner in Victoria between the wars earned him many enemies. It should be added at once that, among his senior officers, he had many supporters also. Some of these subordinates were men of great accomplishment and integrity. Herring went on to be Chief Justice of Victoria. Major General J. E. S. Stevens, who commanded the 5th Division in New Guinea, was a senior public servant who reorganised the Postmaster-General's Department after the war. Lieutenant General Frank Berryman, Blamey's chief of staff, retired as a lieutenant general in 1954 and had been tipped widely (if incorrectly) to be CGS in succession to Sturdee had Labor won the 1949 election.

But the picture was uneven. Some believed that Lieutenant General Stan Savige retained his command of II Australian Corps simply because of his old friendship with Blamey which went back to the latter's troubled period as police commissioner. The sacking of Rowell in Papua, the relegation of Gordon Bennett after his ill-judged escape from Singapore, the feud with Lavarack in North Africa and the sidelining of Robertson in Australia until the last months of the war created and intensified bitterness and jealousies within the senior ranks of the army. Some of those who fell foul of Blamey were brilliant, if occasionally erratic, personalities. Arguably, their absence from senior commands made little difference to the prosecution of the war against the Japanese. The fighting in New Guinea posed enormous problems of logistic management, supply and reinforcement, but in some respects and for much of its duration it was a positional war of a kind well-suited to men who had first learned their trade on the Western Front. There was little requirement for the intuitive grasp of mobile warfare which fighting the Germans demanded. The nature of the terrain in New Guinea meant that operational command was invested often at brigade and battalion level, where tactical control was of the highest order and where the Australian Army could call on a growing number of talented young brigadiers like Dougherty, Chilton, Porter, Eather and Windeyer. Higher Australian command in New Guinea was competent, if at times rather pedestrian. There were periods in the campaign where this was not true, notably during the advance on Lae and Salamaua and in the fighting in the Ramu and Markham valleys. But rapid advances required air and amphibious support and this had to be obtained from the Americans, who of course never had enough of it anyway.

By November the Japanese had been pushed back along the Kokoda track and the Australians began to attack the enemy positions in the Buna–Gona area. American units of the 32nd Division took part in these operations, although General Robert L. Eichelberger, commanding the US I Corps, was uncertain of their ability to face the Japanese without further training, a view justified by events. The American units initially performed poorly at Buna, taking more than 500 casualties for little or no gain; the situation was turned around only when MacArthur sent Eichelberger himself forward to take command. Blamey was able to remind MacArthur of the disparaging remarks he had made about Australian performance earlier, which did not endear him any further to the Supreme Commander. The Japanese defences employed pill-boxes and numerous strong points which were resolutely defended, usually to the death. Casualties were high as the allies attacked again and again in the bitter fighting which continued until January 1943, when the survivors of the Japanese forces were evacuated by sea or broke out overland. Of the 20 000 enemy engaged in Papua, 13 000 were killed or died of disease; 2165 Australians were killed and 3533 wounded; the Americans suffered about 3000 casualties as well. In the same few months the 9th Division, which was still in Egypt, had suffered nearly 6000 casualties during the Alamein offensive. The wastage from battle casualties was exceeded by the inroads made by tropical disease, and the twin pressures which this placed upon manpower led Curtin to raise the issue of conscription for service beyond Australian territory. The 'two armies' policy did not pose serious problems at this stage of the war, since fighting in Papua was on Australian territory in any case.

Any militia unit in which three-quarters of the men volunteered became an AIF unit, and thus liable to service anywhere, but in February 1943 only 530 000 of a total enlistment of 820 000 were volunteers. There was some talk of merging the two forces, but the whole question of conscription for overseas service was likely to prove emotive within the ALP; Curtin himself had been a leading anti-conscriptionist in 1916–17. Legislation was passed successfully on 19 February, extending the areas in which the militia would be liable for service to the whole of SWPA but excluding the Philippines, western Java and northern Borneo.

Militarily, the new provisions were of little use and in the course of the war more than 200 000 men transferred from the CMF to the AIF in any case. Given the situation in which Australia found itself, few people seem to have objected to the extensions made; of 2791 applications for conscientious objector status to August 1944 only 636 were rejected. Curtin's motivation is less clear. It has been suggested that the move was at the behest of MacArthur, who cited the likely consequences in the US if Australia was perceived to be making less than an all-out effort when American conscripts were liable for service anywhere in the world, including Australia. Certainly the Hearst newspaper organisation tried to make this a domestic political issue in the United States. The move may have been made in response to shifts in the domestic political arena, for Australia went to the polls in August 1943 in the middle of the war and domestic politics continued very much in its peacetime manner, something which did not occur in Britain. On balance, both domestic politics and the obligations of alliance played a part in the decision. With memories of the 1916–17 referenda still fresh for many, it is unlikely that a conservative political leader could have forced the legislation through without immense disruption on the home front.

From late 1942 until the end of the war the Australian government faced serious manpower pressures of a kind which would not be ameliorated by the extension of conscription alone. Australia's manufacturing and agricultural base was called upon to supply the needs of Australia's own forces, the Americans in SWPA, and the British home front which continued to rely upon foodstuffs from the empire. The army had been expanded rapidly in early 1942, and was too large to be maintained from Australia's manpower base. By October 1942 eight battalions had, like the 39th Battalion, been disbanded and eleven more were to be broken up. Curtin informed London that the 9th Division, still in North Africa, would have to be recalled. Reinforcements could no longer be supplied at the requisite rate and the formation would cease to function if not maintained. Because of the Alamein battles, however, the decision concerning its withdrawal was put off until after the offensive. On 29 October Curtin informed Churchill that the

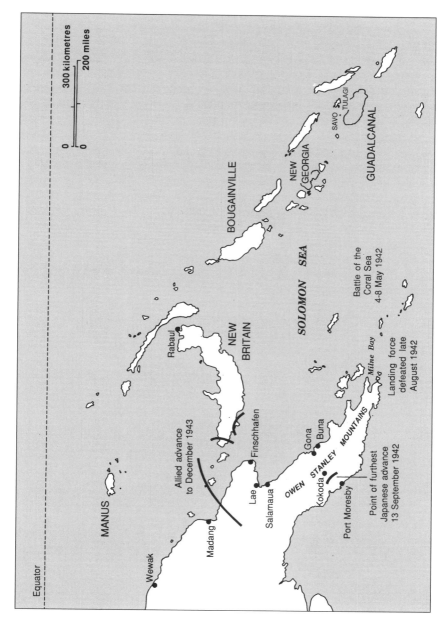

Map 14 Operations in Papua-New Guinea, 1942–43

Table 8.1 Transfer of CMF and AMF personnel to the AIF, 1939–45

Service	Number transferred to AIF
Permanent Military Forces	2 725
Citizen Military Forces	207 041
Australian Army Nursing Service	1 878
Australian Army Medical Women's Service	3 013
Total	214 657

Source: *Australian Year Book*, No. 37, 1946–47, and Gavin Long (ed.),
            Australia in the War of 1939–45, Canberra, 1952–77.

division was required in Australia and in serviceable condition, and although Roosevelt tried to intervene on Churchill's behalf, Curtin insisted and the 9th Division sailed in January 1943 to be retrained and re-equipped for jungle fighting in New Guinea. The 1st Armoured Division was broken up at the end of 1943, never having seen service overseas, while in May 1944 the strength of the Volunteer Defence Corps was cut substantially also.

The Australian government was occupied both with the problems of fighting the war, and with preparing for the peace. The ALP was concerned that there should be no return to the high unemployment and depressed economic conditions of the 1930s, and set up various government regulatory bodies to plan for and oversee a resumption of full peacetime production, even before the peace itself had arrived. In August 1944 it sought as well an extension of the wide-ranging powers which it exercised under the *National Security Act 1939* for five years after the end of hostilities; the matter was put to referendum and defeated comprehensively. A factor in its defeat was the general dissatisfaction with the controls and regulations imposed in the domestic sphere. There were many complaints, for example, about the severity of press and information censorship, which was more rigorous than its counterpart in Britain.

The war brought other changes to Australia. Large numbers of women entered the industrial and agricultural workforce for the first time, but they were paid less than their male counterparts and attracted the disapproval of moral crusaders, although not generally of the unions. Women were employed mostly in four classes of industry during the war: industrial metals and machines, textiles, clothing, and food and drink. The total number of women in factories rose from 147 282 in 1938–39 to 228 600 by June 1943; the number of those involved in direct war work went from about 1000 in 1939 to 74 000 by the outbreak of war with Japan, to more than 190 000 by mid-1943. The total number of women in the workforce and the women's branches of the services peaked at 849 000 in September 1943. To the need to ameliorate pressures on the workforce occasioned by the absence of men was added the attraction of cheap labour – commonly in Australia women received 54 per cent of the male wage.

The great influx of women into war industry came about as much as anything else because of the growth of that industry itself. Between 1939 and 1941 the number of government munitions factories had stayed nearly static, rising from five to just seven. By June 1942 it had increased to seventeen, and by the middle of the following year it had risen again, to thirty-two. A start had been made on developing a capacity to manufacture artillery shells, for example, before the war, but little more had been achieved. The inability of traditional suppliers overseas to meet Australia's needs, the failure of potential new suppliers such as Canada to direct production away from existing markets and towards Australia, and the need to supply the growing US forces in SWPA meant that Australian industry had to meet needs and demands never before experienced. The 25-pounder went into local production following a government decision in January 1940, and more than 1500 were manufactured here, including the not altogether successful variant, the 'short 25', developed for use in jungle terrain in New Guinea. Despite having no automobile industry before the war, Australia even produced a tank prototype, the Cruiser Mark I (AC I). With a crew of five, it weighed twenty-seven tons. Its armour was cast in one piece rather than milled because Australia lacked the necessary plant, and it was undergunned, being equipped with the 2-pounder. Perhaps fortunately it never saw action. A subsequent model, the Mark IV, mounted a 17 pounder, but by the time it went into production the Army had acquired all the tanks and tank replacements it would need for the remainder of the war. The great wartime success story of Australian design and manufacturing was the Owen submachine gun, adopted eventually over bitter opposition from the British, and some Australians, who wished to market the inferior Sten gun to the Australians.

The advent of women and partial demobilisation late in the war could not make up the shortfall in labour in all areas, and in certain restricted employment categories, such as the coal mines, there were strikes for higher wages and better conditions. There was industrial trouble in the transport industry also, partly through labour shortages and partly because the American services, in particular, attempted to circumvent peacetime industrial awards and restrictive practices. Although rationing was strict, there were few real hardships on the home front, and the level of real wages rose considerably in the course of the war. For Australia, unlike Britain or Canada, the great boost to manufacturing industry and the major influx of women into that industry which modern industrial warfare has provided in the twentieth century came in the Second World War, and not in 1914–18. Before the war, primary industry had been the major engine of economic growth; after 1945 and as a result of the changes wrought by the war, manufacturing industry occupied an increasingly prominent place. Gross domestic product grew from £1819 million in 1939 to £2842 million by 1945, an increase of 61 per cent at current prices. Much of the increase in the manufacturing sector came about through the growth in war industry, but even with the withdrawal of substantial numbers of men for military service in the first half of the war, employment in this sector rose by 25 per cent. Less easily quantifiable was the increase in skills levels among a broader section of the workforce which accompanied such expansion. In common with other belligerents, the federal government extended its regulatory powers in the course of the war, epitomised most readily by the increase in the size of the tax take enjoyed by the federal government and the ending of the right of the state governments to levy tax on income. The end of the war, the releasing of unmet consumer demand and Labor's commitment to full employment ensured that many of these gains were extended into the 1950s and 1960s.

The war had an important impact on another group – Aboriginal Australians. Some hundreds of Aborigines had served in the ranks of the AIF in the Great War, but the fact of their service had done them little good in helping to ameliorate their social, economic and political disadvantage in inter-war Australia. (No one knows for certain how many Aborigines served in either world war, because the services did not ask questions about Aboriginality on enlistment forms while recruiters simply ignored the prohibition on enlisting such men in any case.) From September 1939, young Aboriginal men again enlisted in the 2nd AIF; the best known of them, Reg Saunders, was commissioned in the field in 1944 and went on to serve in the postwar Army during the Korean War. More significant, perhaps, were the large numbers of men, and some women, who served in the Army within Australia or worked in the auxiliary services on Army farms or in transport and supply units. While less glamorous than active service, the involvement of indigenous people here was important. For one thing, they were paid in cash and not in kind (as on the pastoral leases in central and northern Australia), although admittedly at a lower rate than white servicemen received. For another, they received training in skills and responsibilities previously believed to be beyond their capacities by many whites. As one such service woman, the noted author Kath Walker, put it, 'the Army didn't give a bugger what colour you were, so long as you did your job'. While that view probably understates the individual and institutional racism which still existed in the services, and while genuine progress in Aboriginal affairs at the national level was still a generation away, the 1942–45 experience of many Aborigines was an important foretaste of what was possible.

The focus of Australian operations now shifted to the mandated territory of New Guinea, but further preparations were necessary before these could begin. Based on Wau, Australian forces maintained pressure against Japanese positions at Salamaua in order to divert the enemy's attention from the real objective of the coming operations, Lae. The operations in New Guinea were part of Cartwheel, an offensive orchestrated between MacArthur's forces and those of Admiral William F. Halsey's South Pacific theatre which was intended to bring about the reduction of Rabaul. In these operations, as later in the war, MacArthur coordinated air superiority and interdiction operations with amphibious landings and limited land campaigns with great skill, achievements which were spoiled by his graceless and egocentric unwillingness to share the credit with others.

MacArthur's eventual strategy in Cartwheel was similar to that of the US Navy in the central Pacific, to bypass strong enemy garrisons and land troops in lightly defended areas resulting in the neutralising of those garrisons and the minimising of allied casualties. Rabaul was too strong to be taken by ground assault and was to be neutralised in this manner, its air and naval units destroyed by preponderant allied forces. The Australians were involved in heavy combat in the Lae-Salamaua area and in the eight months' fighting which gained possession of the Huon peninsula, although now the Japanese disengaged and retreated before superior forces rather than waging the heavy attritional battles which they had fought at Buna. Lae fell relatively easily on 16 September, but the newly arrived 9th Division was involved in bloody fighting in its three-month advance along the northern coast from Finschhafen. Fighting for the Huon peninsula did not end until April the following year, and sizeable enemy forces escaped to the west to take up defensive positions around Aitape–Wewak. But the Japanese position in eastern New Guinea was broken and the great base at Rabaul had been isolated.

On 23 December 1943 Blamey had issued a directive which reorganised the Australian ground forces in recognition of the fact that their role increasingly was to be assumed by American formations. The three AIF divisions in I Australian Corps would return to the Atherton Tableland for retraining and refitting, while the three militia divisions in II Australian Corps would be allocated garrison and training duties in New Guinea and mainland Australia. MacArthur had undertaken to include Australian forces in the advance to the Philippines, a promise which he did not honour and which he probably had no intention of keeping. The problem for Australia in the last eighteen months of the Pacific war was not only that MacArthur's ego would not permit him to share the glory of the final defeat of Japan with others (and this included the US Navy as well as the British, Australians and Dutch), but that the enormous military might which had been mobilised by the United States made the contribution of small allies largely superfluous. In Australia's case, the economic contribution in the form of supplies and services was still significant, and pressure in this area led the government to begin partial demobilisation of the forces in 1944 to meet the demands of production.

The need to maintain an active role in the war was justified in terms of national interest, however. If Australia wished to have a say in the postwar settlement then it had to be perceived by the great power allies to be fully engaged right to the end. It was believed increasingly that the Pacific would be the arena in which Australian postwar interests were most vital, and the government concentrated its forces in the war against Japan accordingly. By the beginning of 1944 the overwhelming majority of Australian servicemen were in SWPA, but by the end of that year MacArthur's forces were in the Philippines and the war was passing out of SWPA. MacArthur now commanded some eighteen American divisions, six of which were tied to defensive roles on Bougainville, New Britain and at Aitape. Since it was now evident that former American territory was to be cleared of the Japanese by American troops only, and since the Australian government had earlier stated that it had a special interest in clearing its territories in New Guinea of the enemy, MacArthur proposed that these American formations be replaced by Australians. This was a means also of keeping the Australians out of the northwards drive to Japan, since he refused to countenance Blamey's proposal that the job be done with just six brigades and insisted on the deployment of four divisions. The 3rd Division and two independent brigades were detailed for Bougainville and the northern Solomons, the 5th Division was allotted New Britain, the 6th Division went to Aitape and the 8th Brigade was to operate between Madang and the Sepik River. This left just the 7th and 9th Divisions for other tasks which, it was finally decided, would involve the Australians in swinging away from the main axis of the allied advance, westward into the Netherlands East Indies, specifically against Borneo. In the last months of the Pacific war there would be six Australian divisions actively engaged with the enemy, a greater proportion than at any other time in the war. Conversely, it has been argued that these peripheral campaigns were unnecessary and wasteful in the lives of Australian soldiers, some of whom had fought right through the North African and SWPA campaigns. In addition, it has been suggested that the form which these campaigns took was entirely at Blamey's behest and for his own glorification.

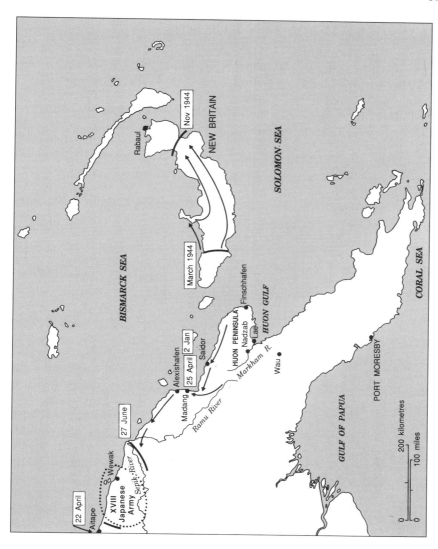

Map 15 Operations in Papua-New Guinea, 1944–45

There is no doubt that these final campaigns made no difference to the outcome of the war and did nothing to hasten the defeat of the Japanese. If that is the only yardstick applied, then indeed they were futile efforts. Against this must be weighed the very real considerations of national interest in the final settlement after the war, the desire of the government to be seen by the indigenous peoples to have restored the Australian imperium in New Guinea, and the compassionate arguments for freeing Australian prisoners of the Japanese as quickly as possible.

(The appalling fate of the men on the Sandakan death march only months before the end of the war highlights this very real concern.) Blamey's role is less clear-cut. In his view, offensive operations should be pursued where the likelihood of casualties was low, but where stiff enemy resistance was offered a 'holding' operation should be initiated. He pointed out that in the southern Philippines the Americans destroyed all Japanese resistance, whether it was in the path of the main advance or not. The operations on Bougainville and at Aitape cost nearly 1000 Australian dead, far too high a price for the negligible strategic advantage gained, and a result which flowed directly from Blamey's policy. But that policy had been given the blessing of both the Cabinet and the Advisory War Council, and if fault is to be found then it lies with the army's political masters and less with its military head. If Curtin and his ministers disagreed then it was concomitant upon them to insist upon a different plan and, if necessary, to impose one from above. They did not do so.

Each of the final campaigns was unrelated to the others as well as being of tenuous relevance to the great conflict to the north. On New Britain the Australians faced nearly 100 000 Japanese, while believing that there were only 38 000 there. Fortunately the local Japanese commander seems to have lacked the will to fight it out, and for a very small cost in casualties the smaller force contained the larger until the end of the war. On Bougainville the fighting against 40 000 Japanese was far heavier as terrain and the enemy conspired to drag this campaign out over seven months. On mainland New Guinea the Japanese XVIII Army was reduced from about 35 000 to just 13 500 survivors, suffering 9000 battle casualties and 14 000 dead from disease. The real question is not whether these campaigns should have been fought but how they should have been conducted. While some justification can be found for the Mandate campaigns, less can be said for the assault on Borneo which clearly was MacArthur's idea. The argument that possession of the oilfields would deny their use to the forces defending the Japanese home islands was spurious, since the American submarine campaign had throttled enemy seaborne trade throughout the Pacific and around Japan itself. The landings began on 1 May at Tarakan followed by assaults at Labuan and Brunei in June and at Balikpapan on 1 July. At Labuan 114 Australians were killed and 221 wounded; at Tarakan the losses were 235 dead and 669 wounded, while at Balikpapan they lost 229 killed and 634 wounded. These were the final engagements of Australian ground forces during the war.

The last stages of the Pacific war barely concerned Australia. The bloody fights for Iwo Jima and Okinawa convinced the Combined Chiefs of Staff that the assaults upon the home islands would incur enormous

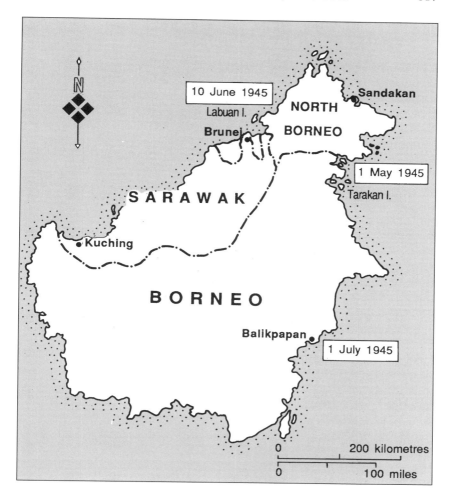

Map 16 Operations in Borneo, 1945

casualties. For this and other reasons the decision to drop the atomic
bombs was made, the existence of which came as a total surprise to most
Australians. On 2 September on board the USS *Missouri* in Tokyo Bay,
the Japanese signed the surrender terms. Blamey signed for Australia.
Throughout SWPA, small surrender ceremonies were conducted as the
remnants of the Japanese forces in what remained of the Greater East
Asian Co-Prosperity Sphere surrendered to Australian forces.

The impression may be taken from the preceding pages that Australia's role in the Pacific war was largely discharged by the army. In part

this was the case. Much of the fighting in SWPA was in New Guinea, where ground combat was decisive. It must be understood at once, however, that the success of ground forces in this war, whether in the Middle East, northwest Europe or SWPA, was dependent upon airpower and local air superiority. In the war against Japan the RAAF played a significant role in this process, but never as much more than an adjunct of the far greater US Far East Air Force. Its major role remained as an auxiliary to both the RAF and the USAAF; in the former case through participation in the Empire Air Training Scheme, in the latter because of poor leadership at the highest level and the willingness of the US command to allot it subsidiary roles – the deployment of the First Tactical Air Force to operations on Morotai from late 1944 being a case in point. The aerial resupply role was probably of greater significance, especially in New Guinea, but was far less glamorous.

Many of the problems in the air force were caused by divided command at the top. The feud between Air Vice-Marshals Jones and Bostock did considerable damage to the fighting efficiency of the service, but the real blame again lies with a government which permitted the situation to last for three years. A divided command is anathema to all sound military principles, and Jones' appointment as Chief of Air Staff and Bostock's as operational commander of RAAF Command should not have been persisted with. This disgraceful business was prolonged for two reasons: the difficulty in obtaining the services of qualified Australian airmen serving in Britain with the RAF, and MacArthur's refusal either to agree to the appointment of Jones in overall command or to approve two alternative appointments put forward by the government. This was as fine an example as any of the manner in which Curtin's administration surrendered questions of national sovereignty to the Supreme Commander.

The navy's performance was disappointing also. It lost a number of its newest and best ships to enemy action, and sank no German or Japanese surface warships, although it did account for an Italian light cruiser and a German raider. Much of the RAN's role was vital of course, in convoy escort, minesweeping, naval gunfire support and supply missions, but in terms of the role which had been assumed for the navy before the war, the results cast doubt upon the RAN's ability to meet the nation's defence needs. Like the air force, it spent the war subsumed within larger allied national formations, and this was poor preparation for an independent role in the postwar world, even if the second half of the war had seen it operating with the US Navy and thus exposed to influences other than those emanating from the Royal Navy. The Navy's influence on strategic policy during the war was marginal, and its profile almost invisible in public eyes. By the war's end, however, steps were being taken which would see the RAN develop a far stronger position in postwar defence policy than wartime outcomes might have suggested, not least in the acquisition and development of a carrier aviation capability.

One other group of Australians merits inclusion when we come to consider the impact of the greatest war in our history: prisoners of war. The greatest number were taken captive by the advancing Japanese forces in the first half of 1942, and their story is generally well known. The Pacific war possessed many of the features of a race war, and Western POWs were starved, beaten, worked to death and denied even rudimentary medical assistance by their captors in ways which have few parallels in modern war. Although it is often overlooked in Australia, similar treatment was meted out to the thousands of local labourers who were impressed into Japanese service on, for example, the Thai–Burma railway. Fully a third of those captured died in captivity. Much smaller numbers of Australians were POWs of the Germans and Italians, and although the lot of the prisoner is never jolly, the death rate of around 5 per cent indicates clearly the distinction to be drawn between those Australians captured in Europe and those held prisoner in the Pacific.

Table 8.2 Wartime defence expenditure, 1939–45 (£)

Area of expenditure	1939–40	1940–41	1941–42	1942–43	1943–44	1944–45
Defence Dept	237 000	335 000	363 000	250 000	323 000	179 000
Army	26 447 000	88 574 000	186 573 000	298 372 000	215 766 000	173 979 000
Navy	11 529 000	21 974 000	22 496 000	39 557 000	38 607 000	38 314 000
Air Force	11 622 000	31 976 000	57 750 000	107 274 000	128 189 000	120 026 000
Munitions	4 409 000	14 942 000	27 871 000	28 182 000	19 529 000	10 051 000
Aircraft Production	484 000	1 205 000	1 527 000	2 969 000	2 051 000	1 856 000
Supply & Shipping	200 000	1 064 000	2 274 000	9 958 000	7 438 000	8 575 000
Home Security	–	–(a)	737 000	1 997 000	254 000	70 000
Other(b)	787 000	10 759 000	21 115 000	26 931 000	66 486 000	77 964 000
Reciprocal Lend Lease	–	–	–	58 957 000	110 426 000	89 133 000

Source: *Australian Year Book*, No. 37, 1946–47, and Gavin Long (ed.), *Australia in the War of 1939–45*, Canberra, 1952–77.

(a)   Included under Defence Department.
(b)   Includes UNRRA, Prices Commission, Department of Labour and National Service, Department of Postwar Reconstruction, Department of Information, War Pensions etc.

Table 8.3 Casualties, 1939–45

Casualties	RAN	AMF	RAAF	All services
Killed in action, died of wounds	2 004	21 558	10 264	33 826
Prisoner of war	263	20 920	1 876	23 059
Wounded in action, etc.	579	177 049	3 236	180 864
Total	2 846	219 527	15 376	237 749

Source: *Australian Year Book*, No. 37, 1946–47, and Gavin Long (ed.), *Australia in the War of 1939–45*, Canberra, 1952–77.

Table 8.4 Battle casualties, by theatre, and non-battle casualties, 1939–45

Casualties	RAN	AMF	RAAF	All services
Battle casualties				
War against Germany				
Killed in action, died of wounds	876	3 539	5 116	9 531
Prisoner of war	26	7 055	1 459	8 540
Wounded in action, etc.	26	8 578	529	9 133
Total	928	19 172	7 104	27 204
War against Japan				
Killed in action, died of wounds	953	15 136	1 331	17 420
Prisoner of war	237	13 865	417	14 519
Wounded in action, etc.	553	13 275	253	14 081
Total	1 743	42 276	2 001	46 020
Non-battle casualties				
All theatres and Australia				
Killed	175	2 883	3 817	6 875
Injured	–	155 196	2 454	157 650
Total	175	158 079	6 271	164 525

Source: *Australian Year Book*, No. 37, 1946–47, and Gavin Long (ed.), *Australia in the War of 1939–45*, Canberra, 1952–77.

After the war the ex-POW associations attempted to convince successive governments that the sheer bastardry visited upon them by their captors had permanently undermined the health of many, to no avail. Edward 'Weary' Dunlop, a former medical officer in Changi and on the railway and later a celebrated public figure (arguably the best known Australian ex-serviceman alive after the publication of his wartime diaries in the mid-1980s), spent many years trying to persuade the Repatriation authorities to conduct systematic surveys of mortality and morbidity among former POWs, without success, but it is clear from such studies as have been done that the period of Japanese captivity, with its attendant physical stress and debilitating diseases, had aged the men affected far more than their cohort at large in the population. They died earlier and in greater numbers, and their experience remains for some at least the single greatest remaining impediment to genuine forgiveness between the two sides.

The Second World War wrought great changes in Australian society. The participation of women in war industry and on the land, the short-term impact of thousands of US service personnel upon a country which until that time had been narrowly British and provincial in its outlook, the early shock of defeat and the fear of invasion, cannot be quantified. Economically, Australia did well from the war as a whole and from the Lend-Lease scheme in particular, far better than any European belligerent. Australian reciprocal aid to America totalled one-quarter of the country's war expenditure in the last two years of the war. Whereas it received 3.3 per cent of total Lend-Lease aid, Australia provided 13 per cent of total reverse Lend-Lease. Unemployment fell significantly in the course of the conflict and manufacturing industry received a boost. Perhaps of greatest long-term effect was the fall in the nation's overseas indebtedness, not least to Britain. Air raids in the north and the odd mini-submarine in Sydney harbour notwithstanding, the country was barely touched physically by one of the most destructive wars ever fought. Australia's fatal battle casualties were 33 826; 21 558 in the army, 10 264 in the RAAF and 2004 in the RAN. These compared with nearly 40 000 battle casualties for Canada and more than 397 000 for Britain. Indeed, it was a smaller total casualty figure from a larger population base than had been the case in the Great War twenty-five years previously.

Australia played a decisive role in only one theatre, the Middle East, where Australian divisions enabled the British to maintain their position against the Italians in two theatres simultaneously, the Greek and Syrian campaigns could not have been fought without them, and the quality of the 9th Division led Montgomery to give it a key role at Alamein. But participation in the Second World War brought with it a greater maturity in Australia's dealings with the rest of the world, as evidenced by the opening of diplomatic relations with many countries both during and after the war, the role played by Australian delegates in the great international conferences in 1944–45, and the tremendous programs of assisted immigration which began after the conclusion of hostilities. Above all else, the Second World War demonstrated both the pitfalls and the advantages of being a medium-sized ally in a war of great power blocs. It was a useful lesson, but not one from which Australians necessarily learnt anything of value.

CHAPTER 9

The Postwar Challenge, 1945–1955

The Second World War marked the most sustained military effort Australia had ever produced, one that proved impossible to maintain. As noted, the Australian government began demobilisation of the forces even before the end of the war, recognising that the country could not support the three services at their existing strengths and also meet the manpower needs of industry and agriculture. Much thought had been given to the needs of postwar reconstruction, again well before the conclusion of hostilities. John Dedman had been made Minister for Post-War Reconstruction in the Curtin ministry in 1945, and received the Defence portfolio in addition following the re-election of the Chifley government in 1946. The administrative and policy-making tensions which existed between the two areas were thus expressed in the person of a single minister, and senior officers subsequently noted that Dedman seemed far more interested in the task of building a postwar Australia than he was in defending it.

The Australian government faced three immediate problems in September 1945. The first, and most obvious, involved the demobilisation and repatriation of Australian servicemen scattered across the Southwest Pacific Area, in Britain, and in prison camps in Europe, Manchuria, Formosa and Japan itself. The second involved the provision of forces to take part in the occupation of Japan in concert with the Americans and other victorious allied powers. Finally, there was the need to decide on the form and type of the postwar forces, and the nature and needs of Australian defence in the aftermath of the war.

The size of the army had fallen by almost 100 000 during the last two years of the war, as a result of the decision to return men to the industrial workforce to cater for the needs of the civilian economy which was still supplying both Australia's forces and those of its allies in the

SWPA. There were still more than half a million men and women in uniform, however. The army fielded six divisions, the RAAF numbered fifty-three squadrons, and the RAN mustered nearly 40 000 all ranks in 1945. Demobilisation proceeded smoothly, and most service personnel had been returned to Australia by the middle of 1946, with the process completed by February 1947.

The general principles governing demobilisation had been agreed by the government in June 1944, with the maximum rate of dispersal set at 3000 per day because of the requirements of pre-discharge medical examinations. The order in which personnel received their discharge was decided on a points system, determined on the basis of length of service, marital status, and age. In contrast to the situation after the Great War, this worked efficiently and well, and by early 1947 the strength of the forces had fallen from 598 300 to just 60 133. The demand for labour meant that men returning to civilian life found jobs readily, even if at the price of forcing women out of the wartime workforce and back into the home. A range of sensible legislation, such as the Re-establishment and Employment Act which enabled ex-servicemen to obtain technical and professional qualifications, fulfilled for a later generation of soldiers the promises made to their fathers in 1914–18. There was no repetition of the callous neglect and ingratitude displayed towards the soldiers of the 1st AIF. This was just and fair, but it was also good politics, for there was also no repetition of the 'Red Flag riots' of 1919 or the openly subversive activities of the New Guard (although the clandestine 'secret armies' made a brief return until the defeat of Labor in 1949. The principal paramilitary body was The Association, and some of its leadership had links back to Campbell's New Guard organisation in the 1930s. Blamey was closely associated with it, but it is difficult to take it as seriously as its counterparts in the 1920s and 1930s because of the very different and generally more positive socio-economic climate after 1945). A mixture of economic buoyancy and full employment, and sensible policies ensured a smooth demobilisation of the large forces which Australia had put into the field.

As the armies disbanded, so many of their leaders also retired, not always voluntarily. Blamey's services were dispensed with in November 1945, against his wishes and in a manner calculated to add insult to a host of injuries, real or imagined. The decision was sparked by no particular incident. There were members of the Labor Party who detested him and, with Curtin dead and the war over, neither benefactor nor pressing need remained to protect his position and retain his services. He remained bitter at his treatment to the end of his life, and protested without avail at the sometimes shabby treatment of those of his senior officers identified as 'Blamey' men. He received the Field Marshal's baton in 1950 from the new prime minister, Menzies, just weeks before he died. Whatever the merits of the case, their behaviour did neither Chifley nor his government much credit.

The decisions made in 1946–47 on the shape of the postwar forces were of enormous significance, and influenced the course of military policy for nearly thirty years. Defence policy in the immediate aftermath of the war was predicated upon three suppositions: first, the security of the Pacific region rested primarily with the United States; second, Britain would continue to play a significant role in Southeast Asia, and third, the run-down of the forces in the inter-war period had been a mistake, the consequences of which had been demonstrated in 1942. Although the needs of postwar reconstruction were accorded a higher priority in fact, if not in rhetoric, both sides of politics endorsed the need for a strong defence capability in the post-1945 period.

The Chifley government instituted a five-year defence program in 1947, one determined as much by the directives of the Treasury as the advice of the Chiefs of Staff. In June 1945 the Treasury had forecast a figure of £60 million as the annual postwar defence vote, without any information concerning the size or needs of the postwar forces since these had not been decided. The Defence Committee met in late 1945 at the instruction of the prime minister to formulate a defence plan and indicate the likely level of expenditure. In late 1946 the committee recommended expenditure over a five-year period of more than £320 million, and set enlistment targets for the three services as follows: RAN, regulars 20 981, citizen force nil; RAAF, regulars 19 095, citizen force 388; army, regulars 33 641, citizen force 42 421. The government was also asked to confirm the new permanent establishments of the forces, particularly of the army, which was running on an 'interim' basis, and to approve a national service scheme to provide adequate reserves for the army and navy.

In the event, Chifley indicated that only £50 million would be allotted annually for defence needs, and directed that the Chiefs should re-submit their plans on this basis. He also made it clear that the Labor government would not entertain a national service scheme. This was a sensible decision at the time, although one taken as much for reasons of party ideology as anything else. Shortages of labour continued to be felt for some years after the war and manifested themselves in shortages in other areas, such as the provision of new housing. In this climate, a national service scheme would have been an unnecessary drain on man-power. Such schemes are expensive, and would have entailed a greater proportion of the defence vote being allocated to the army, which would be the only service to benefit from such a scheme. At a time when the RAN, in particular, was looking to large-scale procurement of new capital ships, specifically two fleet carriers, this would have been hard to justify. Finally, so soon after the end of the war, it must be wondered whether there would have been much enthusiasm for such a proposal among the public at large. The national service scheme in Britain was maintained intact after 1945, and the army there quickly came under great pressure in parliament to reduce the scheme, and even to abolish it altogether, although public support for it remained fairly consistent until the mid-1950s.

The transition from war to peacetime conditions saw the reintroduction of certain pre-war organisational features. For the army, perhaps the most important of these was the reinstitution of the Military Board of Administration and the organisation of commands and military districts in March 1946. The revised postwar plans for the forces were presented to the government in March 1947, and released later that year. As the army plan noted, the forces were designed 'for participation in Empire defence and regional security', to 'cover requirements for local defence of the mainland of Australia and for a possible future commitment under the United Nations Organisation'. It pointed to the need to be able to field forces 'unhampered by the dislocation and inefficiency which result from a major reorganisation on the outbreak of war'. And if that was not a sufficiently broad criticism of the nature of pre-war defence planning, Lieutenant General S. F. Rowell, now Vice-Chief of the General Staff, made such criticism explicit. 'The peace time . . . organisation of 1939 and earlier years', he wrote:

> affords no real basis for consideration of what is needed today. It was based on a conception of local defence against raids on, or invasion of, our own country and carried no commitment, expressed or implied, in a wider strategical sphere. Even for its limited outlook, it was woefully inadequate for its primary task as events were subsequently to prove.

There was to be no question of resurrecting the minimal defence forces maintained between 1919 and 1939, and neither would there be a repetition of the frustrated and stalled careers experienced by regular officers in the 1920s and 1930s.

By the end of the first five-year period, it was intended that the RAN should have a fleet of two light fleet carriers, two cruisers, six destroyers and sixteen other vessels in commission, with a further fifty-two in reserve. The RAAF aimed for a strength of sixteen squadrons, four of them manned by the Citizen Air Force. The army was to field a regular force of 19 000 organised into a regular brigade group of three infantry battalions plus an armoured element, and a CMF, reformed in 1948, of 50 000 organised into two divisions and other units. In contrast to all previous practice, the CMF was to exist alongside a regular force which would be capable of providing a 'ready reaction' capability – a first line of defence. A token of this change was the creation in 1948 of the Australian Regiment of three battalions, the first time in the history of the army in which there had been regular infantry units.

In mid-1949 the government raised the total financial provision of the five-year scheme from £250 million to £295 million, but the additional funding did not overcome the basic problem which faced the services. These were unable to meet their manpower targets, and the government consistently refused to allow them to improve rates of pay and conditions of service which might have made the services a more attractive option in a time of full employment. The army's targets of 19 000 regulars and 50 000 in the CMF fell short by 4000 and 27 000 respectively in 1949–50, while the navy took several ships out of commission and the air force employed 2000 civilians temporarily in service vacancies. The hollowness of the rapid deployment capability was demonstrated by the revelation to the parliament in 1949 that of the 3000 infantrymen planned for the regular brigade, which was to be the nucleus of the army in the event of war, only 1000 existed. As the outbreak of the Korean War was soon to demonstrate, this meant that Australia's entire field force capacity effectively stood at just one battalion.

The major overseas commitment of forces in the immediate aftermath of the Second World War was to the British Commonwealth Occupation Force in Japan. The Pacific war had been fought and won largely by the Americans, with little assistance from the British in any theatre other than Burma. The British were anxious to stake a claim in the postwar settlement in the Far East, in terms of regaining lost colonies such as Malaya and in re-establishing their pre-war economic penetration of the region, not least in Japan, with whom they had enjoyed an extensive trading relationship. To this end, the British raised with the other dominions the desirability of fielding a force for the occupation of Japan alongside the Americans.

The Australian government felt that Australia had not been afforded sufficient recognition for the part it had played as a significant co-belligerent against the Japanese, and was not inclined to agree to participation in a Commonwealth force which would be commanded and run by the British. Accordingly, it proposed sending a separate Australian force independently of the rest of the Commonwealth, to be answerable only to General MacArthur and the Australian government. Whether this would have worked in practice is not clear, and fortunately was not put to the test. The British prime minister, Clement Attlee, understood the problems posed by having two forces from the Commonwealth side by side in Japan, especially in terms of the weakening of prestige and influence with the Americans, and agreed that the command of the force should be exercised by an Australian. The officer chosen was Lieutenant General Sir John Northcott.

Northcott had been Chief of the General Staff for much of the war, and had missed out on an active command as a result. When the question of selecting a commander for the force came up in September 1945, Lieutenant General Vernon Sturdee agreed to resume the post of CGS, which he had held in 1940–42, on the condition that Northcott should be appointed Commander-in-Chief, BCOF. Agreement to the force was duly gained from the Americans, and Northcott was appointed in mid-October. The Canadians were not interested in participating, and BCOF comprised a British–Indian division of two brigades, the Australian 34th Infantry Brigade, and the New Zealand 9th Infantry Brigade, formed from units of the 2nd New Zealand Expeditionary Force in Italy. There was also a British Commonwealth Air Component, commanded by an officer of the Royal Air Force.

As virtual viceroy of occupied Japan, MacArthur insisted that the Commonwealth force operate on his terms, and discussions with Northcott produced the Northcott–MacArthur agreement signed in Tokyo in December 1945. This ensured that the force would not be broken up and distributed in small packets all over Japan, and gave BCOF responsibility for Hiroshima prefecture in the west of the main island, Honshu. Military government responsibilities were to be carried out by US agencies, and the force would operate under the overall command of the US Eighth Army and the US Fifth Air Force. This raised questions of sovereignty and national command of forces, and did not please the British or Indian representatives on the Joint Chiefs of Staff in Australia (JCOSA). This latter body was an attempt to replicate the Joint Chiefs of Staff organisation which had run the Anglo-American war effort. It was not a success, partly because the functions of its members had not been spelt out, more because JCOSA was operated through the Australian Department of Defence, an arrangement which the British Chiefs of Staff refused to accept. A formal directive was not ratified until August 1947, by which time the British had withdrawn their brigade and sent it to Malaya and the Indians had withdrawn their forces following independence and partition. The committee was dissolved accordingly in October. While New Zealand maintained its forces in Japan the New Zealand representative sat by invitation on the Australian Defence Committee whenever matters relating to BCOF were discussed.

The main Australian component of the force was the 34th Infantry Brigade. The brigade comprised three infantry battalions, numbered 65th, 66th and 67th, which were concentrated on Morotai at the end of the war. The battalions were made up of volunteers from the 6th, 7th and 9th Divisions of the AIF respectively, all of whom enlisted in the Interim Army specifically for duty in Japan. The delays in negotiating a basis for the operation of the force led to discontent which blossomed into outright disobedience of lawful authority in January 1946. This was quickly and intelligently dealt with by the commanders present, and in February the brigade sailed finally for Japan, more than six months after the surrender of the Japanese.

BCOF subsequently expanded its area of responsibility to include the island of Shikoku, as well as the five western prefectures of Honshu, an area of 7500 square kilometres. At its height it numbered around 40 000 men, 11 500 of them Australians. There was no resistance on the part of the Japanese, and the duties of the occupation force consisted of disarming such Japanese forces as remained, the demilitarisation of depots and military establishments, and reconstruction of a devastated country. Much of the economic and political reconstruction of the country was conducted by the Americans who, under MacArthur, were much more sympathetic to their defeated enemy than were the Australians. The British and Indians withdrew their forces in the course of 1947, and the 65th and 66th battalions were returned to Australia in 1948. The New Zealanders also withdrew in that year, and BCOF's area of responsibility contracted until it once again centred on Hiroshima prefecture and one district of neighbouring Yamaguchi.

After the initial period of consolidation, conditions were anything but rigorous and one of the biggest problems in later years was to combat the inevitable boredom experienced by troops on long-term occupation duties. Greater challenges were posed at the level of the Commander-in-Chief. Northcott was succeeded in mid-1946 by Lieutenant General H. C. H. Robertson, who was destined to remain in command until late 1951. Robertson placed the force on a sound administrative and logistic footing, although he did not get on well with some of his British officers because of personality clashes and the attempts of some senior British figures, civilian as well as military, to undermine his authority. He did enjoy good relations with MacArthur and the Americans, however, and, in the context of the occupation, this probably was more important.

By the beginning of 1950, the Australian armed forces were run-down, under-trained, and still largely equipped from Second World War stockpiles. They certainly did not possess any great operational capacity. Attempts at developing a carrier force, a mobile army field force, and long-range air capabilities were in hand, but none had yet been realised. The three battalions of the newly designated Royal Australian Regiment could field only one battalion between them, and even this was in doubt because the government refused to change the terms of the Defence

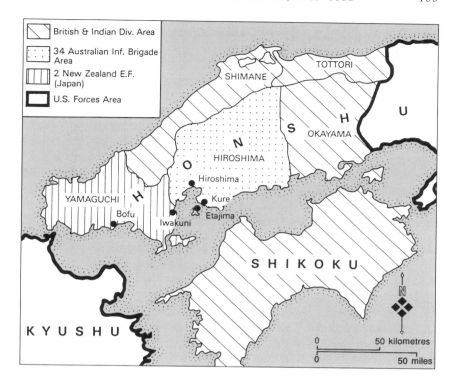

Map 17   British Commonwealth Occupation Force area, Japan, 1946–48

Act, which required that soldiers volunteer specifically for duty outside Australia. The change of government in the elections of December 1949 had made little immediate difference to this state of affairs.

Domestically, the forces had little impact in the early postwar period. As is often the case in the aftermath of major wars, people were more interested in resuming interrupted lives and defence issues, never accorded a high profile in peacetime Australia, were relegated even further to the peripheries of public consciousness. The single exception to this was during the coal strike in 1949, and it affected the army. Communist militants within the miners' union in New South Wales and Queensland took the miners out on strike in mid-1949. The state and federal governments stood firm against the strikers, and in July the Minister for the Army instructed the acting CGS, Rowell, to move troops into the mines to maintain production. As Rowell later recalled, 'there is no magic in the process of open-cut mining, least of all to a corps like the Royal Australian Engineers, skilled in the use of explosives and in handling heavy earthmoving equipment'. The strike was broken in August, not simply because troops had been sent into the mines, although this undoubtedly contributed. Of at least equal importance was the decision of the railways unions to ship coal mined by the army, thus effectively isolating the miners within the trade union movement.

The actual involvement of the troops was relatively uneventful. The larger questions thrown up by the use of troops in strikes and non-violent civil disputes is a different matter, and not one much considered by Australian commentators then or subsequently. Like most military personnel in British-pattern armies, Rowell considered the duty 'a distasteful task'. The Labor government lost the federal election of 1949 due to the maintenance of wartime controls and rationing and the furore over attempted bank nationalisation and not, as is sometimes charged, because it had sent troops against the strikers.

The advent of a Liberal–Country Party coalition government brought a number of changes to defence organisation and, perhaps more significantly, coincided with a period of active military involvement which was to last for some twenty years. On 1 July 1950 the five-year defence program was replaced by a three-year program. The clear onset of the Cold War also led to a revision of the assumptions on which defence thinking was predicated. An 'adequate' Australian contribution to the Cold War was seen as essential to our relations with our allies, and to the allied 'strategic starting point', should a general or world war break out. In practice, in the early 1950s this meant a commitment to the Korean War and the Emergency in Malaya. If a global war broke out, it was recognised that 'no one country could win without the co-operation of all the others', and Australia's role in allied strategy should be recognised and planned for in advance. Finally, it was believed that the security of mainland Australia depended upon control of sea and air communications in the Indian and Pacific oceans. All of this was further influenced by a belief that the time available for mobilisation would be very short, and that as a result 'the degree to which the armed forces were prepared in advance of events must be much greater than had been found necessary in the past'.

As a major part of this preparedness, the government embarked on a national service scheme which became law in March 1951. All male British subjects were liable to call up at eighteen years of age, with the standard exemptions applying for members of religious orders, the mentally unfit, and conscientious objectors. Service was with the Citizen Military Forces, the Citizen Air Force, or the Citizen Naval Forces, but inevitably the vast majority of national servicemen saw service with the CMF both because of the greater numbers required, and because the conditions of the Defence Act continued to apply and only those who volunteered for general service outside Australia were eligible for the CNF and CAF. The total period of obligation was 176 days, or about six months. In the army, this took the form of ninety-eight days' initial continuous training, with fourteen days' full-time camp training and twelve days' part-time training in each of the succeeding three years. For the navy it was 124 days' continuous training and thirteen days' continuous training in each of the following four years, while the air force required the entire 176 days in one continuous period.

Between March 1951 and June 1952, 34 500 young men had been called up, with a further 12 000 scheduled for call-up in the second half of 1952 and 36 000 planned for 1953. This was from a male population of military age (i.e. between eighteen and twenty-six) estimated at around 520 000. All male British subjects normally resident in Australia were eligible for call-up on turning eighteen, and were required to register. The provisions for deferment, as opposed to exemption, were generous, and the provisions for both were widened considerably in the later years of the scheme. The truth was that this level of compulsory induction was almost more than the military system could cope with. National service required the diversion of facilities, equipment and, most important, trained personnel to act as instructors and administrative staff at a time when the services were committed to fighting in Korea and, from 1955, Malaya, and the higher regular personnel establishments approved by the government had yet to be met. One consequence of this manpower squeeze was the re-establishment of the Women's Royal Australian Army Corps in November 1950.

The women's services had been abolished in the aftermath of the Second World War, and despite the manpower shortages there was resistance in the service hierarchies to their re-establishment. The Women's Royal Australian Naval Service was reconstituted as a peace-time service in 1951, but only after much argument arising from the findings of a report, prepared by the Director of Recruiting and Reserve Forces, which had recommended the recruitment of women into the peacetime RAN in March 1948. Even so, the WRANS in particular suffered from a lack of support within senior service circles, and remained a largely token force for the first decade of its existence. The army and the RAAF took a more positive attitude in general, the air force in particular defying government quotas on recruitment of women personnel. Nevertheless, the women's services remained the poor relations of the defence establishment: by 1954 they comprised just 2 per cent of the strength of the RAN, 4 per cent of the army, and 5 per cent of the RAAF, and they were usually the first area to suffer cuts in personnel and finance in an era of tight defence budgets.

Servicewomen also suffered from discriminatory conditions of service which severely restricted the branches and musterings in which they could serve, and which required them to resign upon marriage (although this latter provision was in keeping with the provisions of the Public Service Act).

The national service scheme of the 1950s was of little military value, and drew away resources which might have been better used in keeping the army's one regular brigade at full strength. The inability to send army conscripts overseas on active service severely undercut the practical usefulness of the scheme, while the period of training involved scarcely equipped the men involved for active service without a period of further training. The scheme was popular with the general public, who endorsed it in the opinion polls with an approval rate of between 83 and 88 per cent. There was some scattered opposition amongst those actually liable for call-up, but this was numerically insignificant. The scheme was least popular with the services. In 1955 the period of obligation for the CMF was reduced to 140 days, and to 154 days in the other two services, while in 1957 the annual intake was reduced to just 12 000 and service in the navy and air force was discontinued. The scheme was suspended altogether in 1959. With its suspension ended what might justifiably be described as the last golden age of citizen soldiering in Australia.

For the RAN the decade after 1945 was one of growth and renewal. One of the major lessons of the naval war in the Pacific had been the supersession of the capital ship by carrier-based aviation, and in the early postwar years the Navy embarked upon an ambitious program to acquire two light fleet carriers of the Majestic class from British sources, and to develop a Fleet Air Arm. This was a very resource-intense process, with hindsight one which was probably beyond the RAN's capabilities given the budgetary climate of the time, and in fact the RAN was to sacrifice a number of existing ships and functions in order to maintain the carriers and their air groups. The five year program for the navy approved in June 1947 had set aside £23.4 million for naval aviation from a total outlay of £75 million, with £12 million earmarked for the acquisition of the carriers and their aircraft under highly favourable terms from the British. The Fleet Air Arm was established in August 1948 and the first carrier, *Sydney*, was commissioned at the end of that year. Construction of the second and more modern carrier, *Melbourne*, was delayed and it did not arrive in Australia until 1956. In the interim the British lent HMS *Vengeance* in order that the RAN might consolidate the training and experience which it had begun to acquire. Without the assistance of the Royal Navy, in the form of training, personnel exchanges and equipment, it would have been vastly more difficult for the RAN to develop a maritime aviation capability. *Melbourne* was modernised while under construction, and was thus able to operate jet aircraft, but the funds were not available to do the same for *Sydney* and it was relegated to a training role in 1954 and then paid off in 1958. By the time *Melbourne* joined the fleet, neither carrier was capable of front-line operations, and the RAN was forced to accept, reluctantly, that their primary role would be trade protection.

While these efforts to secure the defence of the Australian homeland proceeded apace, the armed forces were involved in live wars in other parts of Asia, very much as part of the government's concern to con-tribute adequately to the Western effort in the Cold War. This entailed commitments to Malaya and Korea, and later still to the Middle East, although the latter proved short lived and is more important in signifying virtually the last occasion in which Australian forces played a role in defending the Suez Canal zone and imperial communications.

In early 1950 a new Australian government had settled into office and had identified a need to adjust its military commitments overseas. In March that year the decision was taken to withdraw the forces remaining on occupation duty in Japan, both because it was felt that there was nothing gained by keeping them there and because of the anticipated demands of the national service scheme, which would come into force the following year. Under the terms of the Northcott–MacArthur agreement, the Australian government had to give six months' notice of intention to withdraw, which was duly given, but the run-down of the force commenced in May with soldiers of the Interim Army being the first to be shipped home.

In April the British government requested direct Australian assistance in Malaya, where communist insurgency had led to the declaration of a State of Emergency in 1948. Specifically, the British asked for aircraft and aircrew and couched their request in terms of providing assistance in the whole of the Far East theatre, since there was some apprehen-sion that the newly triumphant communists in mainland China might attempt an assault on Hong Kong. In May Menzies announced that a transport squadron of Dakotas and a small squadron of four-engined Lincoln bombers would be sent to Malaya to form a composite Australian wing within Far East Air Force. The British had wanted to incorporate each squadron into an RAF wing but the Chief of the Air Staff, Air Marshal Sir George Jones, insisted that the squadrons be grouped together and commanded by an Australian senior officer.

Menzies also offered to send a team of Australian officers to advise the British on jungle warfare techniques, and to gather information on the progress of the insurgency. Since the Australians' expertise had been gained fighting the Japanese in New Guinea, which was not exactly analogous to the situation pertaining in Malaya, and since the British had derived just as much knowledge in Burma, the rationale for this seems odd. Be that as it may, a relatively high-powered mission under Major General William Bridgeford was dispatched to Malaya in early June. The decision to send the squadrons having been taken, Bridgeford duly recommended that Australia might supply arms and ammunition to the British forces in Malaya, especially the Australian-designed Owen submachine gun which had proved its worth in jungle conditions. He also endorsed a further request for instructors in jungle fighting, and for the provision of a signals intelligence unit, both of which were sent in the course of the year. For the next five years the small army component would consist of this Australian Observers' Unit, while the Lincolns of No. 1 Bomber Squadron would furnish aerial support to British and Malayan ground forces. The Dakotas of No. 38 Transport Squadron were withdrawn in 1952 as a result of the shortage of service transport aircraft in Australia and Korea.

This tiny involvement in Malaya was quickly overshadowed by a larger and far bloodier commitment to the war in Korea which broke out on 25 June when the communist north invaded the south. The country had been divided into Russian and American spheres at the end of the Second World War, and the onset of the Cold War and the inability of either side to devise an acceptable arrangement for the independence and reunification of the country led to the defacto creation of two states whose political allegiances matched those of their occupiers. The Russian boycott of the United Nations Security Council during the crucial sessions which debated the situation in Korea led to the first armed intervention by a United Nations force in the cause of resisting aggression. Australia played a subsidiary part in these debates, but was one of the first member states to volunteer forces to the American-dominated United Nations Command (UNC) which was under the direction of General Douglas MacArthur, who was still running occupied Japan.

It was now that the deficiencies in Australia's postwar defence policy showed themselves clearly. There was no ready-reaction force available, just one half-strength battalion in Japan, under-trained, under-equipped and in no way ready for war. The sole remaining RAAF presence in Japan, No. 77 Fighter Squadron, went into action a few days after the outbreak of war and did vital work alongside its USAF counterparts in blunting the edge of the North Korean offensive, but on top of the commitment to Malaya the RAAF could do no more. The review of capabilities prompted a few weeks earlier by the discussions concerning Malaya meant that the RAN was in a position to identify quickly the units of the fleet which could be sent to Korean waters, and send them there.

None of this altered the fact that Australia could not put men on the ground when they were needed, in the crucial early days of the war when the South Koreans and Americans were pushed down the Korean peninsula by the armoured weight of the Korean People's Army (KPA). It was a poor return for five years of careful planning.

The withdrawal of BCOF was reversed, and drafts of reinforcements were dispatched to Japan to bring the 3rd Battalion, The Royal Australian Regiment (3 RAR), up to war establishment. This was accomplished by further reductions in the establishments of its two sister battalions in Australia, and by a special recruitment campaign for service in Korea, dubbed Kay-Force. By the end of September the battalion was in Korea after a complete refit and some very necessary unit training. It was brigaded with the two under-strength battalions of the British 27th Infantry Brigade, rushed to Korea from Hong Kong in August in response to the worsening tactical situation. This was a happy solution, since a battalion is not a self-sufficient force and service with a British brigade ensured that 3 RAR operated within a familiar tactical and administrative environment. Such would not have been the case had it been attached to an American formation, as happened to most other UN contributed units.

The Australian unit took part in the pursuit of the KPA across the 38th parallel and deep into North Korea. The 27th Brigade, now designated a Commonwealth brigade, was frequently in the van of advancing American divisions and saw action continuously as the enemy was pushed back closer to the Yalu River and the border with China. The advent of the Chinese into the war precipitated a long and debilitating retreat back down the length of the peninsula, with the UNC finally coming to a halt some distance south of the 38th parallel. The Commonwealth Brigade was used regularly as a rearguard for other units, and its battalions quickly became used to finding themselves in dangerous situations. They were among the last units to evacuate the northern capital, Pyongyang, and on a number of occasions were fired upon by retreating American and South Korean troops as discipline broke down and morale in those units slumped. The great advance north had seemed to herald an early end to the war; the great retreat which followed held the promise of a long war, and the potential for a world war should MacArthur widen it geographically to take in the homeland of the new belligerent, China.

MacArthur was sacked in April 1951, the same month that the Australian battalion fought its greatest action of the war. The battle of Kapyong matched the brigade against a Chinese division in a two-day action which helped to blunt the enemy's Fifth Phase Offensive and ensured that he would be unable to push the UNC back into a perimeter on the coast. The Commonwealth was now represented by two brigades in Korea, with a third from Canada on its way. The realisation that the fighting in Korea would be drawn out, together with pressure from the Americans to rationalise their commitment, led to the formation of an integrated Commonwealth division in July that year. Containing units from Britain, Canada, Australia, New Zealand and India, and with integrated staffs and headquarters and a Commonwealth base organisation behind it in Japan erected on the structure of BCOF, the Commonwealth division fought in the line as part of the US I Corps for the rest of the war. When the Australian government acceded to American pressure in October 1951 and announced an increase in its force to two battalions, Australians also gained command of the Commonwealth brigade in which they operated.

The decision to send a second infantry battalion to Korea further illustrated the straitened circumstances in which the Australian army found itself. In February 1951 the Americans had pressured all UN governments with forces in Korea to increase their commitments. Most declined to do so. The position facing Australia and New Zealand was somewhat different. Negotiations had commenced for a tripartite security treaty with the United States, and Australian officials were well aware that the response to American requests for higher troop levels might influence the course of negotiations. The Department of Defence argued against such an increase, on the grounds that the national service scheme required all available officers and NCOs and that a further increase in Korea would be at the expense of the planned expansion of the regular army at home to two brigades. Recruiting rates would not keep pace with casualties and other personnel wastage, either. The calling of a federal election in April allowed the Australian government to defer the decision, but in May it informed the Americans that the small size of Australia's forces and the range of commitments facing them meant that no increase could be made in Korea.

The matter was not allowed to rest. Public and official opinion in the US felt that the other parties to United Nations action were not doing enough on the ground, and commentators pointed to the disparity between the forces fielded only a few years previously and those provided currently. This was not altogether a valid comparison, since the threats posed in the Second World War were somewhat different from those currently faced, but the general feeling that allies must help themselves if they wish for support from others was not unreasonable, and was not lost on key figures in the Australian government and the Department of External Affairs. In August President Truman renewed pressure upon Australia for an increase in troop strengths, and this time the Cabinet acceded to the request in the interests of further cultivating

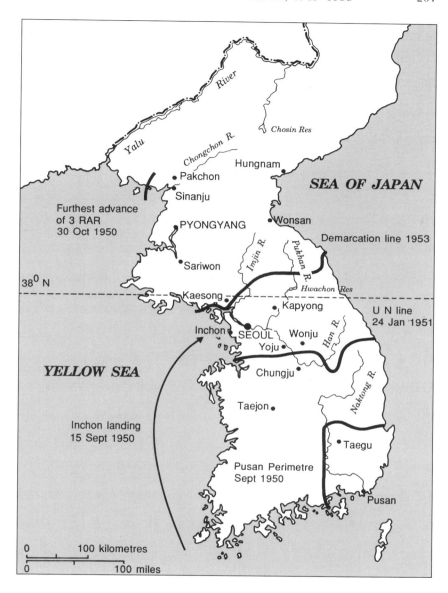

Map 18   Korean War, 1950–53

an alliance relationship with the Americans. Only by taking drafts from
2 RAR, recruiting in Britain, and deferring the planned expansion of
the Field Force was the army able to send 1 RAR to Korea, and then not

until March 1952. The commitment of two battalions was maintained until after the cease-fire in July 1953, with 1 RAR relieved on a unit basis by 2 RAR in March 1953, but the Australian army was now at the absolute limit of its capabilities.

While it was the army which took the vast majority of the casualties and bore the brunt of the fighting, the other services were heavily involved too. No. 77 Fighter Squadron had gone into action in the first days of the war, and had provided valuable support for the American and Korean ground forces in their desperate plight. The squadron's Mustangs were no match for the MiG-15 jet fighters with which the Russians re-equipped the North Korean and Chinese air forces, however, and the RAAF was faced with the problem of upgrading and replacing the aircraft or of withdrawing the squadron from operations. The obvious replacement was the new F86-A Sabre, but American production of this aircraft was fully absorbed by the needs of the US Air Force. The decision was made to purchase the British-made Meteor 8, by then an inferior aircraft developed in prototype during the Second World War. The squadron converted to the Meteor in April 1951, and thereafter was employed in an escort role, because the new aircraft were still inferior to the MiG.

Thirty-six were ordered in December 1950 at a cost of £2.5 million, with a further twenty-two in June the following year. The RAAF had already decided to equip its fighter squadrons with the British-designed though Australian-built Vampire aircraft, but production had not commenced. The British delayed the re-equipping with Meteors of one RAF squadron in Germany in order to meet the urgent demand from Australia. In the same month that the order was placed, the Australian government also resolved to discuss the production of the Sabre in Australia with the British government, since this would have implications for the Vampire production program already agreed to. Sabres were not produced in Australia in volume until 1955, but the question of aircraft procurement was to become an important theme in the postwar air force, especially in terms of the competition between British aircraft manufacturers and their American, and later French, competitors. To some extent the air force was unlucky in that it was caught by the Korean War in the middle of an evaluation and acquisition cycle involving the next generation of modern, high-performance jet aircraft. British generosity in providing the Meteor at short notice and at some inconvenience to their own acquisition process should be acknowledged, but it was nonetheless an expensive exercise for the RAAF, acquiring an aircraft which was already outclassed by its likely opponent and for which there existed no requirement in the RAAF's force structure plan.

Surface units of the RAN played an important but essentially low-key role in the naval operations in Korea. In particular, it was the first occasion on which the new naval aviation capability had been used in action. The second fleet carrier, *Melbourne*, had not yet been delivered, but *Sydney* was deployed in Korean waters as part of the increase in forces which followed on from Truman's request in June 1951. The major tasks of naval units were blockade and ship-to-shore bombardment, and the navies in Korea faced peculiar difficulties posed by the peninsular nature of their war. The greatest risks posed to them were from the forces of nature, since the area is noted for shifting tides, typhoons, storms and ice-bound waters, rather than from enemy fleets. The presence of strong naval forces in Korean waters prevented the enemy from making flanking naval and amphibious movements of the sort which MacArthur had mounted so spectacularly at Inchon, and supported South Korean forces engaged in gathering intelligence and in raiding. The RAN kept two ships on station during the war and, like the army, was fully extended by this modest commitment. The contrast with the capabilities during the Second World War is marked once again. Korea provided the navy with opportunities for active service experience which were not gained again until the Vietnam War in the following decade, and enabled the development and testing of techniques in naval aviation to the benefit of the service.

The services lost 339 killed in the Korean War, 1216 wounded and twenty-nine taken prisoner. The financial cost of war is difficult to gauge, since it depends so much upon the criteria used, but Australian participation is considered officially to have cost £47 763 000. Australian forces remained, in gradually reduced form, until 1956, and Australia remains committed to support the Republic of Korea should the North break the ceasefire agreement which has remained shakily in place for more than forty-five years. The benefits which accrued from involvement in the Korean War can be enumerated readily. The army developed the capacity to maintain two battalions on active service, although it did not long retain this ability after the end of the war. The RAN gained valuable operational experience in new techniques of naval aviation, while the air force refined the tactics of air power in the jet age. A generation of young officers in all three services gained their first operational experience in Korea, while links with the forces of the United States and the Commonwealth were strengthened at both operational and higher command levels.

Domestically, the war had a number of consequences. The price of wool soared, helping to fuel an already expanding economy. The nation's economic performance was further enhanced by the successful negotiation of a $250 million loan from the World Bank, the application

Table 9.1 Casualties, Korean War, 1950–53

Casualties	RAN	ARA(a)	RAAF	All services
Killed in action,				
died of wounds	2	276	28	306
Other deaths	3	17(b)	13	33
Wounded in action	6	1210(c)	n.a.	1216
Prisoner of war	–	23	6	29
Total	11	1526	47	1584

Source: Central Army Records Office, and Robert O'Neill, *Australia in the Korean War, 1950–1953: vol. 2: Combat Operations*, Canberra, 1985.
(a)   Australian Regular Army. 10 657 served in Korea between 1 August 1950 and 18 November 1955.
(b)   Includes 1 death while a POW.
(c)   Includes 36 wounded twice.

backed by the Truman administration in recognition of Australia's willingness to support American policy in the Asia-Pacific region and in the UN. Additionally, the loan was made without restrictions, so that the Australian government could devote the entire amount to the development of an industrial and manufacturing infrastructure. At the strategic level, the signing of the ANZUS Treaty in 1951 appeared to guarantee Australia's security and formalised the alliance relationship with the United States. Contrary to popular belief, the treaty was not given in gratitude for Australian support in Korea, although this influenced American attitudes, but in compensation for Australian and New Zealand agreement to the conclusion of a 'soft' peace treaty with the Japanese in 1952, the Treaty of San Francisco.

The Minister for External Affairs in the Labor government, Dr H. V. Evatt, had sought to bring about a security treaty with the United States after 1945, to no avail. His failure stemmed from a number of factors, not least an often objectionable personal manner which sat ill with the needs of patient diplomacy and negotiations. At the heart of the problem lay American reluctance to extend themselves further strategically through entangling alliances in far corners of the world. The US had fought to defend Australia against the Japanese because Australia was important to allied strategy in the Pacific. With the defeat of Japan Australia's strategic value declined, and the American refusal in 1946 to develop a base on Manus Island to Australia's northeast, as Evatt urged, reflected these altered circumstances.

By the early 1950s the strategic picture had changed again. The Americans sought support among Western nations as the Cold War deepened, and desired to rebuild Japan as a bulwark against communism on the Asian mainland. The thought of a revived Japan was an unpalatable one so soon after the end of the Pacific war, and not only in Australia. The new foreign minister, Percy Spender, took the lead in pushing the Americans for a security pact in the Southwest Pacific, inspired by Article 5 of the recent Atlantic Treaty which viewed an attack upon one signatory as an attack upon all. In doing so he acted without Menzies' support, since the prime minister believed that Australia was unlikely to gain such a treaty and did not need one anyway.

In the course of talks on the Japanese peace treaty in Canberra in February 1951 Spender pressed the American envoy, John Foster Dulles, on the question of a Pacific security pact. The Americans finally acquiesced, reluctantly, and the ANZUS Treaty was signed in September in San Francisco. The changed international climate together with his own ability enabled Spender to succeed where Evatt had failed, but the treaty nonetheless fell short of his desires in that it did not commit the US to underwriting Australian and New Zealand security. The language of the treaty was general, not specific, and there was no secretariat and no standing force as in Europe under NATO. Like NATO, however, ANZUS showed that membership of the American imperium often was both voluntary and sought after. Renewed American interest in the region was reflected further by the Radford–Collins Agreement signed between the Australian CNS and the US Commander-in-Chief, Pacific (CINCPAC) in 1951. This set out areas of responsibility between the Australian and American navies in the waters of the Australia, New Zealand and Malaya (ANZAM) area in the event of hostilities. Its precise dimensions remain classified still. It was a further instance of the ways in which Australian national security policy was being enmeshed more closely with global Cold War strategy.

In a personal sense the Korean War impinged upon the average Australian hardly at all. The early months of the war, with the dramatic movements and manoeuvres up and down the country, had excited press coverage and public interest, but after the war settled into its bloody but static phase in late 1951 interest waned. There was no opposition to the war of any note, other than from communist and fellow-travelling organisations. The fact that the operations were conducted under the aegis of the United Nations certainly helped to foster a spirit of bipartisan support for involvement, but the blatant aggression of the North Koreans and the recent memories of the war in the Pacific inclined Australians to see the war as just, and involvement as proper.

By 1955 the defence vote was set at £190 million, and the strengths of the services stood at 22 895 for the RAN (13 143 regulars and 9752 citizen forces), 152 198 for the army (22 726 regulars and 129 472 citizen forces), and 33 536 for the RAAF (15 411 regulars and 18 125 citizen forces). The avowed basis of defence policy was the maintenance of a defence capacity at a level 'that can reasonably be sustained for a long haul having regard to the essential demands of other sectors of the national economy, including national development'. The local defence of Australia and its territories was seen as the absolute first priority of the services, followed by overseas defence based on a global strategy to defend vital interests in concert with the Western alliance. In practice this meant that defence would receive adequate, but never lavish, budgetary allocations, while the defence of vital interests overseas came to enjoy priority over the development of a defence infrastructure within Australia.

The growing instability in Southeast Asia in the early 1950s, as the French lost ground to the communist and nationalist revolution in Indochina, heightened Australian fears over communist intentions in the Asia-Pacific region, and for the next twenty years these fears were to focus upon the spectre of 'Chinese expansionism'. The Geneva Conference in 1954 failed to resolve the problems of Korea and Indochina, and left both Korea and Vietnam divided into a communist northern state and a non-communist, American-supported southern one. In September that year a regional conference convened in Manila and led to the signing of the South-East Asia Collective Security Treaty (SEATO).

As with ANZUS, the Australian intention in these negotiations was to lock the Americans into a regional equivalent of NATO, something which the Americans, and especially the Congress, did not want. SEATO included the two remaining colonial powers in the region, Britain and France, Australia and New Zealand, the United States, and the acceptable regional governments in Thailand, the Philippines and, somewhat bizarrely, Pakistan. The provisions of the treaty were extended by protocol, and with their agreement, to the newly independent states of Laos, Cambodia, and the Republic of Vietnam, and the Americans specified that the obligations of the treaty related to communist aggression only. (To this end, Pakistan and Thailand were warned by the Australian foreign minister, R. G. Casey, that Australia would not regard the treaty as operative in cases of conflict with a non-communist neighbour.) SEATO headquarters was established in Bangkok in 1956, and some contingency planning was undertaken, but the United States declined to commit specific forces to the organisation prior to the event, with the result that such planning was largely ineffectual.

Anglo-Australian defence cooperation took various forms. The most controversial remains British atomic testing in Australia in the 1950s. Following the refusal of American testing facilities for the British weapons program in October 1950, the Menzies government gave permission for test facilities to be constructed in Australia. Initially conducted at Monte Bello, off the Western Australian coast, where the first British device was fired on 3 October 1952, a series of atomic and later thermonuclear weapons were exploded at the Permanent Proving Ground at Maralinga in South Australia, beginning in 1956. Tests were conducted also at Emu Field, South Australia, and, simultaneously between 1957 and 1964, off Christmas Island. Defence cooperation in testing of guided missiles and long-range weapons also took place at Woomera, beginning in 1950. In the latter case the British provided the weapons, all support and most technical personnel; Australia contributed site facilities and some scientific support at a cost of about £10 million per annum. About 13 000 trials were conducted over the years of the joint project, and six satellites were launched from Woomera, two into earth orbit. Built around the V-bomber force, experiments with the stand-off missile *Blue Streak*, and finally the American *Polaris* missile system, the testing programs in Australia helped create the British independent deterrent. Periodic consideration was given to the proposition that Australia's forces might acquire nuclear weapons of their own, but the suggestion remained just that.

On 1 April 1955 Menzies announced that Australia would participate in the establishment of a strategic reserve in Malaya to which Britain and New Zealand would contribute. The bomber squadron which had been there since 1950 would become part of this reserve, and two fighter squadrons were to be deployed for the air defence of the region. The navy would send two destroyers and two frigates, with occasional visits by an aircraft carrier as well. The army was to dispatch an infantry battalion, an artillery battery, and supporting arms, and these forces were to be available for use in a 'secondary role', combating the communist insurgency. The defence of the region would take precedence henceforth over more distant and traditional imperial needs such as the Middle East, and the Australian forces were about to embark on nearly twenty years of constant warfare in Southeast Asia.

CHAPTER 10

The Wars of Diplomacy, 1955–1972

The years from 1955 until 1972 were characterised by continuous military involvement in Southeast Asian wars and considerable organisational change in both the structure of the forces and the political and civilian bureaucracy which managed them. The demands placed on the services in this period, especially the Army, also saw the regular forces expand to reach a size exceeded only during the two world wars. The Malayan Emergency, a role in the Indonesian Confrontation of the Federation of Malaysia, and the Vietnam War provided almost twenty years of active campaigning for Australian servicemen. While each conflict had unique features, they formed a continuum in Australian postwar military history. From a doctrinal and training viewpoint, many of the men who served in Vietnam had already seen action in Malaya and Borneo and in some cases in Korea as well. From a strategic perspective, this involvement marked the increasing concern with Asia and the region which characterised much of Australia's foreign and defence policy in the postwar period. Military cooperation within the British Commonwealth continued, while ties with the United States were strengthened. Finally, the period saw increasing self-reliance in various areas, administrative as well as operational.

Like the rest of the Commonwealth, Australia had agreed to maintain its forces in Korea after the signing of the ceasefire in July 1953. The Chinese and North Koreans were by no means trusted to keep the agreement which they had signed at Panmunjom, and it was only in August 1954, when the United States decided to reduce its commitment from six divisions to two, that the Commonwealth was able to begin the phased reduction of its own forces there. The Commonwealth Division was broken up and the 28th Commonwealth Infantry Brigade alone remained, with forces from Britain, Australia and New Zealand in its ranks. In September 1954 the Australians reduced their presence there from two battalions to one, and in April 1956 the remaining battalion was withdrawn. Thereafter the Commonwealth was represented by a small Commonwealth Contingent, largely supplied by the United Kingdom.

So long as the ground force commitment to Korea remained, the Australian Army was unable to deploy any other force overseas, so reduced was its capacity after the ceasefire. With the return of the first battalion from Korea, however, and the assumption that the second would not be long delayed, it became possible for Australian defence planners to consider the government's requirements for Australian participation in Malaya. This involvement was to be in the form of a contribution to a British Commonwealth Far East Strategic Reserve. Britain had pressed Australia – and New Zealand – for a troop contribution to Malaya in 1953, when the Chief of the Imperial General Staff, Field Marshal Sir William Slim, had visited for talks on the defence of the region. Further staff talks were held in 1954, but it was only with the reduction in the commitment to Korea that the Australian army could consider seriously deploying units to Malaya. The Menzies government portrayed the involvement as the fulfilment of treaty obligations under SEATO, which was only partly true since Malaya was not an independent nation until 1957 and thereafter showed no inclination to join the Manila pact countries. The colonial power, Britain, was a signatory, and so an act of aggression against Malaya could be construed as an attack upon a member state, at least until 1957. More particularly, the move by Australia and New Zealand into the area was made in recognition of the fact that the United States would not underwrite the security of Britain's Far East colonial assets and would not play a part in the security of Malaya, Singapore or the Straits, regardless of the wishes of its ANZUS partners.

The primary role of the Strategic Reserve was to meet external threats to Malaya, usually thought to be posed by the People's Republic of China. The Strategic Reserve was available for deployment anywhere in Southeast Asia, and in 1962 in fact Australian soldiers operated in Thailand during the crisis there. The secondary role of the formation, and the one on which the battalions were engaged for most of their two-year tours of duty, was combating the Malayan Races Liberation Army, popularly known as Communist Terrorists or CTs, in counter-insurgency operations under the State of Emergency. Menzies had announced this subsidiary role for the force in the Australian parliament in June 1955. The decision provoked opposition from the Labor Party, which believed wrongly that the insurgency was a justified rural protest movement based on legitimate economic grievances. They also argued that Australian involvement would exacerbate the insurgency, and that participation in anti-terrorist operations would damage Australia's reputation in the eyes of its Asian neighbours. Since the forces sent were composed entirely of regular soldiers, and Malayan leaders stated that they welcomed their presence, the matter never really became an issue in Australian domestic politics.

The Australian component of the 28th Commonwealth Infantry Brigade comprised an infantry battalion, an artillery battery, and supporting troops. Australians also held staff positions on the headquarters of Malaya Command, Far East Land Forces, and of course the brigade itself. For the duration of the Emergency the 28th Brigade was commanded by British officers, and the brigade was under the command first of the 1st Federal Division and then, after 1957, of the 17th Gurkha Division, both of which were commanded by British officers. After 1961 the command of the brigade was rotated between officers of all component nationalities. The RAAF squadron of Lincoln bombers which had operated in Malaya since 1950 was transferred to the Strategic Reserve in 1955 before being withdrawn in 1958, and a further squadron of fighter aircraft was earmarked for dispatch to Malaya also, although this did not arrive until 1959 and played no part in the operations against the CTs. Ships of the Royal Australian Navy were placed on station in Malayan waters from 1955, and one of the RAN's new fleet carriers made periodic visits for exercises with ships of the British, American and New Zealand fleets, but the navy played no real part in Emergency operations either.

The first battalion to serve in Malaya was 2 RAR, supported by 105 Battery, RAA, in September 1955. After a two year tour they were relieved by 3 RAR and 100(A) Battery, who were succeeded in turn in September 1959 by 1 RAR and 101 Battery. A Field Troop of the Royal Australian Engineers also served in Malaya as part of an integrated British engineer squadron, and was engaged in building roads and bridges and other similar projects which would come to be known as Civic Action in Vietnam fifteen years later. The principal area of operations for the Australian units was in the north of Malaya, in the states of Perak, Kedah and Perlis. These were rugged areas of deep jungle extending up to the wild and isolated region of the Thai border. The Australians were based around Ipoh and, later, Grik although for approximately one month each year they were withdrawn from Emergency operations for training in their primary role, which usually emphasised conventional operations, sometimes under conditions of atomic attack. The contrast between the primary and secondary roles could not have been greater.

THAILAND

PERLIS

Alor Star

KEDAH

Kota Bharu

SOUTH CHINA SEA

PENANG

Grik

KELANTAN

PROVINCE

PERAK

TRENGGANU

DINDINGS

Ipoh

Cameron Highlands

Kuala Lipis

PAHANG

SELANGOR

KUALA LUMPUR

Strait of Malacca

NEGRI SEMBILAN

MALACCA

Kluang

JOHORE

Johore Bahru

0   100 kilometres

0   100 miles

SINGAPORE

Map 19   Malayan Emergency, 1948–60

By the time the Australians were committed to Malaya the Emergency had been won by the government, although there was still plenty of fighting in the jungle and the Emergency would not end officially until 1960. Anti-terrorist operations consisted of endless jungle patrolling and ambushing, together with measures designed to cut off contact between the CTs and the civil population such as food denial and population control. 2 RAR had a number of major contacts with parties of enemy up to twenty strong, but as the latter years of the Emergency passed the number of incidents dropped, and the size of enemy units encountered became smaller and smaller. During its two-year tour, 1 RAR did not manage a single contact with the communists, although it came close on several occasions. The enemy retreated into the mountainous, jungle-clad fastness of the Thai border region, where operations continued after the official end of the Emergency in cooperation with the Royal Thai Army and police.

Malaya was a platoon commanders' war, and the skills of jungle warfare were relearnt by a new generation of officers and men. A patrol would spend two weeks searching an area, followed by two days' stand-down before returning to operations. Tracker teams with Alsatian and Labrador dogs were used for the first time by the Australians, and each platoon would have a couple of Sarawak rangers attached to it. Drawn from the Iban and Dayak tribes of the interior, these men were invaluable for tracking enemy units, and in dealing with the aboriginal tribes which lived in the deep jungle in which the Australians operated. Patrols were equipped with a variant of the new, Belgian-designed, semi-automatic FN rifle, known as the SLR (self-loading rifle), the trusty Owen gun and Bren light machine gun of Second World War vintage, and even shotguns for use by the forward scouts in a platoon.

The insurgency necessitated the deployment of large forces in Malaya, and the Australian units were a small part of a much larger military organisation made up of battalions from British and Gurkha regiments, imperial units from Fiji and East Africa, battalions of the Royal Malay Regiment and the Federation Regiment, and of course the Malayan police who made up the majority of the Security Forces. A small war of the retreat from empire, it was lethal all the same. Fifty-one Australians were killed in Malaya although only fifteen of these deaths were as a direct result of operations, and twenty-seven were wounded. When the Emergency was declared at an end on 31 July 1960, the battalions of the Strategic Reserve remained in the country under the terms of the *Anglo-Malayan Defence Agreement* (AMDA), negotiated at independence in 1957.

The late 1950s and early 1960s saw notable changes in the Australian defence organisation, and even more notable attempts at change. These must be considered in two principal areas – change within the structure of the forces themselves, and within the control and administration of those forces. The services also initiated large re-equipment programs at this time, although in the nature of things these often experienced long delays in implementation. Beyond the simple fact of their occurrence, these changes were important for what they showed about the strategic

Table 10.1 Casualties, Malayan Emergency, 1950–60

Casualties	RAN	ARA(a)	RAAF	All services
Operational				
Fatal	–	13	2	15
Non-fatal	–	24	3	27
Non-operational				
Fatal	4	21	11	36
Non-fatal (b)	43	111	18	172
Total	47	169	34	250

Source: Central Army Records Office, and Australian Archives A1945, file 48/1/1.
(a)   Approximately 7000 served in theatre.
(b)   Casualties caused by accident or misadventure. The higher incidence in the RAN results from a different system of reporting which includes illnesses.

assumptions of the governments of the day. They also dictated the basis on which Australian defence was predicated in the years immediately before Australia's commitment to the war in Indochina.

Australia in part followed the postwar trend towards greater unity of the armed forces and the centralisation of decision-making within Departments of Defence and away from individual service ministries. Historically the Department of Defence had been small and bureaucratically weak, although the long-serving secretary of the department, Sir Frederick Shedden, had enjoyed great influence under governments of all persuasions during the 1930s and especially during the Second World War. His retirement in 1956 marked the end of an era in several senses. Most particularly, it had become clear during his last years in the position that the sweep of Australian defence issues was becoming too large for one man to oversee, however able the individual. The system whereby the secretary acted as the channel between the minister and the service boards of administration, and was responsible to the minister for the general and financial administration of the Defence Department, had been the final legacy of George Foster Pearce's tenure as minister in 1934. It had replaced an earlier, and much looser, system of administration, and was itself now in need of reform. It was also clear that Shedden's methods, consciously modelled on those of his mentor Sir Maurice Hankey and the old Committee of Imperial Defence, were appropriate no longer, and there is some evidence that the government retired him early in order to bring about necessary administrative and organisational reforms. It would be easier to assert the primacy of the Minister for Defence in matters relating to defence without the formidable alternative centre of authority which Shedden had long represented.

In November 1957 the Cabinet convened a high-powered committee of review under the chairmanship of Lieutenant General Sir Leslie Morshead to advise the Cabinet on the defence group of departments. These numbered six: Defence itself, the three service ministries, Supply, and Defence Production. The committee reported in December, and submitted a supplementary report in February the following year. It made two major recommendations. The first of these was to amalgamate the Departments of Supply and Defence Production on grounds of efficiency and the streamlining of resource allocation, not on substantive issues of policy between the two departments. The savings in fact were modest, but the amalgamation made good management sense and was adopted by the government with little hesitation.

The second major recommendation was for the amalgamation of the three service departments within the Department of Defence, under a single minister. This recommendation was intended to assert the supremacy of the Minister for Defence over all defence policy issues, something which did not happen in a structure in which four departments and four separate ministers exercised control over different aspects of the defence portfolio. It would also have the advantage, the committee felt, of rationalising the position of the service Chiefs of Staff, who would then answer to one minister only. This recommendation had implications for the future of the Service Boards of Administration. The committee's report did not recommend specifically that the boards be phased out, but the clear thrust of the streamlined administration which would result was that the functions of the boards could be assumed by the service chiefs. It was fifteen years before this idea was implemented.

The Menzies government was not prepared to face the more contentious issues squarely, and rejected this recommendation. The benefits of the proposal were obvious, however, and the government did take steps to bring about some of the desirable consequences which would have flowed from implementation of the report, while doing so within the existing structure. An administrative order was issued which established the primacy of the Minister for Defence in the policy area, and in the central coordination of defence matters. The assertion of this authority still depended on the personality of the individual minister until into the next decade, because for some years the minister lacked the statutory powers necessary to enforce the order. It took some years also for the department to develop a capacity in policy formulation and analysis, although this was achieved under the successive secretaries of the department in the 1960s, Sir Edwin Hicks and Sir Henry Bland. It was to reach fruition under a later secretary still, the forceful, autocratic and highly talented Sir Arthur Tange.

The second change implemented by the government and arising out of the Morshead committee report was the creation of the post of Chairman, Chiefs of Staff Committee, a position directly responsible to the Minister for Defence and whose occupant was intended to act as the government's principal military adviser. Again, in the early years the position relied upon the personality of the incumbent for its effectiveness, since although he was Australia's senior serviceman he commanded nothing and had no statutory responsibility for or control over the forces. This problem was to be highlighted during the Vietnam War, while the continuing fragmentation of the defence effort through the continuance of separate service departments was to bedevil the command and administration of the forces into the 1970s.

Without doubt the most far-reaching, and least successful, reorgani-sation within the services themselves was the army's flirtation with the Pentropic Division in the early 1960s. The existing organisational structure of the field force was that of all British-pattern armies, the triangular battalion–brigade–division formation (i.e. three battalions to a brigade, three brigades to a division). Briefly, the pentropic system involved the adoption of a five-sided organisation: five companies made a battalion, with the division containing five infantry battalions, an armoured regiment, a reconnaissance squadron and five artillery regiments. Flexibility and firepower were the keys to the Pentropic Division. Battle groups formed around an infantry battalion from the various elements of the division would enable a force to be tailored to the operational tasks confronting it, while an increase in manpower of 50 per cent over the old battalion organisation was accompanied by the capacity to deploy twice the firepower. In theory, battle groups could operate independently, at less cost, with greater offensive capability. The plan was for two such divisions, one to consist of two regular battle groups and three supplied by the CMF, the other to comprise five battle groups entirely supplied by the CMF and to be expanded to full strength in time of war. The US Army had experi-mented with a Pentomic organisation in the late 1950s, in the belief that it was appropriate to the potential atomic battlefield. The Americans did not persist with the idea, and had abandoned it by the time that the Pentropic Division was introduced into the Australian army in 1960.

The system was introduced in the belief that it matched the changing strategic environment which faced the Australian army, not least the needs of limited war in Southeast Asia. Its introduction coincided with the suspension of the national service scheme in 1959, an overdue move which freed nearly 3000 regular army personnel for other duties. (The scrapping of the scheme was accomplished easily and the objections of the Returned Services League, often thought to be a formidable lobby group, were ignored on this occasion.) Without doubt, the army believed that the financial and manpower resources made available by the ending of national service should be allocated to re-equipping and reorganising the regular force, and Pentropic was a means of ensuring this. Pentropic was certainly a disaster for the CMF, even without the decline in numbers brought about by the suspension of National Service in 1959 (CMF strength more than halved from 50 000 to 20 000 in 1959–60). Seven artillery regiments were disbanded from a total of seventeen, and thirty-one infantry battalions were reduced to seventeen. In New South Wales the reductions left just three battalions from thirteen originals. (Armoured units on the CMF establishment had already been reduced heavily in number in 1957, and thus suffered few additional reductions in 1960.) In place of the old, local and regional ties the Army introduced new, multi-battalion state-based regiments (Royal New South Wales Regiment, Royal Queensland Regiment etc). The number of CMF appointments in senior ranks (colonel and above) was reduced and the post of general officer commanding the 1st Division was transferred to the regular army. The tensions over who controlled the Army – citizen soldier or regular – which went back to the inter-war years had now been resolved in favour of the regular. Many CMF soldiers resigned, and never returned.

There were several things wrong with the Pentropic organisation. The first was that no-one else used it. The regular army's four battalions had to be split, so that two were Pentropic while two were on the old pattern, now called a 'restricted establishment', because Australia still maintained a battalion with the Strategic Reserve in Malaysia. Compatibility with the forces of one's allies is essential to the conduct of allied operations. Likewise the Pacific Islands Regiment in Papua-New Guinea remained on the British establishment. As a result there were two conflicting systems at work within the one small army. A battalion with five rifle companies was a difficult command proposition, and many critics felt that it was too unwieldy in jungle conditions. Finally, the scheme did not increase the number of battalions available, and it maintained a reliance upon the CMF which did not represent a strengthening of the army's capabilities, whatever the citizen soldier lobby might argue. What it did represent was an economy, since a CMF soldier cost the Treasury about £90 per year whereas a regular, and by extension a full-time national serviceman, cost £1200. Once again the Treasury was dictating the form and nature of defence policy. In December 1964 the system was scrapped on the recommendation of the CGS, Lieutenant General Sir John Wilton. In his view it was an idea which never should have been taken up. A more practical step towards compatibility with allied armies was Australia's admission to the existing Standardisation Agreement between the US, Britain and Canada in 1964, creating the ABCA (America, Britain, Canada, Australia) Agreement. New Zealand became associated with ABCA in 1965.

During the 1950s the Australian forces continued to train and fight with equipment drawn from Second World War stockpiles, or developed from Second World War technology. This attracted unfavourable comment in the press in 1956–57, especially in the case of the army. The situation was even more marked in the CMF. The adoption of the semi-automatic SLR by the army, and an aircraft buying spree presided over by the Chief of the Air Staff, Scherger, were indications that by the late 1950s the government had recognised that technological advances in weapons systems necessitated the updating of the services. The decision to buy Belgian rifles and American aircraft also demonstrated a desire to diversify the sources of acquisition away from Britain, together with a recognition that compatibility with American systems would be more important in the coming decade.

Menzies announced the next three-year defence program to the House of Representatives on 4 April 1957, and made this change plain. 'Australia will standardise as far as we can with the Americans', he told the parliament. '[W]e have decided, both in aircraft, in artillery, and in small arms, to fit ourselves for close cooperation with the United States of America in the Southeast Asia area'. Accordingly, the RAAF purchased the Lockheed C-130 transport aircraft, and considered buying the F-104 Starfighter from the US also. Eventually they opted for the French Mirage III to replace the ageing Sabres, but these decisions were resented in RAF and British aerospace circles, the more particularly because Scherger was held by some, wrongly, to be anti-British. He also presided over the acquisition of helicopters for the RAAF, again from US sources, but the most bitter recriminations against him in British circles came with the Australian decision to purchase twenty-four F-111 fighter bombers in mid-1963. It was alleged, untruly, that the 'loss' of the Australian market had led to the scrapping of the British Aircraft Corporation's prototype TSR 2.

Of the three services, the navy did least well in terms of equipment procurement and the definition of a role in the defence of Australia. In a statement on 26 November 1959 the Minister for Defence, Athol Townley, had announced that the government intended to disband the Fleet Air Arm when the fleet carrier *Melbourne* was decommissioned, expected to be some time in 1963. *Melbourne* was of Second World War design, and could not accommodate more sophisticated aircraft on its flight decks, while the cost of a new and more modern carrier was considered prohibitive. In 1961 the role of the Fleet Air Arm was extended by the conversion of *Melbourne* to an antisubmarine role, using Westland Wessex helicopters purchased from Britain. The government steadfastly refused to consider a replacement for either *Sydney* or *Melbourne*, although it did agree to extend the life of the navy's fixed-wing aircraft. The older *Sydney* was not returned to a flying or flying training role, but was commissioned as a fast troop transport in 1962.

In other areas the navy was able to purchase two guided-missile destroyers, but these were to be of the American Charles F. Adams-class and not the County-class vessels which the British were urging on the Australian government. In January 1963 the Minister for the Navy announced the intended purchase of a third Adams-class ship, together with the acquisition of four Oberon-class conventional submarines. These latter were to come from British shipyards, as had the six ex-British minesweepers bought in September 1962. It was becoming clear, however, that British shipyards were beginning to lose the relatively small but lucrative market which the RAN had traditionally provided. It was also clear that, the intended purchase of the submarines notwithstanding, the role of the RAN was still seen as essentially an anti-submarine one, even though this did not match the actual capabilities of other regional navies. The decision on the carriers and the Fleet Air Arm meant that any naval operations conducted beyond the range of land-based RAAF aircraft would have to rely on the air protection provided by the fleets of allied navies.

The decision to acquire the F-111 was a direct result of the deterioration of the strategic situation in Southeast Asia, particularly in relations between the Federation of Malaysia and Indonesia. The history of Australian–Indonesian relations is mostly downhill from the early days of the Indonesian revolution, when Australia advocated the Indonesian cause against their Dutch colonial masters in the UN and other international forums. There had been increasing unease in Australian circles in 1961–62 when Indonesia had incorporated Dutch New Guinea into its territory, with international agreement but against Australia's wishes. The formation of the Federation of Malaysia and the unsuccessful Brunei revolt in 1962 led President Sukarno to adopt a policy of 'confronting' Malaysia, a term which was never really explained but which gave the episode its name, *Konfrontasi* or Confrontation.

Most of the Indonesian incursions into Malaysian territory occurred in Sarawak and, to a lesser extent, Sabah, located in the northern part of the island of Borneo. During the most intense period of Indonesian military activity, July–December 1964, parties of Indonesian soldiers and irregular militia made landings in West Malaysia at Labis and Pontian, in one instance by parachute drop. But the centre of the fighting was in Borneo, and it was here that the Australian units of the Strategic Reserve were deployed in 1965. The end of the Malayan Emergency in July 1960 had seen the 28th Brigade revert to training for its primary role, although 1 RAR continued to engage in sporadic anti-terrorist operations on the Thai border for several months thereafter. From 1961, however, the units of the brigade trained and exercised for more conventional operations, often in a theoretical nuclear environment. In October 1961 1 RAR left Malaysia at the end of its two-year tour, and was replaced by 2 RAR, the first Australian battalion to have served in Malaya during the Emergency seven years earlier. 2 RAR had been organised as a Pentropic battalion, and had been reorganised to conform to the Strategic Reserve establishment before departure, serving to emphasise the organisational and administrative nonsense of having two incompatible establishments within the one small service.

The *Anglo-Malayan Defence Agreement* of 1957 committed the British to the defence of Malaysia, but the Australians were under no such obligation. The Strategic Reserve was intended for deployment on SEATO tasks, and Malaysia was not a member of that organisation. Involvement in the operations in Borneo would mean that the battalions would no longer be available should the Manila pact be invoked elsewhere in Southeast Asia. Equally, if the concept of the 28th Brigade as a strategic reserve was to have any validity, it could not be broken up for use on different operations in different places. On 6 April 1964 the Malaysian government requested the Australian government to make the Australian battalion, now 3 RAR, available for security operations in Borneo if necessary. They also requested other forms of military aid. At the same time, the British government made it clear to Australia that security forces engaged against Indonesian border-crossers would be permitted to cross a certain distance into Indonesian territory in pursuit.

The Australian government was unhappy with this prospect, for a number of reasons. It argued that cross-border operations should be conducted by Malaysian troops to avoid the charge of 'neo-colonialism'. Cross-border operations in the Thai border region against the CTs had been conducted on this basis, with the Malayan Police Field Force or infantry units actually crossing into Thai territory in pursuit of their enemy, and the Australian or British unit acting as a blocking force on the Malayan side of the border. But this was in the context of a neutral state, Thailand, a situation which hardly pertained in Borneo. Initially, however, the Australian government limited the use of its battalion to security tasks on the Malay peninsula, but agreed to provide two minesweepers and some helicopters to act in support of Malaysian forces while Australian naval units from the Strategic Reserve conducted anti-infiltration patrols in the waters between Sumatra, peninsular Malaya and Singapore, and in the waters around northern Borneo. In October that year the Australian battalion was in fact involved in the apprehension of a party of infiltrators in the Terendak area.

The Indonesian incursions in the second half of 1964 brought them closer to outright war, and the British government discussed the use of air and naval strikes against targets in Indonesia. By the end of that year, there were eighteen British and Gurkha battalions, and three Malaysian ones, in Borneo itself, and 65 000 Commonwealth troops throughout the Federation of Malaysia as a whole were engaged in security tasks. On 21 January 1965 the Malaysian government made a direct request for the use of Australian troops in Borneo, and at the end of that month the government agreed to deploy 3 RAR and a squadron of the SAS. The Malaysians had requested a second infantry battalion also, but Australian resources were not capable of such a deployment, especially as the Australian involvement in Vietnam was about to be stepped up.

Like earlier operations in Malaya, the fighting in Borneo was characterised by patrol and ambush actions, with the politically sensitive problem of pursuit across the border – CLARET operations, as they were known – always to the fore. The Indonesians crossed the border in relatively small groups, often of less than platoon size. Of the 152 such incidents in Sarawak and sixty-two in Sabah, only eighteen and three respectively involved groups of more than forty men, and only three of these exceeded fifty men. In the course of 1965 the Indonesians began to build up the strength of their bases in Kalimantan, and appeared to be moving towards company-sized incursions, which would have represented a significant escalation in the military situation. In 1965 and 1966, the Indonesian forces opposing the security forces increasingly were Indonesian regulars, well-equipped and trained. In the view of General Sir Walter Walker, the British Director of Operations in Borneo, this stage of Confrontation came closest to a regular war, akin to fighting the Japanese in Burma.

The Australian units played their part in these operations, mounting some highly successful ambushes on both sides of the border, inflicting casualties and of course incurring them. The fact that these operations in Indonesian territory was not mentioned in the press, nor indeed in the unit records, is an indication of the sensitivity with which they were viewed. When casualties were incurred, the government and the army were at pains to stress that they were suffered on the Malaysian side of the border, even when this was not true. In October 1965, 3 RAR was relieved in Malaysia by 4 RAR, and this battalion served in Borneo in the first half of 1966. Two squadrons of the SAS also served tours in Borneo, the first time that this unit had embarked on active service. The strategic situation was changing, however, with the attempted communist coup in

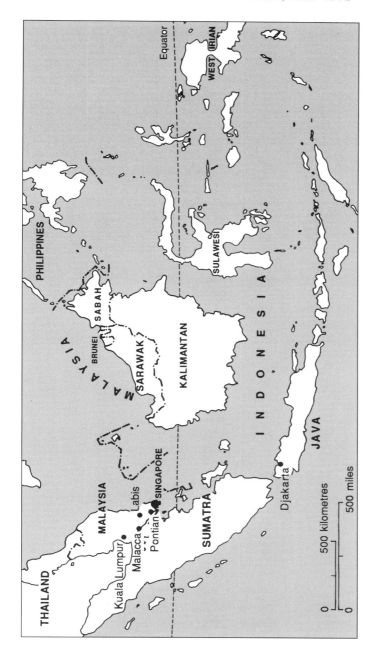

Map 20a   Malaysia and Indonesia, 1962–66

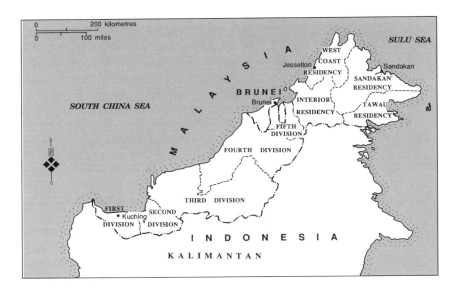

Map 20b   Borneo and Kalimantan, 1964–66

Indonesia on 30 September 1965, and the violent suppression of the PKI (*Partai Komunis Indonesia*) by the Indonesian army thereafter. The army then became so involved in the internal affairs of the country that the tempo of operations against Malaysia slackened, although some cross-border raids continued into 1966. A peace treaty between Malaysia and Indonesia was ratified in Jakarta on 11 August 1966, and Confrontation was at an end.

Twenty-three Australians were killed during Confrontation, only seven of them on operations, and eight were wounded. The Australian battalion reverted to its primary role in the Strategic Reserve, and the focus of Australian military effort now switched to the war in Vietnam. Operations in Borneo had been gruelling, and had called for the high levels of professionalism which the small regular army possessed. There had been little public reaction to them, because the public was told very little about them, but the maintenance of a battalion on active service in Borneo, and of another one in Vietnam after May 1965 together with long-standing commitments in Papua-New Guinea, had been a major commitment for the army. The size of the forces was now to increase dramatically in response to the new demands placed upon them, but the fighting in Borneo had given Australian soldiers a refresher course in the demands of low-intensity conflict which was to stand them in good stead in Phuoc Tuy.

Table 10.2 Casualties during Confrontation, 1964–66

Casualties	RAN	ARA(a)	RAAF	All services
Operational				
Fatal	–	7	–	7
Non-fatal	1	6	1	8
Non-operational				
Fatal	2	10	4	16
Non-fatal (b)	83	14	3	100
Total	86	37	8	131

Source: Central Army Records Office, and Australian Archives A1945, file
48/1/1.
(a) Approximately 3500 served in theatre.
(b) Casualties caused by accident or misadventure. The higher incidence
in the RAN results from a different system of reporting which
includes illnesses.

The United States had indicated its reluctance to underwrite the
security of Malaya during the 1950s, but was prepared to concede that
the operations in Borneo might be regarded as coming under the
provisions of the ANZUS treaty. The Americans were reluctant to
provoke Indonesian hostility, however, and made it clear that there was
no likelihood of committing American troops there. As a result the
Menzies government embarked upon its Vietnam commitment in order
to bind the Americans more closely to Australia, in the expectation that
close support of American actions in Indochina would bring reciprocal
support from the US in Australia's hour of need, should this arise. This
suggests a clear-sighted appreciation of the usual alliance relationship
between greater and lesser powers and of the complexity of the regional
situation which faced the Australian government in the first half of the
1960s. British intentions to withdraw from 'east of Suez' had been
delayed by the need to defeat Indonesian aggression, but they had not
been altered. Given the small size and limited capabilities of the armed
forces and the tendency to reduce defence spending in peace time,
reliance upon alliance structures was the only option open. In any case,
it is important to judge the government's motivation by what it hoped
would be the result of its policy, and not solely in terms of the actual
outcome in 1975. Although the government foresaw the possibility of a
Western defeat in Indochina, the importance of the overall aim was held
to outweigh the risk.

Australia's military commitment to the Republic of Vietnam began
in July 1962 with the dispatch of thirty advisers, the original members
of the Australian Army Training Team, Vietnam. Drawn from junior

officers and senior NCOs, the members of the AATTV were deployed as part of the US advisory system, the majority of them in I Corps in the north. Their initial role was strictly training, and they were barred from accompanying their Vietnamese charges on operations. This greatly reduced the value of their advisory effort. By June 1964 the size of the team had been increased to eighty personnel, and their role was extended to include operational advisory tasks with combat units. They began to move also into the US Special Forces units, working with Montagnard tribesmen. At the same time that the increase in advisers was made, the RAAF dispatched a small squadron of Caribou transport aircraft to operate out of Vung Tau.

The year 1964 was a crisis one for the government of the Republic of Vietnam. The Viet Cong guerrillas, augmented by regular troops of the People's Army of [North] Vietnam (PAVN), were gaining control of large parts of the country and were engaging units of the Army of the Republic of [South] Vietnam (ARVN) in conventional battles, and beating them. By the middle of 1964 it was estimated that the ARVN was losing a battalion a week through battle casualties and desertion. Initially the South Vietnamese had believed that they could defeat the insurgency from their own resources, and that their need for military assistance was small and could be limited to advisers and some equipment. By late 1964 it was evident that the regime could not long survive unless it accepted large-scale external assistance. It is in this context that Australia's decision to commit combat troops must be viewed.

On 10 December 1964 the South Vietnamese prime minister, Tran Van Huong, made a strong request for increased military assistance from Australia. Huong asked for more advisers and increased air support, and argued that Australian security was threatened by the drift of events in Indochina. At the same time that this request was made, the Department of Defence was already considering the question of increased military aid, prompted no doubt by the clear perception that the United States was doing the same thing following the presidential election in November. The Defence Committee considered that Australia might offer an infantry battalion, a squadron of the Special Air Service (SAS), ten more advisers, and a small naval element. On 14 December, however, Menzies received a cable from President Lyndon B. Johnson requesting 200 more combat advisers, minesweepers, hospital ships, and other naval vessels of a type which the RAN did not possess. The Defence Committee recommended the dispatch of a further seventeen advisers, bringing the total to 100, and the government suggested talks with the Americans and New Zealanders to discuss further military aid. Staff talks were finally held in Honolulu in March 1965.

The outcome of these talks was that America wished for an Australian military presence and that, if the Australian government agreed, a request for such assistance would be forthcoming from the South Vietnamese themselves. American authorities were sensitive to the need for 'third countries' to contribute to the defence of South Vietnam, and Johnson stressed the need for 'more flags' on numerous occasions. On 6 April the Defence Committee recommended that Australia should contribute a battalion, a recommendation which was agreed to the following day. The offer was then cabled to President Johnson via the Australian ambassador in Washington.

In the first instance, therefore, the offer of troops was made to the United States and not to the South Vietnamese. This is important because the question of the 'request' from the Vietnamese prime minister, Phan Huy Quat, was to play an important part in the parliamentary debate in Australia over the commitment of troops to Vietnam. There is no doubt that the American ambassador in Saigon, General Maxwell Taylor, together with his Australian counterpart, engineered the request from the Vietnamese government which was finally made on 29 April. The form of the request revealed this clearly, for it stated that the Vietnamese government had received details of Australia's offer of troops, and was pleased to accept the offer. The request was hardly spontaneous. Against it should be set the earlier requests for assistance made by President Diem, General Nguyen Van Khanh and other officials between 1961 and 1964, requests which were not prompted by external pressure. Although the specific incident in April 1965 was based on a grudging acceptance of the weakness of their position, it can be said that the Australian offer of an infantry battalion was made in the context of a succession of non-specific requests for aid going back several years. Over and above this, the Australian military presence in South Vietnam existed with the clear consent of the Saigon government.

Important decisions were made in Australia in 1964–65 which would shape the commitment to Vietnam. The decision to abandon the Pentropic establishment led to the reorganisation of all infantry battalions back to a British-pattern 'Tropic' establishment, and meant also that strong cadres were available for the formation of two additional infantry battalions, designated 5 RAR and 6 RAR. On 10 November 1964, moreover, Menzies announced that the national service scheme, suspended in 1959, would be revived and introduced the legislation into parliament the next day. Both the army and the Department of Labour and National Service had opposed the reintroduction of the scheme, on the grounds that a short-term liability for service with no requirement for overseas service was a waste of resources, and that there was no need for large intakes of national servicemen. The army argued that the shortfall between the projected manpower needs of the services and the rates of enlistment could be made up by improving the pay and conditions of servicemen in a time of full employment, but the Treasury vetoed this. The result was that a selective ballot was introduced to meet the need for additional manpower while avoiding the call-up of large numbers of conscripts who would then pose an unproductive drain upon resources. Inevitably, this was dubbed a 'blood ballot' by its opponents.

The reintroduction of conscription led to the build-up of the Royal Australian Regiment to a total of nine battalions by 1967. The need for the increase was clear, for in 1965 Australia was still engaged in a campaign in Borneo which was showing signs of escalating, the commitment to the Strategic Reserve remained, and there were fears of possible Indonesian military activity in New Guinea also. Although Australian conscripts were to die in Vietnam from 1966, national service was not introduced for service in Vietnam specifically but as a reaction to worsening relations with Indonesia and fears of a wider conflict to our immediate north. Whether national service was the best option available is another matter. The integration of national servicemen into regular units and the commissioning of some national service graduates through the Officer Cadet Unit at Scheyville was a success. They were treated like regulars, although not paid like them, and in general there was little of the disaffection between regulars and conscripts which characterised the American experience in Vietnam. Conscription for overseas service has always been an emotive political issue in Australia, and it must be doubted that the political and social dislocation over conscription from 1967 onwards was a price worth paying when the territorial integrity and security of the country were not directly threatened. But the form which the new scheme took, by directing national servicemen into the regular army rather than the CMF, served further to emphasise the dominance of the regulars at the expense of the citizen soldiers, who were not to be given the chance to serve through activation of their units for war service.

The abandonment of the Pentropic Division meant a reorganisation of the CMF as well. Existing battalions were reduced, as they had been in the regular army, and additional battalions were raised in Queensland, Victoria and New South Wales. The CMF had been reorganised radically with the advent of Pentropic. With the change back, some attempt was made to return to the newly reconstituted battalions in the larger states some measure of the old units' identities through the allocation of particular numerical titles. By way of example, the new battalion based in the Lismore region of New South Wales regained the designation 41 Battalion, while remaining a unit of the Royal New South Wales Regiment. In a final attempt to maintain the old position of the CMF, the Minister for the Army, J. O. Cramer, had attempted to appoint Major General Ivan Dougherty to the position of CGS in 1960, in succession to Lieutenant General Sir Ragnar Garrett. A former CMF member of the Military Board, Dougherty had wide experience as a battalion and brigade commander in the Second World War. Such an appointment would have thrown out the 'succession' to the post, which had been laid down in 1959 for the ensuing fifteen years, and the idea posed a threat to the newly won dominance of the professional military. It was opposed successfully by both the Prime Minister and the Minister for Defence, Athol Townley. However suitable Dougherty would have been, and he was probably the most able of the younger CMF officers of the war generation, Cramer's initiative would have been a retrograde step in the development of the regular forces, and it was as well that it did not proceed. What role remained for the CMF, given the changes which had occurred, was to remain unresolved until the mid-1970s.

The second major change, the reintroduction of conscription, also affected the CMF. Young men balloted for national service were required to serve in the CMF for three years after completion of their two years of full-time duty with the regular army. In addition, men joining the CMF before their age group was balloted were exempt from call-up, but were required to serve six years in the CMF. If they were eligible for call-up but had exercised the CMF option, and left before the full term, they were called up automatically for two years service in the regular army. By 1968, approximately 17 000 of the 35 000 members of the Citizens' Forces were men who had taken the option to avoid the draft. This had a deleterious effect on the CMF. Many of those who took the option of CMF service were motivated by a desire to avoid the possibility of being sent to Vietnam, and were of little value as recruits. Others, who exercised the option and then found that their birth-dates had not been balloted in to national service, became ineffective and avoided parades until finally discharged. As a result, the CMF was viewed by some sections of the community as a haven for draft dodgers. The morale of the genuine citizen soldier was further undermined by the decision not to activate CMF units for service in Vietnam. Voluntary enlistment declined as significantly as morale.

Menzies' statement to parliament on 29 April 1965 led to the dispatch of 1 RAR, together with some logistical and support units, to South Vietnam in June. The New Zealand government contributed an artillery battery to the force, with some reluctance. New Zealand did not believe that a military solution to the Vietnam War was viable, but pressure from the ANZUS partners and the realisation that the country was too small to act alone in defence matters prompted involvement. Although New Zealand also instituted a national service scheme at this time, only regulars served in Vietnam. Although there was some anti-war dissent in New Zealand, it lacked the heat of the dissent in Australia for this reason.

1 RAR was placed under the operational control of the US 173rd Airborne Brigade (Separate) as its third battalion. The brigade was stationed at Bien Hoa, north of Saigon, and the battalion's initial role was to engage in the defence of the giant air base located there. By December its task had been extended to include operations in the whole of III Corps area. A battalion is not a self-contained formation, and cannot operate independently even with the addition of armoured personnel carriers, light aircraft and additional engineering and logistic support; hence the need for attachment to an American parent formation. The Australian battalion group was supplied and maintained by the Americans in all areas save those of specific Australian issue, such as weapons and uniforms, and the Australian government reimbursed the United States in return on the basis of a capitation system. This was also the means by which the Australian advisers in Vietnam were supplied and maintained.

The attachment of an Australian battalion to a US brigade was a mixed success, and the problems encountered added to the pressures upon the Australian government to increase the size of its troop commitment and field a self-contained force able to operate independently. There were differences in tactics and operating procedures, and these proved difficult to reconcile with previous Australian experience in Malaya and Borneo. The Australians insisted upon operating in their own way, and would not follow American practices such as the daily resupply of sub-units by helicopter or the unrestrained use of firepower where the same end could be achieved by manoeuvre. The Airborne was an elite formation, essentially trained for limited conventional war, while the Australians had much experience of unconventional counter-insurgency operations and emphasised stealthy patrolling and patience in finding and eliminating the enemy. Part of the reason for this emphasis upon conducting operations in their own way was the reluctance to risk the high level of casualties which the Americans accepted as routine. The Americans certainly killed more Viet Cong using their methods, but proportionately they took many more casualties themselves.

The battalion group faced other difficulties which had nothing to do with the attachment to an American brigade. Despite the fact that 1 RAR

Map 21 Republic of (South) Vietnam, showing division into military regions and provinces bordering Phuoc Tuy

was to be deployed overseas, the battalion had been issued with old, defective and obsolete equipment. The Owen gun was a good weapon in its day, but the ones issued to the forward scouts in the platoons were twenty years old. The radio equipment was worn out and lacked the range of the American sets, while the uniforms were of coarse material ill-suited to the tropical climate, and ripped easily on the secondary jungle growth. The boots were Second World War issue, and fell apart after a few days on operations. All this naturally caused an outcry back in Australia when it was revealed through the papers, but such deficiencies took some time to rectify and pointed both to the general unpreparedness of the army for operations and to the lack of priority accorded the battalion during the time in which it was prepared for overseas service.

On 8 March 1966 the government announced that 1 RAR would be relieved by a Task Force of two battalions plus supporting units, the whole to operate in the coastal province of Phuoc Tuy. This decision was made both because of dissatisfaction with the previous arrangements, and because the Australian government was under pressure from President Johnson to increase its commitment in line with American increases. Phuoc Tuy was settled on because it had reasonable access by air and sea, it contained significant enemy activity, it was not contiguous with any border areas, and it was a geographically distinct area with which the Australian effort could be identified. Contrary to popular belief, however, the Task Force was not given sole and exclusive responsibility for the province, nor was it to operate in the province only. The force's responsibility was limited largely to the military sphere of operations and outside the major towns. Pacification tasks and relations with the local Vietnamese administration were left to Vietnamese provincial authorities and their American advisers. The Task Force could be, and was, required to operate anywhere in the III Corps area by the US commander of II Field Force, and operations in the more remote border areas of the province itself often involved crossing into neighbouring provinces. This was because the enemy's organisation was not based on individual provinces. The Viet Cong Military Region Seven encompassed not only Phuoc Tuy but also Bien Hoa, Long Khanh and Binh Tuy. The Task Force was supported in Vietnam by the 1st Australian Logistic Support Group because the Australian deployment coincided with the big American build-up, and the US logistics system could not cope with the additional demands made upon it. The Americans continued to supply the Australians with some items not carried normally on the Australian establishment, but for the first time in its military history Australia was forced not merely to field an expeditionary force but largely to supply and maintain it also.

The operations of the Task Force may be divided roughly into three phases. The first of these was between mid-1966 and December 1967. The two-battalion force was engaged against the Viet Cong and weakened their grip upon the province, but without a major expansion in government influence. The Task Force base was established at Nui Dat, and the Australians fought their first big action at Long Tan on 18–19 August 1966 when a company of 6 RAR intercepted 275 VC Regiment as it was preparing a major attack in the base area, although not perhaps on the base itself as is suggested in some accounts. The Australians killed 245 enemy, with an estimated 500 other casualties inflicted, for the loss of seventeen dead and twenty-one wounded. It was an important early victory, in that it ensured the security of the base area and aided the process of asserting the Australians' superiority over their enemy.

The second phase lasted from January 1968 to mid-1969. The Task Force was expanded to include a third infantry battalion, bringing the strength of Australian forces in Vietnam to 8300. This was declared to be the optimum strength which the army could support. During this period the battalions were often called out of Phuoc Tuy to take part in large-scale operations with American and ARVN units, and the Viet Cong achieved some renewal of strength in the province as a result, although this was short-lived. After the action at Long Tan, the VC rarely sought prolonged engagements with Australian companies, and the war in Phuoc Tuy was characterised by search and destroy operations, the cordon and search of villages, patrolling, ambushing, route clearance, and civic action projects. On several occasions the Australians fought larger engagements, such as at Binh Ba in June 1969 when two companies of 5 RAR killed forty-three VC in a 24-hour period, or at Fire Support Base Coral-Balmoral in neighbouring Bien Hoa province in February 1968 during the Tet Offensive. On the latter occasion a North Vietnamese unit overran part of a battalion position in the only action in which the Australians established full battalion defensive positions during the war. Seventy-six enemy were killed for the loss of twenty-three Australians.

During the third phase, from mid-1969 until the withdrawal of the force in December 1971, protracted operations led to a steady decline in the enemy's forces and a strengthening of the government's position. The Viet Cong had been seriously weakened by the failure of the Tet Offensive, but the security position within Phuoc Tuy remained problematic to the end. The main force units had moved out of the province into other parts of the enemy's Military Region Seven, but the nucleus of the tough provincial regiment D 445 was still in existence, while a weak PAVN unit also continued to operate there. It was estimated

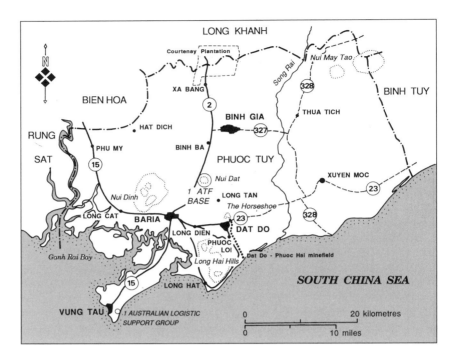

Map 22   Phuoc Tuy province, 1966–72

that upwards of 600 cadre remained in Phuoc Tuy. The province was pacified by day, much less so at night. During the months after the withdrawal of 8 RAR in November 1970, the Task Force again reverted to a two-battalion establishment until its withdrawal between October and December 1971. Small logistic elements were withdrawn in March 1972, and the remaining members of the AATTV were brought home in December that year after the election of a Labor government on 2 December 1972.

The main role in Vietnam was played by the army, as was to be expected in a revolutionary insurgency. Both the RAN and the RAAF had a part, but in the case of the navy this was not large and once again emphasised the navy's search for an operational role in the postwar period. The old carrier *Sydney*, dubbed the 'Vung Tau ferry', was employed as a troop transport and made twenty-three voyages between Australia and Vietnam. A small clearance diving team operated in the Mekong delta and a guided missile destroyer was on station with the US 7th Fleet in the Gulf of Tonkin and the South China Sea, providing naval gunfire support and patrolling the coast. An RAN helicopter flight operated with the US 135th Assault Helicopter Company from 1967. The RAAF flew Canberra bombers of No. 2 Squadron with the 35th Tactical Fighter Wing of the US 7th Air Force out of Phan Rang, and Caribou transports of No. 35 Squadron which were based at Vung Tau. The most important role played by the air force was performed by the helicopters of No. 9 Squadron, which operated with the Task Force and were engaged in medical evacuation, gunship support and troop airlift roles. The Australians never had enough helicopters of their own, and the deficiencies were made good by the US Air Force and the US Army.

The way in which armed forces fight a war is based on their doctrine. In general terms, doctrine is the body of ideas which guides an army's activities in pursuit of its objectives: tactical doctrine guides a force in pursuit of victory in battle, strategic doctrine the pursuit of victory in war. For much of their existence the Australian armed forces used British doctrine, sometimes amended to take account of local conditions. Although the Australian Army had developed its own doctrine for jungle warfare while fighting the Japanese in New Guinea, this had been largely forgotten by the 1960s. Experience in Malaya in the 1950s combined with the reorientation of Australia's strategic policy away from an emphasis on the Middle East and towards Southeast Asia led the Army to develop a body of counter-insurgency doctrine shaped to meet its likely tasks in regional conflicts, beginning in about 1961. When the Pentropic division was abandoned, the doctrine for counter-revolutionary warfare which had been developed was modified to reflect the changed organisation, and it was with this that the Army fought the Vietnam War.

During the period of major ground force involvement, from mid-1965 to the end of 1971, the Army was faced with widely varying operations and operational contexts, and the methods and techniques used to fight the enemy underwent a continuous process of change and modification. Doctrine in 1965–66 was still heavily influenced by the Malayan experience of the 1950s, but the intensity of operations in Vietnam, whether in Bien Hoa or Phuoc Tuy, was far higher than anything experienced during the Emergency. The dramatic conventional battles like Long Tan were a result of the need to establish and consolidate the task force within the province, but they were not characteristic of the war as most Australian soldiers fought it. In particular, pacification operations which were the major part of 1 ATF's activities between 1969 and 1971 involved intensive patrolling and ambushing and placed considerable responsibility at the sub-unit level. There was widespread debate within the Army over doctrinal development during the war, and a heightened process of evaluation and dissemination of information about the enemy's and our own operational and tactical methods was developed.

A notable area of weakness within the forces generally was in the field of joint operations and combined arms warfare. Soldiers in 1 RAR had had little opportunity to practise the techniques of artillery fire support or to train with helicopters before being sent to Vietnam in 1965. In part this reflected shortage of resources in Australia, but the attitudes of some within the RAAF to the provision of close support to the Army were to cause significant friction in Vietnam. No. 9 Squadron operated under flying restrictions imposed from Australia and appeared to some Army observers to be unresponsive to and uninterested in the needs of ground force units. Unfavourable comparisons were made with US helicopter units and with the RAN element operating with the Americans. The comparisons were not always fair, but the attitude of some senior RAAF officers seemed to confirm them. The Iroquois helicopters had been acquired specifically to provide support to the Army, but attempts by the Army to develop methods of cooperation and joint training in 1964–65 were rebuffed by the Chief of the Air Staff. Some of the problems were overcome in time, but the feeling that the RAAF had let the Army down was to influence the outcome of the debate over the next generation of battlefield helicopter, the Black-hawk, in the 1980s and led to these aircraft being transferred from air force to army control.

There had been opposition expressed to the sending of national servicemen to Vietnam from the start, but for the first couple of years this dissenting view was held by a distinct minority only, some of whom had a traditional opposition to compulsory service often based on religious practice while others, especially on the left, opposed the war effort for ideological reasons. Some members of the Labor Party, still in Opposition federally, opposed the involvement in Vietnam from the beginning, but although opposition to the war became stated ALP policy in May 1965, the policy was non-specific on details of how and when troops would be withdrawn. The timing of withdrawal remained a matter of disagreement within the ALP until after the 1969 election. Although little discussed, there was widespread support for involvement also, especially among traditional anti-communist groups like the RSL and some religious groups, especially some sections of the Catholic church. Had Australian military involvement in the Vietnam War consisted of regulars and volunteers, as in Korea and Malaya in the 1950s, there is little reason to believe that anti-war opposition would have been any more widespread than it had been during those campaigns.

For many Australians conscription for overseas service was the issue, the nature or conduct of the war being entirely secondary. For the majority of these Australians this remained the case, as evidenced by the almost complete collapse of the anti-war movement after the withdrawal of Australian forces was announced. (The third and final Moratorium campaign in 1971 focused entirely on the war and did not mention conscription in its six demands. The demise of the movement the following year suggests that the majority of participants did not share this shift in attitude.) Opinion polls indicated a majority of the population continued to support involvement until October 1968. In April 1966 between 63 per cent and 68 per cent of those polled supported the sending of conscripts overseas, but between 45 per cent and 57 per cent opposed their being sent to fight in Vietnam, although more than 60 per cent of the same group indicated support for continuing military efforts there. The greatest objection for many centred on the selective nature of the ballot but, somewhat paradoxically, there was usually overwhelming opposition to draft dodgers and to conscientious objection to service in particular wars. Unlike the United States, a reaction to the casualty figures was not a significant feature of opposition to the war in Australia.

The Moratorium movement, as the anti-conscription, anti-war protest came to be known, never commanded majority support in the Australian community at large. The Liberal government won a comfortable victory in 1966 in an election which the Opposition fought on the Vietnam issue. It won again, less comfortably, in 1969. Support for the protest movement was drawn from 'articulate opinion', journalists, academics, students and intellectuals of various sorts, and generally not from 'grassroots opinion' of the kind that translates into votes and unseats governments. This explains also why many of the features of the Moratorium were derivative, drawn from US models. While the Moratorium movement could sometimes mobilise 700 000 protesters around Australia, it remained a politically weak and divided movement, not least because there were always sections of the ALP unwilling to embrace the anti-American, pro-North Vietnamese rhetoric of the extreme wing of the movement, which was too often the movement's public face. As a result, the ALP never became the parliamentary wing of the protest movement, and the movement's aims were never translated into the mainstream political process. Although disruptive, it is unlikely that the existence and activities of the Moratorium influenced the government to make a decision it would not have made otherwise, or to change a decision already taken. The wind-down of Australia's military commitment in Vietnam came about because the Americans too were beginning to withdraw, and was based on a perception that the war could not be won. It was this same perception of an unwinnable war which sowed doubts in the minds of middle Australia after 1969.

Approximately 50 000 Australians served in Vietnam between 1962 and 1972. Of these, 501 were killed or listed as missing presumed dead,

Table 10.3 Casualties, Vietnam War, 1962–72

Casualties	RAN	RAAF	Army to April 1966	Army from May 1966(a)			All services
				ARA	NS	CMF	
Killed in action, died of wounds	6	4	28	200	184	1	423
Missing, presumed dead	–	2	1	–	1	–	4
Non-battle casualty deaths	2	8	7	42	15	–	74
WIA	13	30	154	986	880	6	2069
Other	37	26	30	567	399	3	1062
Total	58	70	220	1795	1479	10	3632

Source: Central Army Records Office, and Australian Archives A1945, file
            48/1/1.
(a)   After entry of 1 ATF.

and 3131 were wounded. Over 804 000 young men registered for
national service, of whom 35 000 exercised the CMF option. Approximately 63 000 were called up and, of these, 17 424 went to Vietnam. In
financial terms the war was said to have cost Australia $218.4 million,
although the basis on which this was calculated is not clear. Less than
10 per cent of the armed forces were in Vietnam at any one time,
compared with one-sixth of the American services. There were some
strains in the relationship between the army and the control exercised by some ministers, especially Malcolm Fraser when the latter
was Minister for Defence from 1969 to 1971, but the general public was
largely unaware of them and the conduct of operations was not affected
by them. The command and control system, especially as exercised
between the Chairman, Chiefs of Staff Committee in Canberra and
Australian forces in Vietnam, suffered from some shortcomings, and
the changes made in this area over the next ten years were to reflect
this. At a lower level, the professional standards of the forces, and
especially of the army, were enhanced although, as in earlier wars, it
must be doubted that the capability to maintain a multi-battalion commitment overseas was retained for long after the end of that military
commitment.

In the aftermath of the Morshead Committee report, and the government's half-hearted implementation of its recommendations, an
increasing burden had fallen upon the Defence Committee, comprising
the three service chiefs and chaired by the Secretary of the Department
of Defence, although outside participation was extended on an invited
basis. During the 1960s the formulation of strategic policy to a large

Table 10.4   National service 1965–72: final statistics at 31 December 1972

Category	Number
Total number registered	804 286
Balloted out and granted indefinite deferment	567 238
Sub-total (balloted in)	237 048
Exempted from liability (theology students, physically or mentally disabled, conscientious objectors)	3 563
Granted indefinite deferment (married, members of the CMF)	35 548
Served or serving in permanent forces	2 194
Sub-total	195 743
Rejected on medical, psychological or educational grounds	99 926
Not immediately available for call-up (students, apprentices, in breach of the National Service Act, etc.)	32 027
Called up and enlisted in the Army	63 790

Source: Department of Labour and National Service.

extent was the responsibility of this committee. It relied upon a number of joint committees not necessarily subordinate to it; the Joint Intelligence Committee, which provided intelligence studies, and the Joint Planning Committee and Joint Administrative Planning Committee, which provided reports and appreciations on operational and administrative aspects of defence planning. Overall coordination in strategic planning had been assisted by moving the department from Melbourne to Canberra in 1959, so that finally the government and its advisers conducted their affairs in the same city.

The increased military activity prompted by the Vietnam War led to a greater need for centralised control and political direction than had been the case previously. Lieutenant General Sir John Wilton, the Chairman, Chiefs of Staff Committee, suggested a reorganisation of defence administration in 1967. The Naval, Military and Air Boards of Administration still exercised statutory control over the forces while the Chiefs of Staff Committee discharged its functions by administrative direction, the stop-gap measure instituted by Menzies ten years earlier. Not only was the Headquarters of Australian Forces Vietnam a joint headquarters, but the scale of Australian involvement there was greater than anything encountered since the Second World War, as evidenced by the trebling of the defence vote in the first five years of involvement. These pressures on the existing system led to a program of reforms administered by the Minister for Defence, Allan Fairhall, and announced on 1 October 1968. Wilton's recommendation for a Defence Board of Administration and the creation of the post of Chief of Defence Staff was not pursued. The powers of the service boards were left intact, but a new advisory joint staff was created. This ended the practice of relying upon joint committees made up of members representing the interests of their service, and meant that the Secretary of the Department of Defence and the Chairman, Chiefs of Staff Committee would be better served by access to planners and staffs. It did not obviate the need for the Secretary, Sir Henry Bland, to initiate the practice in 1968 of meeting informally with the Chiefs of Staff and the Chairman, Chiefs of Staff Committee to discuss issues such as the size, composition and employment of the forces over which they exercised control. Some necessary changes were also instituted in the Defence Science Organisation.

The skilful use of British forces in Malaysia during Confrontation and the successful prosecution of the war against communist insurgency there in the 1950s, together with the continuing British military presence in Southeast Asia under AMDA, served to obscure the fact that Britain's military effort in the Far Fast was placing enormous strain on its economy and armed forces. By the mid-1960s the balance of payments deficit was becoming chronic and cut-backs were being made in the resources available to defence without concomitant reductions in the commitments of the forces. Increasingly there was talk in Whitehall and Westminster of withdrawal. At the same time that calls were being made for more equitable sharing of the defence burden in Malaysia, directed to Australia and New Zealand, the British Foreign and Defence Secretaries stated in the first half of 1966 that Britain had no intention of 'ratting on our existing commitments', and that they would maintain their military presence in Malaysia and Singapore 'for as long as [those] governments . . . agree that we should do so on acceptable conditions'.

This robust statement of policy did not long survive the continuing failure of the British Labour government's deflationary policies to reverse the balance of payments problem, nor the lack of enthusiasm generally for a continuation of the old imperial role within both the parliamentary Labour Party and British public opinion. By April 1967 Britain had reached a decision on withdrawal, and in July the British announced that half the forces then in Malaysia and Singapore would leave by 1971, with the remainder to follow between 1973 and 1976. Britain's world role was no longer consistent with Britain's actual position, but the wonder is that it took so long for the realisation to be acted upon. Certainly British investments in Malaya were considerable, and had been an important source of foreign earnings in the lean years immediately after the Second World War. But the rationalisation of British military commitments in the Far East had been proposed in the Defence White Paper in 1957 when Duncan Sandys had been Defence Secretary, and the end of conscription in 1963 and the subsequent contraction of the forces had further reduced the capacity of British arms to maintain a presence so far from Europe. And increasingly it was seen that Britain's future lay in Europe, both economically and militarily.

This development was a shock to the relevant governments in the region, despite the fact that Menzies seems to have been emphasising the American link as the only serious means of underwriting Australian security in his last years as prime minister. Recent experience had demonstrated the stabilising effect on the region of a British military presence, but the Australian reaction suggested a lack of understanding and a lack of generosity towards a power which had born a disproportionate share of the regional burden, a burden which Australian governments had shown no desire to share equitably. The changed circumstances now led Australia and New Zealand to consider augmenting the defences of Malaysia and Singapore with force commitments of their own. A five-power conference of senior ministers was held in Kuala Lumpur on 10–11 June 1968; it reached no decision on a framework for the defence of the region after 1971, although the British softened their position a little and agreed to participate in major exercises there in 1971 and to continue to train and exercise in the area after that date. Australia's position was equivocal, in that the prime minister, John Gorton, was attracted to notions of an end to 'Forward Defence' and the development of 'Fortress Australia' as the basis of Australian strategic planning.

The delays in announcing formally the government's decision with regard to Australia's role in the region after 1971 excited unfavourable comment in editorials and the parliament. It was not until a parliamentary statement on 25 February 1969 that Australia's contribution to the Five-Power Defence Arrangements (FPDA) was spelt out. Presenting the decision as a contribution to regional stability, Gorton announced that Australia would commit two squadrons of Mirages (forty-two aircraft, mostly based at Butterworth in Malaysia), a naval vessel additional to the New Zealand ship already allocated, and agreed to the basing of an infantry battalion in Singapore in conjunction with a New Zealand battalion. The RAAF component was the most significant portion of this involvement, since it had a strike capacity unmatched anywhere in Southeast Asia short of the war in Indochina, but the ground force component was of less value, since the government specified that it could only be used in the eventuality of renewed communist insurgency. The decision to base the battalion in Singapore further reduced its significance. At the same time, Australia extended defence aid to Malaysia in the form of military equipment and the training of personnel.

The election of a Conservative government in Britain in November 1970 led to a decision to continue to base British troops in Malaysia and Singapore. With the Heath government's insistence on holding defence expenditure unchanged, this renewed commitment could be of a limited nature only, a fact quickly appreciated in Canberra. Britain now was to be merely an equal partner with the other powers concerned in the FPDA, agreeing to the basing of a number of ships and aircraft and a battalion group in the region. Agreement was reached on a number of outstanding problems in 1971 as a result of continued British participation, notably the formation of an air defence council to supervise the integrated air defence system. After 1970 the response to Britain's policy in the matter was decidedly low-key, an indication that unthinking Australian dependence on the projection of British power in Southeast Asia was now a thing of the past.

The limited nature of the Five-Power Defence Arrangements and the hesitant manner in which Australia entered into them were in contrast to the *Anglo-Malayan Defence Agreement* of 1957, and were as good an indication as any of the way in which the strategic environment had changed in the twenty years encompassed by this chapter. Australia's role in ANZAM had been that of a minor actor, a part well-suited to the small size of her forces and her strategic dependence on Britain, at least until the early 1960s. Australian involvement in operations in Borneo during Confrontation was of little military significance in terms of the final outcome, but was perceived to fulfill a useful diplomatic function. Much the same might be said about participation in the Vietnam War alongside the United States.

The years between 1955 and 1972 were ones of prolonged military activity for the services, although only the war in Vietnam could be characterised as intense. The army underwent great organisational upheaval, particularly in the early 1960s, while the source of defence equipment procurement was oriented away from Britain and towards the United States. This latter change affected the RAAF most of all. The higher direction and organisation of Australian defence underwent substantial changes also, although the full measure of these became obvious only towards the end of the Vietnam period and in the years immediately thereafter, and will be dealt with fully in the next chapter. For the first time since the Second World War, the involvement of Australian servicemen overseas had been a matter of widespread public concern in the late 1960s, and defence and foreign policy issues were just one of the many areas which were thrown open to questioning in the early 1970s; an attitude of mind reflected in the election of the first Labor government for twenty-three years in December 1972.

CHAPTER 11

The Post-Vietnam Era, 1972–2000

Defence was not a high priority for the new Labor administration. Twenty-three years on the Opposition benches had bred a hunger for reformist activity when the party finally regained power, although Gough Whitlam's government was hardly as radical as the rosy glow of nostalgia would have us believe, nor as irresponsible in matters of national security as its domestic critics and an unnecessarily alarmed US administration claimed. The government's failures had more to do with the failings of particular ministers than with any grand design to wreck the Western alliance and Australia's part in it, and for all his ability and dominance over the party machine, Whitlam was unable to control his government in crucial areas. Defence and foreign policy, however, were not fields which suffered conspicuously from this phenomenon, in the latter case because the Prime Minister himself took a personal interest; in the former because defence did not raise much interest in the wider ALP. Indeed, Whitlam's own lengthy and highly detailed account of his government's record devotes just eight pages to defence issues. These were the days of 'no perceivable threat' for at least ten years.

As part of the general spirit of reform, the ALP announced that it would reorganise the Defence group of departments in order to bring about a more integrated approach to defence management. The first step in this process was the appointment of a single Minister for Defence with responsibility for all five departments, to be aided by an assistant minister with responsibilities for the forces themselves. All this did was finally to implement the central recommendation of the Morshead Committee in 1958, and confirm a process which had been under way gradually in the intervening fifteen years. Labor should be given the credit, nonetheless, for implementing a decision which the coalition government had shirked consistently. The creation of an integrated system for formulating policy and the organisational change concomitant upon it was made the responsibility of the Secretary of the Defence Department, the redoubtable Sir Arthur Tange.

Tange is more closely identified with this period than anyone else. A mandarin of the old school, he had been permanent head of the Department of External Affairs between 1954 and 1965. A forceful and irascible man of great ability, his reorganisation aroused great opposition in certain quarters both inside and outside the forces. He dominated the department in much the same manner as Shedden, and his influence was as pervasive. (This is not a comparison which would commend itself necessarily to Tange. Relations between the two permanent heads in the 1950s were less than cordial, Shedden referring caustically to the small External Affairs Department as 'neophyte'.) A centralist by inclination, Tange argued that the separate service organisations served merely to duplicate functions and demands for resources, and allowed the services to equip and organise themselves to fight according to their own assumptions and largely in isolation from one another. He was also highly critical of the quality of policy advice and decision-making on the uniformed side, and argued that service officers were both poorly and narrowly educated which provided inadequate preparation for the senior ranks within the Defence bureaucracy. Central to the Tange Report, delivered to the minister in November 1973, was the abolition of the individual service departments while maintaining the services as separate entities. There was no suggestion of unifying the services in the manner of the Hellyer reforms in Canada.

The Minister for Defence now assumed sole responsibility for the direction of defence policy, the command and administration of the forces and the administration of the department. The separate service ministries, the most junior ministerial posts in government, were abolished. The three chiefs of staff were designated the professional heads of their services and were given full powers to command and administer them along the lines laid down by the higher defence committees. This was at the expense of the service boards of administration, which were abolished. The position of Chief of the Defence Force Staff (CDFS) was created, to command the defence force and to act as the government's principal military adviser with direct access to the minister. The administration of the defence force was divided jointly between the CDFS and the secretary of the department. This move occasioned much criticism, since it was held that the division of responsibility reduced the command powers of the CDFS; in fact, the administrative functions invested in the two senior offices were delegated in their entirety to the service chiefs of staff. The importance of the Secretary's position was enhanced by several factors. He had sole responsibility for advising the minister on matters of defence policy, and either the Secretary or his deputies chaired the majority of the principal committees. Senior civilian officials tend to serve much longer in key posts than either ministers or senior service officers, and this factor heightened the power and influence of the Secretary relative to that enjoyed by the CDFS. The department itself ceased to be a pre-dominantly civilian one as new military positions were created in the central office, but the CDFS continued to operate with insufficient staff support for the range of functions which he now discharged.

The system of higher defence committees to advise the government on matters of policy was continued and strengthened. There were twelve such committees, with membership drawn from both civilian and military staff on all but two, which were entirely military in composition. At the same time the government implemented the five-year defence program in 1972–73, which required that the bids for resources advanced by the individual services should be scrutinised against wider strategic requirements and the overall policy assumptions of the defence force as a whole. This was not a new idea either, but drew upon the work done under Tange's predecessor, Sir Henry Bland. In a bid to improve the educational standards of service officers and to break down the myopic single-service prejudices which inhibited a broad view of defence issues generally, the Australian Defence Force Academy was set up to provide tertiary education to officer aspirants in a tri-service environment. The concept was strongly resisted in various quarters, especially by the RAN, and was forced through by Malcolm Fraser after he became prime minister in 1975. The Academy opened in 1986 and has been the subject of regular review and criticism, much of the latter uninformed and motivated by something other than concern for effective and coherent educational policy within the Australian Defence Force.

The reorganisation was implemented in stages, beginning in November 1973 with the abolition of the service boards and culminating in the passage of the Defence Force Reorganisation Act in 1975. It resulted in a centralised system of defence, and moved Australia in the same direction as most other Western defence bureaucracies in this period. It was not implemented without opposition, but while vociferous in some quarters this did not alter the basic thrust of Tange's changes. The process has proved irreversible, and the Liberal–Country Party Opposition made no attempt to turn back the clock when it returned to government at the end of 1975.

The Whitlam government was active diplomatically throughout its tenure of office, and this activity affected defence policy in a number of areas, principally in terms of Australia's commitments in the region.

Involvement in the Five-Power Defence Arrangements was scaled down in 1973 with the announcement that Australia would withdraw the infantry battalion and artillery battery stationed in Singapore as part of the ANZUK Brigade. The British government decided to withdraw its contribution in 1974 following a defence review, a decision which probably would have been made anyway regardless of the earlier Australian decision. The ANZUK force was disbanded finally in January 1975, the New Zealand government making other arrangements for the continued basing of its infantry unit in Singapore. The remaining Australian detachments in Malaysia and Singapore stayed, however, and the basing of the RAAF Squadrons at Butterworth did not end until 1988. The decision to withdraw part of the force owed more to party ideology than any rational calculation of strategic need or vested interest, and since the force existed at the invitation of the host governments it furnished a good example of the way in which the ALP could allow the presuppositions of one section of the party to dictate national policy regardless of national interest. As a result largely of Australian initiatives, the SEATO Council wound up military planning activity in 1973, the organisation agreeing in September 1975 to phase itself out completely.

Relations with the United States were patchy, a product of the generalised anti-Americanism of the left of the party fuelled by the war in Vietnam, and a fear in Washington, not always soundly based, that the Whitlam government would downgrade ANZUS and threaten the further operation of the communications and monitoring installations which the United States had established on Australian soil with Australian endorsement. In practice, Whitlam had no intention of threatening these facilities and the central role which they played in Western security policy, but he was able to negotiate an agreement with the Americans in 1974 whereby the installation at North West Cape became a joint facility. While the critics were correct in their assertion that hosting the 'bases' increased the likelihood of their becoming nuclear targets in a Soviet–American conflict, they were naive to assume that their removal would allow Australia to opt out of Soviet nuclear target selection while the opposition, with its heavy overlay of anti-American sentiment, ignored the many conventional benefits which accrue to Australia through the allied relationship so nurtured and which have been enhanced, not diminished, since the breakdown of the ANZUS Treaty which followed New Zealand's withdrawal over nuclear ship visits in 1984–85.

Not the least of these conventional benefits, highlighted by the joint facilities themselves, is the access granted to the intelligence resources of both the United States and, through various arrangements, the

United Kingdom and Canada. Renewed priority has been given also to Australian intelligence capabilities in regional matters, on which our assessments may differ from those of our alliance partners. Intelligence priorities are shaped in line with the emphasis upon 'self-reliance', a move welcomed by the Americans. It is said that at the height of the Vietnam War Australian intelligence organisations could provide the government with details of the load-bearing capacities of every bridge in North Vietnam, but were completely unable to do the same for the roads and bridges in northern Australia. Much has changed in the succeeding twenty years.

The other significant regional commitment which ended under Whitlam was responsibility for the defence of Papua-New Guinea. Independence was granted to PNG on 16 September 1975, but the defence power had been transferred in March that year, and the PNG Defence Force (PNGDF) had been created in January 1973 as part of the process of readying the country for independence. The force consisted of two infantry battalions and an engineer company, patrol boat and landing craft squadrons and a flight of transport aircraft. The land component built upon the Pacific Islands Regiment (PIR), raised during the Second World War, disbanded in 1946 and reformed in 1950. The PIR had been upgraded significantly during the period of tense relations with Indonesia in the 1960s, but the force operated as an integral part of the Australian army; until 1964 only three indigenous personnel had been commissioned in its ranks. At the request of the new government of Michael Somare, Australia continued to provide personnel for the training and development of the PNGDF, and its first commander from 1973 until independence was an Australian brigadier who was succeeded in September 1975 by the senior ranking national, Brigadier Ted Diro. The Australian Defence Advisory Group was based in Port Moresby, and at independence numbered 482 personnel acting in support of a Land Element of 2917, a Maritime Element of 431 and an Air Element of 43. The PNGDF was intended deliberately to be a modest force, in keeping with the budgetary limitations which faced a newly independent Papua-New Guinea, and continued to rely upon the Australian forces for logistic support and training facilities.

For obvious reasons, the efficiency of the force and the developments in PNG policy remained of central concern to Australian defence policy makers, reflected by the *Joint Declaration of Principles* on defence matters signed in December 1987. Defence relations in the decade thereafter became increasingly strained. There were a number of causes: Australian attempts to reduce dollar aid were resented in Port Moresby, as was criticism of the conduct of the PNGDF on Bougainville, where the Bougainville Revolutionary Army has waged a secessionist struggle for years. This criticism was tied particularly to the use made of Australian-supplied helicopters, which allegedly were used in a gunship role although this had been forbidden by the Australian government. The growing corruption of public life in PNG, which reached into the armed forces, and increasing crime and violence in the urban centres also helped sour relations. The Sandline mercenary affair in 1997 – when the government introduced a mercenary group into the Bougainville crisis which prompted the intervention of sections of the army and led to the fall of the prime minister, Sir Julius Chan – was the absolute nadir and the logical consequence of the lack of confidence which had developed between the two sides. Personnel from the PNGDF continue to receive education and training in Australia, and the sight of Australian military medical personnel assisting in the aftermath of the tidal wave disaster in northern New Guinea in August 1998 certainly helped to restore Australia's image among the population, but the relationship has a long way to go before it reaches the warmth and closeness of earlier decades.

The Tange Report had concerned itself with the higher levels of defence machinery and with the civil–military policy process; it had said little about the individual services themselves. There was considerable activity on this front also, although again some at least of the changes introduced drew upon earlier initiatives. Thus the internal restructuring of the army which replaced the regional commands, based on the states and in existence since Federation, with functional commands both brought the army into line with the other services and arose from the recommendations of the Hassett Committee which had been convened in 1970–71. The Whitlam government improved markedly the terms and conditions of service in 1973, giving effect to the recommendations of the Kerr–Woodward and Jess Committees, which had begun their inquiries in 1971–72. All three services received additional equipment but, in the nature of these things, these often stemmed from purchasing decisions made years previously. (In the case of the F-111, many years previously. The last of these aircraft to enter service did so in 1974, although the initial order had been placed in 1963.)

Arguably the most contentious of the service reforms affected the army and stemmed from the Millar Report into the CMF. We have noted already that the citizen force had been superseded as the mainstay of the Australian ground forces in the postwar period, and the unfortunate decisions which led to an influx of 'optees' seeking to avoid national service had ruined many CMF units. The Millar Committee found that the CMF was now 'a force heavily depleted in strength at the lower levels and as a result was unable to fulfill adequately any of its tasks'. Amalgamations of understrength units, improvements in conditions of service, closer cooperation between the citizens' force, now designated the Army Reserve, and the Regular Army were all adopted. So too, and most controversially, was the decision to abolish the old CMF divisions thus removing them from the army's order of battle. This more than anything else revived the old animosities between militia and Staff Corps, largely dormant since 1945, and led some senior retired CMF officers, who should have known better, to assert publicly that this move was the Staff Corps' revenge for being denied commands in the Second World War.

Millar's report had many good features, and even those provisions which many in the CMF disliked were necessary if the part-time force was to survive at all. Millar wrote of a 'total force' (later refined into the concept of 'one army') and argued that the Reserve was an essential component of the defence of Australia. It had to have a role, that role had to be clearly defined, and then the measures needed to give it meaning had to be implemented. It was here that the process broke down. Those measures which cut costs were implemented quickly. Thus the recommendation that units and formations be manned on a restricted establishment condemned the Reserve to 'hollowness' – an inability to match actual capabilities to theoretical organisation. Many recommendations lapsed because the will and the resources to implement them were lacking. In 1983 the government decided to tax reservists' pay, which led to a further slump in both retention and recruiting. In 1986, when Paul Dibb undertook his review of Australia's defence capabilities, he was able to write that 'the Army Reserve has suffered over the years from a lack of purpose', comments which were reinforced in the White Paper of 1987 which followed. CMF cynicism over the Millar report would seem to have been justified by events.

The Whitlam period saw far-reaching reforms in the military sector, many of them the natural culmination of earlier decisions under previous governments. The first ALP Defence Minister, Lance Barnard, had promised in 1972 that the level of defence expenditure under Labor would not fall below 3.5 per cent of gross domestic product. This was not sustained in declining economic circumstances; in 1972–73 the level was 3.1 per cent and in 1973–74, 2.8 per cent. In 1974–75 it edged back to 3.1 per cent again, but although defence expenditure increased in absolute terms much of this was taken by inflation, while the overdue reforms in pay and conditions meant that an increasing proportion of the defence allocation would be eaten up in manpower costs. It may well be that the necessary reforms of this period were realised precisely because the Labor Party as a whole paid little attention to defence and was diverted by other issues. Overall, however, the period of ALP rule in

1972–75 should refute the popular notion that Labor governments are somehow 'soft' on defence issues.

The Liberal–Country Party administration which replaced Labor in 1975 built upon the directions set under Whitlam. The Defence White Paper tabled in 1976 accepted many of the assumptions of the last defence report in 1975 with its adoption of 'increased self-reliance' in defence matters. But defence policy was still bedevilled by the absence of a clear and immediate threat. The White Paper's advocacy of a 'core force' concept by which the forces were to acquire and develop 'the structure, equipment and professional skills adequate for timely expansion against a range of contingencies of various types and timings' avoided the question about the nature of the contingencies which might have to be met, and about the type of forces which would be called upon to meet them. Forward defence was discarded, but nothing concrete had been erected in its place. By the beginning of the 1980s the army was incapable of meeting any but the most low-level threat at short notice; the RAN was facing block obsolescence and its role in the defence of Australia was undercut still further in 1983 with the decision not to replace the aircraft carrier *Melbourne*, and hence to phase out the maritime air capacity acquired at such cost; while the RAAF lacked any system of continental radar, an integrated system of air defence, or an airborne early warning capacity.

The Whitlam government and the years immediately thereafter were a period of transition in defence. They were followed by years of wide-ranging and sometimes dramatic changes in the defence sector which have persisted into the second half of the 1990s. Under successive Labor administrations between 1983 and 1996 and then under a renewed period of conservative coalition government the ways in which the Department of Defence and the ADF go about their business have been transformed. This process is exemplified by the very label, 'Australian Defence Force'. The term did not exist before 1975, and it was only formalised in the annual Defence Report in 1980. The change in nomenclature signifies the different ways in which the services and the civilian bureaucracy have had to think about defence issues in the post-Vietnam, and now post-Cold War, eras. Discussion of these developments will encompass organisation; acquisition and force structure; strategic posture; operational deployments; and the civil–military interface. In reality, many of these issues impinged heavily upon each other and it is not possible to deal with each in turn and in isolation.

The reforms associated with Tange were only the first stage in the reorganisation of Australia's defence. In 1981–82 the Defence Review Committee, chaired by a prominent businessman, John Utz, modified the higher organisation which Tange had put in place. The basic structure was confirmed, but a new Department of Defence Support was created and the staff of the CDFS was increased. This was followed in turn in 1984 with a change in nomenclature which saw the title of CDFS replaced by Chief of the Defence Force. The incumbent, General Sir Phillip Bennett, took the opportunity to reorganise his staff into Head-quarters, ADF and to create three new environmental headquarters in order to enhance his ability to command the operational forces in war. Maritime Headquarters was created in July 1985, replacing the old Fleet Headquarters, while Land and Air Headquarters were created in February 1986. Nor was this the final alteration to the higher defence machinery. In March 1988 a report by Brigadier John Baker (a sub-sequent CDF) brought about further changes in the three functional commands designed to enhance the ADF's capacity for joint operations. The service chiefs were now removed from the chain of command and the functional commands made responsible directly to the CDF. In March the following year Major General John Sanderson (a subsequent CGS) headed a review whose aim was to rationalise the existing head-quarters structures and reduce the number of senior officers in Can-berra: HQ ADF had increased in size and importance, but there had been little corresponding diminution of the three service headquarters.

At the same time, there was a major overhaul of the defence intelligence organisation. In February 1997 the three service chiefs were redesignated chiefs of their respective services (i.e. Chief of Army, Chief of Navy, Chief of Air Force) and their functions within the ADF con-fined to raising, training, equipping and maintaining units within their service, and to support the CDF in the 'preparations, sustainment, development and command' of the ADF. Renewed emphasis was placed on joint planning and command arrangements through, for example, the creation of a Headquarters Australian Theatre (HQAST), and functions such as logistic support were placed in peacetime under the joint commands to which they would answer operationally. This process was further emphasised in the Defence Reform Program initiated by the report of the Macintosh committee into defence management, which submitted its findings in March 1997.

Nor has change been merely organisational. In 1985 the recently appointed Labor minister, Kim Beazley, commissioned Paul Dibb to undertake a review of 'the content, priorities and rationale' for Aus-tralian defence planning. Dibb recommended a concentration on the defence of Australia's 'area of direct military interest' (meaning Southeast Asia essentially) and emphasised that with limited resources a country such as Australia should play an appropriately minor and modest supporting role in areas not of primary concern to its own security. Along with identifying the area of direct military interest, Dibb suggested that Australia's defence efforts should be structured to meet three levels of threat (low-level conflict, escalated low-level conflict, and more substantial conflict), and emphasised denial and defence in depth as the bases for countering these threats. The subsequent White Paper, *The Defence of Australia*, published in 1987, accepted many of Dibb's conclusions and arguments, but critics of the government's policy argued that there was still an assumption that Australia would maintain a willingness and a capacity to operate further afield, suggesting that old ideas about 'forward defence' were not really dead after all. Support for this view seemed to be offered by Operation Morris Dance, the Australian response to the coup in Fiji in May 1987, during which a rifle company from the Operational Deployment Force in Townsville was deployed by naval task force to the vicinity to intervene if necessary. The incident demonstrated the need to develop the ADF's strategic lift capacity, and that Australia was prepared to intervene in the South Pacific. Subsequent steps to boost the Five Power Defence Arrangements, and an increase in deployments and joint and combined exercises with the armed forces of the ASEAN member states under the rubric of 'regional engagement', suggested that the basis of Australia's defence policy was more than simply one of 'self reliance'. In the period 1993–98 the budget for defence cooperation activities trebled, from $2.2 million to $6.6 million.

These positions were strengthened with the issue of *Australia's Strategic Planning in the 1990s* (DSP 90), published in 1990, and by the 1994 White Paper, *Defending Australia* (DA 94). The 1987 White Paper had set out the force structure requirements for the three services, and the subsequent statements of policy refined and developed these. The Labor government also undertook a large-scale capital equipment acquisition program, in part a response to the deferment of major equipment purchases under the Fraser government. For the RAN this meant the maintenance of the three Adams-class DDG destroyers and the six FFG guided missile frigates, supplemented by eight Anzac-class light patrol frigates introduced into service in the course of the 1990s. The DDGs, arguably the most cost-effective ship ever acquired by the RAN, will probably be paid off by 2005. Fifteen Fremantle-class patrol boats provide security in coastal waters and police Australia's maritime rights, while six conventional Collins-class submarines will have replaced the ageing Oberon boats in the early years of the 21st century, although there have been significant design and systems problems in the development of the Collins. The 1990 strategic basis document recommended the basing of the submarines and four frigates in the waters of Western Australia, and a fleet base at HMAS *Stirling* has been developed to accommodate them. Likewise arising from the 1994 statement, patrol vessels and hydrographic ships have been based in northern waters. The need to boost the ADF's strategic lift, demonstrated at the time of the Fiji coup, has been met in part by the purchase of two heavy landing ships on favourable terms from the United States, but the purchase has proved controversial because of the extensive and expensive refitting which the ships have required before entering Australian service.

The navy has been the major beneficiary of this process, but the other services have also been affected by the changes brought about under Labor. The RAAF has acquired additional F-111 aircraft to enhance its strike capability, and the transport fleet of C130 Hercules aircraft has been upgraded. The Jindalee Over-the-Horizon radar system, a key element in the defence of the air-sea gap to Australia's north, remains controversially uncompleted while the air force's desire for airborne early warning and control aircraft (AWACS in popular parlance) has been frustrated by budgetary considerations, as has the acquisition of air-to-air refuelling. A replacement for the Army's main battle tank, the obsolescent Leopard acquired in the mid-1970s, has been deferred amidst speculation as to whether tanks have any role to play in Australian defence. A new generation of light armoured reconnaissance vehicles, the LAV 25, has been introduced into service, but the Army still relies on Vietnam-era M113 armoured personnel carriers for battlefield mobility. As part of the reorientation of Australia's strategic posture, significant sections of the army have been deployed to northern Australia, with the brigade which has been based in Townsville since 1964 now matched by another in Darwin. Surveillance across northern Australia is conducted by Army Reserve units – 51 Far North Queensland Regiment in Cape York and the Gulf country, Norforce in the Top End and the Kimberleys, and the Pilbara Regiment in the northwest – and these make extensive use of Aborigines and Torres Straits Islanders in their ranks. They are a telling example of what the Army Reserve might do if properly resourced and given a clearly defined role. In an attempt to lift the standard of the Reserve, in 1991 the government introduced the Ready Reserve scheme, whereby an existing regular brigade based in Brisbane was converted to Ready Reserve status and manned with Reservists who would complete a period of twelve months full-time duty before reverting to regular Reserve status and a four-year part-time commitment. The scheme promised much, but was not given a full testing before being scrapped by the incoming coalition government in 1996.

While all these changes in policy, administration and organisation were underway, the ADF was not standing still. Australia had been a founding member of the United Nations in 1945 and a strong supporter of collective security through involvement in the Korean War under UN

Table 11.1   Australian involvement in multinational peacekeeping, 1947–98

Date(a)	Operation	Acronym
1947–49	UN Good Offices Commission [Indonesia]	UNGOC
1949–51	UN Commission for Indonesia	UNCI
1950–85	UN Military Observer Group in India and Pakistan	UNMOGIP
1950	UN Commission on Korea	UNCOK
1950–56	UN Command – Korea	UNC – K
1950–56	UN Command Military Armistice Commission	UNCMAC
1956–present	UN Truce Supervision Organisation [Sinai]	UNTSO
1960–61	UN Operation in the Congo	ONUC
1962	UN Temporary Executive Authority [West Irian]	UNTEA
1963	UN Yemen Observation Mission	UNYOM
1964–present	UN Force in Cyprus	UNFICYP
1965–66	UN India–Pakistan Observation Mission	UNIPOM
1974	UN Disengagement Observer Force [Syria]	UNDOF
1976–79	Second UN Emergency Force [Sinai]	UNEF II
1979–80	Commonwealth Monitoring Force [Zimbabwe]	CMF
1982–present	Multinational Force and Observers [Sinai]	MFO(b)
1982–84	Commonwealth Military Training Team – Uganda	CMTTU
1988–90	UN Iran–Iraq Military Observer Group	UNIIMOG
1989–90	UN Transition Assistance Force [Namibia]	UNTAG
1990–91	First Maritime Interception Force	MIF I(c)
1991	Multinational Forces in Iraq–Kuwait	MNF (I-K)(c)
1991–present	Second Maritime Interception Force	MIF II(c)
1991–94	UN Mission for the Referendum in Western Sahara	MINURSO(d)
1991–92	UN Advance Mission in Cambodia	UNAMIC(e)
1992–93	UN Transitional Authority in Cambodia	UNTAC
1992–95	UN Protection Force [former Yugoslavia]	UNPROFOR
1995–present	NATO Stabilisation Force in Bosnia	SFOR
1992–93	First UN Operation in Somalia	UNOSOM I
1992–93	Unified Task Force in Somalia	UNITAF(f)
1993–94	Second UN Operation in Somalia	UNOSOM II(g)
1994–95	UN Assistance Mission in Rwanda	UNAMIR
1994–95	UN Operation in Mozambique	UNOMOZ
1994	South Pacific Peacekeeping Force [Bougainville]	SPPKF
1994–95	Multinational Force [Haiti]	MNF
1997–present	UN Mission for the Verification of Human Rights in Guatamala	MINUGUA
1997–98	Truce Monitoring Group [Bougainville]	TMG
1998–present	Peace Monitoring Group [Bougainville]	PMG
Australian Contributions to other UN Operations		
1947–52	UN Special Commission on the Balkans	UNSCOB
1984–87	UN Chemical Warfare Investigation Team	
1989–93	UN Border Relief Operation [Cambodia]	UNBRO
1989–93	UN Mine Clearance Training Team	UNMCTT(h)
1991–	UN Special Commission [Iraq]	UNSCOM(i)
1991	Operation Provide Comfort (j)	

Source: Neil James, 'A Brief History of Australian Participation in Multinational Peacekeeping', in Hugh Smith (ed.), *Peacekeeping: Challenges for the Future*, Canberra, 1993.

(a)   Indicates date range of Australian involvement only.
(b)   Australian involvement in 1982–86 and 1993–present.
(c)   Operation Damask.
(d)   Operation Cedilla.
(e)   Operation Gemini.
(f)   Operation Solace.
(g)   Operation Iguana.
(h)   Operation Salaam.
(i)   Operation Blazer.
(j)   Operation Habitat.

auspices. From the late-1940s to the mid-1960s, Australia had made small but regular contributions to UN peacekeeping missions in various parts of the world, but during the Vietnam War most of these had fallen into abeyance. From the late 1970s Australian involvement in multinational peacekeeping initiatives was revived, and members of the ADF found themselves deployed in a variety of forces around the world, mostly but not necessarily under UN sanction. As a member of the Commonwealth, Australia deployed troops to Rhodesia/Zimbabwe to assist in monitoring the Lancaster House Agreement which brought the long-running bush war to an end in 1979, and from 1982 contributed to the Multinational Force and Observers in the Sinai, under American auspices, to supervise the Camp David peace accords which ended decades of hostilities between Israel and Egypt. In most cases, the numbers contributed were small and their functions specialised, providing communications, transport or engineering support, for example, as in Namibia in 1989–90.

Peacekeeping has provided the ADF with a means of giving some of its members valuable service in a quasi-operational environment and alongside numerous foreign armed forces, but Australia has rarely played a major or leading role in these operations. There are a number of reasons for this. The UN's operating procedures usually call on advanced Western militaries for the higher-level technical and staff support (signals, air transport etc.) in a force while utilising the militaries of less-developed countries to provide the bulk of the rank and file. The Royal Fiji Military Forces have specialised in this latter role for years, regularly deploying infantry battalions on rotation to places like Lebanon. This practice is reinforced by the fact that the language of command and staff work in UN forces is generally English. The slender resource base of the ADF has led to an understandable reluctance on the part of the services to commit too great a proportion of its forces to peacekeeping – the commitment to Cambodia in 1991–93 denuded the ADF of its communications personnel. Finally, there is a widespread belief that peacekeeping is a useful adjunct to the main purpose for which armed forces exist, namely war fighting, and that the balance between the two must be maintained in favour of the latter if the ADF is to fulfill its primary mission if called upon to do so. The Canadian example of recent years suggests that there is merit in this argument.

The only occasion on which Australia has taken a leading role was in Cambodia in 1991–93. The civil war which broke out after the ouster of the Khmer Rouge in 1979 was an issue of considerable regional concern and one in which Australia took a particular interest. In August 1989 the UN attempted to broker a peace agreement and two Australian officers were among a reconnaissance team sent in to lay the ground work for a monitoring force; the collapse of the peace effort led to their withdrawal and the cancellation of the proposed force. Following the Paris Agreements of 1991, the UN established the Transitional Authority in Cambodia to monitor the ceasefire and the planned national election in March 1992. In advance of UNTAC's arrival, the Advance Mission in Cambodia included a communications unit of 65 Australian servicemen and women, and the ADF was to contribute over 500 personnel to Cambodia, including 488 in the Force Communications Unit as well as the force commander, Lieutenant General John Sanderson. At its height UNTAC comprised over 16 000 personnel from thirty-two countries. Members of the Force Communications Unit operated in small groups spread across the country in fifty-six locations, providing electronic communications infrastructure in a country which had none. Six Blackhawk helicopters and their crews were deployed between May and July 1993, and the Australian Federal Police contributed to the civil police component to assist in the restoration of civil law and order. During the election itself, the Australian Electoral Commission provided up to fifty staff to assist with tasks such as voter registration.

Two other UN-sanctioned missions are worth discussing more fully because they represented departures from the norm of peacekeeping operations as the ADF usually experienced them: the Second Gulf War of 1990–91, and the operations in Somalia in 1992–93. Both episodes reflected the continuing importance of the alliance with the United States, and each suggested that the 'area of direct military interest' was being interpreted liberally by the government.

The Iraqi invasion of Kuwait in August 1990 prompted a UN resolution demanding withdrawal followed closely by the imposition of sanctions and a call for UN member states to contribute naval forces to implement them. Planning for a possible Australian contribution began before the UN call for contributions had been made, and it was decided that a naval task group of two FFG guided missile frigates and a replenishment ship would best meet the requirement and be a sustainable contribution. President George Bush made a direct and personal request for support to the prime minister, Bob Hawke, and on 11 August the latter announced publicly the commitment of HMAS *Adelaide*, *Darwin*, and *Success* for duties in the Gulf of Oman. To ensure adequate protection against air attack, *Success* was supported by a detachment from the Army's 16th Air Defence Regiment equipped with anti-aircraft missile systems. The major role of the Maritime Interception Force was the stopping and searching of merchant vessels for illicit cargo bound for Iraqi ports. From the time they began duty at the beginning of September until the end of 1990, the Australian ships conducted 1627 interrogations, eleven interceptions, eight boardings and two diversions of ships to other ports. On 3 December *Adelaide* and *Darwin* were relieved by *Sydney* and *Brisbane*, the latter a DDG guided missile destroyer. *Success* was replaced by *Westralia* in late January 1991.

On 29 November the UN issued a further resolution requiring Iraq to withdraw within six weeks or face expulsion from Kuwait by force, and Hawke announced that the role of the Australian ships would be extended to enable them to take part in Operation Desert Storm. The Australian warships were deployed under US operational control and as part of the escort screen for the American carriers *Midway* and *Ranger*, providing anti-air warfare protection. The most serious threat to the ships in fact came from mines, which the Iraqis had sown liberally, and in late January the ADF deployed Clearance Diving Team 3 to the Gulf to assist in mine counter-measure tasks and explosive ordnance demolition. In addition to the naval task group, Australia contributed a total of six surgical support teams on rotation, serving aboard US Navy hospital ships, and a small Army/RAAF intelligence detachment which served with the US Central Command Headquarters. A small number of men also served with US and British ground and air units on individual exchanges and attachments. Following the end of the ground war and the liberation of Kuwait, the Australian contribution to the Maritime Interception Force was scaled down, and a single FFG continued to participate in maritime interception tasks in the Gulf.

There were no Australian casualties in the Gulf War and the ships all returned undamaged. The Gulf commitment demonstrated a number of things. The contribution was a small one but was important for the navy in testing its ships and their capabilities, although on this score it is worth noting that the Gulf, like Vietnam, brought home the fact that the older classes of surface combatant in the RAN were not equipped to operate in a high intensity threat environment like the Gulf because they lacked modern close-in weapons systems for self-defence. The political and military command and administrative structures which had evolved over the previous decade were given a thorough workout and generally proved effective, although some sections of Defence were placed under considerable strain. The importance to the US of the joint facilities at Nurrungar and Pine Gap was demonstrated again, the one playing an important part in the early detection of Scud missile launchings while the other was involved in electronic intelligence gathering. From a broader perspective, the popular sensitivities to the possibility of casualties – demonstrated by the tearful scenes at the initial departure of the task group and by emotional public comments by some family members of the crews – underscored the importance of preparing public opinion in advance of possible foreign deployments in the post-Vietnam era.

If the dispatch of Australian forces to the Middle East seemed to reprise a familiar theme in our history, the deployment to Somalia

Map 23a Area of operations, RAN Task Group, Desert Shield, 1990

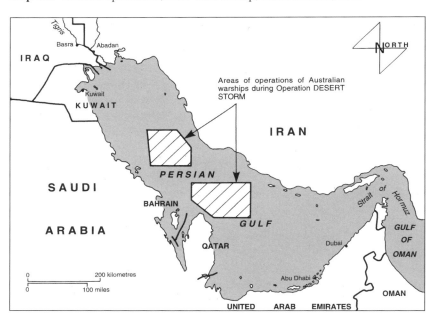

Map 23b Area of operations, RAN Task Group, Desert Storm, 1990–91. *Source: Oxford Companion to Australian Military History,* Melbourne, 1995.

was much more exotic. The UN intervention in Somalia was in some respects driven by the international media and western public opinion; as the country collapsed into internecine clan warfare, mass starvation and the attendant destruction of the civil infrastructure, pressure grew to intervene in the country's internal affairs. In particular, this took the form initially of providing support and protection for international humanitarian organisations attempting to provide food, medical and other aid. The further deterioration of conditions soon outstripped the UN's capacity to provide this, and at the beginning of December 1992 the United States was authorised to form a force from a coalition of member states to protect the aid effort and restore (not merely keep) the peace. Once again, the trigger for the commitment was a request from the United States, but there had been a feeling in some quarters within the army that part of the Operational Deployment Force should be utilised in a peacekeeping role for morale and readiness reasons. The anticipated level of violence within Somalia – there were estimated to be 15 000 armed Somalis in Mogadishu alone – lent weight to the suggestion that an infantry battalion group be sent on this occasion, able to protect the aid workers and fight if required.

The battalion group consisted of 1 RAR and a squadron of the 3rd/4th Cavalry Regiment with field engineer, signals and intelligence elements and civil–military liaison teams attached. The total size of the force was 937 personnel, and they deployed to Somalia in mid-January 1993. The Australian government set a strict time limit on the deployment – seventeen weeks – and a financial cap on costs – under $20 million. The Australians took over the Humanitarian Relief Sector based on Baidoa in the country's southwest, and were regarded generally as one of the most effective of the contingents deployed to protect the humanitarian relief efforts. They were withdrawn on schedule in May, and thus must be said to have contributed rather less to the longer-term goals of nation-building since these required the maintenance of security and civil law and order which the Australian force had begun to establish but which they could not maintain by virtue of their departure. Greatly to their credit, they established good relations with the ordinary people in their sector and there were none of the appalling cases of brutality and murder inflicted on Somali civilians by elements of the Canadian, Italian and Belgian forces. One junior NCO was accidentally shot and killed while on patrol in early April.

The 1990s have proven a stressful time for the ADF. The dangers implicit in realistic training were brought home when two Blackhawk helicopters taking part in a night insertion exercise with the SAS crashed in June 1996, killing fourteen servicemen. Two sailors died aboard the submarine HMAS *Otama* in August 1987 when the boat dived while they were outside, and another four were killed in a fire aboard HMAS *Westralia* in May 1998 following the failure of a fuel line in the engine room. There is some suggestion that this accident was related to the privatisation of support services, and a corresponding decline in maintenance standards. The Defence Reform Program submitted to the government by the Macintosh Committee in March 1997 created considerable turmoil in Headquarters ADF and reinforced many of the moves towards the privatisation of support services which had begun under the Commercial Support Program which has been in place since the early 1990s. The size of the ADF has also declined further, with a total strength projected in early 1998 of about 50 000, regarded by many observers as the absolute minimum for organisational viability.

Unhappiness over the reductions in the services provoked heated arguments between the service chiefs and the government, and these disagreements became public in late 1998 when various high-level documents critical of government policy were leaked to the media. Such tension in civil–military relations in Australia is unusual, though not unknown, and was a symptom of a wider dissatisfaction felt by many service personnel of all ranks. This was reinforced further by the perception that several senior army officers were retired or moved because of their strong internal criticism of the drift in defence policy since 1996, and by an increase in resignations among middle-ranking officers.

The introduction of women into many 'non-traditional' branches and musterings within the services has brought problems, as it has to all Western militaries which have opened their organisations in this manner. Sexual harassment incidents have attracted widespread media and public interest, especially that relating to the assault of a female medical officer on board HMAS *Swan* in August 1992. In 1998 the government commissioned a wide-ranging report into incidents of sexual harassment within the ADF, and its recommendations are due for implementation in the closing years of the decade.

In early 1999 the question of opening combat positions in the army to women was raised again, this time by the Chief of the Defence Force, Admiral Barrie. While women have been eligible for combat positions in the RAN and RAAF for some time as well as for non-combat positions in the army, the physical demands attendant upon service in the infantry, for example, are generally regarded as being beyond most women (and many men). It is not clear that such attempts at social engineering, whatever other agendas they satisfy, will do anything to enhance combat effectiveness. Despite much speculation about the impact of the information revolution on the conduct of future war, it seems highly likely that close quarter combat will remain a feature of war fighting for the foreseeable future, and that this has apparently been lost to sight merely reflects the fact that the ADF of the late 1990s now has very few combat veterans in its ranks.

Meanwhile, in November 1992, the Labor government removed the ban on homosexuals serving in the armed forces, against considerable opposition from the chiefs of staff and some public outcry and after an earlier review of the policy in 1989 had recommended that no change be made. The ADF in the 1990s has been forced to accept and adapt to societal change around it, while at the same time the traditional pressures and demands of the service life have in no way diminished. It has meant an uncomfortable process of adjustment for many. Equally, the ADF has probably worked harder and more consistently to eliminate harassment and discrimination within its ranks than any other public institution in Australia.

The European colonial empires have been dissolved and the Cold War has been won. Two of the three most important influences on Australian security policy in the second half of this century (the third being the American alliance) are no longer factors in the formulation of national defence and military policy. Australian society in its complexity, its ethnic composition, and its engagement with the global economy is unrecognisable in comparison with the Australia of the 1950s, much less the 1930s. Probably for the first time this century, a sizeable majority of Australians have no experience of military service or connections, even indirectly, with the armed forces. The Returned and Services League and other veterans' lobby groups, though still powerful in terms of total membership, have less direct influence on policy than at any time since the 1920s.

In an article published in 1976 Sir Arthur Tange suggested that in thinking about Australia's defence needs, Australia's military history 'may be a distraction rather than – as history often is in other matters – a signpost to the future'. If one assumed that the rhetoric of 'defence self-reliance' was to be taken entirely at face value, then perhaps he would be right (and his remark must be understood in the context of the immediate aftermath of Vietnam). In fact, no government of either persuasion has believed that Australians can concentrate on the defence of this continent and its immediately contiguous waters to the exclusion of all else, as the modifications to the Dibb report under Labor and the policy of 'self reliance within an alliance framework' make clear. National security must be, and for most of our history has been, defined in terms other than those of simple geography. We have not simply gone off to fight 'other people's wars', as some critics charge. Rather, generations of Australian politicians, officials and chiefs of staff have understood that there was little point in defending the periphery if the centre itself was threatened, as occurred in both world wars and during the Cold War. A world dominated by German militarism after 1919, or by Hitler and the Japanese militarists of the 1940s, would have been one with which Australians would have had to make some very unpalatable compromises, and without a single German or Japanese soldier necessarily setting foot in Collins Street or on Circular Quay.

It is a simple fact that strategic threats do not necessarily diminish with distance. Nor is certainty a given in an uncertain world, as the financial crisis in East Asia in 1997–98, after years of 'tiger economies' and 'Asian economic miracles', makes clear. We have emerged at the end of the most strife-torn century in human history essentially intact as a society. We owe this outcome in part to our own efforts, but in equal parts to good luck and the good judgement and generosity of others. We may not always be so fortunate.

Appendix 1
Chronological List of Chiefs of Staff of the Armed Forces

Chairman, Chiefs of Staff Committee

Lieutenant General Sir Henry Wells	23 March 1958 – 22 March 1959
Vice-Admiral Sir Roy Dowling	23 March 1959 – 27 May 1961
Air Chief Marshal	
Sir Frederick Scherger	28 May 1961 – 18 May 1966
General Sir John Wilton	19 May 1966 – 22 November 1970
Admiral Sir Victor Smith	23 November 1970 – 22 November 1975
General Sir Francis Hassett	24 November 1975 – 8 February 1976

Chief of Defence Force Staff

General Sir Francis Hassett	9 February 1976 – 20 April 1977
General Sir Arthur MacDonald	21 April 1977 – 20 April 1979
Admiral Sir Anthony Synnot	21 April 1979 – 20 April 1982
Air Chief Marshal	
Sir Neville McNamara	21 April 1982 – 12 April 1984
General Sir Phillip Bennett	13 April 1984 – 25 October 1986

Chief of Defence Force

General Sir Phillip Bennett	26 October 1986 – 12 April 1987
General P. C. Gration	13 April 1987 – 16 April 1993
Admiral A. L. Beaumont	17 April 1993 – 6 July 1995
General J. S. Baker	7 July 1995 – 3 July 1998
Admiral C. A. Barrie	4 July 1998 –

Chief of Naval Staff

Rear Admiral Sir William Creswell, RN	1 March 1911 – 9 June 1919
Rear Admiral Sir Edmund Grant, RN	10 June 1919 – 14 February 1921

Commodore C. T. Hardy, RN (acting)	15 February 1921 – 23 November 1921
Vice-Admiral Sir Allan Everett, RN	24 November 1921 – 29 August 1923
Commodore G. F. Hyde, RAN (acting)	30 August 1923 – 24 February 1924
Rear Admiral P. N. Hall-Thompson, RN	25 February 1924 – 4 February 1925
Commodore H. P. Cayley, RN	5 February 1925 – 25 April 1925
Rear Admiral P. N. Hall-Thompson, RN	26 April 1925 – 28 June 1926
Rear Admiral W. R. Napier, RN	29 June 1926 – 11 June 1929
Commodore J. B. Stevenson, RAN (acting)	12 June 1929 – 29 October 1929
Vice-Admiral W. M. Kerr, RN	21 October 1929 – 19 October 1931
Admiral Sir George Hyde, RAN	20 October 1931 – 28 July 1937
Commodore G. P. Thompson, RN (acting)	29 July 1937 – 31 October 1937
Admiral Sir Ragnar Colvin, RN	1 November 1937 – 3 March 1941
Commodore J. W. Durnford, RN (acting)	4 March 1941 – 17 July 1941
Admiral Sir Guy Royle, RN	18 July 1941 – 28 June 1945
Vice-Admiral Sir Louis Hamilton, RN	29 June 1945 – 1 August 1945
Commodore G. D. Moore, RAN (acting)	2 August 1945 – 20 September 1945
Admiral Sir Louis Hamilton, RN	21 September 1945 – 23 February 1948
Vice-Admiral Sir John Collins, RAN	24 February 1948 – 23 February 1955
Vice-Admiral Sir Roy Dowling, RAN	24 February 1955 – 23 February 1959
Vice-Admiral Sir Henry Burrell, RAN	24 February 1959 – 23 February 1962
Vice-Admiral Sir Hastings Harrington, RAN	24 February 1962 – 23 February 1965
Vice-Admiral Sir Alan McNicoll, RAN	24 February 1965 – 2 April 1968
Vice-Admiral Sir Victor Smith, RAN	3 April 1968 – 22 November 1970
Vice-Admiral Sir Richard Peek, RAN	23 November 1970 – 22 November 1973
Vice-Admiral H. D. Stevenson, RAN	23 November 1973 – 22 November 1976
Vice-Admiral Sir Anthony Synnot, RAN	23 November 1976 – 20 April 1979
Vice-Admiral Sir James Willis, RAN	21 April 1979 – 20 April 1982
Vice-Admiral D. W. Leach, RAN	21 April 1982 – 20 April 1985
Vice-Admiral M. W. Hudson, RAN	21 April 1985 – 8 March 1991
Vice-Admiral I. D. G. McDougall, RAN	9 March 1991 – 9 March 1994
Vice-Admiral R. G. Taylor, RAN	10 April 1994 – 18 February 1997

Chief of Navy

Vice-Admiral R. G Taylor, RAN	19 February 1997 – 30 June 1997
Vice-Admiral D. B. Chalmers, RAN	1 July 1997 –

Chief of the General Staff

Colonel W. T. Bridges	1 January 1909 – 25 May 1909
Major General J. C. Hoad	26 May 1909 – 30 May 1911
Lieutenant Colonel A. F. Wilson (acting)	1 June 1911 – 10 May 1912

Brigadier General J. M. Gordon	11 May 1912 – 31 July 1914
Colonel J. G. Legge	1 August 1914 – 19 May 1915
Colonel G. G. H. Irving (temporary)	24 May 1915 – 1 December 1915
Colonel H. J. Foster (temporary)	1 January 1916 – 30 September 1917
Major General J. G. Legge	1 October 1917 – 31 May 1920
Major General Sir Brudenell White	1 June 1920 – 10 June 1923
General Sir Harry Chauvel	11 June 1923 – 15 April 1930
Major General W. A. Coxen	1 May 1930 – 30 September 1931
Major General J. H. Bruche	1 October 1931 – 20 April 1935
Major General J. D. Lavarack	21 April 1935 – 12 October 1939
Lieutenant General E. K. Squires	13 October 1939 – 26 January 1940
Major General J. Northcott (acting)	27 January 1940 – 17 March 1940
General Sir Brudenell White	18 March 1940 – 13 August 1940
Lieutenant General V. A. H. Sturdee	30 August 1940 – 9 September 1942
Lieutenant General J. Northcott	10 September 1942 – 30 November 1945
Lieutenant General V. A. H. Sturdee	1 March 1946 – 16 April 1950
Lieutenant General Sir Sydney Rowell	17 April 1950 – 15 December 1954
Lieutenant General Sir Henry Wells	16 December 1954 – 22 March 1958
Lieutenant General Sir Ragnar Garrett	23 March 1958 – 30 June 1960
Lieutenant General Sir Reginald Pollard	1 July 1960 – 20 January 1963
Lieutenant General Sir John Wilton	21 January 1963 – 18 May 1966
Lieutenant General Sir Thomas Daly	19 May 1966 – 18 May 1971
Lieutenant General Sir Mervyn Brogan	19 May 1971 – 19 November 1973
Lieutenant General F. G. Hassett	20 November 1973 – 23 November 1975
Lieutenant General A. L. MacDonald	24 November 1975 – 20 April 1977
Lieutenant General Sir Donald Dunstan	21 April 1977 – 14 February 1982
Lieutenant General P. H. Bennett	15 February 1982 – 12 February 1984
Lieutenant General P. C. Gration	13 April 1984 – 12 April 1987
Lieutenant General L. G. O'Donnell	13 April 1987 – 15 April 1990
Lieutenant General H. J. Coates	16 April 1990 – 30 April 1992
Lieutenant General J. C. Grey	1 May 1992 – 7 July 1995
Lieutenant General J. M. Sanderson	8 July 1995 – 18 February 1997

Chief of Army

Lieutenant General J. M. Sanderson	19 February 1997 – 23 June 1998
Lieutenant General F. J. Hickling	24 June 1998 –

Chief of the Air Staff

Australian Air Corps

Brevet Major R. Williams	12 November 1920 – 30 March 1921

Australian Air Force

Wing Commander R. Williams	31 March 1921 – 12 August 1921

Royal Australian Air Force

Wing Commander R. Williams	13 August 1921 – 14 December 1922
Wing Commander S. J. Goble (acting)	15 December 1922 – 9 February 1925
Air Commodore R. Williams	10 February 1925 – 6 December 1932
Air Commodore S. J. Goble (acting)	7 December 1932 – 12 June 1934
Air Vice Marshal R. Williams	13 June 1934 – 27 February 1939
Air Vice Marshal S. J. Goble (acting)	28 February 1939 – 8 January 1940
Air Commodore W. H. Anderson (acting)	9 January 1940 – 10 February 1940
Air Chief Marshal Sir Charles Burnett, RAF	11 February 1940 – 4 May 1942
Air Marshal G. Jones	5 May 1942 – 13 January 1952
Air Marshal Sir Donald Hardman, RAF	14 January 1952 – 17 January 1954
Air Marshal Sir John McCauley	18 January 1954 – 18 March 1957
Air Marshal Sir Frederick Scherger	19 March 1957 – 28 May 1961
Air Marshal Sir Valston Hancock	29 May 1961 – 31 May 1965
Air Marshal Sir Alister Murdoch	1 June 1965 – 31 December 1969
Air Marshal Sir Colin Hannah	1 January 1970 – 20 March 1972
Air Marshal C. F. Read	21 March 1972 – 20 March 1975
Air Marshal Sir James Rowland	21 March 1975 – 20 March 1979
Air Marshal Sir Neville McNamara	21 March 1979 – 20 April 1982
Air Marshal S. D. Evans	21 April 1982 – 20 May 1985
Air Marshal J. W. Newham	21 May 1985 – 2 July 1987
Air Marshal R. G. Funnell	3 July 1987 – 1 October 1992
Air Marshal I. B. Gration	2 October 1992 – 29 November 1994
Air Marshal L. B. Fisher	30 November 1994 – 18 February 1997

Chief of Air Force

Air Marshal L. B. Fisher	19 February 1997 – 11 May 1998
Air Marshal E. J. McCormack	12 May 1998 –

Appendix 2
Strength of the Armed Forces, 1901–1995

Table A2.1 Strength of the armed forces, 1901–95

Year	RAN	Army	RAAF
1901	n.a.	28 886	
1905	n.a.	20 499	
1910	n.a.	23 509	
1915	9 423	60 972(a)	
1920	10 325(b)	102 665	
1925	4 674(c)	38 889	524(d)
1930	4 475(c)	27 454	1 242(e)
1935	4 177(f)	29 262	1 450(g)
1940	11 600(h)	91 802(i)	32 083(j)
1945	39 650(k)	377 598(l)	154 511(m)
1950	15 195	32 779	9 594
1955	18 155	108 275	18 400
1960	18 414	59 714(n)	16 178
1965	17 708	55 163	18 470
1970	19 472	77 829	24 151
1975	17 396	51 888	22 100
1980	16 961	32 321	22 249
1985	16 059	32 460	22 863
1990	13 404	27 298	19 770
1995	12 563	23 377	14 747

Source: *Australian Year Book*, various numbers, and 'Defence Statistics, 1950–60/61', AWM 21, item 33/A/1.

(a) Does not include AIF – see separate listing, Table 5.1.
(b) 1919 figure.
(c) Excludes reservists.
(d) Permanent Air Force only. RAAF formed as an independent service in 1921.
(e) Includes 350 Citizens' Air Force.

(f)   Plus 5113 reservists.
(g)   Includes 378 Citizens' Air Force.
(h)   April 1940. Gross enlistments to June 1940: 13 173.
(i)   Approximation only at December 1940. Includes 117 502 AIF, 62 300
        militia, 12 000 PMF and garrison battalions.
(j)   December 1940. 1896 officers, 30 187 airmen, including 12 576 Empire
        Air Training Scheme personnel.
(k)   September 1945. Includes 2617 WRANS and 57 nursing sisters.
(l)   September 1945. Includes 286 000 AIF, 69 044 militia, 365 VDC,
        2517 AANS, 4945 AAMWS and 14 727 AWAS.
(m)   September 1945. 137 208 serving in SWPA.
(n)   Includes 14 342 national service part-time trainees discharged on
        30 June 1960.

Table A2.2 Defence expenditure, 1901–95

Financial year	Expenditure (a)
	£
1901–02	861 218
1905–06	970 345
1910–11	3 006 026
1915–16	46 274 129
1920–21	70 732 730(b)
1925–26	6 430 847
1930–31	3 859 069
1935–36	7 014 432
1940–41	170 828 573
1945–46	378 735 000
1950–51	158 750 000
1955–56	190 716 000
1960–61	198 167 000
	$
1965–66	747 983 000
1970–71	1 132 642 000
1975–76	1 943 257 000
1980–81	3 659 143 000
1985–86	6 981 000 000
1990–91	9 065 759 000
1995–96	10 010 610 000

Source: *Australian Year Book*, various numbers, and 'Defence Statistics,
            1950–60/61', AWM 21, item 33/A/1.

(a)   Figures are not adjusted for inflation.
(b)   War expenditure and war gratuity: £65 469 800.

Appendix 3
Defence Expenditure, 1901–1996

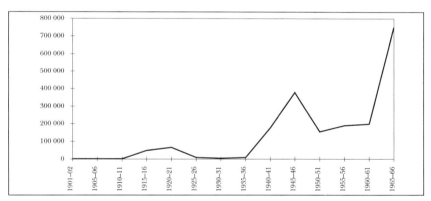

Figure A3.1 Defence expenditure, 1901–66, in £ million

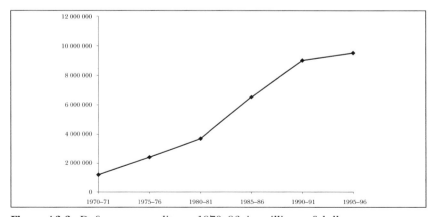

Figure A3.2 Defence expenditure, 1970–96, in millions of dollars

273

Select and Annotated Bibliography

This is not intended to provide an exhaustive guide to the whole literature, nor to literature on every topic related to the themes of this book. In addition, a lot of important work in the field remains unpublished.

Introduction

The standard reference work in Australian military history is Peter Dennis, Jeffrey Grey, Ewan Morris and Robin Prior (with John Connor), *The Oxford Companion to Australian Military History*, Melbourne, 1995. For a guide to Australian sites of conflict see Chris Coulthard-Clark, *Where Australians Fought: The Encyclopaedia of Australia's Battles*, Sydney, 1998. Bibliographies in the field include: Syd Trigellis-Smith, Sergio Zampatti and Max Parsons, *Shaping History: A Bibliography of Australian Army Unit Histories*, Braeside, 1996; Jean Fielding and Robert O'Neill, *A Select Bibliography of Australian Military History 1891–1939*, Canberra, 1978; Hugh Smith and Sue Moss (eds), *A Bibliography of Armed Forces and Society in Australia*, Canberra, 1987.

Anzac Day and the Australian military tradition have attracted some perceptive commentators, foremost amongst them Ken Inglis. See his 'ANZAC Day and the Australian Military Tradition', *Current Affairs Bulletin*, 64:11, April 1988. Together with various of his writings on related themes, this essay is also in John Lack (ed.), *Anzac Remembered: Selected Writings of K. S. Inglis*, Melbourne, 1998. An earlier debate on the role of ANZAC in the creation of Australian national feeling may be followed in K. S. Inglis, 'The Anzac Tradition', *Meanjin*, March 1965; Geoffrey Serle, 'The Digger Tradition and Australian Nationalism', *Meanjin*, June 1965; and Noel McLachlan, 'Nationalism and the Divisive Digger: Three Comments', *Meanjin*, September 1968. For a stimulating general essay about the place of war in Australian history, see Richard White, 'War and Australian Society' in Michael McKernan and Margaret Browne (eds), *Australia: Two Centuries of War and Peace*, Canberra, 1988. For the development of the professional military tradition, Richard A. Preston and Ian Wards, 'Military and Defence Development in Canada, Australia and New Zealand: A Three-Way Comparison', *War & Society*, 5:1, May 1987. The amateur and natural soldier traditions are analysed by Jane Ross, *The Myth of the Digger: The Australian Soldier in Two World Wars*, Sydney, 1985. One aspect of the development of military heroism for popular consumption is analysed by Peter Cochrane, *Simpson and the Donkey: The Making of a Legend*, Melbourne, 1992, although no-one yet seems ready to analyse the erosion of the more traditional or conventional notions of martial heroism which were once so widespread. The memorialising process more generally is discussed and analysed in K. S. Inglis, *Sacred Places: War Memorials in the Australian Landscape*, Melbourne, 1998.

For general comparisons with analogous national cases, see Desmond Morton, *A Military History of Canada*, Edmonton, 3rd edn, 1995, and Allan Millett and Peter Maslowski, *For the Common Defense: A Military History of the United States of America*, New York, 2nd edn, 1994.

Chapter 1

The military in colonial Australia has not attracted anything like the attention which has been devoted to the twentieth century. Good standard guides to the subject are lacking in general. An exception is John Bach, *The Australia Station: A History of the Royal Navy in the South West Pacific, 1821–1913*, Kensington, 1986. The British army is not as well served. Perhaps the most knowledgeable historian of the subject was Brigadier Maurice Austin, whose *The Army in Australia 1840–50: Prelude to the Golden Years*, Canberra, 1979, is an important source for the subject which sadly deals with only a single decade, and arguably the least important one in terms of the British Army's tenure of the Australasian colonies. Austin's other work is scattered through the journal literature; worth consulting are, 'The Foundation of Australia's Army Reserves, 1788–1854', *Defence Force Journal*, 33–37, March/April–November/December 1982, and 'Bayonet and Baton', *Defence Force Journal*, 20–21, January/February March–April 1980. Clem Sargent, *The Colonial Garrison 1817–1824: The 48th Foot The Northamptonshire Regiment in the Colony of New South Wales*, Canberra, 1996 examines the experience of a single British battalion on colonial service in the early 1820s. A short guide to the subject overall is provided by Peter Stanley, *The Remote Garrison: The British Army in Australia, 1788–1870*, Kenthurst, 1986. The role of the Royal Engineers is encompassed in R. R. McNicoll, *The Royal Australian Engineers, 1835–1902: The Colonial Engineers*, Canberra, 1977. The early development of the local forces is in Bob Nicholls, *The Colonial Volunteers: The Defence Forces of the Australian Colonies, 1836–1905*, Sydney, 1988. This should be supplemented with Craig Wilcox, *For Hearths and Homes: Citizen Soldiering in Australia 1854–1945*, Sydney, 1998. An excellent essay on the influence of the military generally is Gerald Walsh, 'The Military and Colonial Development, 1788–1888', in Michael McKernan and Margaret Browne (eds), *Australia: Two Centuries of War and Peace*, Canberra, 1988.

The conditions which faced British soldiers in Australia may be gleaned from Peter Stanley, '"Oh, The Sufferings of my Men": The 80th Regiment in New South Wales in 1838', *Push from the Bush*, 11, November 1981; '"A Mere Point of Military Etiquette": The Norfolk Island Mutiny of 1839', *Push from the Bush*, 7, September 1980, and 'Soldiers and Fellow-Countrymen in Colonial Australia', in McKernan and Browne (eds), *Australia: Two Centuries of War and Peace*. The condition of the rank and file is covered also in Peter Burroughs, 'The Human Cost of Imperial Defence in the Early Victorian Age', *Victorian Studies*, 24:1, Autumn 1980; Burroughs deals with the role of the Board of Ordnance in colonial affairs in 'The Ordnance Department and Colonial Defence,

1821–1855', *Journal of Imperial and Commonwealth History*, 10:2, 1982. Something of the wider role of this department in the creation of colonial infrastructure is given in George Raudzens, *The British Ordnance Department and Canada's Canals, 1815–1855*, Waterloo, 1979. For the origins of the remount trade with India see A. T. Yarwood, 'The "Indian Business": An Outline of the Origins of Horse Exports from Australia to India, 1834–1847', *Journal of the Royal Australian Historical Society*, 73:1, June 1987. The pattern of war scares and colonial social attitudes to war and organised violence are dealt with in K. S. Inglis, *The Australian Colonists: An Exploration of Social History, 1788–1870*, Melbourne, 1974.

The debate on Australia's origins is neatly summarised in Ged Martin (ed.), *The Founding of Australia: The Argument about Australia's Origins*, Sydney, 1978. Of particular importance is Alan Frost, *Convicts and Empire: A Naval Question, 1776–1811*, Melbourne, 1980. See also his 'Towards Australia: The Coming of the Europeans 1400 to 1788', in D. J. Mulvaney and J. Peter White (eds), *Australians to 1788*, in the series, Alan Gilbert and K. S. Inglis (eds), *Australians: A Historical Library*, Broadway, 1987. Most of the early colonial governors lack good modern biographies which evaluate their military careers as well as their gubernatorial ones. Alan Frost, *Arthur Phillip, 1738–1814: His Voyaging*, Melbourne, 1987, John Ritchie, *Lachlan Macquarie: A Biography*, Melbourne, 1986, and A. G. L. Shaw, *Sir George Arthur, Bart, 1784–1854*, Melbourne, 1980, are exceptions.

Strangely, there is no detailed history of the often reviled New South Wales Corps, although the question of its composition has been much discussed. The best and most recent scholarship on the subject is provided by Pamela Statham; see *A Colonial Regiment: New Sources Relating to the New South Wales Corps*, Canberra, 1992; *Ins and Outs: The Composition and Disposal of the NSW Corps, 1790–1810*, Working Papers in Economic History No. 105, Canberra, 1988; 'A New Look at the New South Wales Corps, 1790–1810', *Australian Economic History Review*, 30:1, 1990. For the earlier debate see T. G. Parsons, 'The Social Composition of the Men of the New South Wales Corps', *Royal Australian Historical Society Journal*, 50:4, October 1964 and M. Austin, 'Paint My Picture Truly', *Journal of the Royal Australian Historical Society*, 51:4, December 1965. See also R. H. Montague, 'The Men of the New South Wales Corps: a comparison?', *Journal of the Royal Australian Historical Society*, 62:4, March 1977 and T. G. Parsons, 'Courts Martial, The Savoy Military Prison and the New South Wales Corps', *Journal of the Royal Australian Historical Society*, 63:4, March 1978. As well, consult William Foster, 'Francis Grose and the Officers', *Journal of the Royal Australian Historical Society*, 51:2, September 1965. The Corps' sole 'battle honour', Vinegar Hill, is examined by R. W. Connell, 'The Convict Rebellion of 1804', *Melbourne Historical Journal*, 5, 1965, and by L. R. Silver, *The Battle of Vinegar Hill*, Sydney, 1989. The historiography of the 'Rum rebellion' does not inspire much confidence. John Ritchie (ed.), *A Charge of Mutiny: The Court Martial of Lieutenant Colonel George Johnston for Deposing Governor William Bligh in the Rebellion of 26 January 1808*, Canberra, 1987, provides some important insights, not least through his introductory essay.

An interesting argument concerning the social background to the military in early Australia is provided by J. J. Auchmuty, 'The Background to the Early Australian Governors', *Historical Studies*, 6, 1953–55. This should be augmented by Alan J. Guy, *Oeconomy and Discipline: Officership and Administration in the British Army, 1714–1763*, Manchester, 1985, which, although it stops short of the early colonial period in Australia, examines the relationship between administration, authority and officers' discipline in the eighteenth century British army. Later patterns of indiscipline in the British military are analysed in Peter Stanley, *White Mutiny: British Military Culture in India 1825–1875*, London, 1998. For the broader context of the army and navy in the late eighteenth and nineteenth centuries see Richard Glover, *Peninsular Preparation: The Reform of the British Army, 1795–1809*, Cambridge, 1963; Michael Lewis, *A Social History of the Navy, 1793–1815*, London, 1960, and *The Navy in Transition, 1814–1864: A Social History*, London, 1965.

Chapter 2

Much of the modern literature on Aboriginal resistance has been framed in the context of the history of race relations. While it has reclaimed an important element of Australian history successfully, much of it is written with little regard for or understanding of European military realities in the nineteenth century, or the nature of war in general. The history of black–white conflict in Australia has yet to receive the level of sophisticated treatment found in James Belich, *The New Zealand Wars and the Victorian Interpretation of Racial Conflict*, Auckland, 1986. A good overview of the subject is given by Richard Broome, 'The Struggle for Australia: Aboriginal–European warfare, 1770–1930', in Michael McKernan and Margaret Browne (eds), *Australia: Two Centuries of War and Peace*, Canberra, 1988, while a provocative general argument about the nature of black–white conflict is provided by David Denholm, *The Colonial Australians*, Ringwood, 1979.

The major starting point is the work of Henry Reynolds, especially *The Other Side of the Frontier: Aboriginal Resistance to the European Invasion of Australia*, Ringwood, 1982. His article 'Violence, the Aboriginals, and the Australian Historian', *Meanjin Quarterly*, December 1972, sets out the historiographical problem neatly. See also his 'Aboriginal–European Contact History: Problems and Issues', *Journal of Australian Studies*, 3, June 1978. Much of the work in the field deals with Queensland and has been produced by students and colleagues of Reynolds in Townsville. Of note here is Noel Loos, *Invasion and Resistance: Aboriginal–European relations on the North Queensland frontier, 1861–1897*, Canberra, 1982, and Henry Reynolds (ed.), *Race Relations in North Queensland*, Townsville, 1978.

The major work on the earlier conflict between blacks and whites in New South Wales, focussed on the massacre at Waterloo Creek, is Roger Millis, *Waterloo Creek: The Australia Day massacre of 1838, George Gipps and the British conquest of New South Wales*, Ringwood, 1992, a massive 965 page indictment of white behaviour on the frontier of settlement. On other incidents see David Denholm, 'The Myall Creek Massacre', *Push from the Bush*, 9, July 1981, and David Carment, 'The Wills Massacre of 1861: Aboriginal–European Conflict on the Colonial Australian Frontier', *Journal of Australian Studies*, 6, June 1980. An attempt at a regional study of incidents outside Queensland is provided in Neville Green, 'Aboriginal and Settler Conflict in Western Australia, 1826–1852', *Push from the Bush*, 3, May 1979. Beverley Nance, 'The level of violence: Europeans and Aborigines in Port Phillip, 1835–1850', *Historical Studies*, 19:77, October 1981, argues for a pattern of non-violence towards white settlement in some areas, and the use of traditional methods, especially sorcery. For the Wiradjuri war see Bill Gammage, 'The Wiradjuri War, 1838–40', *Push from the Bush*, 16, October 1983. The role of disease, contact and traditional society is discussed in James Urry, 'Beyond the Frontier: European Influence, Aborigines and the Concept of Traditional Culture', *Journal of Australian Studies*,

5, 1979. An important source on traditional society in general is D. J. Mulvaney and J. Peter White (eds), *Australians to 1788*, in the series, Alan Gilbert and K. S. Inglis (eds), *Australians: A Historical Library*, Broadway, 1987.

The pattern of early contact can be followed in the journals and writings of the officers of the First Fleet, of which Captain John Hunter, *An Historical Journal of Events at Sydney and at Sea*, Sydney, 1968, is one of the best. The fate of those tribes which first came into contact with the whites is described by Keith Willey, *When the Sky Fell Down: The Destruction of the Tribes of the Sydney Region, 1788–1850s*, Sydney, 1979. A good example of attempts to recast the mould of Aboriginal resistance is Eric Willmot, *Pemulwuy: The Rainbow Warrior*, McMahon's Point, 1987, which makes some silly claims about the nature and effectiveness of military activity on both sides.

Surprisingly little has been written on the Native Police, although there are references to them scattered through books by Loos and Reynolds. The early force in Victoria is treated extensively, if controversially, in Marie Hansen Fels, *Good Men and True: The Aboriginal Police of the Port Phillip District, 1837–1853*, Melbourne, 1988, and by Barry Bridges, 'The Native Police Corps, Port Phillip District and Victoria, 1837–1853', *Journal of the Royal Australian Historical Society*, 57:2, June 1971. For the early use of Aborigines in this manner see also Jan Critchett, *A 'distant field of murder': Western District frontiers, 1834–1848*, Carlton, 1990. For Queensland, see L. E. Skinner, *Police of the Pastoral Frontier: Native Police, 1849–59*, St. Lucia, 1975. There is a chapter on the Native Police in the 'top end' in Gordon Reid, *A picnic with the natives: Aboriginal–European relations in the Northern Territory to 1910*, Carlton, 1990. The Mounted Police is examined in M. Austin, 'Bayonet and Baton', *Defence Force Journal*, 20–21, January/ February–March/April 1980.

Chapter 3

Defence in the late colonial period in Australia must be understood in its imperial context, and several good books meet this need: Donald C. Gordon, *The Dominion Partnership in Imperial Defense, 1870–1914*, Baltimore, 1965, and Richard A. Preston, *Canada and 'Imperial Defense'. A Study of the Origins of the British Commonwealth's Defense Organisation, 1867–1919*, Durham, 1967. For a more recent view see Peter Burroughs, 'Imperial Defence and the Victorian Army', *Journal of Imperial and Commonwealth History*, XV:1, October 1986. See also Luke Trainor, 'British Imperial Defence Policy and the Australian Colonies, 1892–96', *Historical Studies*, 14:54, April 1970; R. A. Shields, 'Australian Opinion and the Defence of the Empire: A Study in Imperial Relations 1880–1890', *Australian Journal of Politics and History*, 1, 1964; Meredith Hooper, 'The Naval Defence Agreement of 1887', *Australian Journal of Politics and History*, 14:1, 1968.

The role of the imperial forces in Australia is treated unevenly still. John Bach, *The Australia Station. A History of the Royal Navy in the South West Pacific, 1821–1913*, Sydney, 1986 is an excellent treatment of the Royal Navy. Ray Jones, 'Tryon in Australia: the 1887 Naval Agreement', *Journal of the Australian War Memorial*, 10, April 1987, is useful on the negotiations between Tryon and the colonial leadership. Work on the colonial forces is problematic likewise. Bob Nicholls, *The Colonial Volunteers: The Defence Forces of the Australian Colonies, 1836–1901*, Sydney, 1988, is the only treatment of the colonies as a whole. D. H. Johnson, *Volunteers at Heart: The Queensland Defence Forces, 1860–1901*, St Lucia,

1975, is the only published treatment of the defence forces of an individual colony, although several other studies exist in unpublished theses. For discussion of citizen soldiering in this period, see Craig Wilcox, *For Hearths and Homes: Citizen Soldiering in Australia 1854–1945*. Colin Jones, *Australian Colonial Navies*, Canberra, 1986, is a good technical guide to organisation and capabilities, while Bob Nicholls, *Statesmen & Sailors: A History of Australian Maritime Defence 1870–1920*, Balmain, 1995 has considerable detail on the policy level. Although a number of the fortifications built after 1870 have been restored and are open to public inspection, there are few studies of military architecture or fortification in the Pacific colonies; see Lewis Carey and others, *Fort Scratchley*, Newcastle, 1986.

The centenary of the Sudan contingent produced a rush of publications, many not worth bothering with. K. S. Inglis, *The Rehearsal: Australians at War in the Sudan, 1885*, Sydney, 1985, is elegant and beautifully illustrated, and sets the contingent into the context of colonial society from which it sprang. Malcolm Saunders, *Britain, the Australian Colonies, and the Sudan Campaigns of 1884–85*, Armidale, 1985, covers familiar ground, but adds important new material on the question of anti-war opposition to the expedition. He rehearsed his arguments in 'Public Opinion and the New South Wales Contingent to the Sudan in 1885', *Journal of the Royal Australian Historical Society*, 69:3, December 1983. Still worth reading is B. R. Penny, 'The Age of Empire: An Australian Episode', *Historical Studies: Australia and New Zealand*, 11:41, 1963, and John McCarthy, 'Australia and the Sudan War: Some Recent Issues in an Older Setting', *RMC Historical Journal*, 1, 1972. The roles of two imperial officers may be followed in G. P. Walsh, 'Sir Edward Strickland. A Commissariat Officer's Contribution to Australia', *RMC Historical Journal*, 5, 1976, and Gregory Pemberton, 'Major General Richardson in New South Wales, 1858–1892', *RMC Historical Journal*, 4, 1975.

The role of defence in the move toward Federation is covered in Ronald Norris, *The Emergent Commonwealth: Australian Federation: Expectations and Fulfilment, 1889–1910*, Melbourne, 1975. In general, the standard biographies of Federation era politicians pay scant attention to the question. Defence and imperial relations receive good treatment in Geoffrey Serle, *The Rush to be Rich: A History of the Colony of Victoria, 1883–1889*, Melbourne, 1971.

Studies of the Boer War vary also. The best modern general history, Thomas Pakenham, *The Boer War*, London, 1979, confirms the marginal role overall of the Australian contingents. L. M. Field, *The Forgotten War: Australian Involvement in the South African Conflict of 1899–1902*, Melbourne, 1979, combines analysis of colonial politics and public opinion with the experience of the contingents, but is over-critical in tone. R. L. Wallace, *The Australians at the Boer War*, Canberra, 1976, errs on the side of antiquarianism but contains much useful campaign detail not found elsewhere. B. R. Penny, 'The Australian Debate on the Boer War', *Historical Studies*, 56, 1971, and 'Australia's Reactions to the Boer War: a Study in Colonial Imperialism', *Journal of British Studies*, 7, 1967, argue along traditional lines, while C. N. Connolly, 'Class, Birthplace, Loyalty: Australian Attitudes to the Boer War', *Historical Studies*, 71, 1978, and 'Manufacturing "Spontaneity": The Australian Offers of Troops for the Boer War', *Historical Studies*, 70, 1978, put a revisionist case. A. P. Haydon, 'South Australia's First War', *Historical Studies: Australia and New Zealand*, 42, 1964, examines the reactions in that colony. Responsibility for the execution of Australian officers is examined in Barry Bridges, 'Lord Kitchener and the Morant–Handcock Executions', *Journal of the Royal Australian Historical Society*, 73:1, June 1987.

Chapter 4

This period of peacetime development is better served by the secondary literature than virtually any other comparable period, perhaps because the official records have been available to scholars for longer under the relevant archival legislation. An important overview of the topic which argues for the existence of a clearly defined Australian defence and foreign policy is provided by Neville Meaney, *The Search for Security in the Pacific, 1901–14*, Sydney, 1976. A good brief survey is presented by Chris Coulthard-Clark, 'Formation of the Australian Armed Services, 1901–14', in Michael McKernan and Margaret Browne (eds), *Australia: Two Centuries of War and Peace*, Canberra, 1988. The context of Australian military policy may be followed in several good books on imperial defence and empire relations, especially D. C. Gordon, *The Dominion Partnership in Imperial Defence, 1870–1914*, Baltimore, 1965 and Richard A. Preston, *Canada and 'Imperial Defense'. A Study of the Origins of the British Commonwealth's Defense Organisation, 1867–1919*, Durham, 1967. A good guide to the sources is Gordon Greenwood and Charles Grimshaw (eds), *Documents on Australian International Affairs, 1901–1918*, Melbourne, 1977.

The army is better served than the navy, especially through the work of Chris Coulthard-Clark. See his *The Citizen General Staff: The Australian Intelligence Corps, 1907–1914*, Canberra, 1976; *Duntroon: The Royal Military College of Australia, 1911–1986*, Sydney, 1986; and his biographies *A Heritage of Spirit: A Biography of Major-General Sir William Throsby Bridges*, Melbourne, 1979; and *No Australian Need Apply: The Troubled Career of Lieutenant-General Gordon Legge*, Sydney, 1988. Military policy generally, and Hutton's role specifically, are treated in John Mordike, *An Army for a Nation: A History of Australian Military Developments 1880–1914*, Sydney, 1992, although it needs to be read alongside Craig Wilcox, 'Relinquishing the Past: John Mordike's "An Army for a Nation"', *Australian Journal of Politics and History*, 40:1, 1994. The compulsory military training scheme has been analysed in John Barrett, *Falling In: Australians and 'Boy Conscription', 1911–1915*, Sydney, 1979. The role of defence issues in the government of the early Commonwealth is covered by Ronald Norris, *The Emergent Commonwealth: Australian Federation: Expectations and Fulfilment, 1889–1910*, Melbourne, 1975. J. A. La Nauze, *Alfred Deakin: A Biography*, Melbourne, 1965, covers Deakin's role in defence issues as well as much else; the same applies to L. M. Fitzhardinge, *That Fiery Particle, 1862–1914: William Morris Hughes: A Political Biography*, Sydney, 1964. An important study of an early Commonwealth defence minister is Peter Heydon, *Quiet Decision: A Study of George Foster Pearce*, Melbourne, 1963, although much more could be said on that topic. For the genesis of the RAN see G. Hermon Gill, 'The Australian Navy: Origins, Growth and Development', *Royal Australian Historical Society Journal*, 45:3, November 1959, which is old but still serviceable.

For the Russo-Japanese War and its impact see M. B. Hayne, 'The Impact of the Battle of Tsushima on Australian Defence and Foreign Policy, 1905–1909', *Journal of the Royal Australian Historical Society*, 72:4, April 1987 and I. H. Nish, 'Australia and the Anglo-Japanese Alliance, 1901–1911', *Australian Journal of Politics and History*, 9:2, 1963. The visit of the Great White Fleet is dealt with in Ruth Megaw, 'Australia and the Great White Fleet 1908', *Journal of the Royal Australian Historical Society*, 56:2, June 1970.

The early Australian army awaits its analyst, although Mordike and Wilcox have gone some way towards filling in the blanks. Some details of the pre-1914 officer corps can be found in P. A. Pedersen, 'Some Thoughts on the Prewar

Military Career of John Monash', *Journal of the Royal Australian Historical Society*, 67:3, December 1981, and in A. J. Hill, *Chauvel of the Light Horse*, Melbourne, 1978. There are no biographies of Creswell or Hutton, but see Stephen Webster, 'Vice-Admiral Sir William Creswell: First Naval Member of the Australian Naval Board, 1911–19' in D. M. Horner (ed.), *The Commanders: Australian Military Command in the Twentieth Century*, Sydney, 1984.

Chapter 5

The starting point for any consideration of the Australian role in the Great War is Joan Beaumont (ed.), *Australia's War 1914–18*, Sydney, 1995, which is especially good on economic and social issues. The massive official series edited and largely written by C. E. W. Bean, *The Official History of Australia in the War of 1914–1918*, comprises: C. E. W. Bean, *The Story of Anzac: From the Outbreak of the War to the End of the First Phase of the Gallipoli Landing, May 4, 1915*, Sydney, 1921; *The Story of Anzac: From May 4, 1915 to the Evacuation of the Gallipoli Peninsula*, Sydney, 1924; *The AIF in France, 1916*, Sydney, 1929; *The AIF in France, 1917*, Sydney, 1933; *The AIF in France During the Main German Offensive, 1918*, Sydney, 1937; and *The AIF in France During the Allied Offensive, 1918*, Sydney, 1942. The remaining volumes in the series are: H. S. Gullett, *The AIF in Sinai and Palestine, 1914–1918*, Sydney, 1923; F. M. Cutlack, *The Australian Flying Corps in the Western and Eastern Theatres of War, 1914–1918*, Sydney, 1923; A. W. Jose, *The Royal Australian Navy, 1914–1918*, Sydney, 1928; S. S. Mackenzie, *The Australians at Rabaul: The Capture and Administration of the German Possessions in the Southern Pacific*, Sydney, 1927; Ernest Scott, *Australia During the War*, Sydney, 1936; and C. E. W. Bean and H. S. Gullett, *Photographic Record of the War: Reproductions of Pictures taken by the Australian Official Photographers . . . and others*, Sydney, 1923. The medical series comprised three volumes written by A. G. Butler, published in Sydney, 1930–43. These are particularly valuable for their statistical content, much of it not included in the main volumes by Bean.

The Great War is probably the most written-about subject in Australian military historiography. For an analysis of this literature, see Peter Dennis and Jeffrey Grey, 'Australian and New Zealand Writing on the First World War', in Jürgen Rohwer (ed.), *Neue Forschungen zum Ersten Weltkrieg*, Koblenz, 1985. Bean himself has been examined by K. S. Inglis, *C. E. W. Bean, Australian Historian*, John Murtagh Macrossan lecture, St Lucia, 1969, and by John Barrett, 'No Straw Man: C. E. W. Bean and Some Critics', *Australian Historical Studies*, 23:89, April 1988. Dudley McCarthy, *Gallipoli to the Somme: The story of C. E. W. Bean*, Sydney, 1983, is good on details of Bean's war experience but is uncritical in its judgements and has little to say about the official history itself. An interesting aspect of the production of the history is essayed in Stephen Ellis, 'The Censorship of the Official Naval History of Australia in the Great War', *Historical Studies*, 20:80, April 1983. The raw material of the history, Bean's diaries, has been published in part in Kevin Fewster (ed.), *Gallipoli Correspondent: The Frontline Diary of C. E. W. Bean*, Sydney, 1983. Eric Andrews, 'The Media and the Military: Australian war correspondents and the appointment of a corps commander, 1918', *War & Society*, 8:2, October 1990, examines Bean's role in the politics of the Australian high command in France. Stuart Macintyre, *A History for a Nation: Ernest Scott and the Making of Australian History*, Melbourne, 1994, is a sympathetic and nuanced study of the official historian of the home front.

There are few good modern studies of the campaigns in which the Australians participated, probably because it seems to the average reader, and writer, that Bean has left little uncovered. John Robertson, *Anzac and Empire: The Tragedy and Glory of Gallipoli*, Darlinghurst, 1990, is both the last word on the subject in this generation and a careful, scholarly refutation of many prevalent and popular interpretations. A useful counter to most popular treatments of the August offensive on Gallipoli is Robin Prior, 'The Suvla Bay Tea Party: A Reassessment', *Journal of the Australian War Memorial*, 7, October 1985. Third Ypres has been analysed in Robin Prior and Trevor Wilson, *Passchendaele: the untold story*, New Haven, 1996. Eric Andrews, 'Second Bullecourt Revisited: The Australians in France, 3 May 1917', *Journal of the Australian War Memorial*, 15, October 1989 looks at the reasons why the second assault succeeded where the first had failed so miserably, and offers a critique of Bean's account of the two battles. The brief involvement in the Russian Civil War is dealt with in Jeffrey Grey, '"A Pathetic Sideshow": Australians and the Russian Intervention, 1918–19', *Journal of the Australian War Memorial*, 7, October 1985. Several important studies of the AIF have appeared. Bill Gammage, *The Broken Years: Australian Soldiers in the Great War*, Canberra, 1974, had the effect of placing the Great War on the popular and scholarly agenda for a new generation of readers, although his actual argument does not add anything much to the positions advanced by Bean fifty years previously. L. L. Robson, *The First AIF: A Study of its Recruitment, 1914–1918*, Melbourne, 1970, discusses both the voluntary enlistment system and the conscription referenda, written from the viewpoint of an opponent of conscription for the Vietnam War. J. N. I. Dawes and L. L. Robson, *Citizen to Soldier: Australia before the Great War: Recollections of Members of the First AIF*, Melbourne, 1977, adds valuable anecdotal flesh to the bones of the earlier study. Robson's 'The Origins and Character of the First AIF, 1914–1918: Some Statistical Evidence', *Historical Studies*, 15:61, October 1973, must be treated with caution since it samples only 0.5 per cent of the total enlistment group, and some of Robson's comments upon Bean are dubious at best. A fine example of the more sophisticated approach possible in the field generally is Peter Pedersen, 'The AIF on the Western Front: the Role of Training and Command', in Michael McKernan and Margaret Brown (eds), *Australia: Two Centuries of War and Peace*, Canberra, 1988. Suzanne Brugger, *Australians and Egypt, 1914–1919*, Melbourne, 1980, is excellent on the role of the light horse as enforcers of empire in the Egyptian revolt, and is a model of scholarship and erudition.

Leading personalities are reasonably well served, although most of the Australian generals of the Great War generation lack biographers. Monash has received superb handling by the late Geoffrey Serle in *John Monash: A Biography*, Melbourne, 1982, while his generalship has been scrutinised professionally in Peter Pedersen, *Monash as Military Commander*, Melbourne, 1985. A. J. Hill, *Chauvel of the Light Horse*, Melbourne, 1978, was the first of the modern biographies of Australian generals of this war. It was closely followed by C. D. Coulthard-Clark, *A Heritage of Spirit: A Biography of Major-General Sir William Throsby Bridges*, Melbourne, 1979, and later by the same author's *No Australian Need Apply: The Troubled Career of Lieutenant-General James Gordon Legge*, Sydney, 1987. Bean wrote of both Bridges and White in *Two Men I Knew: William Bridges and Brudenell White, founders of the AIF*, Sydney, 1957, but this is uncritical in certain crucial respects. Guy Verney, 'General Sir Brudenell White: The Staff Officer as Commander', in D. M. Horner (ed.), *The Commanders*, Sydney, 1984, is better, but White deserves a full-length study. Hughes is treated by L. F. Fitzhardinge, *The Little Digger, 1914–1952: William Morris Hughes: A Political Biography*, Sydney, 1979.

Studies of the home front and domestic affairs are numerous, although many tend to concentrate upon the conscription referenda and political dissent. An overview is provided by Michael McKernan, *The Australian People and the Great War*, Melbourne, 1980, which is good also on the experiences and views of the AIF in Britain. The same author's *Australian Churches at War: Attitudes and Activities of the Major Churches, 1914–1918*, Sydney, 1980, is better on the role of the churches in Australia than on the neglected subject of military chaplaincy. The conscription issue has been analysed from varying perspectives: F. B. Smith, *The Conscription Plebiscites in Australia, 1916–1917*, Melbourne, 1966; Alan D. Gilbert, 'The Conscription Referenda, 1916–17; the Impact of the Irish Crisis', *Historical Studies*, 14:53, October 1969, and 'Protestants, Catholics and Loyalty: an Aspect of the Conscription Controversies 1916–17', *Politics*, 6:1, 1971; Michael McKernan, 'Catholics, Conscription and Archbishop Mannix', *Historical Studies*, 17:68, April 1977; D. J. Murphy, 'Religion, Race and Conscription in World War I', *Australian Journal of Politics and History*, 20:2, 1974. Regional studies of the issue include J. R. Robertson, 'The Conscription Issue and the National Movement in Western Australia: June 1916–December 1917', *University Studies in Politics and History*, 3, 1959; A. R. Pearson, 'Western Australia and the Conscription Plebiscites of 1916 and 1917', *RMC Historical Journal*, 3, 1974; and P. M. Gibson, 'The Conscription Issue in South Australia, 1916–1917', *University Studies in Politics and History*, 4, 1963–64. Regional studies of the Australian home front and war effort in general include Bobbie Oliver, *War and Peace in Western Australia: The Social and Political Impact of the Great War 1914–1926*, Nedlands, 1995; Marilyn Lake, *A Divided Society: Tasmania during World War I*, Melbourne, 1975; Suzanne Welborn, *Lords of Death: A People, a Place, a Legend*, Fremantle, 1982; Raymond Evans, *Loyalty and Disloyalty: Social Conflict on the Queensland Home Front, 1914–1918*, Sydney, 1987; and John McQuilton, 'A Shire at War: Yackandandah 1914–18', *Journal of the Australian War Memorial*, 11, October 1987. Bobbie Oliver, *Peacemongers: Conscientious Objectors to Military Service in Australia, 1911–1945*, Fremantle, 1997, examines aspects of dissent in this period from a slightly different perspective to that usually provided. The role of some Australian women is discussed by Joy Damousi, 'Socialist women and gendered space: Anti-conscription and anti-war campaigns 1914–1918', *Labour History*, 60, May 1991, and by Judith Smart, 'Feminists, food and the fair price: the cost-of-living demonstrations in Melbourne, August–September 1917', *Labour History*, 50, May 1986, but little attention has been paid to conservative women, just as little has been written on pro-conscription groups.

The cost of the war in social and human terms is an area of increasing interest. Clem Lloyd and Jacqui Rees, *The Last Shilling: A History of Repatriation in Australia*, Canberra, 1994, is a detailed study of the 'parallel system of welfare' for returned servicemen which sprang out of the Great War experience. G. L. Kristianson, *The Politics of Patriotism: The Pressure Group Activities of the Returned Servicemen's League*, Canberra, 1966, though somewhat dated, is still valuable for its account of the origins of the major veterans' organisation which likewise emerged from the war; it must be supplemented by Peter Sekuless and Jacqueline Rees, *Lest We Forget: The History of the Returned Services League 1916–1986*, Sydney, 1986, which has all the strengths and weaknesses of commissioned institutional history. Marilyn Lake, 'The Power of Anzac', in McKernan and Browne (eds), *Australia: Two Centuries of War and Peace*, provides a dissenting interpretation. Stephen Garton, *The Cost of War: Australians Return*, Melbourne, 1996, examines the post-conflict experiences of those who did return.

Australia had little role in the strategic and higher direction of the war, and literature on this aspect is correspondingly sparse. Wm. Roger Louis, 'Australia and German Colonies in the Pacific, 1914–1919', *Journal of Modern History*, XXXVIII, 1968; L. F. Fitzhardinge, 'Australia, Japan and Great Britain, 1914–18: A Study in Triangular Diplomacy', *Historical Studies*, 14:54, April 1970; Robert Thornton, 'Invaluable Ally or Imminent Aggressor? Australia and Japanese Naval Assistance, 1914–18', *Journal of Australian Studies*, 12, June 1983, deal with this aspect in the Pacific.

A comparative treatment of Australia's participation in the war, especially in the dominion context, is provided by Eric Andrews, *The Anzac Illusion: Anglo-Australian Relations during World War I*, Melbourne, 1993. Useful comparisons might be drawn here with Desmond Morton, '"Junior but Sovereign Allies": The Transformation of the Canadian Expeditionary Force, 1914–1918', *Journal of Contemporary History*, 8:1, October 1979, and Christopher Pugsley, *Gallipoli: The New Zealand Story*, Wellington, 1984.

Chapter 6

The literature on this period is uneven. Some subjects, especially the Singapore strategy, are well covered while others have barely been touched. For a brief overview of the development of policy and practice in Australian interwar defence, see John Robertson, 'The Distant War: Australia and Imperial Defence, 1919–41', in Michael McKernan and Margaret Browne (eds), *Australia: Two Centuries of War and Peace*, Canberra, 1988. The opening chapter of Paul Hasluck, *The Government and the People: 1939–41*, Canberra, 1952, discusses defence policy between the wars. For treatment of the services in this period, recourse may be had to the opening chapters in the first volume in each of the services series of *Australia in the War of 1939–45*. For the army, Gavin Long, *To Benghazi*, Canberra, 1952; for the RAN, G. Hermon Gill, *Royal Australian Navy, 1939–42*, Canberra, 1957; for the RAAF, Douglas Gillison, *Royal Australian Air Force, 1939–1942*, Canberra, 1962. These are dated, but still serviceable.

The Singapore strategy has generated an enormous literature. Good general works include James Neidpath, *The Singapore Naval Base and the Defence of Britain's Eastern Empire, 1919–1941*, Oxford, 1981, and W. David McIntyre, *The Rise and Fall of the Singapore Naval Base*, London, 1979. The standard work on Australian involvement is John McCarthy, *Australia and Imperial Defence: A Study in Air and Sea Power*, St Lucia, 1976. McCarthy's articles on the subject should be consulted also, as should I. C. McGibbon, *Blue Water Rationale: The Naval Defence of New Zealand, 1914–1942*, Wellington, 1981, and W. David McIntyre, *New Zealand Prepares for War: Defence Policy, 1919–1939*, Christchurch, 1988.

Little of value has appeared on the individual services in this period. A unique work in Australian military studies is Robert Hyslop, *Australian Naval Administration, 1900–1939*, Melbourne, 1973. Its focus is administration, not policy, but it is especially good on the nature of the formal and legal links between the RAN and the RN in this period. Chris Coulthard-Clark, *The Third Brother: The Royal Australian Air Force 1921–1939*, Sydney, 1991 is a heavily detailed account of the development of the air force and suggests what might be done with the other two services in this formative period. S. F. Rowell, *Full Circle*, Melbourne, 1974, contains a short chapter on the army, and offers comments on the Squires report from first-hand knowledge. R. N. L. Hopkins, *Australian Armour: A History of the Royal Australian Armoured Corps, 1927–1972*, Canberra, 1978 has material on the army's early brushes with armour and mechanisation. Paramilitary political activity in the interwar period is covered by Keith Amos, *The New Guard Movement 1931–1935*, Melbourne, 1976; Michael Cathcart, *Defending the National Tuckshop: Australia's secret army intrigue of 1931*, Melbourne, 1988; Andrew Moore, *The Secret Army and the Premier: Conservative Paramilitary Organisations in New South Wales 1930–32*, Kensington, 1989. For Spain, see Amirah Inglis, *Australians in the Spanish Civil War*, Sydney, 1987 while Stuart MacIntyre, *The Reds: The Communist Party in Australia from origins to illegality*, Sydney, 1998 sets out Australian attitudes to the Spanish Civil War in a wider political context.

There are a number of articles which look at the defence implications of the imperial conferences between the wars, and at the disarmament conference in Washington. Australian foreign policy and external relations in this period are better served still, but most of this work has little to say about defence or military policy. See Philip Wigley, 'Whitehall and the 1923 Imperial Conference', *Journal of Imperial and Commonwealth History*, 1:2, January 1973; J. C. Vinson, 'The Problem of Australian Representation at the Washington Conference for the Limitation of Naval Armament', *Australian Journal of Politics and History*, 4:2, 1958; Ann Trotter, 'The Dominions and Imperial Defence: Hankey's Tour in 1934', *Journal of Imperial and Commonwealth History*, 2:3, May 1974. Paul Twomey, 'Munich' in Carl Bridge (ed.), *Munich to Vietnam: Australia's Relations with Britain and the United States since the 1930s*, Melbourne, 1991 is good on reactions to the impending crisis in Europe, and recourse should be had as well to Carl Bridge and Bernard Attard (eds), *Between Empire and Nation: Australia's External Relations, 1901–40*, Melbourne, 1999. Some light is shed on defence policy at the end of the period in R. G. Neale (ed.), *Documents on Australian Foreign Policy, 1937–49: Volume I: 1937–38*, Canberra, 1975.

Only one leading military figure in this period has written for publication. Air Marshal Sir Richard Williams, *These are Facts*, Canberra, 1977, does not always live up to its title, but the perspective of the founding father of the RAAF is invaluable. Would that the other services were as well served.

Chapter 7

The Second World War is one of the great watersheds in Australian history, and is well served by the secondary literature. The best guides to Australian involvement in the war are Joan Beaumont (ed.), *Australia's War 1939–1945*, Sydney, 1996, and John Robertson, *Australia at War, 1939–1945*, Melbourne, 1981. The single volume survey by the official historian, Gavin Long, *The Six Years War: Australia in the 1939–45 War*, Canberra, 1973, repays reading still. Long's book is primarily campaign history, Beaumont's collection is especially strong on the social, economic and political dimensions of the topic, while Robertson provides a useful analysis of the strategic and high policy issues.

In the official series *Australia in the War of 1939–45*, the following are relevant to the concerns of this chapter: Gavin Long, *To Benghazi*, Canberra, 1952 and *Greece, Crete and Syria*, Canberra, 1953; G. Hermon Gill, *Royal Australian Navy, 1939–42*, Canberra, 1957; Douglas Gillison, *Royal Australian Air Force, 1939–42*, Canberra, 1962; John Herington, *Air War Against Germany and Italy, 1939–43*, Canberra, 1954; Paul Hasluck, *The Government and the People, 1939–41*, Canberra, 1952; J. Butlin, *War Economy, 1939–42*, Canberra, 1955. See also *Documents on Australian Foreign Policy, 1937–49*, Volumes II–IV, Canberra, 1976–83. Long had intended that a volume of the official history should deal with military and strategic policy. For various reasons this never eventuated, but the gap has been filled by D. M. Horner, *High Command: Australia and Allied Strategy, 1939–1945*, Sydney, 1982. Particular aspects of war policy and strategy are treated in John Robertson, 'Australia and the "Beat Hitler First" Strategy, 1941–42: A Problem of Wartime Consultation', *Journal of Imperial and Commonwealth History*, 11:3, May 1983; and 'Australian War Policy, 1939–1945', *Historical Studies*, 17:69, October 1977; P. G. Edwards, 'S. M. Bruce, R. G. Menzies and Australia's War Aims and Peace Aims, 1939–40', *Historical Studies*, 17:66, April 1976; and 'R. G. Menzies's Appeals to the United States, May–June 1940', *Australian Outlook*, April 1974; John McCarthy, 'The Imperial Commitment, 1939–41', *Australian Journal of Politics and History*, 23:2, 1977; Carl Bridge, 'Casey, Menzies, and the Politics of Australia's Participation in the European War, October 1939 to January 1940', *Flinders Journal of Politics and History*, 11, 1985; and Ian Hamill, 'An Expeditionary Force Mentality? The Despatch of Australian Troops to the Middle East, 1939–1940', *Australian Outlook*, 31:2, 1977.

For the home front see Michael McKernan, *All In! Australia during the Second World War*, Melbourne, 1983, while the control of news and information is covered in John Hilvert, *Blue Pencil Warriors: Censorship and Propaganda in World War II*, St Lucia, Qld, 1984. See also John McCarthy, 'Australian Responses to the European War, 1939–41', *Australian Journal of Defence Studies*, 1:2, October 1977. Menzies and his wartime prime ministership are ably analysed in A. W. Martin, *Robert Menzies: A Life*, vol. 1, Melbourne, 1993. The soldiers of the AIF speak for themselves in John Barrett, *We Were There: Australian Soldiers of World War II Tell Their Stories*, Ringwood, Vic., 1987, although this needs to be read in conjunction with Mark Johnson, *At the Front Line: Experiences of Australian Soldiers in World War II*, Melbourne, 1996. The early volunteers of the 6th Division are examined in Peter Charlton, *The Thirty-Niners*, Melbourne, 1981. On the Greek campaign, see D. F. Woodward, 'Australian Diplomacy with Regard to the Greek Campaign, February–March 1941', *Australian Journal of Politics and History*, 24:2, 1978. McCarthy has written on the Empire Air Training Scheme in 'The Defence of Australia and the Empire Air Training Scheme, 1939–1942', *Australian Journal of Politics and History*, 20:3, 1974 and in *Last Call of Empire: Australia and the Empire Air Training Scheme*, Canberra, 1988.

Personalities loom large in the discussion of Australia and the Second World War. The first commander of the 6th Division is treated by Ivan Chapman, *Iven G. Mackay: Citizen and Soldier*, Melbourne, 1975. John Hetherington, *Blamey: Controversial Soldier*, Canberra, 1973, for long the standard biography of Australia's most senior soldier, is superficial and defensive and in any case is now superseded by David Horner, *Blamey*, Sydney, 1998, which crowns a long and distinguished list of writings by this author on the higher command and decision-making processes during the war. Brett Lodge, *Lavarack: Rival General*, Sydney, 1998 examines one of Blamey's rivals, as does Jeffrey Grey, *Australian Brass: The Military Career of Lieutenant General Sir Horace Robertson*, Melbourne, 1992. David Horner, *General Vasey's War*, Melbourne, 1992 looks at one of the best of the divisional commanders thrown up by the war.

Chapter 8

For a short bibliographic essay on the period, readers are directed to John Robertson and Jeffrey Grey, 'Australian and New Zealand Writing on the Second World War', in Jürgen Rowher (ed.), *New Research on the Second World War: Literature Surveys and Bibliographies*, in the series *Schriften der Bibliothek für*

Zeitgeschichte, Stuttgart, 1990. The starting point for consideration of Australia's role in the period is Beaumont, *Australia's War, 1939–45.* Relevant volumes of the official history are: Barton Maughan, *Tobruk and El Alamein,* 1967; Lionel, Wigmore, *The Japanese Thrust,* 1957; Dudley McCarthy, *South West Pacific Area: First Year,* 1959; David Dexter, *The New Guinea Offensives,* 1961; Gavin Long, *The Final Campaigns,* 1963; G. Hermon Gill, *Royal Australian Navy, 1942–45,* 1969; George Odgers, *Air War Against Japan, 1943–45,* 1957; Paul Hasluck, *The Government and the People, 1942–45,* 1970; S. J. Butlin and C. B. Schedvin, *War Economy, 1942–45,* 1976; and V. D. P. Mellor, *The Role of Science and Industry,* 1958. Government policy is to be followed through W. J. Hudson et al., *Documents on Australian Foreign Policy, 1937–49,* Volumes IV–VIII, Canberra, 1982–89.

There are a number of decent studies of individual campaigns outside the official history. Worth reading are Raymond Paull, *Retreat From Kokoda,* Melbourne, 1958; Victor Austin, *To Kokoda and Beyond: The Story of the 39th Battalion, 1941–1943,* Melbourne, 1988; a trilogy by Peter Brune, *Those Ragged Bloody Heroes: From the Kokoda Trail to Gona Beach 1942,* Sydney, 1991; *Gona's Gone: The Battle for the Beach-head 1942,* Sydney, 1994; *The Spell Broken: Exploding the Myth of Japanese Invincibility,* Sydney, 1997; and Bernard Callinan, *Independent Company: The 2/2 and 2/4 Australian Independent Companies in Portuguese Timor, 1941–1943,* Melbourne, 1953. Peter Charlton, *The Unnecessary War: Island Campaigns of the South West Pacific, 1944–45,* Melbourne, 1983, presents the case for the prosecution. Horner's study of Australian military leadership in Papua, *Crisis of Command: Australian Generalship and the Japanese Threat, 1941–1943,* Canberra, 1978, and Peter Stanley, *Tarakan: An Australian Tragedy,* Sydney, 1997 are two of the best books written on Australian operations in recent times. Although written from an American perspective, Lida Mayo, *Bloody Buna,* New York, 1974, J. Miller, Jr, *Cartwheel: The Reduction of Rabaul,* Washington, 1959, and S. Milner, *Victory in Papua,* Washington, 1957, the latter both volumes in the series *The United States Army in World War II,* are worth consulting for the big picture. A valuable tactical analysis of Buna is provided by Jay Luvaas, 'Buna: A "Leavenworth Nightmare"', in Charles F. Heller and William A. Stofft (eds), *America's First Battles, 1776–1965,* Lawrence, 1986.

The politics of alliance, command relations and the higher direction of the war may be followed in D. M. Horner, *High Command: Australia and Allied Strategy, 1939–1945,* Sydney, 1982, and in his *Inside the War Cabinet: Directing Australia's War Effort 1939–1945,* Sydney, 1996. A different view is offered in Roger J. Bell, *Unequal Allies: Australian–American Relations and the Pacific War,* Melbourne, 1977, which is weak on the military aspects but good on the politics of Lend-Lease. Paul Burns, *The Brisbane Line Controversy: Political Opportunism versus National Security 1942–45,* Sydney, 1998 provides a long account of the genesis of the political controversy, but also has something to say about the preparations for the defence of the Australian mainland in 1942. On the defence of Australia, David Jenkins, *Battle Surface: Japan's Submarine War Against Australia 1942–44,* Sydney, 1992, is very good on both the analysis and the detail of the flawed submarine campaign waged in Australian waters. Also worth a look is Alan Powell, *War by Stealth: Australians and the Allied Intelligence Bureau 1942–1945,* Melbourne, 1996. P. G. Edwards has edited the reports on wartime Australia of senior American diplomatic personnel in *Australia through American Eyes, 1935–1945,* St Lucia, 1977. Much of the relevant literature remains in the journals; see Joseph Forbes, 'General Douglas MacArthur and the Implementation of American and Australian Civilian Policy Decisions in 1944 and 1945', *Military Affairs,* January 1985; J. M. McCarthy, 'Australia: A View from Whitehall',

Australian Outlook, 28:3, December 1974; P. G. Edwards, 'Evatt and the Americans', *Historical Studies*, 18:73, October 1979.

Personalities loom large in many episodes discussed here, but few of the available biographies match the complexity and seriousness of the issues involved. The definitive biography of MacArthur is D. Clayton James, *The Years of MacArthur: Volume II: 1941–1945*, Boston, 1975, although Gavin Long, *MacArthur as Military Commander*, Sydney, 1969, is useful for an Australian perspective. A. B. Lodge, *The Fall of General Gordon Bennett*, Sydney, 1986, is both a penetrating study of its subject and a serious analysis of the Malayan and Singapore campaigns. The best of the rest include Ivan Chapman, *Iven G. Mackay: Citizen and Soldier*, Melbourne, 1975; Stuart Sayers, *Ned Herring*, Melbourne, 1980; F. Kingsley Norris, *No Memory for Pain*, Melbourne, 1970. S. F. Rowell, *Full Circle*, Melbourne, 1974, gives his side of the sacking incident in Papua, and is distinguished by being the only serious set of memoirs written by a senior Australian general. Harry Rayner, *Scherger*, Canberra, 1984, is useful on its subject's wartime role during the Darwin air raids and as commander of the First Tactical Air Force towards the end of the war. Air Marshal Sir George Jones, *From Private to Air Marshal*, Richmond, 1988, is slight and reveals little not covered elsewhere.

Little of consequence has been written about the services themselves during the war. Notable exceptions are R. N. L. Hopkins, *Australian Armour: A History of the Royal Australian Armoured Corps, 1927–1972*, Canberra, 1978, which devotes nearly half its space to the war years, and D. M. Horner, 'Staff Corps versus Militia: The Australian Experience in World War II', *Defence Force Journal*, 26, January/February 1981. F. W. Perry, *The Commonwealth Armies: Manpower and Organisation in Two World Wars*, Manchester, 1988, is useful on the fluctuations in strength of the services. The essays in David Stevens (ed.), *The Royal Australian Navy in World War II*, Sydney, 1996 range widely in quality and subject matter, but the best are very good indeed. The home front is better served: Michael McKernan, *All In! Australia during the Second World War*, Melbourne, 1983, John Hilvert, *Blue Pencil Warriors: Censorship and Propaganda in World War II*, St Lucia, 1984, and Peter Love, 'Curtin, MacArthur and Conscription, 1942–43', *Historical Studies*, 17:69, October 1977, are worth consulting. There are good regional and particular studies in Kate Darian-Smith, *On the Home Front: Melbourne in Wartime 1939–1945*, Melbourne, 1990; Kay Saunders, *War on the Homefront: State Intervention in Queensland 1938–1948*, St Lucia, 1993; and Margaret Bevege, *Behind Barbed Wire: Internment in Australia during World War II*, St Lucia, 1993. An example of what might be done in this field is provided by Alan Powell, *The Shadow's Edge: Australia's Northern War*, Melbourne, 1988, which provides an exhaustively researched and ably written analysis of the war as it affected the Northern Territory. On the experience of indigenous Australians see Robert A. Hall, *The Black Diggers: Aborigines and Torres Strait Islanders in the Second World War*, Sydney, 1989. It is unfortunate that much of the thesis work on women in wartime industry and the armed forces remains unpublished. However, see Jan Bassett, *Guns and Brooches: Australian Army Nursing from the Boer War to the Gulf War*, Melbourne, 1992; Joyce Thomson, *The WAAAF in Wartime Australia*, Melbourne, 1991; and Ann Howard, *You'll be Sorry: Reflections of the AWAS from 1941–1945*, Sydney, 1990. Several books have been written on the impact of American service personnel in Australia during the war; like the several books written on the Cowra outbreak, they are of indifferent quality.

One of the single finest memoirs ever written by an Australian soldier about the nature of Australian soldiers is Henry ('Jo') Gullett, *Not as a Duty Only: An*

Infantryman's War, Melbourne, 1976, which is in a class of its own. The experience of prisoners of war, especially of those captured by the Japanese, has spawned a considerable literature. In addition to the numerous memoirs which may be consulted via Robin Gerster, 'The Rise of the Prisoner-of-War Writers', *Australian Literary Studies*, 12:2, October 1985, see Hank Nelson, *Prisoners of War: Australians under Nippon*, Sydney, 1985. The best single book on the Australian POW experience is Joan Beaumont, *Gull Force, Survival and Leadership in Captivity, 1941–1945*, Sydney, 1988, which uses the experiences of Gull Force, captured after the short-lived defence of Ambon, as a vehicle for exploring morale, leadership, mortality and survival among prisoners of the Japanese. It should be matched with Peter Henning, *Doomed Battalion: The Australian 2/40 Battalion 1940–1945: Mateship and Leadership in War and Captivity*, Sydney, 1995, on Sparrow Force, and Gavan McCormack and Hank Nelson (eds), *The Burma–Thailand Railway: Memory and History*, Sydney, 1993. Australian prisoners of the Germans and Italians await scholarly treatment.

Chapter 9

The post-1945 period is not well served in the secondary literature, especially before the involvement in Vietnam. A major interpretation of the foreign and defence policies in the earlier years is provided by Robert O'Neill, *Australia in the Korean War, 1950–53: Volume I: Strategy and Diplomacy*, Canberra, 1981. Older works which repay reading are Alan Watt, *The Evolution of Australian Foreign Policy, 1938–1965*, London, 1967, and T. B. Millar, *Australia in Peace and War*, Canberra, 1978. Both concentrate upon foreign policy, however, and military policy is generally ignored. Of interest here as well is David Lee, *Search for Security: The Political Economy of Australia's Postwar Foreign and Defence Policy*, Sydney, 1995.

Little has been written on the Commonwealth role in the occupation of Japan and the best examination is provided by Roger Buckley, *Occupation Diplomacy: Britain, the United States and Japan, 1945–1952*, Cambridge, 1982. The book's principal shortcomings are that it focuses upon Britain to the neglect of the Commonwealth, and looks at most aspects of the topic only up to 1947, when Britain withdrew its occupation forces. The long-serving Commander-in-Chief of the force is discussed at some length, as is his command, in Jeffrey Grey, *Australian Brass: The Military Career of Lieutenant General Sir Horace Robertson*, Melbourne, 1992. An excellent compilation of documents is provided by Robin Kay (ed.), *Documents on New Zealand External Relations: Volume II: The Surrender and Occupation of Japan*, Wellington, 1982.

On Australian participation in the Korean War, Robert O'Neill, *Australia in the Korean War, 1950–53: Volume II: Combat Operations*, Canberra, 1985, is essential reading, although the level of detail is not necessary for the general reader. Jeffrey Grey, *The Commonwealth Armies and the Korean War: An Alliance Study*, Manchester, 1988, examines Australian participation in its Commonwealth context, and from an alliance viewpoint. George Odgers, *Across the Parallel*, Melbourne, 1952, although old, is worth consulting for Australia's part in the air war; David Wilson, *Lion over Korea: 77 Fighter Squadron RAAF 1950–53*, Canberra, 1994 is a more recent account of the same subject. The services themselves are covered more generally in Anthony Wright, *Australian Carrier Decisions: The Acquisitions of HMA Ships Albatross, Sydney and Melbourne*, Canberra, 1998; by some of the essays in T. R. Frame, J. P. V. Goldrick and P. D. Jones (eds),

Reflections on the Royal Australian Navy, Kenthurst, 1991; and in Alan Stephens' magisterial account of the postwar air force, *Going Solo: The Royal Australian Air Force 1946–1971*, Canberra, 1995.

Australian military figures do not write much for public consumption, and this period is no exception. S. F. Rowell, *Full Circle*, Melbourne, 1974, covers his period as CGS from 1949 to 1954, but is frustratingly brief and circumspect on most issues. Harry Rayner, *Scherger: A Biography*, Canberra, 1984, devotes a chapter to Scherger's command of Commonwealth air units in Malaya from 1952 to 1954, but does little to analyse policy issues in this period. Australian foreign ministers have fared little better. Evatt awaits a biographer able to disengage himself from his subject. In the interim, P. G. Edwards, 'On Assessing H. V. Evatt', *Historical Studies*, 21:83, October 1984, is still the best starting point. Percy Spender awaits his student, but R. G. Casey has been well served by W. J. Hudson, *Casey*, Melbourne, 1986, although the evolution of SEATO is dealt with in passing only.

Demobilisation in 1945–46 is covered briefly in S. J. Butlin and C. B. Schedvin, *War Economy, 1942–1945*, Canberra, 1977. For the miners' strike of 1949, see Philip Deery, *Labour in Conflict: The 1949 Coal Strike*, Sydney, 1978. Aid to the civil power is placed in its wider context by Eric Andrews, 'Civil–Military Relations in the Twentieth Century', in Michael McKernan and Margaret Browne (eds), *Australia: Two Centuries of War and Peace*, Canberra, 1988. Andrew Moore has looked briefly at the postwar secret armies in 'Fascism Revived? The Association Stands Guard, 1947–52', *Labour History*, 74, May 1998. *Collective Defence in South East Asia: The Manila Treaty and its Implications*, London, 1956, is a useful introduction by a contemporary Chatham House study group. A more modern analysis is Leszek Buszynski, *SEATO: The Failure of an Alliance Strategy*, Singapore, 1983. The best source available on the genesis of ANZUS is W. David McIntyre, *Background to the ANZUS Pact: Policy-Making, Strategy and Diplomacy, 1945–55*, London, 1995. See also *Documents on New Zealand External Relations*; Robin Kay (ed.), *The Anzus Pact and the Treaty of Peace with Japan*, Wellington, 1985. On atomic testing consult Lorna Arnold, *A Very Special Relationship: British Atomic Weapons Trials in Australia*, London, 1987. The official history of the long-range weapons program is Peter Morton, *Fire Across the Desert: Woomera and the Anglo-Australian Joint Project 1946–80*, Canberra, 1989.

Chapter 10

There is no good overall guide to the defence policy of the period, of the kind provided by O'Neill for the Korean War. Coral Bell, *Dependent Ally: A Study in Australian Foreign Policy*, Melbourne, 1988, ranges more widely than defence issues, but is good on the higher-level decision making. Two essays with reasonable policy coverage are J. L. Richardson, 'Australian Strategic and Defence Policies', in Gordon Greenwood and Norman Harper (eds), *Australia in World Affairs, 1966–1970*, Melbourne, 1974, and T. B. Millar, 'Australian Defence, 1945–1965', in Gordon Greenwood and Norman Harper (eds), *Australia in World Affairs, 1961–1965*, Melbourne, 1968.

Australian involvement in the Malayan Emergency and Confrontation with Indonesia is treated in Peter Dennis and Jeffrey Grey, *Emergency and Confrontation: Australian Military Operations, Malaya and Borneo, 1950–1966*, Sydney, 1996, while the naval dimension of both is discussed in Jeffrey Grey, *Up Top: The Royal Australian Navy in Southeast Asian Conflicts, 1955–1972*, Sydney, 1998. Discussion of diplomacy and government policy is to be found in Peter Edwards,

Crises and Commitments: The Politics and Diplomacy of Australia's Involvement in Southeast Asian Conflicts 1948–1965, Sydney, 1992. Because of the relatively small role they played, more general histories of these conflicts do not mention Australian forces. See J. A. C. Mackie, *Low-Level Military Incursions: Lessons of the Indonesia–Malaysia 'Confrontation' Episode, 1963–66*, Canberra, 1986. An interesting personal account of service with 3 RAR in Malaya is offered in Colin Bannister, *An Inch of Bravery: 3 RAR in the Malayan Emergency 1957–59*, Canberra, 1994.

The organisational changes during the period have not been fully dealt with either, but several sources are available. F. A. Mediansky, 'Defence Reorganisation, 1957–1975' in W. J. Hudson (ed.), *Australia in World Affairs, 1971–1975*, Sydney, 1980, deals with the Morshead Committee and changes in the 1960s. Harry Rayner, *Scherger: A Biography*, Canberra, 1984, discusses the changes as they affected Scherger as, successively, Chief of the Air Staff and Chairman, Chiefs of Staff Committee, but was written without access to official files. He includes some material on the changes in equipment procurement policy also. John Blaxland, *Organising an Army: The Australian Experience, 1957–1965*, Canberra, 1989, provides a thorough analysis of the Pentropic experiment. On doctrinal development, see M. C. J. Welburn, *The Development of Australian Army Doctrine 1945–1964*, Canberra, 1994 and Richard Bushby, *Educating an Army: Australian Army Doctrinal Development and the Operational Experience in South Vietnam, 1965–1972*, Canberra, 1998. Ian McNeill, 'General Sir John Wilton: A Commander for his Time', in D. M. Horner (ed.), *The Commanders: Australian Military Leadership in the Twentieth Century*, Sydney, 1984, has a brief discussion of Pentropic and Wilton's part in ending it, and is as yet one of the few published analyses of a postwar chief of any of the services. On the RAN, Tom Frame, *Where Fate Calls: The HMAS Voyager Tragedy*, Sydney, 1992 is excellent on the institutional culture and imperatives of a service approaching organisational crisis in the early 1960s.

We are much better served with literature on Australia and the Vietnam War. There is no uniformly good, single-volume synopsis of the Australian war, though one will doubtless follow the completion of the official history. In the meantime, John Murphy, *Harvest of Fear: A History of Australia's Vietnam War*, Sydney, 1993 does a good job although it is not so strong on the military dimension. See as well Peter Pierce, Jeffrey Grey, Jeff Doyle (eds), *Vietnam Days: Australia and the Impact of Vietnam*, Ringwood, 1990 and Jeffrey Grey and Jeff Doyle (eds), *Vietnam: War, Myth and Memory*, Sydney, 1992. The official series, *The Official History of Australia in Southeast Asian Conflicts 1948–1975*, under the general editorship of Peter Edwards, consists of: Peter Edwards, *Crises and Commitments: The Politics and Diplomacy of Australia's Involvement in Southeast Asian Conflicts 1948–1965*, Sydney, 1992; Ian McNeill, *To Long Tan: The Australian Army and the Vietnam War 1950–1966*, Sydney, 1993; Brendan O'Keefe and F. B. Smith, *Medicine at War: Medical Aspects of Australia's Involvement in Southeast Asian Conflicts 1950–1972*, Sydney, 1994; Chris Coulthard-Clark, *The RAAF in Vietnam: Australian Air Involvement in the Vietnam War 1962–1975*, Sydney, 1995; Peter Edwards, *A Nation at War: Australian Politics, Society and Diplomacy during the Vietnam War 1965–1975*, Sydney, 1997; Jeffrey Grey, *Up Top: The Royal Australian Navy and Southeast Asian Conflicts 1955–1972*, Sydney, 1998; Ian McNeill, *A Province for a Battlefield: The Australian Army in the Vietnam War 1967–1972*, Sydney, 2000. Of value is Dennis L. Cuddy, 'The American Role in Australian Involvement in the Vietnam War', *Australian Journal of Politics and History*, 28:3, 1982, while David McCraw, 'Reluctant Ally: New Zealand's Entry into the Vietnam War', *New Zealand Journal of History*, 15:1, 1981, examines the pressure which the

Australian government brought to bear upon its smaller ANZUS partner. A finely detailed if overly long study of the strategic and diplomatic context in which the Vietnam commitment was played out is Gregory Pemberton, *All the Way: Australia's Road to Vietnam*, Sydney, 1988.

Discussion of Australian Task Force operations appears in Frank Frost, *Australia's War in Vietnam*, Sydney, 1987. Frost presents a highly critical picture of the aims and achievements of the Australian force, and his judgements will be ameliorated as the official records are released gradually. The experiences of the AATTV are fully covered in Ian McNeill, *The Team: Australian Army Advisers in Vietnam, 1962–1972*, Canberra, 1984. The best account of an individual unit is Michael O'Brien, *Regulars and Conscripts: With the Seventh Battalion in Vietnam*, Sydney, 1995, which follows 7 RAR through two tours during the war and thus demonstrates the ways in which the fighting, and the unit, developed over time; see also Robert O'Neill, *Vietnam Task: The 5th Battalion, Royal Australian Regiment, 1966–67*, Melbourne, 1968; Lex McAulay, *The Battle of Long Tan*, Melbourne, 1986; and *The Battle of Coral*, Hawthorn, Vic., 1988; Terry Burstall, *The Soldier's Story: The Battle of Xa Long Tan*, St Lucia, Qld, 1986. R. J. Breen, *First to Fight*, Sydney, 1988, examines the problems experienced by the first Australian regular battalion operating as part of a US airborne brigade, while Robert O'Neill, 'Australian Military Problems in Vietnam', *Australian Outlook*, 23:1, 1969, examines the situation of the Australian Task Force at the onset of the 'Vietnamisation' period. D. M. Horner has discussed the problems of command and control of Australian forces in *Australian Higher Command in the Vietnam War*, Canberra, 1986. Accounts of the other two services which appeared shortly after the end of the Australian commitment can be found in Denis Fairfax, *Navy in Vietnam: A Record of the Royal Australian Navy in the Vietnam War*, Canberra, 1980, and George Odgers, *Mission Vietnam: RAAF Operations, 1964–1972*, Canberra, 1974.

Nothing has been written on conscription from an institutional or administrative perspective. Jane Ross, 'The Australian Army – Some Views from the Bottom', *Australian Quarterly*, 46:3, 1974; 'The Conscript Experience in Vietnam', *Australian Outlook*, 29:3, 1975; 'Australian Soldiers in Vietnam: Product and Performance', in Peter King (ed.), *Australia's Vietnam: Australia in the Second Indochina War*, Sydney, 1983, looks at the experience and attitudes of national servicemen from a sociological perspective, but the treatment relegates the regulars to a minor place. Of value still in a wider perspective is Henry Albinski, *Politics and Foreign Policy: The Impact of Vietnam and Conscription*, Durham, North Carolina, 1970, although written without access to official sources and before the end of the Australian commitment.

On shifts in public perception of the war see Murray Goot and Rodney Tiffen, 'Public Opinion and the Politics of the Polls', in King (ed.), *Australia's Vietnam*. The only serious analyses of the Australian media are by Tiffen, 'News Coverage of Vietnam', in King, (ed.), *Australia's Vietnam*, and Lyn Gorman, 'Television and War: Australia's *Four Corners* Programme and Vietnam, 1963–1975', *War & Society*, 15:1, May 1997. There are several articles on aspects of opposition to the war and conscription for it, but as yet no overall treatment of the movements or their membership, although Greg Langley, *A Decade of Dissent: Vietnam and the Conflict on the Australian Home Front*, Sydney, 1992 is a good starting point. See as well: Malcolm Saunders, ' "Law and Order" and the Anti-Vietnam War Movement, 1965–1972', *Australian Journal of Politics and History*, 28:3, 1982; 'The ALP's Response to the Anti-Vietnam War Movement, 1965–1972', *Labour History*, 44, 1983; 'The Trade Unions in Australia and Opposition to Vietnam and Conscription', *Labour History*, 43, 1982; Kim Beazley, 'Federal Labor and the

Vietnam Commitment', in King (ed.), *Australia's Vietnam*. The context of anti-war dissent and the anti-conscription movements is provided by Alan Gilbert and A.-M. Jordens, 'Traditions of Dissent', in Michael McKernan and Margaret Browne (eds), *Australia: Two Centuries of War and Peace*, Canberra, 1988.

Chapter 11

Most of the secondary literature dealing with this period has been produced by political scientists and defence commentators, whose concerns are different from those of the historian. The absence of historical writing is explained almost entirely by the lack of access to the official documentary record controlled by the relevant archival legislation.

Graeme Cheeseman, *The Search for Self-Reliance: Australian Defence Since Vietnam*, Melbourne, 1993, is arguable in its advocacy but reliable in its factual basis. On the Whitlam period, see Gough Whitlam, *The Whitlam Government, 1972–75*, Ringwood, 1985, although this has comparatively little to say about defence issues. Better are R. J. O'Neill, 'Defence Policy' and F. A. Mediansky, 'Defence Reorganisation, 1957–75', both in W. J. Hudson, *Australia in World Affairs, 1971–75*, Sydney, 1980. Little has been written on the Pacific Islands Regiment or the fostering of the Papua New Guinea Defence Force. James Sinclair, *To Find a Path: Volume 1: The life and times of the Royal Pacific Islands Regiment*; Volume 2: *The Papua New Guinea Defence Force and the Australians to Independence*, Spring Hill, 1990 only takes the story to 1975. Ian Downs, *The Australian Trusteeship: Papua New Guinea, 1945–75*, Canberra, 1980, devotes a few pages to the transfer of defence powers. See also F. A. Mediansky, 'Defence' in W. J. Hudson (ed.), *Australia's New Guinea Question*, Melbourne, 1975, and R. J. O'Neill, *The Army in Papua-New Guinea. Current Role and Implications for Independence*, Canberra, 1971.

Post-Whitlam, recourse should be had to Hugh Smith, 'Defence Policy' in P. J. Boyce and J. R. Angel (eds), *Independence and Alliance: Australia in World Affairs, 1976–80*, Sydney, 1983, and Coral Bell, *Dependent Ally: A Study in Australian Foreign Policy*, Melbourne, 1988. The ubiquitous David Horner is a reliable guide to Australian involvement in the Gulf War, and has a good account of the early development of the ADF: see *The Gulf Commitment: The Australian Defence Force's First War*, Melbourne, 1992, written with high level access to both records and personalities. Michael McKinley, *The Gulf War: Critical Perspectives*, Sydney, 1994 provides exactly that. There is no accessible history of Australian involvement in peacekeeping. For the deployment to Somalia see Bob Breen, *A Little Bit of Hope: Australian Force Somalia*, Sydney, 1998 which is much too long for the size of its subject, but which contains interesting detail on the ways in which the force was mounted and sustained from Australia.

A timely and judicious overview of the forces after Vietnam is provided by Brian Beddie, 'The Australian Armed Forces in Transition', *Armed Forces and Society*, 5:3, Spring 1979. The question of public attitudes to defence and the services is essayed by Henry S. Albinski, 'The Armed Forces and the Community in Post-Vietnam Australia', *Politics*, XIV:2, November 1979. A subtle and stimulating essay which sets recent changes in defence thinking into a longer perspective is Michael Evans, 'From Defence to Security: Continuity and Change in Australian Strategic Planning in the Twentieth Century', in Peter Dennis and Jeffrey Grey (eds), *Serving Vital Interests: Australia's Strategic Planning in Peace and War*, Canberra, 1996.

Index